Lila
with good wishes
Michael
Tristram Out '13

MW01030681

In Memory of Irving Louis Horowitz

It is an honor to dedicate this work to a dear friend who is sadly missed. In the great lottery of life his personal and scholarly contributions were towering, and his sagacity manifested itself in everything he touched. He embodied the aphorism of Aristotle that courage is the first of human qualities because it is the quality that guarantees the others.

Contents

Bias in the International Community; Bias in Geneva; The Durban Follies; Animosity or Hatred?; The Accusation of Apartheid; Apartheid Used as a Cultural Weapon; The Big Lie; Israel Is Not a Colonial Power; The Bizarre Alliance against Israel; The Weapon of Boycott; Zionist Thinkers; What the BBC Did Not Know and Should Have Known about Jerusalem; Justice for the Kurds; Secretary-General Ban Goes to Teheran; International Dithering over Syria; The New Potemkin Village: Syria Disguised; Multiculturalism Revisited; An End to Appeasement

The Devil's Advocate and Free Speech; The Blood Libel Charge in Hungary; Antisemitism on the Rise in Europe; Antisemitism Is Alive and Well in Romania; Aimez-Vous Wagner?; Charles de Gaulle, Raymond Aron, and Israel; The Heroic Italian and the Vel d'Hiv; The New Trojan Horse for Democracies; France Condemns the Holocaust and the Antisemitic Atrocities of the Past; The French Railroad and the Holocaust; A Convenient Hatred; The Hilsner Case and Ritual Murder; Against All Odds: A Profile of Jewish Survival; Where Is the Art?

Acknowledgments

It is a pleasure to acknowledge the advice and counsel of a number of friends and colleagues who have read parts of this book at various stages. I am particularly grateful to Ken Bialkin, Fred Gottheil, Fred Balitzer, Norm Goldman, Nina Rosenwald, Leonard Moss, and above all my wife, Judith K. Brodsky. I am grateful to Gatestone Institute and the *American Thinker* for posting parts of the essays published here.

Introduction

Will the animosity toward Jews and the State of Israel never end? This book consists of commentaries and essays that examine the noises and sounds uttered about Jews and Middle East issues. The essays venture to rectify the misrepresentations, propaganda, obsessions, and falsifications contained in the utterances and attempt to explain the motivations for them. The issues scrutinized here, like people, are complicated and controversial, sometimes baffling, but the essays attempt to review them in as objective and rigorous a manner as possible.

The essays, some or parts of some previously published, are organized in chapters pertaining to five themes. These themes are (1) Political Correctness and the Obsessive Attack on Israel; (2) The Surprising and Disturbing Rise of Antisemitism; (3) The Arab World and the Islamist Threat; (4) The Palestinian Narrative; and (5) The Israeli/Palestinian Conflict.

1. Political Correctness and the Obsessive Attack on Israel

These essays assay the censorious attitude toward Israel of many in the international community, in both official and unofficial organizations. The State of Israel has faced and is still threatened by physical attacks. It now also faces unremitting verbal attacks by political and diplomatic entities and individuals, and by the abuse of international law. This criticism has led to endless denunciations and condemnations of Israel, to calls for boycott, divestment, and sanctions that have had an impact on tourism and foreign investment in the country, and even to denial of the legitimacy of the State of Israel and passion for its elimination.

Why do the animus and intellectually reckless assaults against Israel exist? The essays challenge the views of those politicians, academics, diplomats, and journalists, as well as Palestinian and Arab spokespersons, who have been immoderately critical of events, personalities, and politics relating to Jews and the State of Israel. A considerable number of those intellectuals, politicians, and the media, those in the halls of power and in universities, have forsaken self-discipline in the extent of their bias, prejudice, and hypocrisy toward Israel and Jews in general. Too many have lacked a disinterested concern for truth and reason. They exemplify what social psychologists have termed "motivated reasoning," the process by which people form and cling to false beliefs, despite overwhelming evidence to the contrary.

Equally dispiriting is the fact that some politicians and intellectuals adopt, at best, an attitude of neutrality toward acts of terror committed against Israel. Or they may posit a moral equivalence, in actuality an immoral equivalence, between the military actions of Israel seeking to defend itself against terrorist attacks and making considerable effort to minimize civilian casualties on the other side, and jihadist groups indiscriminately and deliberately firing rockets and missiles launched from public buildings against Israeli civilians, hiding weapons in homes, and using their own population as human shields.

Why otherwise intelligent individuals, especially those who regard themselves as liberals or on the political left, adhere to fallacious and biased opinions about Israel or hold antisemitic beliefs remains an enigma. Why, for example, does an individual like Clare Short, British member of Parliament, 1983–2010, and former minister for international development in the Labour Government, who incidentally admitted to overstating her parliamentary expenses in order to pay for her mortgage, find Israel guilty of "bloody, brutal, and systematic annexation of land, destruction of homes, and the deliberation creation of an apartheid system"?

It is equally puzzling that a respected politician like Shirley Williams, former British Labour Party member of Parliament and cabinet minister and a founder of the Social Democratic Party, should in a BBC broadcast program on November 16, 2012, have remarked that Gaza was "full of people who see their land slowly eaten up by more and more Israeli settlements." The moderator of the program did not explain to her that all Israeli settlements had been pulled out in 2005, and that the only Israeli who remained in Gaza since that time was the soldier Gilad Shalit, who had been kidnapped by Hamas on June 25, 2008, and not released until October 18, 2011.

From a rational point of view it is astonishing that so many academics and other writers are fixated on the so-called crimes of Israel while oblivious to the genocidal horrors of various countries in Africa. This fixation may be explained by the position of postcolonial critics, who are disinclined to criticize Arab countries or non-Western countries in general. They willfully ignore the reality that Israel today, as in the biblical past, is surrounded by large numbers of hostile enemies with military power. Israel, with its eight thousand square miles containing seven million people, is surrounded by an Arab world occupying 5.14 million square miles with a population of four hundred million.

It is a bitter truth that the State of Israel since its establishment in May 1948 has been subjected to constant condemnation for its very existence and legitimacy. This assessment goes far beyond appropriate and merited criticism about the behavior of the State of Israel or its citizens, in relation to specific actions or nonactions.

Using disproportionately harsh language, critics of this kind concentrate on what they depict as racism, discrimination, ethnic cleansing, violations of human rights, colonialism, and improper occupation of territory by Israel, which they denounce as an apartheid state. One well-known example of this inordinate criticism of Israel are the proceedings of international bodies such as the United Nations General Assembly, which has devoted six of its ten emergency special sessions to Israel; none has been devoted to Rwanda or the Sudan with their appalling acts of genocide. The imbalance in the behavior of the UN was again shown in November 2012, when the UN General Assembly elected Sudan, by 176 of 193 members, to a three-year term on the UN Economic and Social Council, which is supposed to promote respect for the observance of human rights and fundamental freedoms for all.

The imbalance and the international double standard applied to Israel, and the Islamic obsession for its destruction, become even more conspicuous when the very existence of the country is threatened. The primary concern of nation states is to protect its citizens. This principle of international law is enshrined in Article 51 of the United Nations Charter, which refers to "the inherent right of individual or collective self-defense" if an armed attack occurs against a member state. No sovereign nation can tolerate attacks or planned attacks on its territory or population.

The United States acted on this principle in October 1962. The Kennedy Administration took action to protect the country when the former Soviet Union threatened to place medium-range and intermediate-range nuclear missiles in Cuba. It imposed a quarantine, a euphemism for military blockade, to prevent the weapons from being delivered to Cuba. Israel claims a similar right to defend itself when faced with rockets and missiles from adjoining territories. The international community has usually condemned the Israeli response to these attacks while remaining silent about the provocations.

Rhetorical attacks on Israel have not been limited to external sources. Throughout history, political systems have come to an end when citizens lose faith in their countries. The State of Israel has been challenged internally as well as externally by academics and others who have come to be referred to as "post-Zionists." Among the themes derogatory toward Israel are the following. Zionism—the movement of Jewish self-determination that led to the establishment of the State of Israel—is a colonial enterprise. A Jewish state is by nature undemocratic. Israel is immoral, having been founded on the domination, or even the ouster—by force and other means—of another people. The creation of the state caused a catastrophe for Palestinian Arabs. Israeli occupation of disputed territory is a violation of human rights. Israel is an imperialistic power and a threat to world peace.

It is difficult to say whether this obsession with the deficiencies of Israel and anguish about its defective soul are sincere, inspired by partisan motives or by financial interests. Some of the essays in this chapter suggest that the naysayers—who wallow in what they term the crisis of Zionism, or the doubting Thomases among the academics and international and national bureaucrats living in Oxford, Geneva, and Washington, who are troubled by the perilous state of the soul of Israel—should take notice of the fact that the miracle in the desert is not only flourishing but is making extraordinary innovative, scientific, and economic contributions to the world.

These critics misinterpret and distort both the nature and behavior of the state of Israel and the ideology of Zionism. It is all the more surprising because the founders of Israel, and indeed the principal theorists of the various schools of Zionism itself, never suggested that the recreation of a Jewish state in its ancient homeland, where the kingdom of Judea was established circa 1010 BC under David, who united the Jewish tribes and created a single nation, would be a shining beacon devoid of blemishes or of the necessary compromises required for survival. Israel, in theory and in practice, has not, in Alexander Hamilton's words in *The Federalist Papers*, engaged in chimerical pursuit of a perfect plan.

These immoderate detractors might also be reminded of the words of Bartley Crum, the American lawyer, in his foreword to the book *This is Israel*, written by I. F. Stone: "They [Israelis] have built beautiful modern cities, such as Tel Aviv and Haifa on the edge of the wilderness. . . . They have set up a government which is a model of democracy." They might also remember Winston Churchill's statement concerning the proposed Arab veto on all Jewish immigration into Palestine after 1944: "Now, there is the breach, there is the violation of the pledge, there is the abandonment of the Balfour Declaration, there is the end of the vision, of the hope, of the dream."

Apart from this lack of a perfect society (and what democratic society is perfect) how can one explain the change in Western countries from admiration to criticism or condemnation? Certainly, the existence and prevalence of the historical prejudices of antisemitism, to which modern forms have been added, explain the change to some extent.

One can also look to the alliance between the Soviet Union and Arab states starting in the 1970s, a partnership that introduced propaganda and international resolutions castigating Israel as a racist and discriminatory state. The alliance cast both the United States and Israel in the role of imperialist, capitalist countries dominating less fortunate nations. The statements and actions of the alliance enhanced the position of the European and American anticolonialists who identified with the Palestinian cause rather than with westernized Israel. Based on this view, a specious argument has been made that Israeli settlements built after 1967 were a manifestation of imperialism.

In a second alliance, called in an essay here a "bizarre alliance," idealists, environmentalists, and human rights groups have joined together with Arab and Islamist states and groups in their animosity to Israel. They promote the point of view that the United States and Israel consider the less developed Third World countries, the nonaligned nations, as weak and in need of their control. The condition of those countries contrasts with the State of Israel, which has not only been able to survive military attacks but has also been capable of remarkable modernization, and achievements in scientific and technological research. The entrepreneurial spirit in Israel, with a population of seven million—and a highly educated population—has produced more Israeli companies on the NASDAQ exchange in New York than all companies from Europe with its population of 503 million.

In some cases perhaps mercenary factors also account for part of the anti-Israel hostility. The increase in the wealth of Arab oil-producing countries like Saudi Arabia and Libya has affected political and intellectual behavior and media reporting.

Among the essays in this chapter is one about the plight of the Kurds. The critics of Israel focus primarily on the situation of the Palestinians. They are blind to other populations who have not achieved self-determination. The Kurds are the largest ethnic group without a state of their own. They constitute perhaps thirteen million in southeast Turkey, where there is a Kurdistan Workers' Party that agitates for their rights. In Syria the Kurds, some three million, account for about 10 percent of the population and until recently had some degree of autonomy in the towns in northeast Syria where they form a majority. In Iraq they account for about five million. Nevertheless, in spite of their numbers, perhaps six or seven times larger than the number of Palestinians and their political organizations, the Kurds have not been able, as the essay here shows, to gain international support for Kurdish self-determination and a state of their own, in a fashion similar to that of the Palestinians.

In another essay, the silence of long regarding the ruthlessness in Syria in recent years is measured against the wild false claims by Israel detractors of the oppression they accuse Israel of imposing on the Palestinians. While the UN scrutinizes every Israeli response to aggression on the part of the Palestinians, it has done little to halt the obscene behavior of the Syrian leader, Bashar Assad, who has butchered more than seventy thousand of his own people.

It was well known that Bashar's father, Hafez Assad, after taking power in 1970 established a strong state and brutally maintained that power partly through the alliances he made between his Alawite regime and some Sunnis and Christian minorities in Syria. It took longer for the world to recognize the equal brutality of Bashar and the links he made with Iran and Islamist movements, perhaps because he was partly educated in London and thus appeared to be Westernized. At the start of his rule Bashar was seen by some observers as the Lion of Damascus, as the reformer who would end the automatic and corrupt regime of his father. The essay here discusses the refusal of the international community to stop Bashar's viciousness, even when eighteen of the twenty-two members (twenty-one states and the Palestinian Authority) of the Arab League voted to suspend Syria from its membership, impose sanctions, and announced that Syrian assets in Arab countries would be frozen.

One essay comments on the lack of serious action by the UN on the containment of Iran. The UN Secretary General, the well-meaning Mr. Ban, undertook what turned out to be a fruitless mission to that country. If he believed his presence in Teheran and the fact he was there because of his leadership of the United Nations would have some impact on Iranian policies, he was soon disabused of that idea. Instead, his visit was used for political advantage by Mahmoud Ahmadinejad, the Iranian president, who makes no secret of his call for the destruction of the State of Israel or his determination that Iran will have a nuclear weapon.

In this age of political correctness, the essays suggest there should be a more honest discussion of the real differences of values among societies and peoples. At least since the Vietnam War, there has been a loss of confidence in Western societies, as well as little appetite for foreign wars. Among other things, this uneasiness about whether the principles and political attitudes encountered in democratic countries and in the State of Israel, secular societies that are characterized by the rule of law, concern for freedom and human rights, and by pluralism are still valid has led to a lack of balance in political commentary, especially about Middle East affairs.

This uneasy attitude about their own societies has tended to end in a stance of appeasement by apologists in Western countries, who express contrition toward those such as the Palestinians who claim to have suffered from Western actions or who feel resentment toward the West. That resentment often includes Israel because of its identification as a Western democratic society. Western advocates of appeasement have also been influenced by other factors: a certain sense of fatigue with what they see as an unsolvable Israeli-Arab conflict and a growing concern about the demographics and the behavior of the Muslims who have entered their countries in recent years and increased in numbers and proportion of the population, complicating policy decisions.

The essays contend that it is unwarranted to bestow admiration automatically on countries or groups that adhere to traditional culture. They suggest that not all cultures are equally admirable, as the essay on gender illustrates. To argue that differences in religions, languages, and traditions are important is not equivalent to being a bigot or a racist. Furthermore, societies need a shared culture, even if people maintain different faiths. The essay on multiculturalism in Western countries indicates the deficiencies of applying a multicultural approach toward all aspects of society.

Another essay presents the example of France to reveal how Islam presents difficulties for democratic societies. The refusal of Muslims to integrate fully into French society may turn that community into a Trojan horse, destroying French culture from within.

This chapter also chronicles how Arab and Islamic countries censor criticism and sometimes promote terrorism. The Palestinian Authority, as well as those countries, detains journalists and political opponents for criticizing its leadership and investigating corruption. The resorting to, justifying of, and honoring of terrorists by Arab groups, is familiar. Between 1993 and 2012, terrorists murdered almost 1,500 Israelis. Totally insensitive to this fact, the Palestinians sponsored a soccer tournament named after a suicide bomber who killed twenty Israelis in a restaurant. In 2010 the Palestinian Authority (PA) heralded as a heroine a woman terrorist, Dalal Mugrabi, who participated in 1978 in the murder of thirty-seven Israeli bus passengers, and named a city square in Ramallah after her. By being apologetic for this kind of behavior, otherwise dependable commentators compromise their integrity and credibility.

2. The Surprising and Disturbing Rise of Contemporary Antisemitism

This second chapter consists of essays on the surprising and disturbing increase of contemporary antisemitism not only in Arab and Muslim countries but also in European democracies. These essays address the lies, disinformation, and misstatements associated with the new antisemitism of the twenty-first century, the increasing physical violence against Jews, and the calls for boycotts—economic, cultural, and academic—of Israelis and Jews within and outside Israel. Some of the pieces here deal not only with the campaign of words against Israel and Jews but also with the continuing military campaign against Israel. While at the moment, when the turmoil within and among Arab states means they are unlikely at present to mount any coordinated military attack on Israel, there is still a continuous armed conflict against the state involving Hamas and Islamic Jihad terrorists in the Gaza Strip and from Hezbollah in Lebanon, with its sixty thousand rockets, antiaircraft cannons, antitank missiles, and sophisticated communications equipment.

Discrimination, prejudice, bigotry, intolerance, persecution, racism, and xenophobia have been present in all historical eras and in all countries. However, there is something altogether distinctive in the extraordinary persistence of antisemitism, the hateful and hostile perceptions and persecution of Jews as individuals and as a collective group that has existed for thousands of years up to the present throughout the world. Antisemitism has been displayed in public life, the media, school textbooks, the workplace, and religious institutions.

Pejorative commentaries on Jews have ranged throughout history, from the Roman historian Tacitus around 100 BC and the Greek writer Philostratus three centuries later, until the present day. It is bewildering that hostile antisemitic views have been espoused by intelligent, well-educated individuals. Lawyers, philosophers, economists, intellectuals were among the principal proponents involved in abetting the antisemitic Nazi Holocaust. Heinrich Himmler, the SS leader, and Hassan al-Banna, founder of the Muslim Brotherhood in 1928, were both schoolteachers. Important cultural and literary personalities in the past—Chaucer, Voltaire, Degas, André Gide, T. S. Eliot, among so many others—have not been immune to antisemitic beliefs. Karl Marx, himself of Jewish origin, in his essay "On the Jewish Question," wrote of Judaism as a religion of money and called for the emancipation of mankind from Judaism. Antisemitic expressions do not disappear even when no Jews are present; after the expulsion of Jews from England in 1290, Jews were still excoriated in poetry, art, and sermons.

Antisemitism is a viral specter that persists in haunting Europe despite the guilt over the Holocaust. British Prime Minister Tony Blair was accused of being "unduly influenced by a cabal of Jewish advisers." In 2011, France was the scene for the murder of Jewish schoolchildren in Toulouse, attacks on Jewish property in Paris and Dijon, desecration of Jewish graves in Nice, and antisemitic graffiti. Other notable outbreaks have been in the Kreuzberg, the area of Berlin populated by Palestinians and Turks, and in many countries and places such as Stockholm, Malmo, Amsterdam, Corfu, Greece, and Rome. This rise has been accompanied by a growing tendency to deny or minimize the Holocaust or to argue that Jews have exploited it for political purposes. In the light of present-day declarations by Islamist extremists of their intention to eliminate the State of Israel, one must remember that the Nazis followed up their rhetoric about eliminating Jews with actions that almost achieved that objective.

An interesting offshoot of the contemporary rise of antisemitism is the situation in Israel, where there is still a relatively substantial community of Holocaust survivors (although they are rapidly dying off). An essay in this chapter addresses how the issue of the limits of free speech was recently tested, when Wagner's music was to be played. The essay raises the question of how to balance the memory of the Holocaust against the upholding of the principle of free speech in a democratic society.

From a rational point of view, this persistence of antisemitism is baffling because of the contradictory nature of the negative assertions about Jews, the way in which they are assessed by a standard not applied to others, and because that hostility is manifested irrespective of any particular behavior on the part of Jews. No other group of people in the world has been subjected to this kind of bigotry. A repugnant example of the thoughtlessness and the stereotypes of antisemitism was evident in the police report in July 2006 on the actor Mel Gibson, when he was arrested for drunken driving. He is alleged to have asserted in the course of his arrest that "The Jews are responsible for all the wars in the world."

Essays here address not only the current expressions of dislike or hatred of Jews but also the interrelationship between this hatred and the condemnation of the State of Israel. Antisemitism and anti-Zionism merge. Vehement opponents of Israel have compared the Israeli government to the Nazi regime and equated the Israeli Star of David with the Nazi Swastika, thus transmuting antisemitism into anti-Zionism. British poet Tom Paulin, comparing Israel to Nazi Germany, referred to it as "the Zionist SS."

The fusion between antisemitism and anti-Zionism is clear in Arab and Islamic declarations. The Preamble to the Hamas Covenant of August 18, 1988, proclaims "our struggle against the Jews is very great and very serious . . . it must be reinforced . . . until the enemies are defeated and Allah's victory is revealed." A similar, if somewhat confused, utterance came from Hassan Nasrallah, leader of Hezbollah in Lebanon: "If we searched the entire world for a person more cowardly, despicable, weak, and feeble in psyche, mind, ideology, and religion, we would not find anyone like the Jew. Notice I do not say the Israeli."

The union between antisemitism and hatred of Israel has manifested itself in concrete actions. One illustration is the suicide bombing on July 18, 1994, of the Jewish Community Center in Buenos Aires, Argentina, where eighty-seven Jews were killed and more than a hundred injured; those responsible were believed to be anti-Israel extremists associated with Iran—which was behind the planning and financing of the operation—and with Hezbollah, which carried it out. More recently, Malmo, Sweden, with a now considerable Muslim population, has become the milieu for increasing outbreaks of violence against Jews under the banner of anti-Zionism. Ilmar Reepalu, the mayor of the city, denied the occurrence of these manifest attacks and dismissed criticism of his denials as the work of the "Israel lobby."

Though this interrelationship may be arguable, Martin Luther King, Jr. was and is not alone in believing that "when people criticize Israel, they mean Jews." The poison of antisemitism has led to irresponsible and excessive condemnation of Israel for its very existence rather than for any specific action. Of course, not all critics of Israel are to be regarded as antisemitic. They may fairly criticize deficiencies or defects in the actions and policies of Israel or its citizens, but it is unreasonable, though it has become fashionable, to condemn Israel for not embodying the absolute or undiluted implementation of any Zionist ideal.

It is not surprising that the antisemitic views of Muslim authorities and their hatred of Israel are constantly voiced. It is less understandable that some in the European left, in their enthusiasm to support the Palestinian cause, have also not differentiated between hostility to Israel and to Jews. One might expect to see a distasteful Arab cartoon, such as the one that appeared in 2003 showing Israeli prime minister Ariel Sharon devouring a Palestinian child. But to find Ken Livingstone, former Labour Party mayor of London in 1982, publishing a cartoon of Menachem Begin, then Israeli prime minister, in Nazi uniform on top of a number of Palestinian bodies is repellent.

Several essays in this chapter address antisemitism in France from an historical perspective, providing background to the troubling contemporary situation in which the growth of the Muslim population in France has aggravated and led to the rise of antisemitism. French political history and thought can be characterized as diverse. The country has long experienced strong and bitter political and social divisions over Jews and other groups that the French consider non-French, the most intense and passionate division perhaps being the Dreyfus Affair in the 1890s. Since then, the period that has been most divisive among the French are the years of the Vichy regime, the French State headed by Marshal Philippe Pétain, which governed France during World War II.

Jews have been present in the territory of France for nearly two thousand years. The charge against Vichy, discussed in several essays in this book, is its responsibility for both the civil death of Jews in France—by legal exclusion from the French community, by removal from economic life, by spoliation and Aryanization—and their physical death by internment in camps where they died and by arresting and transporting seventy-six thousand to their death in Nazi extermination camps.

On this sad history there was virtual silence by many who should have been outspoken. One example of this muteness was Raymond Aron, the brilliant French commentator of Jewish origin, who wrote fifty-seven articles on national and international affairs in the periodical *La France Libre*, published in London from November 1940 until the end of 1944. He made only an occasional reference to the persecution of Jews in France, and then only regarding the action of the Nazi occupiers, not the French authorities or police. He explained later that between 1940 and 1943 he was more concerned with the pro- or anti-German feelings of the authorities of the Vichy regime than with their opinions on domestic politics.

Acknowledgment of French participation in the Holocaust was long in coming. It finally did with the admission and apology in July 1995 by Jacques Chirac, then president of the Republic, "for the dark hours which will forever tarnish our history." One of the essays discusses the even more fulsome apology made by President François Hollande in 2012.

Interconnected with the rise of antisemitism in France is the ambivalence in French foreign policy toward Israel. An essay concerning the rhetoric and policy of President de Gaulle in 1967 provides the background for recent displays of anti-Zionist attitudes, as shown by the hostility to Prime Minister Ariel Sharon on his visit to France in July 2001, and by the French criticism of Israel's operation in Gaza in 2009.

But the development with the most impact on antisemitism in France and the issue of relations with Israel is now related to the increasingly complex problem also addressed in the previous part, the presence in France of several million Muslims. These immigrants have experienced high unemployment, poor housing, and inadequate education. Some of them have become a threat to general law and order, as displayed in the riots in Paris in November 2005, and members of the Muslim community have been a source of antisemitic behavior and violence, the most egregious being the murders of Jews in March 2012 by a French-Algerian Islamist. To its credit, when the French government became aware of the antisemitic violence in September 2000, it began programs of physical protection for Jewish institutions and introduced both educational programs about the Holocaust and a law punishing Holocaust denial.

3. The Arab World and the Islamist Threat

This third chapter addresses the recent changes in the Arab world, the threat of Iranian ambitions, the new alliance of Sunni Islamist states, and the growing strength and danger of Islamic fundamentalism and extremist behavior, not only in the Middle East but also in Western societies, thus posing a threat to democratic values. Connected to this theme are essays about the adherence of Muslims to the traditional values of Islam, resulting in problems that arise from lack of integration among Muslim communities in European countries. Examples of Muslim refusal to integrate are plentiful. France faces demands by Muslim female students who insist on wearing headscarves in public secondary schools that have been secular institutions since 1905. A town close to Copenhagen, Denmark was forced to cancel Christmas celebrations in December 2012 as a result of pressure by Muslim immigrants who comprised more than half of the population.

Among other issues, the essays in the third chapter discuss the concept of jihad, a concept subject to different interpretations but which most Islamic theologians interpret in a military sense. Those interpretations have become important distinctions in the division between the majority Sunni countries in the Middle East, especially Saudi Arabia and Egypt, and the Shiite communities, especially the country of Iran, the latter having become more assertive in recent years. Since the ascent to power of Ayatollah Khomeini in 1979, Shiite Iran has aspired to regional hegemony. With its ambition to build nuclear weapons and with its capacity to block the flow of oil through its control of the Strait of Hormuz—only twenty-one nautical miles wide and the only entrance to the Persian Gulf—Iran may become the dominant power in the region.

John Keats sang, "Where are the songs of spring? Ay, where are they?" The Arab world is in turmoil today, and the uprisings that began with the Arab spring have had unintended consequences. They are drastically altering the social and political structures of the Arab countries through the shift in balance between secular and religious factions resulting from the rise of Islamist political power, the fluctuating alliances among the Arab countries, and the prominence of sectarian and tribal loyalties. A significant aspect of the uprisings has been that they are not concerned or interested in the Palestinian cause often used by previous Arab rulers for their own political advantage. Rather, they are focused on internal issues: the overthrow of corrupt and inefficient rulers with a thirst for power, the concentration of wealth among a few with resulting widespread poverty, and the lack of political rights. Thus the uprisings lay bare the claim of the Arab countries that their problems are instigated by the existence of Israel.

Certain recent political changes are particularly critical. The first change is the disintegration or weakening of a number of the existing Arab states, all of which except Egypt were artificially created by British and French diplomats after World War I; their existence has become more fragile as a result of internal divisions. Those divisions are the result of the greater assertiveness of tribal, sectarian, ethnic, and religious factions in all the countries. Another activity disturbing the situation is the use by jihadist groups of the Sinai Peninsula, which since 1979 has been semi-demilitarized, to smuggle arms and provide a haven for terrorist infrastructure. Because of the relationship of these groups to the Muslim Brotherhood, Egypt is caught in a dilemma and wavers in its efforts to control those groups and the use they are making of Sinai as a staging area for attacks on Israel. Moreover, in Sinai a growing problem is the increasing assertiveness of the four hundred thousand Bedouins there engaged in tribal vendettas against each other. An additional problem that has become more acute in recent years is the decline, and the greater persecution, of non-Muslim minorities in Arab countries.

To these political issues may be added the practical problems referred to above: the dire poverty, high rate of unemployment, the high proportion of unemployed youth in the population, and low rate of economic growth in the non-oil producing Arab countries. A recent development that is crucial to the explosiveness of the situation is the increase in the Arab and Muslim worlds of the role of social media, digital technology, the Internet and smartphones, which have disseminated information and are allowing many voices to participate in shaping opinions about religion and politics.

Most significant is the fact that the Arab and Islamic worlds are merging, thus resulting in the greater role of political Islam. Bernard Lewis cogently remarked that for Muslims, religion traditionally was not only spiritual but also central for daily existence, in the sense that it constituted the essential basis and focus of identity and loyalty. As early as the years just after World War II, a more assertive form of Islam began to challenge and sometimes displace the nationalist and pan-Arab secular movements that developed in some of the Arab countries during the earlier part of the century. The Arab world is now increasingly divided both on sectarian lines between Sunnis and Shiites and between moderates and extremists who can be regarded as Islamists. This rise in Islamist political power has resulted in the rise of militant jihadists, including the ideologically extreme Salafist group, which gained about a quarter of the seats in the Egyptian parliamentary election in 2011.

In this book the term "Islamist," rather than fundamentalist, has been used to indicate those who invoke Islam in this assertive and aggressive way and who propound both the necessity of Sharia law and the concept of jihad. It also contends that jihad can more properly be interpreted as "war against unbelievers" than as "striving in the path of God." That concept of jihad can be linked to the terrorist attacks and suicide bombings sponsored by Islamist organizations. The connection between Islam and terrorism is apparent in Article 15 of the charter of Hamas (Islamic Resistance Movement) proclaimed on August 18, 1988: "The day the enemies conquer some part of the Muslim land, jihad becomes a practical duty of every Muslim. In the face of the Jewish population of Palestine, it is necessary to raise the banner of jihad." Hamas, the controlling power in Gaza, has not only raised the banner but has accompanied it with hundreds of rocket and mortar attacks against the civilian Jewish population of Israel.

The beginning of a change to a more religious focus was evident when President Gamal Abdel Nasser of Egypt, a secular ruler, after the Arab defeat in the Six-Day War released a thousand members of the Muslim Brotherhood who had been arrested for plotting to avenge the execution of Sayyid Qutb, who in the twentieth century laid the ideological basis for jihad. The Brotherhood thus became a political force, while more public attention was given to Islamic doctrines and the promotion of Islamic fundamentalism. Saudi Arabia provided finances for the building of mosques, for religious schools, and for Islamic groups, even though it has political differences with the Brotherhood.

The increase in religious observance and influential sermons led in 1980 to the change in the constitution of Egypt, declaring that Islam was the state religion and Sharia was the main source of law. For political reasons President Anwar Sadat released more members of the Brotherhood who were still imprisoned, though ironically he was assassinated by an Islamist officer belonging to an offshoot group of the Brotherhood, and one that a few years later established ties with al-Qaeda. Alliance between these groups was strengthened by their mobilization to fight the Soviet Union's invasion of Afghanistan in December 1980. From this alliance al-Qaeda emerged as a significant Islamist force.

Recent years have witnessed the success of Islamist parties and groups in Tunisia, Morocco, Egypt, Libya, Iraq, and Jordan. Wahhabism, the most extreme and coercive of Islamic beliefs and sects, emphasizing the renewal and purification of authentic and uncorrupted Islam, remains significant in Saudi Arabia. Since that country was established in 1932 by the combination of the al-Saud family and the Abd al-Wahhab clan in their revolt against Ottoman rule, the kingdom of Saudi Arabia has been ruled as an absolute monarchy and one in which religious edicts are rigidly enforced. The kingdom is unusual in that there is really no formal method to determine the successor to the deceased king. Some prominent figures in the kingdom have been critical of the Brotherhood, partly because of its supposed moderation and partly because it has come to power in Egypt through legal, electoral methods and appeared to renounce violence.

The extremist groups such as al Qaeda, the group formed by Osama bin Laden, himself of Saudi origin, and the Salafists, who have been obtaining financing from private individuals in the Gulf countries, are another source of unrest and political violence. The Salafists, who glorify death as they cause others to die, have influenced the Taliban in Afghanistan and Pakistan. Some fundamentalists seek to purge their countries of parts of their history; in Egypt they seek to destroy the Pyramids and the Great Sphinx of Gaza, while the Taliban in Afghanistan have destroyed historical artifacts.

Yet, in the Arab world of diplomatic rivalries, national differences, and different approaches, not all countries favor an Islamist policy or common policy. Within that world there is evident tension between pragmatic politicians willing to govern with moderation and the more extreme leaders allied to the Islamic ideology of Iran, in spite of its being a Shiite state, and intent on the elimination of the State of Israel. The Muslim Brotherhood broke away from other Arab groups by supporting Iraq's occupation of Kuwait. Saudi Arabia disagreed with the overthrowing of Hosni Mubarak in Egypt and Ben Ali in Tunisia. If Islamists want an Islamic state, Saudi Arabia insists on one that is loyal to the royal Saudi family.

The essays in this chapter also deal with the issue of Sharia law, both for itself and for its implications in regard to European countries. The spread and acceptance of Sharia law in the West suggests that the Islamization of Europe may occur before the Europeanization of Islam. The French situation enters into the picture again. It is revealing that in France today there are more practicing Muslims (about 2.5 million, or 40 percent of the Muslim population) than practicing Catholics (1.9 million, or 4.5 percent of the Catholic population).

The essay on the work of Bat Ye'or discusses her controversial argument on the growing presence and influence of Muslims in European countries, and implicitly the Islamic objective of installing the legal system of Sharia law in those countries and re-establishing a Caliphate to enforce Sharia. Some of the essays here indicate that in most of the Arab monarchies and republics Sharia law is the main basis for legislation. Islam is the religion of the state, except in Syria, where, according to the 2012 constitution, it is the religion of the president.

European countries now face the issue of Sharia law in their own territory. Muslim politicians, candidates of the Islam Party, who have been elected in 2012 to municipalities in Brussels, Belgium, have declared their intention to introduce Sharia law in Belgium. The Muslims in Brussels in 2012 account for more than three hundred thousand people. Predictions made by the sociologist Felice Dassetto in her book *L'Iris et le Croissant* suggest that by 2030 they will constitute a majority in this city, "the capital of the European Union." Already, the most popular name for a newborn boy in Brussels, as well as in Amsterdam, Rotterdam, and other European cities, is Muhammad. One calculation is that by 2050 about one-third of all children born in Europe will be born to Muslim families.

In neighboring Germany, the city of Hamburg has made an agreement with its Muslim communities to grant them rights and privileges, the most significant of which is the promotion of teaching of Islam in the city's public schools, together with the right of Muslim officials to decide on the teachers of the subject. The question has been raised in the country as to whether Islam should be officially recognized as a religious community.

Moreover, the economic power of Arab Muslim countries is being used to influence the financial structures and cultures of European countries. Qatar, a former British protectorate, is spreading its economic tentacles in Europe. It already owns part of Volkswagen and Porsche in Germany, Valentino fashion in Italy, and in Britain part of the Canary Wharf financial district and the Shard Tower skyscraper in London, as well as 20 percent of the London Stock Exchange. Qatar's ruler, the Emir Sheikh Hamad bin Khalifa al-Thani, a Wahhabi fundamentalist, by using a combination of money and ideology has become an international political player. He not only funded the Al Jazeera television network in 1996 but also was, in October 2012, the first head of state to visit Gaza; he also gave it $400 million. Though not a French-speaking country, Qatar has joined the International Organization of La Francophonie (a body organizing relations between states and governments that share the use of the French language) as an associate member.

The attempt by Islamic authorities to censor any critical comments on Islam has become more pronounced. King Abdullah of Saudi Arabia in October 2012 demanded a United Nations resolution condemning any country or group that insults religions and prophets. It was, he said, the duty of every Muslim to protect Islam and to defend the prophets. In their book *Silenced*, Paul Marshall and Nina Shea remark that in Muslim-majority countries and areas, restrictions on freedom of religion and expression—based on prohibitions of blasphemy, apostasy, and "insulting Islam"—are pervasive, thwart freedom, and cause suffering to millions of people. In a number of European countries, blasphemy and religious insult are criminal offences.

One of the essays here raises the question of whether Islamist ideology can be considered totalitarian. It points out the similarity of contemporary Islamist themes, attacks on liberal democracies, antisemitism, anti-Americanism, limitation of individual freedoms of expression, justification of violence on ideological grounds, and lack of equal rights of women, with those of the former Nazi and Stalinist systems.

The objective of the upsurge in Islamic extremism in Europe as elsewhere is either to influence decision-making in those countries or to destroy democratic states. In particular, Islamic fundamentalism sees the United States in its role as the leading liberal democratic country as its main enemy, and Israel, which it would like to eliminate, as its vassal. While most of the mainstream Christian churches pay little heed to or do not condemn the violence implicit in the upsurge, in contrast many Christian evangelicals, as one of the essays shows, are concerned both for the State of Israel and the preservation of the Jewish people.

Underlying many of these essays is the question of whether the Western democratic countries will defend their cultural and political legacies and preserve their societies, even admitting existing faults, in the face of threats of Islamism. The use of power as well as legal methods, as in the case of the terrorist Hamza discussed in one of the essays, is appropriate to meet the challenge of inexcusable violence and terrorism. To comment critically on the doctrines of Islam or the behavior of its adherents or to address the extremism of some of them is not an act of bigotry, certainly not against those who themselves attempt to prevent free speech.

Surrender to the force of Islamic bigotry is not an option if fundamental values are to survive. Nor is pacifism or a refusal to respond an option when faced with romanticized violence and believers in a myth of historical destiny, which they passionately seek to implement. An attitude of this kind, and the accompanying corollary that no war is just, implies blindness to the reality of historical conflict, as well as to the present mix of ideology and theology that is threatening violence against democratic countries including Israel.

4. The Palestinian Narrative

This fourth theme concerns the acceptance by many critics of Israel and the international media of the Palestinian narrative of victimhood. Doubtless, this projected image of a victimized people, a central feature of the anti-Israel campaign, has produced emotional overtones that have influenced people and events as much or more than rational deliberation on the reality of Middle Eastern affairs. The Palestinians have been successful in using what Abraham Lincoln called "a drop of honey that catches his heart which is the great highway to his reason" and which will convince people of the justice of the cause.

The Palestinian account of history and politics, expressed in both positive and negative terms, has occasioned more heat than light. This narrative propounds the view that the Palestinian people are victims of a racist, colonialist Israel. Palestinians sometimes make this view the central factor in describing their identity, explaining that they are prevented from economic and social development because of Israeli oppression.

The tale propounds the false postulation that the Arab people living in the area comprise the nation of Palestine and that Palestine has a seven-thousand-year history in the land of Canaan, which according to the narrative extended from the Mediterranean to the Jordan River. In fact, the term "Palestine" never appears in the Bible. The territory of Palestine has been conquered by many different armies and settled by different peoples throughout history. This historical snapshot reveals that the present Arab population is not wholly indigenous; the roots of the majority of that population are no deeper than that of the Jewish population; and the whole of Palestine never belonged to an Arab population. Only comparatively recently has the adjective "Palestinian" been used to distinguish those now in the land from other Arabs in the Middle East region.

Arab nationalism in general is of recent vintage. No independent state with Arabic as its official language existed before World War I. Palestinian Arab nationalism is even more recent. It has lacked the comprehensive coherence, the positive approach, and cooperative spirit that characterized Zionism. Indeed, it is fair to suggest that a major impetus to the development of Palestinian nationalism came from response to the growing Jewish settlement in the area, and then to the State of Israel.

The Palestinian narrative has not only asserted an inaccurate picture of Palestinian presence in the disputed land but has also denied the reality of the long Jewish history in the area, refusing to acknowledge the meaningfulness of Jewish sites, holy places, and the Temple in Jerusalem. The objective of the account is to erase Jewish history and to dismiss any claim of relationship between the Jewish people who lived three thousand years ago and the present Jewish community in Israel.

At an extreme, Palestinians and Islamists continue to invoke a reminder of the battle of Khaybar of 629, at which the Prophet Muhammad defeated and eliminated many of the Jews in the area. Chanting, "Khaybar, Khaybar, O Jews, the army of Muhammad will return," the Islamists are calling for aggression against Israel, the destruction of Jews in general, and the seizure of their property.

More pertinent to present concerns has been the refusal of Palestinian leaders to enter into unconditional negotiations with Israel, even after the creation of the Palestinian Authority subsequent to the 1993 Oslo Accords. The question arises whether any agreement will be regarded as a *hudna*, or truce, or as a valid permanent peace. Rather, the leaders have waged continual hostility, terrorist and guerrilla actions, and two intifadas, the first from 1987 to 1992 and the second which ended in 2005, as well as attacks in 2012.

In any case, a peaceful settlement has become more difficult, not simply because of diplomatic deadlock, but more because of the internal dissent among the Palestinians, between Fatah and the Palestine Liberation Organization (PLO) on the one hand and Hamas on the other. Hamas, started in 1987, has always been outside of the PLO structure. It now constitutes a political, military, and ideological threat to the more moderate Fatah body. It won both the election in Gaza in 2006 and the civil war against Fatah in June 2007 for control of Gaza. It gained more international prominence as a result of its rocket attacks on Israel, especially those of November 2012.

While the PA, the Fatah administration in the West Bank, largely controlled outbreaks of violence and any significant terrorist activity, Hamas, more Islamist than Fatah, has been the constant source of terrorist attacks from Gaza against Israel. Palestinian terrorist assaults have included suicide bombings and attacks on hotels, restaurants, and especially on buses, which have resulted in the killing of about one thousand Israelis. Rocket attacks by Hamas from Gaza continued after the Israeli Operation Cast Lead of winter 2008–2009; between 2009 and 2011 there were 1,400 such attacks against Israeli civilians.

Weapons used in those attacks have become more sophisticated, with two consequences: Israel has had to spend millions of dollars on bomb shelters and make constant improvements in its missile defense system. The latest in this system are the five Iron Dome rocket-defense batteries, each costing about $50 million, stationed in a number of towns including Ashdod, Ashkelon, and Beersheba. The domes protect crowded civilian areas from attacks by short-range missiles. The combat between the 1,500 Hamas-launched missiles, many fired against unpopulated Israeli areas, and the Israeli missile defense system, which shot down over 85 percent of assigned targets, took place for eight days in November 2012 over the skies of Israel.

While engaging in its military activity, Hamas tends to talk not of the establishment of a Palestinian state as an objective, but of liberation of the land and jihad against the infidels. In its perspective, all of the disputed area belongs to Palestinian Arabs. This uncompromising view does not bode well for peace.

5. The Israeli/Palestinian Conflict

The four chapters above are interrelated with a fifth chapter on the prolonged Arab-Israeli and the Palestinian-Israeli conflict. Hostile critics of Israel seem to have little hesitation in making judgments and casting responsibility for these conflicts on Israel. In contrast, where are their judgments in relation to the Sunni-Shiite conflicts in the Middle East, the Arab–non-Arab Iran conflict, the belligerence of Saddam Hussein against Kuwait or President Nasser against Yemen, or the constant terrorist attacks on United States personnel as well as Israelis by Hezbollah, located in Lebanon but in essence an extension of Iran, rather than a national Lebanese movement?

These essays suggest that two points should be kept in mind. The first is the fact that it is not the presence of settlements in the West Bank, but rather the refusal of so many Arab and Palestinian leaders to acknowledge officially the existence of Israel and to accept its legitimacy that prevents a solution to the Israeli-Palestinian conflict. The second point is the fact as indicated earlier that the Israeli-Palestinian conflict is not the only one in the Middle East.

The conflict between Israel and the Arab states and the Palestinians has gone on for over a hundred years, since the aliyah (immigration) of Jews began into the historic land of Israel. In the early twentieth century,

Jews, Antisemitism, and the Middle East

murders of Jewish settlers took place, and they were followed by a series of Arab attacks in 1920, 1921, and 1929. In the attack of 1929, 133 Jews were murdered, including 66 in Hebron. The attackers claimed their land was being lost to the Jewish settlers, but the last Land Survey made by British Mandate authorities in 1947 suggests otherwise. It showed that only 5.2 million dunams were actually owned by Arabs and Jews. Arabs possessed about 20 percent of the land and Jews about 6 percent. The rest was public or state land and therefore open to dispute.

In his testimony to the Anglo-American Committee of Inquiry in 1946, David Ben Gurion explained that Jews coming to the Palestine area had found hundreds of Arab villages inhabited by Muslims and Christians. They did not take them away, but built new Jewish villages on virgin soil. He said, "We did not merely buy the land, we re-fashioned it. It was rocky hill . . . the land [was] reclaimed by our own efforts."

The conflict in the area was intensified with the creation of the State of Israel in May 1948, when the neighboring Arab states—Egypt, Syria, Lebanon, Jordan, and Iraq—attacked and attempted to destroy it. In keeping with the intent of this book to focus on objective discussion, it is necessary to lift the veil of obfuscation about that attempt and tell the truth. The war was instigated not by Israelis or Jews, as in the Palestinian narrative, but by Arabs. It began on May 4, 1948. Unprovoked by any Israeli action, an Arab Legion column attacked the Etzion Bloc, an area important for supply routes to Hebron and Jerusalem, killing forty Jewish defenders. On May 12, another column with artillery and armored cars attacked that area, murdering 133 Jewish men and women *after* their surrender.

The day after the establishment of the State of Israel, attacks were made on May 15 on Jerusalem, on the Jewish Quarter which was razed by the Arab forces, and on Jewish settlements including Beit Ha'arava. The war against the new State of Israel was brutal, leading to the death of six thousand Israelis, 1 percent of the population. Paradoxically, the invasion and the fighting led to the refugee problem of Palestinians, who were propelled to move as a result of the invading Arab armies rather than forced out by Israel. Israel—without oil, gas, precious metals, or mineral resources including water—survived, and began the process of development and the integration of immigrants from more than seventy countries.

This birth in the crucible of fire also led to the building of a new country in its own particular manner, in which the emblem was the sabra, the tough and strong Israeli, named after the prickly cactus.

xxxii

The country and the people were transformed. The leading political figure set the example; David Grun became David Ben Gurion, and was prominent in ushering in a pluralistic, secular, democratic political system. In its sixty-four years Israel has known thirty-two governments, twelve prime ministers, and nineteen parliaments, all of which have contained at least ten political parties.

After four wars, a war of attrition by Egypt against Israel, countless terrorist acts and continual violence, and attempts to impose economic, cultural, diplomatic, and academic boycotts against Israel and its citizens, Israel has survived, but the conflict remains unresolved. The attacks on Israel have come from suicide bombers, rockets, airplane bombings, hijackings, and border raids. For some time Israel has been confronted with terrorist attacks from the Gaza Strip by Hamas, which has governed Gaza for more than five years and which calls for the destruction of the "Zionist entity." Iran has been a major arms supplier to Hezbollah in Lebanon and to Hamas and the Palestinian Islamic Jihad, which operate out of Gaza using sophisticated weapons. They include Fajr-5 rockets (named after the Persian word for dawn) with a range of forty-six miles and can be fired from underground launching pads, enhanced Grad rockets with big warheads, Russian SA-7 (Stella) shoulder-fired antiaircraft missiles, and the Russian-made Kornet, a laser-guided antitank missile with a range of 3.4 miles.

The international community and media have largely ignored the attacks against Israel that inevitably provoke justifiable responses, but have been critical of the responses. They have also largely disregarded objective comments on Israeli military behavior. In an article in June 2009 and in testimony in October 2009 before the United Nations Human Rights Council, Colonel Richard Kemp, former commander of British troops in Afghanistan, refuted allegations that Israel had engaged in war crimes or crimes against humanity during Operation Cast Lead, the Israeli response in December 2008–January 2009 attacks from Gaza. He testified, "During its operation in Gaza, *Israel did more to safeguard the rights of civilians in the combat zones than any other army in the history of warfare.* Israel took extraordinary measures to give Gaza civilians notice of targeted areas, dropping over two million leaflets, and making over 100,000 phone calls" (emphasis mine).

Once again, in an article in the *Jewish Chronicle* of November 22, 2012, Colonel Kemp countered the shrill accusations made by members of the media. In reporting on Operation Pillar of Defense, they accused Israel of making indiscriminate air strikes and deliberately targeting Palestinian civilians in response to the intense barrage of rocket attacks from Gaza that took place in November 2012. On the contrary, Kemp emphasized that extraordinary steps had been taken to minimize civilian casualties, by leaflet drops, text and radio messages, and phone calls.

In this regard it is enlightening to compare the ratio of civilian to combat deaths in recent conflicts. The limited number of civilian casualties caused by the proportionate response by Israel is striking. While opinion legitimately varies on the degree to which a state can resort to self-defense, it appears that Israel in Operation Pillar of Defense did balance appropriately the anticipated military advantage with the risks to civilians and property, even if the international community did not recognize it for the high moral standing it deserved. Members of the international media empathize with the Palestinians and are therefore blind to the Palestinian manipulation of evidence about events or non-events, the deliberate staging of events for propaganda purposes, and the deliberate use of the camera to portray events are more dramatic than they really are.

The Arab-Israeli conflict initially resulted from the competing claims to rights and justice in the same land. It became more intense with the refusal of the Arab states—until the peace treaties with Egypt in 1979 and with Jordan in 1994—and some informal commercial and diplomatic contacts, to acknowledge the existence and legitimacy of the State of Israel and to accept it as a member of the family of nations in the Middle East.

It is this refusal to accept the existence of Israel that makes serious negotiation impossible. More recently, those opposing Israel have begun to focus on questioning the nature and degree of democracy in Israel, refusing to accept that Israel can be both a Jewish state and a democratic one, and calling for the removal of Israeli settlements, or a halt to future construction. For them the tough sabra and the social democrats who were once central in the life of the country have been transformed into imperialist colonizers.

Those opponents often ignore or minimize the reality that conflict has not prevented interaction or offers of compromise by Israelis. One significant example is the treatment of Palestinian Arabs in Israeli hospitals. No distinction is made between Arabs and Jews seeking medical help. However, the opposite behavior was displayed when Palestinians prevented Israeli physicians from visiting Ramallah to provide medical services there.

More significant have been Israeli proposals for a compromise peace settlement. In 2008, then Prime Minister Ehud Olmert presented a proposal for Palestinian control over most of the West Bank that would include transfer of 327 square kilometers of territory from inside Israel. As a result, Israel would retain only 6.3 percent of the West Bank and would evacuate many Israel settlements as well as build a safe passage from the West Bank to the Gaza Strip. The proposal was rejected by the Palestinian Authority, despite the fact it might have enhanced their ability to control the 1.4 million Palestinians currently under the rule of Hamas in Gaza.

Resolution of the conflict is difficult because of the complex history of the area; the tangled web of inter-Arab rivalries, civil wars, and feuds; the divisions and factions among the Palestinians; tribal, ethnic, and religious rivalries; the Islamist upsurge; the intricate maneuvering and ambition of outside powers; and the bitter intransigence that has led to a refusal to enter into compromises and make concessions. Outstanding issues remain: differences over territory that may be considered occupied or disputed; debate about Jerusalem; a just settlement of the refugee issue—not only Palestinian refugees but also Jews who fled from Arab countries; control of terrorist activity; statehood of the contending parties; secure and permanent borders to be determined in final status negotiations between Israel and Palestinian representatives.

All the essays in this chapter are concerned, in one way or another, with these issues and the need for peaceful negotiations to end the Israeli-Palestinian conflict.

Some of them suggest that attempts by Palestinian representatives to formulate and seek international approval for a unilateral declaration of independence are misguided. Such attempts suffer from two problems. One is that they are counterproductive, leading to mistrust between the parties and intensifying rather than reducing the existing animosity. The second problem is that these attempts not only bypass negotiations with Israel but also repudiate already negotiated understandings. It was agreed at the Oslo II Accords of September 1995 that "neither side shall initiate or take any step that will change the status of the West Bank or the Gaza Strip pending the outcome of permanent status negotiations."

The essays further argue that Palestinian representatives have constantly been unwilling to enter into negotiations. It would be helpful if they would agree that a compromise solution is not a perpetuation of any gross injustice. Other essays discuss accusations that Israel is a colonial or occupying power. Both accusations are implicitly a denial of Jewish rights and history in the disputed areas. They refuse to accept the reality that Jews form a nation, not simply a religious community.

It is not pedantic but relevant here to suggest that discussion of the territories should be in appropriate language. It would be preferable for negotiators on both sides to use the language of UN Security Council 242, which referred to "territories occupied in the recent conflict," rather than refer to "the occupied territories." The Palestinian representatives might accentuate the positive as suggested in one of the essays. A compromise settlement is unlikely to lead to a happy marriage but it might lead to a pleasant divorce with both parties living peacefully in close proximity.

Perhaps the wisest advice came from Golda Meir: "Peace will come when the Arabs will love their children more than they hate us."

1

Political Correctness and the Obsessive Attack on Israel

1. Bias in the International Community

It is difficult to avoid cynicism when considering the nature of the discussion of the policies and actions of Israel by international bodies that were ostensibly created for and purportedly engaged in furthering the existence of peace and justice in the world. To paraphrase Lord Macaulay, no spectacle is as ridiculous as the international community in its periodical fits of morality concerning Israel. Many of these organizations, both nongovernmental bodies—such as Amnesty International, Oxfam, War on Want, and the French group FIDH (International Federation for Human Rights)—and governmental bodies, particularly the organs of the United Nations, especially the United Nations Human Rights Council, have dishonored themselves and violated the principles on which they were established through their institutional bias, tendentious reports, and pejorative language concerning Israel.

It is startling to recall that Israel has been the subject of more critical resolutions in the UN General Assembly (UNGA) than any other nation. A telling illustration of this lack of balance is that while the UNGA has passed over a hundred resolutions on Palestinian refugees, it has not addressed a single one concerning the 850,000 Jewish refugees who fled or were forced to flee from Arab countries when Israel was established. Nor does any resolution address the legitimate rights of Jewish refugees who were forced to flee from Arab countries, or the issue of compensation for those Jewish refugees as part of the final negotiating process between Israel and the Arab countries and the Palestinians.

The disproportionate amount of time devoted to critical resolutions devoted to Israel has been evident in the activity of the UNGA. The institutional bias against Israel within the United Nations is reinforced by some of the very units it has created. A UNGA resolution in 1968 created a Special Committee to investigate Israeli practices affecting the human rights of the Palestinian people and other Arabs. One of the General Assembly's secretarial units, the Division for Palestinian Rights, serves as staff for the UN Committee on the Exercise of the Inalienable Rights of the Palestinian People created in 1975. This Division, together with some other UN offices, disseminates information critical of Israel and has as its main function advocacy of Palestinian rights and mobilizing international support for that policy. That objective has largely been continued in the UN Human Rights Council (UNHRC) that replaced the Commission on Human Rights in March 2006.

This bias continues, if in slightly more guarded form than in earlier years. In 2008, Israel was the subject of 120 resolutions, compared with 47 on Sudan, the second country in the list, with 37 on the Democratic Republic of the Congo, and with 32 in Myanmar. Even though the US State Department in 2009 reported that in all areas of the Congo the government's human rights record remained poor and security forces continued to act with impunity, the UNHRC in June 2009 characteristically decided that it would discontinue consideration of the situation in the Democratic Republic of the Congo.

At its eleventh session at that time, the Council spent six hours in critical discussion of Israel; it spent one minute on the Congo. In another report, Israel was, next to the Islamic Republic of Iran, declared guilty of the largest number of violations of human rights in the world. With this state of the moral conscience of the world, the general response to the action of Israel in December 2008 in Gaza against the forces of Hamas (The Islamic Resistance Movement formed in 1987) that had launched over six thousand rockets against Israeli civilians was entirely predictable.

Rather than seeing the Israeli action as a legitimate response to aggression, many commentators saw it as an unprecedented use of force and as collective punishment or, in moderated language, usually used as a disproportionate attack. Those commentators have not yet defined what a proportionate response might be to unprovoked Arab attacks on innocent civilians. They also had no comment on the attacks by Hamas inside Israel in June 2006, during which one Israeli soldier was kidnapped, and the attack by the Hamas's Popular Resistance Committees on southern Israel on August 18, 2011, in which eight Israelis were killed.

By dint of the constant reiteration of a biased narrative of events in the Middle East, and particularly of the interactions between Israel and Palestinians, and the deliberate unsympathetic interpretation of Israeli actions, the world is well aware of problems in the West Bank. One may ask if it is similarly aware of much worse problems in East Timor. Advocates of human rights have frequently been culpable of selective morality in their analysis of instances of injustices and flagrant violations of rights.

Consider the outrage expressed by international bodies over actions by Israeli authorities compared with the response, either minimal or none, about those in a few other countries: the thirty-five thousand killed in the brutal civil war in Syria; the twenty thousand civilians, part of the total of seventy thousand, killed by Sri Lankan troops fighting against the Tamil Tigers; the cleansing of Bahai's in Iran; discrimination against Berbers in North Africa; the killing of over two million in Darfur; the genocide by Hutus in Rwanda; the turmoil in Zimbabwe; the slaughters in Somalia; the elimination of the entire community of Bodo inhabitants of Takimari in northeast India by Muslims; the lack of freedom in North Korea, the world's remaining totalitarian state; violence in the Congo; the forty thousand killed in Chechnya; discrimination against Tibetans; massacres in the Balkans, especially in Srebrenica; and the discrimination within the Arab world, particularly against women and children, and also against Christians. The international community has paid scant attention to the practice in Syria and other Arab countries of men murdering female relatives for besmirching the honor of the family by having sex outside marriage, or by having been raped, or by wearing immodest clothes. Little has been said about the practice in Muslim countries of stoning women to death for adultery. Nor has attention been drawn to the lack of freedom of travel or choice of residence in Saudi Arabia.

Surprisingly little attention has been paid by the international bodies interested in violations of human rights and by those ostensibly concerned about the treatment and condition of Arabs in Middle East countries to help remedy the deficiencies pointed out by the Arab intellectuals who wrote the United Nations Arab Human Development Report of 2002, which has largely been ignored.

That Report concluded that Arab nations suffer not so much from any actions of Israel as from a deficit of freedom, gender inequality, weak commitment to education, and denial of human rights in their own countries. That deficit of freedom meant that out of seven world regions, the Arab countries had the lowest freedom score in the late 1990s.

In those countries women suffer from unequal citizenship and legal entitlements, often evident in voting rights and legal codes. Those nations apparently are reluctant to tackle their domestic economic and political problems. According to the 2009 UN Arab Development Report, Arab countries are less industrialized today than they were four decades ago.

2. Bias in Geneva

Perhaps the most ridiculous organization in the contemporary world is the misnamed United Nations Human Rights Council (UNHRC), which meets in Geneva, Switzerland. It purports to be responsible for the promotion and protection of all human rights around the world. Supposedly a forum and a springboard for action for all victims of human rights abuses, its membership alone would disabuse anyone that this remotely resembled the reality. Among its forty-seven current or recent members are countries whose record of human rights are not universally admired, such as Libya, Mauritania, where slavery still prevails, Saudi Arabia, Cuba, Kuwait, Qatar, Jordan, Burkina Faso, and Russia. Syria applied for admission in July 2012 but, under pressure, withdrew its application two months later. Surprisingly, the United States became a member three years ago and has again applied and been admitted for another three-year term.

That the UNHRC has become a major and unrelenting critic of Israel has been evident for some years. Some two-thirds of its critical resolutions and special sessions have been focused on the State of Israel and its policies. It reached a new low point with the adoption of eleven resolutions of March 22, 2012, primarily concerned with the impact of Israeli settlements on "the Occupied Palestinian Territory, including East Jerusalem, and the occupied Syria Golan." These resolutions have resulted in yet another inquiry, the sixth so far, into alleged Israeli violations of human rights. The resolutions barely mentioned any issue other than those regarding Israel. Moreover, these resolutions provide for the issue of human rights in Israel to be debated every year.

A survey of these resolutions would make clear the total bias of the UNHRC. In one of them, the Council decided at the March 2012 meeting to dispatch an independent international fact-finding mission to investigate the implications of the Israeli settlements on the civil, political, economic, social, and cultural rights of the Palestinian people throughout the Occupied Arab Territories, including East Jerusalem. On July 6, the mission was in fact appointed, with the naming of three women jurists as its members: Christine Chanet of France, Unity Dow of Botswana, and Asma Jahangir of Pakistan. The mission will examine only Israeli actions and their alleged impact on the human rights of Palestinians. The constant attacks by Palestinians on Israeli civilians, and their violations of Israeli human rights will not be part of the inquiry.

All of the eleven resolutions betray the bias of UNHRC, as is shown in the following language used. One resolution, regarding human rights in the "occupied Syrian Golan," calls on Israel to stop a number of activities: building settlements, imposing Israeli citizenship and Israeli identity cards, allowing the Syrian population of the "occupied Syrian Golan" to visit their families. Another resolution called on Israel to stop all settlement activities in the Occupied Palestinian territory, including East Jerusalem, and to cease prolonged closures and economic and movement restrictions, including those amounting to a blockade on the Gaza Strip.

What is disconcerting about all these resolutions is not only the level of hypocrisy and double standards in the UNHRC and the distorted and prejudiced language concentrated against Israel, and not against any other country, but also the considerable and sometimes near-unanimous majority they received. One resolution (A/HRC/19/L.34) stated that all measures and actions taken by Israel in the Occupied Palestinian territory, including East Jerusalem, in violation of the relevant provisions of the Geneva Convention and contrary to the relevant resolutions of the Security Council, are illegal and have no validity. It was adopted by a vote of forty-four in favor, two abstentions (Cameroon and Guatemala), and only one against (United States).

The resolution (A/HRC/19/L.35) condemning the plan to construct new housing units for Israeli settlers in the West Bank and around occupied East Jerusalem was adopted by a vote of thirty-six in favor, ten abstentions, and one against (US). In this there was delightful irony. Syria, where the slaughter—including among other methods the use of fighter jets in major cities—of its own citizens has so far amounted to over 70,000 people; where street battles have been fought in the Old City of Aleppo, a UNESCO World Heritage Site; where more than 500,000 have fled the country, about half to Turkey; and where the government has refused to agree to cease-fire efforts, said that Israel was sabotaging peace efforts. In contrast, the United States argued that it was inappropriate to prejudge final status issues that could only be resolved through bilateral negotiations between Israel and the Palestinians.

A third resolution (A/HRC/19/L.36), referring to a previous report on the Gaza conflict, called for the reconvening of a conference to enforce the Fourth Geneva Convention in the Occupied Palestinian Territory, including East Jerusalem. This resolution, which was in essence a call for inquiry into alleged violations of human rights by Israel and improper use of certain munitions, was adopted by a vote of twenty-nine in favor, seventeen abstentions, and one against (US). On this resolution, Belgium, speaking on behalf of the European Union, had the grace to abstain.

What is perhaps most troubling about these selective and politicized resolutions, all purportedly concerned about the plight of the Palestinians, is that none of them called on the Palestinian Authority to resume bilateral relations with the State of Israel, which is the only way to lead to a peaceful resolution of the Israeli-Palestinian conflict. It is unlikely that the new one-sided inquiry into alleged Israeli violations of human rights to be made by the three named women jurists, whose impartiality remains to be tested, will lead to a useful conclusion that will forward a peaceful resolution. Indeed, Christine Chanet, the head of the new inquiry, is reported to have said in July 2012 that "In Israel's written response to the committee [she was heading] one could see a total discrimination in the sense that settlers benefitted from the pact." Commenting on a country, one of the freest in the world that has so many political parties and points of view expressed without reserve, she may be one of the few people in the world to find "it was very difficult to have a real dialogue with Israel." The United States should have reconsidered the desirability of its membership of the UNHRC, a body committed to disproportionate and one-sided resolutions.

3. The Durban Follies

In similar fashion to the working of the UNHRC, the inherent and automatic bias by a majority of the international community has been illustrated by the Durban meetings, the so-called World Conferences against Racism, Racial Discrimination, Xenophobia, and Related Intolerance, in essence an extension of the UN Human Rights Council. It is ironic that the Durban meetings should have been the forum for ugly displays of intolerance and antisemitism. The main thrust of the outcomes of Durban I, held in September 2001, and Durban II, held in Geneva in April 2009, was the repeated charge against Israel of racism and apartheid. One consequence of this charge was the impetus given to the campaign for boycott, disinvestment, and sanctions against Israel.

The Durban statements led countries to have fewer specific contacts with Israel; the overall objective was to isolate Israel from the world community.

Durban I was hosted by the United Nations Human Rights Council (UNHRC), a body that, since it was set up in 2006, has condemned Israel in about half of its resolutions. Durban I was attended by representatives not only of states but also of about 1,500 nongovernmental organizations (NGOs), some of which helped shape the critical language later used about Israel at the Conference. Indeed it was the NGO Forum during the meeting that used a strategy of advocating human rights claims as a device to attack Israel. The conference of Durban II itself was prepared by a committee whose chairs were representatives from Libya and Cuba.

The objective of Durban II was to examine and undertake a comprehensive implementation of the conclusions and recommendations of the UN Durban I (World Conference against Racism, Racial Discrimination, Xenophobia, and Related Intolerance), held in September 2001. One can take some comfort that highly critical and disparaging remarks about Israel written in the Preparatory Committee Report for Durban II were eliminated in the final Outcome Document of the Conference.

Nevertheless, the first paragraph of that Document of April 2009 affirms the statement of the earlier Durban I Conference. That statement in Article 72, which implicitly refers to Israel, "reaffirms that a foreign occupation founded on settlements, its laws based on racial discrimination with the aim of continuing domination of the occupied territory, as well as its practices, which consist of reinforcing a total military blockade, isolating towns, cities and villages under occupation from each other, totally contradict the purposes and principles of the Charter of the United Nations and constitute a serious violation of international human rights and humanitarian law, a new kind of apartheid, a crime against humanity, a form of genocide and a serious threat to international peace and security." Moreover, paragraph 63, mentioning only one group, states that "We are concerned about the plight of the Palestinian people under foreign occupation," and paragraph 65, again implicitly confining itself to one group, says, "We recognize the right of refugees to return voluntarily to their homes and properties in dignity and safety." No other group is mentioned specifically. An even stronger statement emerged from the NGO Forum at Durban I. Article 162 of its final statement says, "We declare Israel as a racist, apartheid state."

A number of countries, including the United States, Canada, Italy, Czech Republic, Austria, Australia, the Netherlands, and Israel, announced they would not attend Durban III. All realized that the Durban process, I and II, had been a travesty of human rights concerns and that it has promoted rather than combatted racism. Instead, it has been a platform for relentless attacks on Zionism.

The conclusions of the Durban process are a sad commentary on the bias within the international community. Though Israel was not directly named, those conclusions, which clearly referred to it, stated that a foreign occupation founded on settlements, with laws based on racial discrimination to maintain domination of the occupied territory, totally contradicted the purposes and principles of the Charter of the United Nations.

In their immoderate language, the documents held that Israeli policy was a violation of international human rights and humanitarian law, a new kind of apartheid, a form of genocide. Mentioning only one group in the world, the Durban process was concerned about "the plight of the Palestinian people under foreign occupation." It recognized the right of refugees to their homes and properties. Israel was charged with occupation, but obvious violations of human rights such as China's occupation of Tibet and Russia's occupation of Japanese Kuril islands since the end of World War II remained unmentioned.

The spurious nature of the Conferences was clearly shown at Durban II, which provided an official platform for Iranian President Mahmoud Ahmadinejad, the only head of government to attend the meeting. In his customary manner and extravagant rhetoric, he declared that Israel was a racist state masquerading as a religious one and that it was the most cruel and repressive racist regime in existence. This, of course, was before the Arab Spring and the revelations of the absence of human rights in the Arab countries. The Iranian leader in his raucous declaration accused the West of using the Holocaust as a pretext for aggression against the Palestinians. If he was more careful in referring to the Holocaust as an "ambiguous and dubious position," he did advocate the end of the State of Israel.

The very timing of Durban III on September 21, 2011, in New York, was a gratuitous insult to the sensibilities to the United States and to freedom-loving countries. The Durban process has not been a milestone in the inherent struggle against racism but rather the reverse in its manifestation of political hatred. Predictably, Durban III issued a statement that the Palestinians were "victims of racism." Equally predicable was the utterance of the foreign minister of Iran about "the human rights violations perpetrated by the Zionist regime" against the Palestinians.

The United States did well to absent itself from this travesty. It might have gone further in using the occasion to start a prosecution against Ahmadinejad, based on the Convention on the Prevention and Punishment of the Crime of Genocide, adopted by the United Nations General Assembly (Resolution 260) on December 9, 1948. This would be based not on his relatively mild comments in New York in 2008 that the so-called Zionists dominated an important part of the financial centers as well as the political decision-making centers of the United States and some European countries, but on his call for the elimination of the State of Israel.

4. Animosity or Hatred?

On October 6, 2011 Tzipi Livni, former Israeli foreign minister and then leader of the Kadima party, met in London with British Foreign Secretary William Hague. Her previous attempt to attend a conference in Britain in December 2009 was prevented when an intended arrest warrant was issued by the Westminster magistrates' court. She was to be arrested for her alleged involvement as Israeli foreign minister in Operation Cast Lead, the Israeli response to the incessant shelling from Gaza, between December 27, 2008, and January 18, 2009. The issuing of the warrant was based on the principle of universal jurisdiction. The difference for Livni in October 2011 was a change in British law, a month earlier, concerning that principle.

However, the change in the law has not stopped the harassment of Israeli officials. Mr. Hague, on behalf of the British Foreign Office, was obliged to give the Crown Prosecution Service a certificate that Livni was on a "special mission." That meant that the visit included diplomatic functions, thus providing immunity from legal action during the visit. A court cannot challenge the classification of a visit as a "special mission."

The principle of universal jurisdiction provides for national courts to adjudicate cases against foreigners alleged to have committed crimes against humanity, war crimes, genocide, and torture, irrespective of where the alleged crimes were committed or the nationality of the accused, or whether the actions had done damage to the citizens or interests in the country of the court. Under the Geneva Conventions Act of 1957, war crimes and other grave offences are subject to universal jurisdiction. Some form of legal provision regarding these offences is now present in most countries in the world.

The principle seems eminently reasonable on the premise that such crimes are so serious that they should be prosecuted everywhere. It provided the rationale for the trial in Jerusalem in 1962 of Adolf Eichmann, who had been living with forged papers as Ricardo Klement in Argentina since July 1950. Eichmann and other senior Nazi officials such as Josef Mengele, the camp doctor at Auschwitz, had escaped prosecution in Europe by fleeing to South America. In the postwar years, the menace of Communism appeared to officials and groups—including the CIA, the Catholic Church, and the International Red Cross—as more imperative than prosecuting former Nazi leaders.

The Israeli court held that the crimes committed by Eichmann, one of the major Nazi figures responsible for the Holocaust, not only bore an international character but also that their widespread harmful effects shook the international community to its very foundation. It held that the State of Israel was therefore entitled to try and to punish him. Likewise, Prime Minister Ben Gurion argued that Israel, the land of Jews, could legitimately try and punish Eichmann for his crimes in the genocide against Jews.

The principle of universal jurisdiction also seems equally reasonable as embodying the rule of law that perpetrators of serious violations of human rights should not use foreign countries as a haven to escape punishment. Thus, international tribunals since the Nuremberg trials have examined actions by individuals in the former Yugoslavia in 1993 and Rwanda in 1994. The Rome Statute of the International Criminal Court, 1999, declared that the most serious crimes of concern to the international community as a whole must not go unpunished. Effective prosecution would be ensured by action at the national level and by enhancing international cooperation.

Desirable though the use of the principle has been on some occasions, the essential problem is that it has been used not only for legal reasons but also abused for political purposes. The chief targets of the abuse have been citizens of Israel. Ariel Sharon, Israeli minister of defense during the civil war in Lebanon, when Christian Phalangists Maronites killed eight hundred Palestinians in the refugee camps of Sabra and Shatila in Beirut, was not only held morally responsible for these murders by others but was also accused of war crimes in a court in Brussels in 2003. Two Israeli military figures, Doron Almog in September 2005 and Moshe Ya'alon in October 2009, could not visit Britain also for fear of being charged with war crimes.

An arrest of Ehud Barak, then defense minister, was only prevented in Britain in September 2009 because the British Foreign Office said he had diplomatic immunity. Several other Israeli generals or former generals have decided not to visit European countries because of the fear of being arrested for war crimes. Among them were General Yohannan Locker, military secretary to prime minister Netanyahu, and General Aviv Kochavi, head of Israel's Intelligence Corps. While some attempts have also been made to issue warrants against other individuals such as Henry Kissinger and Bo Xilai, Chinese trade minister, most warrants have been against Israelis.

To remedy this abuse of its justice system, the British Parliament on September 15, 2011, passed the Police Reform and Social Responsibility Act. By British law, in cases of universal jurisdiction, anyone may apply to a magistrate or to the courts for a summons or an arrest warrant of those alleged to have committed war crimes anywhere. The essence of the reform is that now the director of public prosecutions is required to consent when an individual or group calls for an arrest warrant. He can decline issues of warrants made on scant evidence or for the purposes of making a political statement or causing embarrassment, or when there is no realistic chance of prosecution.

The legal dilemma is that arrest warrants need less evidence than a case for prosecution. Thus they have been increasingly used for harassment. The change in British law is intended to ensure that visitors to the country would be protected from malicious and politically motivated arrests and that alleged violations will only be pursued on the basis of solid evidence likely to lead to a successful prosecution.

Though the intention of the legal change is well meaning, the problem of harassment of Israelis and the depths of animosity toward Israel remains. Two incidents are particularly revealing. One was the behavior of Baroness (Jenny) Tonge, Liberal Democrat, during the debate on the Police Reform Bill in the House of Lords, in which the Bill passed by only a single vote majority. The second was the publication of a letter in the newspaper *The Guardian* on December 12, 2010.

Lady Tonge is well-known for her anti-Israeli position. In February 2010 she resembled a performer in the theater of the absurd by arguing that Israel should set up an inquiry to disprove that its medical team sent to help in the disaster in Haiti was trafficking in the organs of earthquake victims. In the 2011 House of Lords debate she argued that the real reason for the change in law was the incident relating to allegations of war crimes against Tzipi Livni in 2009. She attacked the British foreign secretary for not having thoroughly examined the evidence against Livni at that time. After being called to order for her intemperate remarks, she ran out of the chamber. She was officially chastised for disobeying the normal rules of the House of Lords and acting in an inappropriate manner.

The letter in *The Guardian*, signed by more than fifty people—including many familiar and automatic critics of Israel such as the filmmaker Ken Loach, the playwright Caryl Churchill, and Labour Party members of Parliament Martin Linton and Jeremy Corbyn—opposed the changes in the Police Reform Bill. The changes, they wrote, would "risk creating a culture of impunity in the minds of those politicians and military leaders who already treat international law with cavalier disregard" and would allow people suspected of war crimes to escape justice. It is not irrelevant in explaining their attitude that Mr. Linton had warned on March 23, 2010, of the "long tentacles of Israel" interfering in the forthcoming British parliamentary election, and that Mr. Corbyn was reprimanded for breaching standards of impartiality by his charges against Israel in a television program. Corbyn had always made the absurd allegation that Israel in 2008–9 had used phosphorous bombs against an unarmed and defenseless Palestinian civilian population.

Equally critical of the reform of the law was a conference entitled "Universal Jurisdiction against Israeli War Criminals" hosted by the Middle East Monitor in London on December 7, 2009. The keynote address was given by John Duggard, a South African–born professor of international law. He was the former, unpaid, supposedly impartial Special Rapporteur to the UN Commission on Human Rights (now the UN Human Rights Council) in the Occupied Palestinian Territories. On this occasion he repeated the title of the conference, emphasizing the importance of implementing universal jurisdiction against Israeli war criminals.

Earlier, Duggard had compared Israel to Apartheid South Africa, stating, "Both regimes were/are characterized by discrimination, repression, and territorial fragmentation [that is, land seizures]." Apartheid's security police, he said, practiced torture on a large scale as did the Israeli security forces. In his report of February 2007 as Special Rapporteur this professor of law, using unscholarly language, asked rhetorically, "Can it seriously be denied that the purpose [of Israeli actions in the West Bank] is to establish and maintain domination by one racial group [Jews] over another racial group [Palestinians] and systematically oppressing them?"

A number of British lawyers known for their partisan opinions participated in the general campaign against Israel, and specifically against Livni. They argued that the Police Reform Act did not provide protection of the Israeli politician. Hague's action in allowing Livni to visit London is commendable, but it illustrates the remaining problem that he had to find a way to prevent her arrest and allow Livni to enter Britain. Animosity, and perhaps hatred, toward Israel will, for various reasons, probably be manifested for some time, and the reform in British law has not eliminated that animosity.

The anti-Israeli lobby is made up of domestic political groups in the US and European countries; individual lobbyists paid by Arab countries and executives of oil companies; direct participation by Saudi Arabia by its expenditure of hundreds of millions of dollars in building mosques and Islamic centers in the US and its impact on school curriculum, financing of Wahhabist literature, and funds given to US universities and thousands of Muslim students, domestic and foreign, attending US universities. Among other things, this essentially informal anti-Israeli lobby has used or endorsed the use of international law, under the guise of universal jurisdiction, for political expediency and for harassing Israelis. It is making a mockery of the Fourth Geneva Convention and the Universal Declaration of Human Rights.

5. The Accusation of Apartheid

The indiscriminate, hermetic criticism of Israel, especially since 1967, reached its apogee by denouncing Israel not simply as a racist but even more as an apartheid state, thus evoking the injustices of the infamous former South African regime. This indictment initially appeared at the Assembly of Heads of State and Government of the Organization of African Unity, July 28–August 1, 1975 which compared "the racist regime in occupied Palestine" with the racist regimes in Zimbabwe and South Africa.

The criticism was repeated in the UN General Assembly Resolution 3379 of November 10, 1975, which determined "that Zionism is a form of racism and racial discrimination." The Resolution was carried by a large majority that included all the Islamic and communist countries and which in fact was inspired by propaganda and pressure of the then Soviet Union.

13

Other organizations repeated the charge. One was the League of Arab States, which on May 22, 2004, adopted an Arab Charter on Human Rights, which came into force in March 2008. Article 2(3) of the Charter states, "All forms of racism, Zionism, and foreign occupation and dominion constitute an impediment to human dignity and a major barrier to the fundamental rights of peoples; all such practices must be condemned and efforts must be deployed for their elimination." The Charter held that racism and Zionism constituted a "violation of human rights and a threat to international peace and security."

It was disconcerting that celebrated individuals such as the novelist Alice Walker in 2012 and Nobel Peace Prize winner Archbishop Desmond Tutu in 2002 should have compared the treatment of Palestinians by Israel with the treatment of native Africans by the former South African regime. Others went further than Tutu in criticism. Israel was said to be the embodiment of evils: apartheid, occupation, colonialism. Thus it could be the object of a boycott, divestment, and sanctions against it.

Any reasonable objective observer could appreciate the falsity and absurdity of equating contemporary Israel, faults and all, with the specific and empirical behavior of the former South African regime. Controversial Israeli actions in the West Bank such as house demolitions and some expulsions of people do not constitute a behavior pattern comparable to that in South Africa, whose apartheid policy was systematically grounded on legal racism and segregation of people of different races. People there were officially recorded on the basis of race ranging from white to seven other population groups, and laws there created and maintained a society of legal, economic, and residential discrimination.

The very word apartheid derives from an Afrikaner term meaning separateness or apartness. It is generally defined as "an institutionalized regime of systematic oppression and domination by one racial group over any other racial group or groups and committed with the intention of maintaining that regime." But its definition has been deliberately changed by international bodies to fit the case of relations between Israel and Palestinians.

To illustrate the issue it is helpful to examine the exact nature of apartheid as it existed in the South African political and social system from its introduction in 1948 by the ruling National Party under its leader D. F. Malan until 1994, when Nelson Mandela, leader of the African National Congress who had spent twenty-seven years in prison, became president of the country.

The first major edict of discrimination was the prohibition in 1949 of mixed marriages between white people and people of other races. A year later, sexual relationships between white and black people were forbidden. In 1950, a national register was created in which each person's race was recorded, and tests were made of physical and linguistic factors. In the same year different residential areas were established for different races. Over three million were thus relocated by forced removal. By other statutes, blacks could not perform any skilled labor in urban areas except in those areas designated for black occupation, and they could be removed from public or privately owned land and resettled in special camps.

Starting in the 1950s, statutes created a system of territorial segregation. In 1951 black homelands, or Bantustans (coined from the name for "people" in Bantu language), with some measure of self-government and regional authority were set up in South Africa and in Southwest Africa (now Namibia). In time, the area of the Bantustans constituted about 13 percent of the country. As a corollary, the possibility of blacks having the right of permanent residence in towns was narrowed to those who had lived or worked there for not less than fifteen years. By the Pass Laws of 1952, black people over age sixteen were obliged to carry identification at all times. Anyone unable to produce a pass could be arrested. No black could leave a rural area for an urban one without official permission; in urban areas a black had to obtain a work permit within seventy-two hours of arrival. By the Bantu Education Act of 1953 a curriculum was to be compiled to suit "the nature and requirements of the black people." The aim of this was to limit educational opportunities for blacks through schooling that would only provide them with skills to serve their fellow blacks in the homelands or to work in jobs under whites.

Probably the most egregious of the statutes was the 1953 Reservation of Separate Amenities Act that imposed forced segregation in all public amenities, public buildings and transport, in order to prevent contact between white and other races. Facilities provided for the different races did not have to be of equal quality. By an act of 1959, black students could no longer attend white universities, mainly those of Cape Town and Witwatersrand. The Promotion of Bantu Self-Government Act of 1959 classified black people into eight ethnic groups. Each was to live in a homeland developed for it and could govern itself without white intervention.

The overall objective of the South African system was to codify and further segregate the black homelands that had been established in

1951 by making them self-governing political units. People became citizens of their homelands and thus were deprived of South African citizenship. The 1970 Bantu Homelands Citizens Act went even further. All black people were compelled to become citizens of the homelands relevant to their ethnic group, irrespective of whether or not they lived there. They would now be considered as aliens without South African nationality or the right to live or work in South Africa. Between 1976 and 1981, four of the ten Bantustans that were set up were granted independence, with a government and a flag of their own. But they were not recognized internationally.

For forty years no genuine negotiations were undertaken to change or modify the oppressive laws. Beginning in the mid-1980s some of the restrictions began to be removed, and the dismantling of the apartheid system began. After the release of Nelson Mandela in 1990 and the first democratic election in 1994, with all people able to vote, and the ensuing National Unity government, apartheid was officially ended.

Can the real relations between Israel and Palestinians be justly or even remotely compared with this picture of the nature of an apartheid regime? Israel has been criticized for the unequal place of Israeli Arabs within its territory, for the existence of separate roads, checkpoints, roadblocks, curfews, clearing of olive groves used for ambushes, and border defenses outside the Green Line (the cease-fire line between Israel and Jordan between 1949 and 1967); for limited access for Palestinians to land and resources; and for Israeli settlements in the disputed areas of the West Bank and Golan Heights. It is true that in the Teudat Zehut (compulsory national identification card), which all legal residents in Israel over sixteen must carry, the Hebrew date of birth is included, thus indicating if the holder is or is not Jewish. But to term this apartheid or foreign occupation may be deemed rhetorical excess or linguistic partisanship. Whatever the validity of some or all of the criticisms, Israeli policies are not based on racial criteria or animated by racist ideology, nor do they seek to create Bantustans. Israeli Arabs have not been deported to the West Bank or Gaza or anywhere else. They have not been denied access to universities, hospitals, or political organizations, or to international bodies, or movement to and from the outside world without cause.

The struggle of local Africans against the oppressive Afrikaner colonization cannot be considered comparable to the friction between Palestinians and Jews who have returned to their ancient homeland.

A deliberate legal policy of segregation and discrimination in South Africa is not equivalent to a tragic clash of two national movements competing for self-determination in the same area of Palestine or *Eretz Israel* (the land of Israel). In contrast to the South African case, negotiations have been sought by Israel since 1949 to reach a just and lasting peace between the two sides.

Lewis Carroll immortalized the adage that words mean what you want them to mean. In November 1973, the UN General Assembly (Resolution 3068) adopted the International Convention on the Suppression and Punishment of the Crime of Apartheid, which became enforced in July 1976. Implicit in it was that a condition of apartheid was not limited to the South African regime but was to be considered a crime against humanity. It was now defined as policies and practices of racial segregation and discrimination which have the purpose of establishing and maintaining domination by one racial group of persons over another group of persons and systematically oppressing them, in particular by means such as segregation, expropriation of land, denial of the right to leave and return to one's country, the right to a nationality, and the right to freedom of movement and residence.

The Rome Statute of the International Criminal Court, which was established as a tribunal to prosecute persons for genocide, crimes against humanity, and war crimes, was adopted in July 1998 and became enforced in July 2002. In its Article 7, it listed apartheid as one of the crimes against humanity and defined it as inhumane acts "committed in the context of an institutionalized regime of systematic oppression and domination by one racial group over any other racial group or groups, and committed with the intention of maintaining that regime." Accordingly, organizations and agents of an apartheid state are subject to criminal prosecution, irrespective of motives involved. The crucial change in definition of apartheid from the 1973 formula was that persecution was now said to be on political, national, ethnic, cultural and religious grounds, not merely racial ones. This definition could thus be seen as applicable to Israeli actions in the territories. One perhaps unintended consequence was that Jimmy Carter entitled his 2006 book *Palestine: Peace not Apartheid.*

A fair commentary would be that international law has been used, or misused, for partisan purposes to attack Israel. It is worth pointing out in this connection the paradox that since 1999 the UN, at the urging of the Organization of the Islamic Conference of fifty-seven states, has every year passed a resolution on Combating Defamation of Religions which in effect attempts to prevent criticism of Islam, a religion usually defined as "submission to God."[1]

In what may well be considered its lowest point the United Nations approved the General Assembly Resolution 3379 on November 10, 1975. The Zionist ideology was thus denounced as embodying racist exclusiveness by a people, Jews, whose colonial intentions were to create a nation, and to occupy by military means the land of Palestine and to dominate the Arabs living there. This extraordinary Resolution ignored or misunderstood the diversity of the Zionist movement, which was never monolithic, and its aspirations for a Jewish independent state in the ancient homeland of the Jewish people which, among other things, would be both an endeavor of national renewal and a safe haven for Jews. For critics, the original sin of Zionism was the Zionist call for Jewish settlement in that territory by immigrants and the injunction not to depend for survival on Arab labor. For those critics such settlement and the injunction meant displacing non-Jewish Palestinians. Yet this was not the original intention of the Zionist pioneers, nor was it the objective of Israeli military actions in 1947–48, when the settlers were attacked before and immediately following the establishment of the State of Israel in May 1948, consequent on the UN General Assembly Resolution of November 29, 1947. Palestinian leaders tried to prevent Jewish settlement by calling on Britain, which was the Mandatory power, to limit immigration, and by refusing to sell land to Jews, as well as engaging in violence against those settlements.

Following the 1948–49 war, Israel did not create any legal system of territorial segregation, though for understandable security purposes it did, between 1948 and 1967, control the movements of Israeli Arabs. Yet, with the conflict between Israel and Palestinians still unresolved, a cogent reply to the criticism of this control was given by Professor Ruth Gavison, who argued that the "contiguity of Arab settlement both within Israel and with the Arab states across the border . . . invites irredentism and secessionist claims, and neutralizing the threat of secession is a legitimate goal."[2]

6. Apartheid Used as a Cultural Weapon

The constant reference to Israel as an apartheid state has affected some commentators, who have used the charge as a political instrument to criticize the state and its citizens and to call for a boycott of them. Among these commentators have recently been individuals in the arts, individuals hardly politically sophisticated but eager to condemn Israel. This was shown in events in 2012 relating to the performances in Britain given by the Israeli Habima theater company and the Batsheva dance company, and by the unusually strong denouncing of the State of Israel by Alice Walker, the distinguished novelist.

Shylock in *The Merchant of Venice* rightly protested against injustice toward Jews and to manifestations of malignant antisemitism. One might expect fair-minded people to protest against the unjust assault on Israeli institutions, its culture, and its people being waged by some European professionals against Israeli fellow professionals, as well by those groups accustomed on all occasions to supporting Palestinians and condemning Israel. Those groups always apply a double standard in their automatic critical comments on Israel's behavior and actions, while rarely mentioning violations of human rights by other countries. Yet, consciously or otherwise, the European professionals mentioned have tended to accept the Palestinian narrative of history and of their present conditions, a narrative that is based on negative images, myths, and malicious stereotypes about Israel and Jews.

Those participating in the campaign against Israel should heed Shylock's words to his accusers: "You have among you many a purchased slave which . . . you use in abject and in slavish parts." European and American academics who have for some time called for a boycott of Israeli universities and teachers ought to be conscious of the double standard implied in Shylock's remark. More recently, some cultural performers have joined this campaign, calling for a boycott of specific Israeli activities, which they believe will exert pressure on Israel to change its policies, especially on the issue of what they charge is "illegal occupation of occupied land." They forget that culture should foster international dialogue, regardless of external events.

On March 29, 2012, the British newspaper *The Guardian* published a letter signed by thirty-seven actors, playwrights, and producers, including individuals prominent in the theater such as Emma Thompson, Mark Rylance, Mike Leigh, David Calder, and Jonathan Miller. The letter asked the Globe Theater in London to withdraw its invitation to Habima, (The Stage) Israel's National Theater since 1958, to perform *The Merchant of Venice* in its World Festival of thirty-seven Shakespeare plays to be performed in thirty-seven languages starting in May 2012. To his great credit, the director of the Globe did not agree. The performances took place in spite of the fact they were disrupted by Palestinians and activists inside and outside the theater.

The ostensible reason for this call to boycott Habima was that the company had performed in the halls of culture in two unnamed Israeli settlements. The two, in fact, were Kiryat Arba, founded in 1968 on the site near Hebron, where Jews were massacred by Arabs in 1929, and Ariel, which was founded in 1978 about eleven miles east of the Green Line.

This was not the first time that groups have tried to prevent Israelis from performing. The letter in *The Guardian* had been preceded by a letter to the director of the Globe in January 2012, written by a group in Israel, apparently Jewish and Arab citizens, calling itself Boycott from Within, founded in 2009. A year earlier, in August 2011, a performance sponsored by the BBC at the Royal Albert Hall in London by the Israel Philharmonic Orchestra, (IPO), which played works by Anton Webern, Max Bruch, and Nikolai Rimsky-Korsakov, was disrupted by Palestinian protestors and their allies. This churlish behavior led to the cancellation for the first time of a live radio broadcast by the BBC. At that time twenty-three professional musicians published a letter in the British paper *The Independent* castigating the BBC for inviting the IPO. The displays of ignorance, malice and blinded ideology have become farce. It is difficult to accept the view of these twenty-three musicians that the IPO in its concert was Israel's prime weapon in any denial of human rights.

Equally fatuous was the letter written in October 2012 by fifty writers and artists to the head of Carnegie Hall in New York to ban a performance by the Israel Philharmonic Orchestra conducted by Zubin Mehta on the grounds that Israel was an apartheid state. This is especially ironic since Mehta, a non-Jewish Parsi from Bombay, is active in promoting musical education for Israeli Arabs and gives free concerts in Israel towns that have a predominantly Arab population.

It was equally difficult to accept the view that performances in Israel by American jazz artists such as McCoy Tyner and Cassandra Wilson can be regarded as supporting Israeli policies of "ethno-racial segregation and apartheid," as protestors proclaimed. It is even more difficult to take seriously the actor David Calder, one of the signers of the March 29, 2012, letter, and who himself has played the role of Shylock with the Royal Shakespeare Company, who is quoted as saying that Habima was part of a "cultural fig leaf for Israel's daily brutality."

The Guardian letter speaks of the Globe Theater "associating itself with policies of exclusion practiced by the Israeli state and endorsed by its national theatre company." Any objective, especially theatrical, observer should have been familiar, though the thirty-seven signers apparently were not, with the broad range of productions of Habima, which has staged plays on a variety of themes, some critical of Israel, and which as a group has no political policies of its own, nor acts on outside instructions.

Though some of the signatories of the letter, such as Emma Thompson and Mark Rylance, fine actors on the stage and screen, are unlikely to be regarded as knowledgeable, sophisticated analysts of Middle East history and politics, others such as Caryl Churchill and Mike Leigh are well-known for their habitual and relentless criticism of Israel, regardless of any specific actions. It is regrettable, though understandable, that Thompson and others should not be fully aware of the complex issues concerning the disputed territories or the historic connection of the Jewish people to that land. One wonders if she is aware of the size and location of the two Israeli settlements that were, supposedly, the reason for the call for the banning of a great theatrical company whose performance she might have admired. She and her fellow writers know well the location of the Globe Theater, on the South Bank of the river in London, but are they equally familiar with the nature of the West Bank?

The argument in the letter that the Habima performance would be complicit with human rights violations and the illegal colonization of occupied land by Israel suggests three things; the writers need tutoring in the niceties of international law and Middle East affairs; they are, by their silence on the issues, implicitly condoning the human rights violations of the companies from China, a country that occupies Tibet, which performed *Richard III* in Mandarin; from Turkey, a country that represses the Kurds and occupies part of Cyprus, which performed *Anthony and Cleopatra*; and from Russia, which presented *Measure for Measure*, and they are disrespecting the fact that Habima is the most well-known and respected Hebrew-language theater in the world.

It is saddening that the prominent members of the theatrical and musical professions should be so benighted in their biased view of Israeli policies and their lack of understanding of the realities of Middle East politics. It is perhaps most ironic that the controversy they have created is about the disinterested decision of the Globe Theater. The thirty-seven signatories of the letter should be reminded of the blue plaque outside the Theater honoring Sam Wanamaker, the American Jewish actor who was blacklisted in 1952 during the McCarthy years despite his distinguished service in US forces in World War II, and who is the person most responsible in his time, energy, and enthusiasm for the rebuilding of the Globe as an exact replica of the one in which Shakespeare acted. What would the visionary Wanamaker, who made the Globe an international symbol of high culture, have thought of the biased, ungenerous thirty-seven? Echoing Shylock, probably "I am not bound to please you with my answers."

Since 2004 the Palestinians and their supporters, as part of their campaign against Israel, have called for a boycott of all cultural performances and exhibitions associated with Israel. This offensive has been expanded into a general campaign for boycott, divestment, and sanctions (BDS) against Israeli companies and personnel, and against those interacting with Israel in any way. That strategy has now become a ritual in the ongoing campaign of attacks using misrepresentation and distortion as substitutes for military aggression.

The cultural warfare against Israel continued in conjunction with the prestigious Edinburgh International Festival in August and September 2012. The Israeli Batsheva Dance Company was invited to give three performances at the Festival between August 30 and September 1, and would later perform in other British cities including London and Manchester. The Batsheva Company is world renowned, generally regarded as one of the great contemporary dance companies in the world, and incarnates the high standard of Israeli culture and art.

But in a perverse fashion a Palestinian group in Dundee, Scotland called for Batsheva to be disinvited because it has been "actively complicit in whitewashing Israeli human rights abuses, apartheid, and occupation of Palestinian land." The Scottish film director Ken Loach, well known for his strong anti-Israel utterances, through the Scottish Palestine Solidarity Campaign urged people to stay away from the Festival.

The absurd charges of apartheid and violations of human rights were taken up in an open letter to Jonathan Millis, the Australian Edinburgh Festival director, endorsed by over seventy international organizations and individuals, and later by Liz Lochhead, Scotland's national poet. It made broad allegations. Batsheva was accused of "willingly collaborating with the propaganda exercise, known as 'Brand Israel' that was conceived by Israel's Ministry of Foreign Affairs. This cynically aims to present positive spin about Israel and whitewash its oppressive regime and human rights abuses." The Batsheva performances did take place, though they were interrupted by protestors, Palestinians and others.

Most important in all this is the Big Lie. Palestinians are said to face restrictions and harassment because of Israel's occupation (place unsaid) and its system of "apartheid . . . an aggravated and state-directed form of racial discrimination in which one group dominates and oppresses another." Palestinian organizations and activists, under the banner of "Don't Dance with Israeli Apartheid," planned to protest all the Batsheva performances if they took place. This was intended to be a repetition of the hostile protests by Palestinians against Batsheva during the tours of the Company in the United States in 2009 and 2010.

It is saddening that one of the latest celebrities to succumb to the fallacious Palestinian narrative of the relationship between the Palestinian population and Israel is Alice Walker, the distinguished Afro-American writer whose book *The Color Purple* was a prize-winning contribution to American literature. In a letter of June 9, 2012, to the Israeli publisher Yediot Books she refused to allow the publication of a Hebrew translation of her renowned book dealing with racism in the United States South, which won the Pulitzer Prize for Fiction in 1983.

Her letter is more based on fiction and misconceptions than on fact. She argues "Israel is guilty of apartheid and persecution of the Palestinian people, both inside Israel and also in the Occupied Territories." This goes even further than most of those who charge Israel with the appellation *apartheid*, since they apply the term only to the Occupied Territories. In addition, she writes that she supports the boycott, divestment, and sanctions movement (BDS) because it will, she hopes, have an impact on Israeli society to change the situation.

Walker, who has visited Gaza and has participated in recent years in anti-Israeli activity, takes an unusually extreme viewpoint in her pronouncement by saying that Israel's policies were worse than the segregation she suffered in her youth. She also relates conversations with unnamed South Africans who told her that those Israeli policies were worse than apartheid.

Like so many others, Walker does not appreciate that the goal of many of the supporters of BDS is not to improve the lot of the Palestinian population or to achieve peace between the contending parties but rather to eliminate totally the State of Israel.

Factual evidence and reasoned argument seem to have little impact on the critics and haters of Israel. Over and over again, objective analysis has shown that apartheid, defined internationally as "inhumane acts committed for the purpose of establishing and maintaining domination by one racial group . . . over another racial group . . . and systematically oppressing them," has no application to and is not consonant with the policies and actions of Israel.

Everyone will agree that inequities and problems exist in the relationship between Israel and Palestinian Arabs. The relationship exists in an imperfect society and imperfect people. Israel is a democratic society and like the United States is imperfect. Class and ethnic issues exist and are discussed freely in the Israeli press and on the floor of the parliament, and are acted upon, the only caveat being the need to protect the citizens of Israel from attack.

Imperfections do not constitute a situation of racism, discrimination, or segregation legally enforced. Reason is unlikely to persuade those who are the slave of passions or ideologically extreme, or those who are pathologically addicted to dislike or hatred of Jews. One can understand the moral value of empathy for those who are suffering. Walker, like so many other persons of good intentions, has swallowed the Palestinian assertion of victimhood, that they are an innocent people oppressed by a powerful country, supported by an international conspiracy on its behalf. If Palestinians are suffering, this has been largely due to Arab unwillingness to reach a peaceful solution with Israel.

We need an explanation from Alice Walker of her passionate assault on Israel. Is she aware of the political and religion freedom of Arabs, Muslims and Christians, in the areas controlled by Israel? Arabs can build mosques and Christians can build churches in Israel, a religious freedom denied to Christians in many Muslim countries. Arabs are members of political parties, are members of the Israeli Parliament (Knesset), hold political executive positions throughout the country, are diplomatic representatives of the state, can study and teach at all Israeli universities, and can enter in to all professions. If she used public transport she would find that passengers, Arabs and Jews, are not segregated, as they were in South Africa or in her American South, but travel together freely.

If there is racism and discrimination in the area it is more pertinent to the words and actions of Palestinians than those of Israelis. One example may suffice. In a speech on July 11, 2010, Mahmoud Abbas, head of the Palestinian Authority, denied Israel's link to Jerusalem. Judaization, he said, was stealing Jerusalem's "cultural, human, and Islamic-Christian religious history. . . . This land is Allah's best land, for which He chooses the finest of His believers, as it is written in the words of the Prophet."

How does Alice Walker's accusation of apartheid apply to the reality of the recent Israeli case where a supreme court of two women and an Arab, George Kara, who chaired the panel, convicted a former president of the State of Israel of sexual offenses? Does she know that Israeli Arabs have held positions of deputy foreign minister, commander of border police, ambassadors, and consuls?

Alice Walker appears to be so entrenched in her anti-Israeli views that she is apparently preparing to take part in another flotilla to Gaza. On the way there she may witness the ten thousand rockets held by Hama in Gaza, some of which are deployed daily against Israeli civilians, especially in November 2012; the sixty thousand missiles, including surface-to-air missiles with a range of one hundred kilometers; and an arsenal of tanks with a range of three hundred kilometers, in the hands of Hezbollah and its leader Hassan Nasrallah in Lebanon; the absence of Israeli settlers in Gaza and in Sinai; the Arab attacks on the pipeline in Sinai that exports gas to Jordan and Israel; and the fence that Israel is building to prevent the entrance of drugs and illegal immigrants.

Finally, Alice Walker may see some of the one hundred twenty thousand black Africans from Ethiopia who are now citizens of the State of Israel, or the two thousand members of the Jewish Bnei Menashe community who came from northeast India, or the two thousand Muslim Gypsies in Jerusalem, or the fifty thousand people from Sudan and other countries who have sought refuge in Israel. Whatever this remarkable assimilation and hospitality means it is not apartheid.

7. The Big Lie

The Big Lie, with its emotional resonance, that Israel is an apartheid state, is continually being used as a weapon in the continuous non-military propaganda war against Israel. Though the false allegation has been discredited on many occasions, Palestinians and their supporters persist in using it to inflame criticism of Israel, irrespective of the truth. The charge of apartheid, implying identification of Israel with the infamous former racist regime in South Africa, is one of the most histrionic weapons in the arsenal of those seeking to delegitimize and eliminate the State of Israel.

Since 2004 the Palestinians and their supporters, as part of their campaign against Israel, have called for a boycott for all cultural performances and exhibitions associated with Israel. This offensive has been expanded into a general campaign for boycott, divestment, and sanctions (BDS) against Israeli companies and personnel, and against those interacting with Israel in any way. That strategy has now become a ritual in the ongoing campaign of attacks using misrepresentation and distortion as substitutes for military aggression.

Why has the Big Lie been repeated endlessly and accepted even by some well-meaning people? It is especially puzzling because all these false Palestinian charges are happening in an international fantasy world of which individuals such as Ken Loach and Emma Thompson seem to be unaware. A few absurdities of the many that illustrate the double standard used in the international world may be sufficient.

One absurdity includes the allegations made, contrary to all evidence, that the death of PLO leader Yasser Arafat was due to poisoning by some unnamed Israeli. This kind of accusation is reminiscent of the famous case of Rudolf Hess, one of the Nazis closest to Hitler, who flew in May 1941 to Britain, purportedly hoping to arrange a peace between Germany and the British government, which to his surprise treated him as a diagnostic problem. Whether a genuine lunatic or not, Hess then claimed that British authorities were trying to poison him.

The possible cause of Arafat's death is discussed in another article here. One intriguing aspect of this farcical accusation against Israel is that the grieving widow, Suha Arafat, living in luxury in Paris and Malta on an income of about $500,000 a month, refuses to release the medical records of her husband. In the past, when meeting Hillary Clinton, who remained silent, Mrs. Arafat accused Israel of poisoning water used by Palestinians. These absurd allegations are akin to those made by the Iranian Vice President, Mohammad Reza Rahimi, at the United Nations Anti-drugs International Conference in Teheran in June 2012, that Jewish gynecologists were killing black babies.

A second irresponsible action is the behavior of a group of African states in agreeing to endorse Sudan, which has slaughtered over a million of its own people, for one of the five seats allocated to Africa in the United Nations Human Rights Council, an organization of forty-seven states that has spent most of its time in criticism and condemnations of the State of Israel, rather than in condemning violations of human rights in Sudan and other places.

In the international fantasy world, another agency of the United Nations is prone to make questionable decisions. The United Nations Educational, Scientific and Cultural Organization (UNESCO) recently endowed a professorial chair in science at the Islamic University of Gaza. That University no doubt has some academic credentials, but it has not only been an institution for anti-Israeli and antisemitic indoctrination, but, more importantly, it has been used by the Hamas organization to develop and produce explosives and rockets, weapons that have been used against Israel. It is not coincidental that, in the same week as the announcement of the decision, Saudi Arabia gave $20 million to UNESCO.

In a second action, UNESCO decided to award a prize financed by President Teodoro Obiang, the dictator of Equatorial Guinea, who provided $3 million for it. The fifty-eight members of the executive board of UNESCO apparently appeared ignorant of the fact that the donor has been accused by human rights groups of embezzling hundreds of millions of dollars from his impoverished, though oil rich, West African state.

The campaign for the banning, mentioned above, of the Israeli Batsheva Company at the Edinburgh Festival was ironic in many ways. One is that the Company's artistic director, far from being a tool of the Israel government, has been critical of some of Israel's specific policies. Another is that the visceral hatred of any Israeli cultural activity expressed by the Palestinians and supporters like Ken Loach is not only a violation of free artistic and intellectual expression but also exacerbates conflict rather than furthering peace. It also tends to increase antisemitism.

Any reasonable objective observer took for granted that the director of the Edinburgh Festival would disregard the pressure to ban the Batsheva Company and allow its performances to take place. But the time is long overdue for individuals of good will and for all people interested in a genuine peace settlement between Israel and its Arab neighbors to call for an end to the incessant, unrelenting calls for boycotts and banning of Israeli intellectual and cultural expression that can do nothing but prevent such a peace settlement.

8. Israel Is Not a Colonial Power

Colonialism, in the same way as *racism* and *imperialism*, has become a loaded buzz word in the lexicon of politics, seeking by accusation to prevent discussion of complex political issues. Certainly throughout history strong or dominant powers—such as Rome, Greece, Arab dynasties, Britain, France, Spain, the Netherlands, Belgium, Ottoman Empire, Russia, Japan, the United States—have sought colonial possessions for political or economic reasons. Israel is not one of them. Unlike the peoples of past and present colonial powers, Jews were historically in exile, and for the most part were a persecuted minority. It would be a travesty or a fallacious historical narrative to argue that Israel falls into this pattern of an outside power eager to impose its will on or to conquer an indigenous population.

Allegations of this kind, based on Israeli occupation of territory, have arisen as a result of deliberate distortions of historical events and present day politics, resulting in Arab and Palestinian refusal to enter into peace negotiations and thus acquire self-determination. It was self-defeating for the Arab leaders meeting at the important summit conference on September 1, 1967, in Khartoum to declare, in response to the Israeli proposal for a compromise solution, that the basic principles by which the Arab states adhered were "no peace with Israel, no recognition of Israel, no negotiation with Israel, and adherence to the rights of the Palestinian people in their country," thus preventing any compromise agreement on territory captured as a result of the Six-Day War.[3] A singular development had occurred; the Israeli victors sued for peace, while the defeated Arabs called for Israeli surrender.

Israel was thus left with the function of control over this captured territory. That control has been seen by critics as "belligerent occupation," a status defined by the Hague Regulations of 1899 and 1907, to which Israel is not a party but which the Israeli Supreme Court regards as part of customary international law. These Regulations outline what constitutes occupation; the Regulations are supplemented by the Fourth Geneva Convention.

The relevant Regulations are Articles 42 and 43. The first states that "Territory is considered occupied when it is actually placed under the authority of the hostile army. The occupation extends only to the territory where such authority has been established and can be exercised." Regulation 43 states that "The authority of the legitimate power having in fact passed into the hands of the occupant, the latter shall take all the measures in his power to restore, and ensure, as far as possible, public order and safety, while respecting, unless absolutely prevented, the laws in force in the country." That has meant Israel following Jordan law in the West Bank, though Jordan had illegally occupied the area.

A major problem is that these Regulations are subject to legitimate differences in interpretation. Israel dealt with the captured territories in different ways. Also pertinent in interpretation of the complex law on the subject is the definition in a Nuremberg trial in 1949 that "an occupation indicates the exercise of governmental authority to the exclusion of the established government."[4]

Can Israel's actions relating to the territories captured in 1967 be regarded on any impartial assessment as colonialism, particularly now that substantial control of them, including the Gaza Strip and parts of the West Bank, is now in the hands of Palestinians, the PA, and Hamas?

Since the Six-Day War, Israel used different procedures toward the territories, many of which were concerned with security and ability to defend itself against terrorist attacks as well as responsibility for the life of Palestinians. Israeli civilian law was employed for all of Jerusalem and, after a while, in the Golan Heights, previously ruled by Syria.

However, the West Bank and Gaza Strip has never had recognized legitimate rulers. Since in those two areas a "prior legitimate sovereign" was lacking, Israel did not regard its control over them as constituting colonialism or occupation, as defined in customary law. For security reasons, from the end of the 1967 war until 1993 most people in the West Bank were subject to Israeli military administration, which at first ruled on the basis of the system of government inherited from Jordan, the ruler from 1949–67.

After the series of Letters of Recognition in September 9, 1993—the series of letters between the government of Israel and the Palestine Liberation Organization (PLO) headed by Yasser Arafat—in which the two sides formally recognized each other, and the Interim Agreement in September 1995 between Israel and the PLO, which created the Palestinian Authority (PA), the areas from which Israel withdrew its military forces have been under the jurisdiction of the PA.

Since then, the PA controls most of Palestinian life in those areas: schools, medical facilities, civic and political organizations, passports, an international airport, and a flag. The Interim Agreement stated that "redeployments of Israeli military forces to specified military locations" would begin, but Israel does not govern the areas. These troops are not an occupying force, since the area is under Palestinian control. Israel did not annex the West Bank, nor does Israeli law apply in it. It has also applied the humanitarian aspects of the Fourth Geneva Convention, rules of substantive and procedural fairness, and rules of proportionality. (The Jami' at Ascan Case, HCJ 393/82).

One pertinent, if somewhat puzzling, factor concerning the future of the West Bank stems from the 1994 Peace Treaty between Israel and Jordan. Acknowledging that the Treaty establishes the international boundary between the two countries, Article 3(2) states that "The boundary is the permanent, secure and recognized international boundary between Israel and Jordan, without prejudice to the status of any territories that came under Israeli military government control in 1967." By implication, the Green Line is not necessarily the boundary between Israel and a future Palestinian state. As a result of Israeli annexation of east Jerusalem, some Israelis regard the division between

Jerusalem and the West Bank as "the blue line," as a de facto border that will be considered as a subject for negotiation in the future.

Nevertheless, some in the international community still refer to the occupation of Gaza even though Israel has withdrawn all its military personnel, civilian authority, and settlements from it. From 1994 the Palestinian Authority had been responsible for setting and collecting all taxes in that area; since 1997 this has been done by Hamas, which now rules Gaza. Israel does collect customs duties on goods entering the Palestinian territories via Israeli-controlled ports and land borders on behalf of the PA, but to term this an act of occupation would appear unreasonable since no Israeli hostile army exercises the function of governmental authority. Moreover, the argument that Israel remains in control of Gaza's borders and of Gaza's airspace and territorial waters ignores the reality that Egypt can open its border with Gaza to the free flow of people, weapons, and goods.

The second Palestinian intifada (uprising) started in September 2000. By mid-2005 almost one thousand attacks had occurred within Israel and about nine thousand in the West Bank, mostly against civilians. Israel combat operations had not been able to end all the activity, suicide attacks, bombings, mortar fire, and rocket fire against its communities, which had cost over a thousand Israeli lives. To prevent or minimize Arab attacks, and to deter additional acts of terrorism, especially suicide bombing attacks from the West Bank, Israel decided in June 2002 to build a multi-layered separation fence system, which Arabs see as a wall, between Israel proper and some settlements, and the West Bank. No doubt this has caused inconveniences for some Palestinians and restricted their mobility to some degree, and led to some disputes over the loss of land. Recognizing this, the Israeli government did try to minimize the effect on the daily lives of Palestinians.

The fence has greatly improved security, been an effective defensive deterrent, and has successfully reduced the threats to Israeli citizens and the loss of life. Nevertheless, by the advisory opinion of the International Court of Justice (ICJ) in July 2004 the building of the fence or barrier or wall was held to be a violation of international law. In the same month a UN General Assembly Resolution, with 150 countries supporting it, condemned the fence; only 6 countries, including the US, voted against it. The European Union similarly condemned it, as also did the World Council of Churches.

In response to the issue, the Israeli Supreme Court (in *Beit Sourik Council v. The Government of Israel*, HCJ 2056/04, and later in High

Court Ruling Docket HCJ 7957/04 of September 2005) ruled there was no authorization to build a fence if the goal was a political one of annexing territory or drawing political borders. But the Israeli military commander did have proper authorization since this was not the case and it was a military necessity to erect the fence. The fence was a security measure and did not reflect a political border or any other border. Moreover, the fence was not a permanent one, but was erected temporarily for security needs to provide a solution to existing and future threats of terrorism. Nevertheless, the Court, in Docket HCJ 7957/04, also held that some segments of the fence route violated the rights of Palestinian residents disproportionately, and that the needs of the local population must be considered. As a result, Israel altered some segments of the existing route and changed some of the plans for the extension of the fence. In a second case in 2005, the Court again determined that the government must change the route of the fence to lessen the impact on the rights of the resident Palestinian residents.

However, the basic problem remained, was the separation fence legal? This was examined in Israel High Court Ruling Docket HCJ 7957/04, and a decision rendered on September 15, 2005. The Court outlined the attempts that Israel had made to counter the attacks against civilians since the start of the intifada. The Court criticized the ICJ for disregarding the reality that the Israel defenses of military exigencies, national security, or public order were applicable to the fence as a whole or to individual parts of it.

The ICJ had almost totally ignored the security problems facing Israel, and perhaps its opinion was colored by a political hue. The Court pointed out that construction of the fence was unrelated to any concept of colonialism, expropriation, confiscation, or transfer of ownership of land, and that Israeli possession for the construction was accompanied by payment of compensation for the damage caused. The rationale for the construction of a fence to defend the lives and safety of Israeli settlers in the area is derived from the need, made clear in The Hague Regulation 43, to preserve public order and safety. The fence went beyond the Green Line and into the West Bank because the topography of the area—mountain ridge, riverbeds, thick vegetation—did not allow for defense of the Israeli soldiers patrolling the area if it was confined to construction within Israel. On a number of occasions the Israeli Supreme Court has grappled with the two conflicting considerations for the military command: legitimate security interests and safety of Israeli citizens, and the rights, needs, and interests of the local Arab population. It has called for a proper balance between the two (Hess Case, pp. 455–6; HCJ 953/83 *Levy v. The Commander of the Southern District of the Israeli Police*, 38(2) P.D. 393). No simple answer is available to resolve how the balance should be performed; the starting approach is using the principle of proportionality.

9. The Bizarre Alliance against Israel

The optimism of Arab Spring, which seemed to promise desirable change, has vanished into autumnal disenchantment. Among other things it has also become a winter with less protection for minority groups, including Christians, in Arab countries and in the Gaza Strip. Hopes for political changes and reforms have dwindled, and the fundamental political, economic, and social dysfunction of most of the Arab countries in the Middle East remains.

The most committed idealist can find no more comfort in the present behavior of the twenty-one countries (and the PLO) of the Arab League than in the past, divided as they are by civil wars and religious tensions, as daily displayed in Syria, Egypt, Iraq, Libya, and Lebanon. They are beset with Islamist insurgencies, enmity between Sunni and Shiite Muslims, and discord between mainstream and extremist Sunnis.

All their governments suffer from a deficit of freedom and political rights. All are nondemocratic in character, often corrupt, and are still based on systems that are autocracies, military dictatorships, hereditary family rule, presidencies for life, tribal elders, or edicts of Islamic dignitaries in a theocratic regime. This results in policies that deny basic human rights to women, minorities, and even the general population.

Yet much of the focus of European and American commentators on the Middle East remains concentrated not on the glaring problems of the Arab societies but on Israel. They are more interested in indicating that in Israel the rate of female illiteracy is about 4 percent rather than to analyze why the rate is 45 percent in Egypt or 55 percent in Yemen. They hesitate to point out that at least three Israeli institutions of higher learning rank among the best in the world, and that Israeli policies and actions have nothing to do with the fact that the Arab world still lacks a single world-class university. No one can justifiably argue that Western imperialism in the past or the existence of Israel in the present can be held responsible for the Arab lack of achievement today.

George Orwell offered the pertinent remark that "even an idealistic politics, perhaps especially an idealistic politics, can pervert itself." Armchair revolutionaries in San Francisco, New York, London, and

Paris for twenty years saw Yasser Arafat as the embodiment of anti-colonial heroism, and endorsed the ideology of Third Worldism. In their animosity to Israel, the European and American self-proclaimed idealists, personifications of political correctness, and earnest environmentalists, are now joined in alliance with Arab and Islamist groups. Both sides in this bizarre relationship of these otherwise dissimilar groups of people tend to see Israel as at best misguided, or at worst as a formidable and oppressive power. Environmentalists are surprisingly oblivious of Israeli research and achievements in desalination and drip irrigation techniques, better agricultural technology and fuel alternatives, that are benefitting the world.

One of the many ironies in this situation is that, with the end of the hateful regime of apartheid in South Africa, radical leftists—many in the academic world, the media, as well as partisan Arab spokesmen—have shifted their image of the existing most demonic state to Israel, which they see as an apartheid nation. The result is a bizarre red-brown-green alliance of Western leftists and liberals—including Christian humanitarians, antiglobalists, and environmentalists—with Islamic fundamentalists and Arab nationalists. With little else in common, they share a common motif: dislike, even hatred of Israel. They depict Israel both as a criminal state in itself and also as the accomplice or lackey of American imperialism.

This attitude goes so far that some academics in European and American universities even register more support for Hamas, the ruling party in Gaza, than does the Palestinian population, including the PLO in the West Bank. Some of the most extreme critics, perhaps of sound mind, have suggested not only that the actions of the Islamic suicide bombers in New York on 9/11 and elsewhere resulted from alleged control over the United States government and media by Jewish interests—again the Jewish conspiracy at work—but also argue that Israel provoked the wars against terrorism in Iraq and Afghanistan in which the United States is involved. Critics, some in high official positions, of less than sound mind in Iran have proclaimed that the "Zionist regime is deliberately spreading homosexuality" to pursue Zionism's real goal of world domination. Forgetting that Zionism really was first articulated in the 1880s, the Iranian President Ahmadinejad, who will probably not receive the Nobel Prize for History, remarked in August 2012, "It has now been some 400 years that a horrendous Zionist clan has been ruling the major world affairs."

The kindest thing one can say about the bizarre alliance is that it stems from idealism, from an ideology that seeks to rectify the supposed wrongs of European and American colonialism. This is an ideology of Third Worldism, which has become familiar since the formation of the Non-Aligned Movement in 1955. It is grounded in the conviction that a division exists between the developed nations of the West and the developing nations, and that the latter should be supported.

Few today are likely to echo the extravagant rhetoric of the famous writer H. G. Wells that "The Soviet Union upholds the tattered banner of world collectivity and remains something splendid and hopeful in the spectacle of mankind." Now that the bloodbaths of the Stalinist era and the brutal murders of seventy million Chinese people by the revolutionary hero Mao Zedong have become known, pessimistic critics of Western culture, espousing cultural relativism, have redirected their enthusiasm for change to the cause of revolutionary insurgencies and violent energy in non-Western countries. An early comment by Bertrand Russell is appropriate to these views. In one of his *Unpopular Essays* he sardonically addressed those moralists who believe in the "superior virtue of the oppressed."

Expectations of the Utopia to be established in the Soviet Union, now discredited, have been replaced by gullible assertions by intellectuals of the virtues of non-Western countries or groups. A prominent example of this state of mind is the French philosopher Michel Foucault. In his article "What are the Iranians dreaming about?" he praised the attempt of the Iranian Islamic regime under Ayatollah Khomeini in opening "a spiritual dimension in politics."

This ideology of Third Worldism postulates a hypocritical, even violent, West eternally to be held guilty for its past colonial activity that is alleged to have been destructive of non-Western indigenous cultures. It is noticeable that in this blanket condemnation the proponents of this ideology pay little attention to the important differences among the individual indigenous cultures, but rather lump them all together in one vast Third World.

The usual and automatic guilty party for these ideologists is Israel, a country that they see, after the United States, as the main embodiment of present-day colonialism and imperialism. The essential irony is that for members of the bizarre alliance the non-West, and Palestinians in particular, is lauded not for positive reasons, or for love of its inhabitants, but because it is not Western and does not adhere to Western practices such as liberal democracy, an open economy, rule of law, free elections, personal autonomy, individual and sexual freedom, emancipation of women, and constitutional rights, all which Israel embodies, if sometimes in imperfect form. The critics ignore that imperfection is an inevitable consequence of the activities and policies of all nations, and indeed of all organizations, even their own.

Critics of Israel and European and American values posture as idealists with high moral standards, but their actions or non-actions reveal a lack of consistency about those standards. Western radicals, including academics, have shown more compassion for Arab dictators, especially in Libya and Syria, than for democratic Israel. Western feminists, gay and lesbian groups have been silent about the place and treatment of women and homosexuals in Muslim Arab countries. No woman in an Arab country has yet been elected to a prominent position, as was Golda Meir in Israel, the first woman prime minister elected anywhere who was not the wife or daughter of a previous head of government.

Criticism of the actions of the State of Israel and its personnel is wholly appropriate, but it serves no purpose if it is based not on objective appraisal of those actions but on the endless search for new saviors of humanity who will overcome the imagined evils of Western civilization.

10. The Weapon of Boycott

It is now universally acknowledged by objective commentators that the real underlying purpose of the calls for boycotts against Israel and its citizens is not a concern for the human rights or welfare of Palestinians but is to challenge the legitimacy and ultimately to eliminate the State of Israel. The calls are in essence a racist response to the existence of the Jewish state, in the call for action against one people in the world, a branding of a whole people as if they were wearing a yellow star in Nazi-like fashion. Even Noam Chomsky and Norman Finkelstein, well-known critics of Israel and pro-Palestinian activists, have characterized the boycott, divestment, and sanctions movement against Israel as "hypocritical" and run by individuals who falsely claim to represent the Palestinian people. Those who truly seek peace between Israel and the Palestinians regard the boycotts as unhelpful, as totally negative, and argue they should be ended.

Whether the calls for boycott are the product of leftist posturing, antisemitism, or simple ignorance is a matter of judgment. In their disingenuousness nature they are simplistic responses to complex, unresolved problems that ignore the distinctions between different kind of activities and issues. They are counterproductive in that they create an atmosphere in which attempts at any political compromise between Israel and Palestinians becomes impossible. The boycott calls have been and are an obstacle to the start of real negotiations between the parties. They are a significant example of cognitive dissonance, the inability of the boycotters to distinguish between actual facts and their perceptions, perhaps their indifference to those facts, or perhaps reluctance to put those facts in the context of the real relationship between the parties.

Boycotts of Jews and Jewish interests and merchandise by Arab groups goes back almost a hundred years, and became more prominent with the declaration of the newly formed Arab League Council in December 1945 that "Jewish products and manufactured goods shall be considered undesirable to the Arab countries." Hypocrisy was present from the start. The Arab states were less interested in helping Palestinian Arabs than in preventing Jewish products from entering their own countries and competing with them.

This boycott, administered by the Central Boycott Office in Damascus and covering three facets—primary, secondary, and tertiary elements—attempted to isolate Israel economically as well as diplomatically. It did some harm to the economy of Israel after the state was established in 1948. In addition to the Arab states, some non-Arab businesses—among them Pepsi, McDonald's, and most Japanese cars— abided by the boycott, but it was more honored in the breach than in the observance. Arab states themselves suffered economic harm by losing the opportunity to export their goods to the new State of Israel.

Since the 1980s a number of Arab states, starting with Egypt, and except Syria, have abandoned the boycott, wholly or in part. They could not ignore the new world of globalization, international trade, and binding international trade agreements, particularly the World Trade Organization. As a result, Arab countries have, through legal channels and clandestinely through third parties, been trading with Israeli companies in a considerable fashion, including in irrigation and security systems, and have accepted Israeli investment. Nevertheless, though Israel has been economically prosperous, it has been handicapped by the impact of the animosity toward it created by the boycott: its per capita income would have doubled over the last ten years, and tourist revenue would have increased by over $15 billion, if the political conflict had been resolved.

The boycott is still technically in force by Arab countries, though often bypassed, ineffective, and negligible. Its impact now is less in economic affairs than in becoming a major polemical weapon in the hands of those non-Arabs who are critical of or want to condemn Israel, ostensibly because of their opposition to Israeli settlements. One can understand the politically motivated logic of Arabs, inside Israel as well as outside, calling for a ban on products made in Israeli settlements, including Ahava Dead Sea health products, Beigel and Beigel pretzels, Super Drink soft drinks, Oppenheimer chocolates, fruits, vegetables, and computers, and many other products. It is an illustration of democracy in Israel that a major advocate of the boycott is Ahmad Tibi, the Arab-Israeli deputy speaker of the Knesset.

It often goes unmentioned that the boycott called for by the Palestinian Authority is a violation of the April 29, 1994, Paris Agreement between Israel and the PLO, which expresses respect of "each other's economic interests," and recognizes "the need to create a better economic environment for their people's and individuals." The essential fallacy in the Palestinian logic is not only that the boycott is a violation of signed agreements, but also that it is difficult, if not impossible, to separate the economy of the settlements from that of Israel as a whole.

What is now surprising is the acceptance of this hostile strategy by non-Arabs, particularly citizens of Britain and other European countries. The campaign of boycott, divestment, and sanctions (BDS) began in July 2005 by 171 Palestinian nongovernmental organizations (NGOs), arguing that they support the Palestinian cause because Israel was not complying with international law and universal principles of human rights. It appeared somewhat duplicitous that Omar Barghouti, one of the founders of BDS, who called for an academic boycott of Israel, was at the time a student at Tel Aviv University.

The campaign has led to various kinds of actions: in the academic area, in economy, in mainstream churches, in the media, in cultural activity, and by nongovernmental organizations. Some actions are bizarre. What can explain the mindset of the individuals who obeyed the order of the Philadelphia BDS movement in December 2011 to sing outside a store Christmas carols with lyrics urging people not to buy Israeli products?

In extraordinary fashion and contrary to self-proclaimed liberal ideas of free speech and opposition to censorship, academic and cultural groups have expressed their support. The annual Israeli Apartheid Week in the United States and Europe has led to demonstrations on university campuses in which anti-Israeli advocates have prevented the expression of dissent, and also stimulated antisemitic manifestations.

A few examples of boycott actions suffice to illustrate the anti-Israeli malice. The British Association of University Teachers (AUT) Council voted in April 2005 for different reasons to boycott two Israeli universities, Haifa and Bar-Ilan; under pressure from members supporting academic freedom, the boycott was cancelled. However, the British National Association of Teachers in Further and Higher Education (NATFHE) in 2006 also called for a boycott of Israeli academics and universities, and the new group, the British academic union (UCU) in 2009 passed a resolution to the same effect.

Moty Cristal, a well-known Israel expert on negotiation theory and mediation, and a person who had in the past worked with Arab and human rights organizations, was disinvited in April 2012 from the conference on conflict resolution held in Britain and arranged by the Manchester Mental Health and Social Care Trust because of the objection by the Unison trade union, which has been a constant and open critic of Israel. Two Israeli scholars were dismissed from editorial boards of scientific journals published in Manchester by the Arab editor.

The action of Unison, the largest public sector union in Britain with 1.3 million members, was particularly disturbing. In 2010 it decided to suspend normal bilateral relations with the two public service federations of the Histadrut, the Israeli trade union. This decision was reaffirmed in 2012. It means that Unison will not invite these federations of Histadrut to attend meetings, nor accept invitations from them, nor agree to work on any joint projects.

Another problem in the academic world came to court in 2012 when Ronnie Fraser, a lecturer in mathematics at a London college who had been a member of the British University and College Union for eleven years, brought suit against the Union for alleged harassment about his Jewish identity, which had created a hostile environment for him.

Economic businesses have entered the picture. In April 2012 the British Co-operative Group, the fifth largest supermarket group in Britain, said it would no longer do business with any supplier of produce from Israeli settlements. It is probably the first major supermarket group in Europe to implement such a boycott. Its customers will miss the Arava export growers, Mehadrin, Agrexco, and Adafresh collective exports of fruits and vegetables. Paradoxically, these companies have employed Arab workers in the fields and packing-houses. Moreover, Histadrut, the Israel trade union, has had good relations with PGFTU, the Palestinian counterpart for Palestinian workers.

Most surprising has been the activity of mainstream Churches and individuals in the cultural and entertainment sections of society, as mentioned earlier. Many in the latter group are hardly likely to be sophisticated analysts of Middle Eastern affairs, yet well-known musicians Elvis Costello, the Pixies, Cassandra Wilson, Gil Scott Heron; performers including Emma Thompson and Mark Rylance; and film-makers Ken Loach and Jean-Luc Godard have expressed support for a boycott, or refused to visit Israel. This attitude is more likely to result from fear, intimidation, or a desire to be seen as politically correct among their peers, than from any political or moral conviction. A group of anti-Israeli activists tried to stop the Toronto Film Festival in 2009 from featuring Israeli films, and the films of Steven Spielberg have been banned in fourteen Arab countries because he made a $1 million donation to Israel in 2006.

Recent studies by psychologists and neuroscientists investigating the causes of the denial of reality by individuals suggest that liberals display higher levels of openness to experience and to new ideas than do conservatives, who are more concerned with order and structure. Sadly, this does not appear the case with the boycott advocates, who seem to be prevented by their preexisting beliefs, whether they are anti-Israeli or antisemitic attitudes, from appreciating the facts on the ground or the context in which those facts can be understood. If they truly wanted to help the Palestinians, their time and energy would be better spent in encouraging Arab states and Palestinians to normalize political and trade relations with Israel, rather than supporting actions that derive from a prejudiced anti-Israeli view. The argument that the boycott should remain in place until the Arab-Israeli conflict is resolved is the exact opposite of the path to a settlement. Relaxation of the boycott leading to its complete abolition is the way forward to peaceful negotiations.

11. Zionist Thinkers

Appropriate criticism of the actions and policies of the State of Israel and its citizens is certainly justifiable, but, as has been already suggested, many of the charges against and condemnations of the State go far beyond any reasonable commentary. They stem from a misrepresentation or deliberate distortion of the concept of Zionism, the movement of Jewish self-determination that led to the establishment of the State in May 1948.

Some of the criticism of Zionism, fashionably termed post–Zionism, has come from academics and the media in Israel, and usually from the political left. Even if some of the criticism is justified, the post-Zionist argument is deficient in many respects. It is a quaintly insular view of Israel—a country in a world of globalization and complex interdependence, confronted by continual hatred so that it must always be prepared to defend itself. Its proponents are singularly naive in their expectations of a perfect social and politically egalitarian, secular society and are guilty of prejudice against devout religious believers. Moreover, these critics misunderstand Zionism, which has never been a monolithic concept but always includes a pluralistic variety of approaches.

What particular aspects of the different views of Zionism are unacceptable to the critics? Do they want to eliminate the State of Israel? Proponents of Zionism argued that Jews in the Diaspora had been excluded from world history, and that for the Jewish people to exercise power it was necessary to establish a state for them as a national unit. The Israeli Declaration of Independence speaks of "the natural right of the Jewish people to be masters of their own fate like other nations." Advocates varied about where and how this should happen: territorialists wanted any suitable areas, including Uganda, where persecuted Jews might go as "asylum for the night"; others demanded a state in Palestine or *Eretz Israel* (the Biblical Land of Israel); practical Zionists proposed settlements; others urged a solution by political and diplomatic means; socialists disputed with the political right; nationalists disagreed with internationalists; and the religious coexisted with the free-thinkers.

The post-Zionists argue that Zionism is a colonialist concept essentially founded on injustice toward the local Arabs, and that the differences in Israel now in status, income, and rights between Jews and Israeli Arabs means that the state is therefore undemocratic. The logical conclusion for these critics would be that Israel would be more democratic if it were less Jewish. Herzl and many others would have disagreed with this conclusion. He wrote in his diary in 1895 that Jewish settlement would bring immediate benefits to the land and that "we shall respectfully tolerate persons of other faiths and protect their property, their honor, and their freedom with the harshest means of coercion."

The fundamental external reality—which seems to escape those who challenge the legitimacy of Israel—is that many Arab countries and Palestinians, having warred and engaged in constant hostility, still refuse to recognize Israel's legitimacy. Necessarily, security is vital; the problem is to what extent should this interfere with Arab claims to the land and rights? The present mainstream view is that a secure Israel is better than a territorially extended one.

Certainly a variety of opinions exist within Israel on the nature of the economy and the free market, on the cultural identities that make up the mosaic of its society, and on the inequalities both within the Jewish community and between Jews and non-Jews. Although attitudes toward the Arabs in the territory differ, there never has been any official policy to expel them from the territory. In spite of this, critics of Israel persist in the allegation that Zionism has promoted this view. They are as mistaken in this belief as they are in their aversion to the exercise of Israeli power to defend itself, while at the same time shirking any realistic alternative proposals.

The main assertions of critics are that Israel is too nationalistic—that it should no longer be a Jewish state but rather a democratic one, implying an incompatibility between the two, and that Israel should end its occupation of captured territory. These critics conveniently ignore the continual Arab rejection of any compromise solution to the conflict and their repeated rejection of all partition proposals and resolutions. Post-Zionism tends to become anti-Zionism—the denial that Israel has a legitimate right to exist.

It is fortuitous that the book *The Founding Fathers of Zionism* by Benzion Netanyahu, the eminent historian who died in 2012 at the age of 102, has been translated from Hebrew and has been published for the first time in English by Balfour Books. He was the patriarch of an important Israeli family, including Jonathan, the celebrated hero who was killed while leading the mission to rescue Jewish hostages held by the PLO at Entebbe airport in Nigeria on July 4, 1976; Benjamin, prime minister of Israel; and Iddo, a prominent physician. Benzion, born in Poland in 1910, the son of a rabbi, went to Eretz Israel in 1920. His career embodied a rare combination of characteristics: an original, if controversial, scholar, and a passionate advocate of a minority Zionist political point of view on whose behalf he was a strong advocate.

The scholarly opinions of Benzion were consonant with his more overtly political ones. His advocacy began with his revulsion at the murder by Arabs of sixty-seven Jews in Hebron in 1929. Believing that the mainstream Zionist organization did not react strongly enough to this outrage, he became an activist in the Revisionist Zionist movement that was the rival of the mainstream Zionist Organization. The Revisionist group was founded and led by Vladimir (Zeev) Jabotinsky, whom Benzion served for a time as secretary. He was also editor of the Revisionist paper HaYarden in the 1930s. In 1940 Benzion supported Jabotinsky's campaign to create a Jewish military force to fight against Nazi Germany and helped create a Committee for a Jewish Army. Jabotinsky had already formed the Haganah in 1920 as an independent Jewish army to protect settlements in the Yishuv, the area of Jewish settlements in Palestine.

Benzion was part of a group, which included Peter Bergson (Hillel Kook), that went to the United States in 1940 to seek funds and support both to rescue Jews in Europe and to create a Jewish state in Palestine. As a result he became director of the American branch of the Revisionist movement and editor of its magazine. His editorials were critical of mainstream American Jewish leaders, such as Rabbi Stephen Wise, a friend of President Roosevelt, for being too cautious and too willing to accept Western appeasement policies toward Nazi Germany. Benzion attempted to influence the leaders of the Republican Party during the 1944 Presidential election to demand their support for a Jewish state as a refuge for the millions of European distressed Jews.

At the same time as this engagement in political activity Benzion had completed a doctorate in medieval Jewish history and began teaching in the US, where he remained until 1976. His scholarship is closely related to his political outlook. His first major work in 1953, stemming from his dissertation, was a biography of Don Isaac Abravanel, philosopher and financial expert who was the leader of the Jews in Spain in 1492. Benzion describes the inability of Abravenel to prevent the expulsion of the Jews from Spain and their sad fate as they sought refuge elsewhere. Reading the work, it is not possible to avoid the parallel inherent in it between the Spanish episode and the Holocaust and the fate of Jews attempting to seek refuge after escaping from Nazi Germany.

Even more telling was the argument in his major 1,400-page controversial, revisionist, and tendentious book, *The Origins of the Inquisition in 15th-Century Spain*, published in English in 1995, which is dedicated to Jonathan. This book challenged the prevailing scholarly view that the accusations by the Inquisition about *conversos* (Christianized Jews) were true. The Inquisition accusation was that these conversos and their descendants who supposedly had converted to Christianity were still secretly Jews, and therefore could be tortured, deprived of their wealth, and murdered. Benzion disagreed with this interpretation and argued that the Inquisitors were motivated not so much by religious passion or profession of faith but more by racial hatred of Jews. They killed loyal Christians because of their Jewish blood.

The Inquisition, in Benzion's view, had introduced and laid the groundwork for a racial argument for antisemitism. According to this, Jews were different; they did not have purity of Christian blood, *limpieza de sangre.* The relevance of this argument to the contemporary world of Nazism and twentieth-century antisemitism is clear. The actions of the Inquisition were a forerunner of genocidal Nazism and of the racial laws in Vichy France during World War II. Netanyahu's argument is compelling; for racial reasons those people regarded by others as Jews would never be accepted as equals.

Another controversial aspect of Benzion's book was his criticism of the conversos themselves. Instead of praising the conversos as the British historian Cecil Roth had done in writing of the "incredible romance" of their story because of their unique devotion to tradition, which they transmitted from generation to generation, Benzion censured them for their lack of loyalty as traitors to Judaism. Indeed, Benzion, in a powerful comparison with the conversos of Spain, praised the Jews of medieval Germany for their religious devotion and readiness for martyrdom. His criticism can be construed as a comment on the inactivity of American Jews during World War II regarding the suffering of European Jews.

Netanyahu's book *The Founding Fathers of Zionism* is a series of essays, some based on lectures, written before and after the Holocaust. They deal with five major writers—Leo Pinsker, Theodore Herzl, Max Nordau, Israel Zangwill, and Vladimir Jabotinsky—who are seen as contributing to the intellectual foundation of Zionism and thus to the establishment of the State of Israel. In spite of Benzion's own political stance in favor of Jabotinsky, the essays, elegantly written and highly original, are also eminently fair in the evaluation of the five individuals, their policies and personalities.

Benzion traces Zionism back to late nineteenth-century Russia and the rise in Eastern Europe of Jewish nationalism and national consciousness, partly the outcome of religious longings and aspirations but largely as a result of the pogroms and manifest antisemitism. He views the dawning of Zionism, the emergence of a Jewish national consciousness, in the context not only of the pogroms in Eastern Europe but also as relevant to international issues of the time, especially the role of Britain in gaining Cyprus after the Russo-Turkish war, its control over Egypt in 1882, and general British interest in the Palestine area.

All five writers he chose were conscious of the problems of assimilation and Jewish identity in modern states. One solution to these problems has been total assimilation, along with abandonment of traditional ritual. A more moderate and difficult approach was integration into mainstream society while retaining religious faith and the distinctiveness of a separate culture. This approach has long perplexed the Jewish community in the past and still does today. Moses Mendelssohn, in his work *Jerusalem* (1783), was one of the first of many thinkers beginning in the Emancipation period to address the complex problem of remaining distinctive in the modern world, whether it is based on religious or ethnic or cultural factors. At the core is the tension between Jewish particularism and universalism, a dialogue between concern for Jewish national interests and preference as a priority for human emancipation.

It is of course true that some in the Jewish community in the past and in the present do not approve of Zionism. Some significant scholars preferred other resolutions of the Jewish problem. Simon Rawidowicz wrote of global Hebraism, the idea that language and culture, not a territorial state, would link the Jewish people; Mordecai Kaplan, the founder of the Reconstructionist Movement, wrote of Jewish national civilization, the outcome of history, culture, and religion; Hans Kohn of cultural humanism; Simon Dubnow and Chaim Zhitlovsky of Jewish identity and communal or cultural autonomy in political entities. Essentially these views, if not a denial of the existence of a Jewish people, are a rejection of the principle of Jewish self-determination, of Zionism as a solution to the Jewish question, and do not acknowledge the land that is now Israel as the necessary homeland for all Jews.

The five founders in Netanyahu's book thought otherwise. Their arguments, which played a major part in shaping the intellectual foundations on which the State of Israel was built, were based on the prescient understanding that European Jews would be doomed without a Jewish state in which they would be protected and could defend themselves. For Netanyahu, the motivation of Zionism as expressed by his founders was political, not religious.

Leo Pinsker, a doctor for the Russian army during the Crimean War in 1854, who was decorated for bravery, wanted to make the world conscious of the Jewish problem. Instead of using the word *antisemitism*, a term said to have been first used in 1879 by Wilhelm Marr, a German journalist, Pinsker coined the word *Judeophobia*, a psychological disease to refer to the pathological fear, disrespect, and dread of Jews. This was part of the general disease of the age. The 1871 pogrom in his hometown of Odessa, instigated by the Russian and Greek intelligentsia and more vehement than previous outbreaks, led him to believe that assimilation was futile. At this time and during the 1881 pogrom, Jews received no protection from the Russian police. Pinsker's pamphlet, *Auto-Emancipation*, written in 1882, was a call for a Jewish national movement based on the view that the Jews were a race and a historical group, not a religious sect. He argued that the Jewish people at the time had no fatherland, no center of gravity, no government of its own, and no official representation.

In view of the ongoing persecution, there was an immediate need for national salvation and territorial concentration. Anticipating the Holocaust, Pinsker argued that it was necessary for Jews to act or it would be too late. That was why at first Pinsker suggested Argentina as the place for the Jewish homeland. His appearance at the first Jewish National Congress in Kattowitz (Upper Silesia) in November 1884 was in effect the start of a political national movement, organizing Jews in Europe and petitioning the great powers to help the establishment of a national home. Pinsker wanted to put the Jewish question on the international agenda rather than be satisfied with the purchases of land and settlement by small groups in Palestine.

The generally acknowledged founder of Zionism is Theodor Herzl, the charismatic secular playwright and journalist for the *Neue Freie Presse* who was in Paris during the Dreyfus Affair. The cosmopolitan Herzl, born in Hungary but immersed in Viennese culture, was largely uninterested in Jewish matters until he became personally aware of the outbreaks of antisemitism in Europe. This led him to the belief that assimilation was not possible due to the fact that there was continuing hostility toward Jews because they were regarded as aliens.

What is important about Herzl is that while others preceded him in understanding the Jewish problem, he with his powerful personality put the national idea into practice with his founding of the Zionist movement in Basel in August 1897 and with his call in *Der Judenstaat* (1896) for the creation of a Jewish state, rather than gradual immigration of Jews into the selected area.

Herzl believed that the Jewish problem had to be solved on the political level. The agricultural settlements founded in Palestine by European Jewish philanthropists were important but insufficient. The declaration at the First Zionist Congress that Herzl convened in Basel was that "Zionism seeks to establish a home for the Jewish people in Palestine secured under public law." This statement implied an international charter for Jews to return to Palestine: the result, Herzl believed, would be not only a state but also the ending of antisemitism. In this, of course, he was sadly mistaken.

Herzl later wrote that in Basel he had founded the Jewish State. Herzl emphasized the need for the Jewish people to rule, to believe in their own powers. Netanyahu sums up Herzl in three words: believe, dare, and desire. Indeed, in Herzl's novel, *Altneuland*, a character concludes, "If you will it, it is no dream."

Herzl's contributions to Zionism combined realism and optimism. He appreciated a fact that post-Zionists question, that Jews "are a people, one people." Affliction, he said, "binds us together, and thus united, we suddenly discover our strength." With historical allusions, he urged the restoration of the Jewish state, one in which a normal society would exist. The new state must have an assured right of sovereignty, a legal right, agreed to by the international community. That explains his persistent diplomatic efforts to get international approval. At first Herzl was prepared to accept areas other than Palestine; Cyprus, South America, and especially Uganda were mentioned as the location of the state on a temporary basis. At first he thought that because of the continuing pogroms it was essential to find a location that was immediately available, but he soon realized this was unsatisfactory and that the state must be in Palestine.

Interestingly, Lord Balfour expressed a similar view. In his introduction to the book by Nahum Sokolow, *History of Zionism, 1600–1919*, Balfour recounts that he first supported creating a Jewish settlement in East Africa under the British flag to avoid any further persecution of European Jews. Well-intentioned though this might be, it was not Zionism. Balfour realized in 1906, two years after the early death of Herzl, that the Jewish national home had to be in Palestine, the historical and religious location associated with Jews.

One of the people converted to Zionism by Herzl was the Hungarian physician and psychiatrist, an avowed atheist, the strong and stubborn character Max Nordau (1849–1923). A talented writer, Nordau's earliest writings focused on the corruption of Parisian life, on modern civilization as a disease, on degeneration in society, and on decadence in Europe, the mental and moral pathology of modern civilization. He had been present at the event on January 4, 1895, when Alfred Dreyfus was stripped of his army colors after being falsely convicted of espionage.

Nordau realized that emancipation, specifically in France, had not ended antisemitism, a worldwide disease, and he foresaw that Jews had to leave Europe quickly for their survival. In their own historic country Jews would be able to employ all their powers and skills for development. Even after their emancipation in European states, Nordau argued, Jews were suffering from alienation from labor and led an unhealthy life. With their return to Palestine they would be transformed, physically and spiritually. He was unconcerned about Judaism in that transformation. With a state of their own, Jews could participate in a European progressive culture from which they were precluded. Zionism was good for that non-Jewish culture and the countries in which Jews would no longer be present, as well as for the Jews themselves. Like Herzl, he thought that antisemitism would decline. Nordau, a persuasive speaker, influenced a number of important figures in literature and politics, including Georges Clemenceau, and was in effect the unofficial head of the Zionist Organization after the premature death of Herzl.

Israel Zangwill, the noted British journalist, publicist, and author, is a surprising choice for Netanyahu's fourth founder. Though well known for his novels on British Jewish life in the ghetto, as well as for his political activism on feminism and other issues, he was a strong Jewish nationalist who made the Jewish question central to his work. For him it was crucial for Jews to get out of the social and spiritual ghetto. At first he worked to accomplish this goal by helping to form the Maccabi club in 1893, and bringing artists and writers together to participate in British patriotism and thus become an integral part of the larger society. He soon realized this direction would never result in full acceptance of Jews, and with Herzl as his hero he became an advocate of Zionism. He promoted Zionism to prominent political and literary figures, including David Lloyd George, Winston Churchill, Lord Robert Cecil, Lord Lansdowne, Theodore Roosevelt, and Hall Caine, and perhaps influenced Lord Balfour. Zangwill was not loath to attack British Jewish leaders for their subservience to government civil servants. On the contrary, independent action was necessary, and the Zionist movement, he thought, must follow the route of national liberation; the model was what Garibaldi had done for Italians.

Where would that route lead? The Ottoman Empire controlled Palestine. Zangwill recognized the need to rescue Jews from persecution in Europe. As a result he broke with the official Zionist movement and founded in 1905 the Jewish Territorial Organization, looked for an emergency solution anywhere. He first advocated Uganda as a home for the Jews, a proposal that was rejected by the 7th Zionist Congress. When Zangwill realized that the Ottoman Empire would soon come to an end, he argued for Palestine as the site for a Jewish homeland.

It was Zangwill who echoed the words of Lord Shaftesbury and wrote in 1901 that "Palestine is a country without a people; the Jews are a people without a country." It is worth pointing out that he did not write, as commonly supposed, that Palestine was "a land without a people for a people without a land." Nor did any other Zionist leader. In 1915 Zangwill proposed that Jewish brigades be part of the Allied Forces in World War I. After the Balfour Declaration he called not simply for a home for Jews in Palestine but for a state to be established in Palestine for the Jewish people. He was critical of Zionist leaders who had not demanded the establishment of a state. Zangwill's most controversial argument was for Arabs in the area to be transferred to neighboring Arab countries. Understandingly, Zangwill wrote after World War I that in view of the vast territories freed for the Arabs from the Ottoman Empire, the Allied Powers surely had the right "to ask the Arabs not to grudge the petty strip [of Palestine] necessary for the renaissance of a still more downtrodden people."

Not surprisingly, the longest essay in Netanyahu's book is on his hero Jabotinsky: orator, writer, and philosopher, a master of languages, literature, and history. That hero welcomed Herzl as a liberated, strong personality who was a model of the proud, independent, Jew able to command, qualities necessary in a new Jewish entity to be established. Jabotinsky was disappointed by the official Zionist organization, especially its chairman Chaim Weizmann, whom he believed did not speak of the establishment of a state in Palestine with sufficient urgency. Both Herzl and Jabotinsky saw as unacceptable the poverty and the powerlessness of Jews in the Diaspora.

Jabotinsky is important for a number of reasons, but particularly for advocacy of aggressive policies and resistance to subjugation. He was a realist regarding politics as tests of strength, aspiration, and domination. He spoke on behalf of Jewish resistance, calling to action people who had not known resistance for hundreds of years. He demanded political and military resistance to concession of any right to which Jews were entitled, as individuals or as a people.

To this end he championed Jewish self-defense in Russia, created the Jewish Legions in World War I as a private individual, and after the war the Irgun Zva'i Leumi (National Military Organization). Netanyahu points out that he urged both a political and military struggle against British rule. The political struggle would be one of constant public pressure, going beyond diplomatic niceties. The military one would be a way of educating Jewish youth; at an extreme it would be the basis for an armed uprising against Britain. In this aggressive attitude he differed with Weizmann on tactics and strategy, especially on the question of putting pressure on the British. As a result he resigned from the Zionist Organization, which he found too cautious, too moderate, too self-restrained, and founded his organization in January 1923.

The most controversial argument of Jabotinsky was his policy toward local Arabs. He had predicted the Arab pogroms against Jews of April 1920, and he organized defense against them, an act for which he was jailed for fifteen years, though soon released. He recognized that Arabs would not voluntarily consent to the establishment of a Jewish state and would fight against Jewish immigration, even though it would bring them cultural and economic benefits. Hence his famous advocacy of an Iron Wall, which Arabs would be "powerless to break down," and a strong legal military and political force to convince the Arabs that they could not force Jews to leave the area.

For him the land of Israel would be obtained only through force. This forthright view of Arab opposition was not agreeable to many, but Jabotinsky was realistic in his appraisal of worldwide historical processes. In history, he argued in his article *The Iron Wall* of November 4, 1923, there was not a solitary instance of any colonization being carried on with the consent of the native population. That population not only refuses to admit new masters but also new partners or collaborators. This was true of the Arabs as it was of all other peoples, and they would never peacefully allow a Jewish state to be established.

In the late 1930s he predicted the Holocaust when he argued that catastrophe was coming closer for the Jews. He argued strongly for a state in which the Jewish majority would exercise self-determination, but this state would not be exclusively Jewish. In 1938 he wrote, "It must be hateful for any Jew to think that the rebirth of a Jewish state should ever be linked with such an odious suggestion as the removal of its non-Jewish citizens."

All these Zionist writers called for a national home, a state for the Jewish people. They believed that normalization of Jews would only occur if Jews were citizens of a sovereign state that could exercise power. At the present time the question is how Zionism is related to the State of Israel in both internal and external matters. The inescapable internal problem is the presence of a considerable and growing Arab minority. The Zionist pioneers were aware of this problem and proposed different policies. The State of Israel still grapples with the problem of Arab assimilation and with the implementation of individual and collective rights for that minority.

Post-Zionists argue that Zionism is a colonialist concept built on a foundation that institutionalizes injustice toward local Arabs and that the differences in Israel now in status, income, and rights between Jews and Israeli Arabs means that the state is undemocratic. These critics argue that Israel would be more democratic if it were less Jewish. For them the fact that Israel is a Jewish state means it is undemocratic.

Certainly there are extreme Zionist religious elements, such as the followers of Rabbi Zvi Yehuda Kook, with their belief in redemptive religious Zionism and emphasis on settlements and possession of the land. At the same time, some ultra-Orthodox rabbis, particularly those of Neturei Karta, oppose the existence of the State of Israel. Herzl would have disagreed with both sides. He wrote in his diary on June 12, 1895, that Jewish settlement in the area of Palestine would bring immediate benefits to the land, and that "we shall respectfully tolerate persons of other faiths and protect their property, their honor, and their freedom with the harshest means of coercion." In a famous letter of March 19, 1899, to Yussuf Ziah el-Khaldi, former mayor of Jerusalem and then member of the Ottoman parliament, Herzl wrote regarding the non-Jewish population in Palestine, "their well-being and individual prosperity will increase as we bring in our own."

The fundamental external reality that seems to escape post-Zionists, who challenge the legitimacy of Zionism and of Israel itself, is that Arab countries, with some exceptions, and Palestinians who have warred and engaged in constant hostility still refuse to recognize the legitimacy of the State of Israel. Necessarily, security is vital, and the problem is to what extent this should interfere with Arab claims to the land and rights.

Whatever the different formulations of Zionism, all proponents share the view that the area, whether one calls it Palestine, the Holy Land, or Eretz Israel, is the birthplace and the ancestral homeland of the Jewish people, linked by historical ties and by religious and cultural traditions shared by all Jews. Zionism is a national movement, not a colonialist one. It classes with Arab opposition and with the relatively new Palestinian nationalist movement. But it does not call for expelling the non-Jewish population in the disputed land. Neither is Zionism a racist concept, in spite of the declaration of the United Nations General Assembly Resolution 3379 that "Zionism is a form of racism and racial discrimination," a Resolution that was revoked in 1991.

Nor is Zionism, except in the eyes of those who are antisemitic, based on the concept of the Chosen People, a people engaged in a conspiracy to rule the world. This concept of the Chosen People, often evoked in derogatory fashion by those hostile to Jews, does not mean that Jews claim a racial or genetic superiority, but rather that Jews adhere to the covenant made by God with the Jewish people at Mount Sinai. Obeying the covenant (Exodus, 19–20) would make Israel a "holy nation." Genesis (12:3) relates that the Lord blessed Abraham and those who in turn blessed Abraham. Moses instructed the Israelites to "observe these statutes and judgments, for these are your wisdom and understanding in the sight of the nations which will hear them." Nevertheless, a secular ruler was needed, and Saul became the king of Israel. (Samuel I).

Netanyahu's book makes a persuasive case for the idealism of the Zionist founders, although its comprehensiveness suffers from omission of others who have contributed to the Zionist mansion, such as Ahad Ha'am (Asher Ginsberg), Ber Borochov, A. D. Gordon, Rabbi Kook, and Nahman Syrkin. A number of conclusions can be drawn from his work. Implicitly by his choice of thinkers, Netanyahu emphasized the political aspect of Zionism. Jews have been, since the days of David and Solomon, and after the Bar Kochba Revolt (132–135), a homeless and politically powerless people. Benzion believed that Zionism is national, not religious. Netanyahu's five founders were not observant Jews. He also clarifies that the suggestions of these early Zionists for a Jewish home outside Palestine was always seen as a temporary proposal due to the immediate need to remove Jews from the increasing persecution in Russia and Eastern and Central Europe. The ultimate goal was always Palestine. The Zionist writers differed in attitudes toward and proposals about the Arabs in the territory, but there was no official Zionist policy to expel them.

Nevertheless, critics of Israel persist in the allegation that Zionism promoted this view. They are also averse to the exercise of Israeli power to defend the country, while at the same time neglecting to propose any alternative realistic proposals. Furthermore, these critics deplore the decline in socialist ideology in the country and the diminishing role of early institutions and policies associated with left-wing politics; the Histadrut; the kibbutzim, dating back to Degania, started by socialists in 1910; the moshav or semicooperative; the role of the state in the economy; and the increasing place and electoral power of the orthodox religious groups, but again do not offer alternative proposals.

Left-wing groups (the Poale Zion party, which was affiliated with the Socialist International, the Mapai party, and its successor, Ma'arach), leftist ideas pronounced by academics and in the media, and the exuberant heralding of the kibbutz with its egalitarian identity did dominate from the early years of settlement in Palestine and then in Israel, with social democrats from David Ben Gurion to Yitzhak Rabin, assassinated in 1995, as leaders, until 1977 when Menachem Begin, leader of Likud, the party influenced by Vladimir Jabotinsky's New Zionist Organization, became prime minister. The kibbutz, with its communal child rearing and small-scale operation, became less pivotal in the Israeli self-assertive social structure.

Present-day critics of Israel, Western leftists, radicals, and the so-called post-Zionists tend to see the social democratic groups as the good Zionists, rather than Begin and later leaders like Ariel Sharon in 2001 and Benjamin Netanyahu. The expectation of those groups, influenced by Nahman Syrkin, Ber Borochov, and Berl Katznelson, was the creation of a secular socialist state that would be part of the international socialist movement. The main assertions of critics now is that Israel is too nationalistic; that it should no longer be a Jewish state but rather a democratic one, implying an incompatibility between the two; and that it should end its occupation of captured territory. Usually forgotten in these assertions is the continual Arab rejection of any compromise solution to end the conflict and Arab rejection of partition proposals and resolutions. Benzion Netanyahu has played a valuable role in reminding us of the motivation behind the Zionist movement and of the concern of his five founders for a safe and secure state in which Jews can live a healthy and normal life.

12. What the BBC Did Not Know and Should Have Known about Jerusalem

To say the least, the British Broadcasting Corporation (BBC) is not known for its positive advocacy of the policies and actions of Israel, and once again it displayed its unrelenting bias against the State of Israel. For some years it has forsworn the political neutrality demanded by the Royal Charter given it. In conjunction with the Olympics in London in summer 2012 it posted a BBC Olympic website containing basic information about the competing countries, including a map indicating the capital of each country. In its text of Israel the site listed Jerusalem as "the seat of government though most foreign embassies are in Tel Aviv."

Of course this is factually correct, but as the same time it appears that Israel has no capital, certainly not Jerusalem. By comparison, the BBC listed "East Jerusalem" as "the intended seat of government of Palestine," a state which is not yet in existence. The question must be raised whether the BBC intentionally described Jerusalem in this way in order to add its voice to the ongoing campaign of many international bodies to delegitimize the State of Israel. To help the BBC and any other media in any future depictions of Jerusalem, a brief explanation of its political and religious significance might be useful.

Politics and religion have always been intertwined in the story of Jerusalem, a city that bears the weight of history. The long history of the city started about three thousand years ago. David became the king of Judea around 1010 BC, unifying the Israelite tribes and establishing Jerusalem as his capital in the city of David. In 964 BC, during the reign of David's son, Solomon, the Israelites built the Temple, establishing a physical expression of their religion in the city they considered sacred. Jerusalem thus became both the political capital and the religious capital, the Holy Place for Jews. The Temple was destroyed in 586 BC during the Babylonian invasion that led to the exile of many Jews. King Cyrus allowed them to return to Jerusalem in 539. Immediately, they began building the Second Temple in the sacred city, an edifice that became the political symbol of a Jewish state. Jerusalem was central to Jewish aspirations, still recited in Psalm 137: "If I forget thee, O Jerusalem, let my right hand forget her cunning."

Though Jerusalem was captured numerous times by invading armies—Roman, Byzantine, Umayyad, Mameluke, Crusader—the Jewish people retained its identity in the area until the destruction of the Temple in AD 70 and the banning of Jews from the city in 135. For Jews, the daily liturgy hopes for a return to Jerusalem and the Temple. Jews say their prayers facing the direction of Jerusalem. In the Bible, Jerusalem is mentioned almost 350 times, and Zion more than a hundred times.

The two other major religions have also established a presence in Jerusalem. It was the place where Jesus was crucified, but the city only became holy for Christians in the fourth century AD, after Emperor Constantine and his mother, Helen, converted, and ordered the building of the Basilica of Saint-Sepulcre in AD 326, which through the centuries has become for many Christians the most important pilgrimage destination. After the revolt led by Simon Bar Kochba in 132 against the Roman Empire and his creation of a State of Israel, the Romans made a determined effort to "dejudaise" the area. They renamed the area of Israel *Syria Palaestina* and the city of Jerusalem now became *Aelia Capitolina*. With Constantine, the city again became Jerusalem.

Muslims, commemorating the Prophet's experience in the city, about which there are different versions, began building there, on the Temple Mount, the Dome of the Rock, in AD 638. This is not a mosque, but the Al-Aqsa mosque has been built close to it. Mecca and Medina are the two important Holy Places for Muslims; only in recent years have some Muslims regarded Jerusalem as a third Holy Place. Unlike Jews, who pray toward Jerusalem, Muslims pray toward Mecca. The Koran never mentions Jerusalem. The city was not mentioned in the original 1964 National Covenant of the Palestine Liberation Organization.

For many years, especially during the Abbasid Caliphate, starting in the eighth century, Jerusalem had little significance for Muslims. After a brief period of rule by the Christian Crusaders, started by Goffrey of Bouillion in 1099, the city was retaken by Saladin in 1187 after the battle of Hattin and remained under various kinds of Islamic control until the end of the Ottoman Empire after World War I. As a result of the 1967 war and its capture of east Jerusalem, Israel gave the Waqf, the Muslim religious administration, control over the Temple Mount, where no Jew is allowed to pray.

Political rivalries over the Middle East have always existed among the great powers. With the demise of the Ottoman Empire, the Holy Places became rallying points for Zionists and Arab nationalists. Political passions were exhibited at the Western Wall and at the Dome of the Rock. But after it was given the League of Nations Mandate for Palestine in 1920 at the San Remo conference, Britain in 1922 established Jerusalem as the capital. Jews had been the majority population in the city for over a century; by 1922 they accounted for 65 percent of the total.

The decisive proposal for settlement of the Arab-Israel conflict was the UN General Assembly Resolution (181) of November 29, 1947, which partitioned the area between Jews and Arabs. However, Jerusalem was to become a *corpus separatum*, under a special international regime and the administration of the United Nations. Whether this was a feasible solution or not was never tested because of the Arab invasion of the new State of Israel in May 1948. Instead, as a result of the 1948–49 war, Jerusalem was divided; the Arab Legion captured the Jewish Quarter of the Old City, the site of many synagogues and of the Western Wall, part of the retaining wall of the Temple Mount compound, which remained after the Temple was destroyed by the Romans in AD 70. The only time that Jerusalem has been divided is between 1948 and 1967.

This division was the so-called Green Line in April 1949, between Israel and Jordan. The latter continued to control the Old City, including the Jewish Quarter, between 1949 and 1967. The Jewish inhabitants were expelled, and destruction and desecration of Jewish sites took place, including the Hurva synagogue and thirty-three other houses of worship and the ancient cemetery on the Mount of Olives.

Arabs controlled the Holy Places of all three religions. For eighteen years Jews were not able to go to and pray at the Western Wall. For the first time in two thousand years, no Jew remained in the Jewish Quarter. At this time, West Jerusalem was officially declared the capital of Israel, and the Israeli Parliament, the Knesset, moved to Jerusalem in January 1950.

During the Six-Day War in June 1967, Israeli parachutists on June 8, 1967, seized east Jerusalem, which remains in Israeli hands. The area was not annexed, but Israeli law and jurisdiction was on July 27, 1967, extended to east Jerusalem and to a few miles of the West Bank. The Israeli Protection of Holy Places Law provided for the protection of churches and mosques as well as synagogues. Jordan continued to administer the Muslim holy sites in the city. On July 30, 1980, a fundamental law adopted by the Knesset declared that "Jerusalem complete and unified is the capital of Israel." It is the seat of the president of the State, the Knesset, the government, and the Supreme Court.

Palestinian leaders have also claimed Jerusalem. Their statement on November 15, 1988, about the establishment of a state proclaimed the capital as Jerusalem, Al-Quds Ash-Sharif. Yasser Arafat, head of the PLO, even denied that a Jewish Temple had existed in Jerusalem.

It is ironic that the BBC should be aware of this declaration that has not been implemented but appears to be unaware of the three thousand years of Jewish history in which Jerusalem has been the cardinal and capital feature, politically and religiously.

13. Justice for the Kurds

In the topsy-turvey world of international relations much ink has been spilled about the desirability or even the inevitability of a Palestinian state. Such a state would encompass five to six million people, the separate identity of whom stems only from the middle of the twentieth century. Until that time, those living in the area of Palestine did not consider themselves as Palestinians. They associated themselves with the Pan-Arab or Pan-Islamist movement rather than as a separate people of Palestinians. A Palestinian identity was not regarded as distinct from the identities of other Arabs who inhabited adjacent regions. The concept of such a separate identity arose, among other reasons, partly as a response to the Zionist movement. The result now is a demand, which has international support, for a Palestinian state separate from that of other Arabs.

What has been much less discussed by the international community, and for the most part ignored, is a similar claim by the Kurds, a frequently forgotten people with a long history and a distinct identity pleading for—and literally fighting and dying for—an independent state of their own. The Arab League with its twenty-two members, along with Turkey and many countries and groups in the international community have passionately advocated that a part of the disputed land in the Palestine area become a Palestinian state. The same individuals and groups, however, have opposed the creation of a Kurdish non-Arab state on territory it claims as its own.

Yet by any reasonable and objective historical and cultural criteria the claim of the Kurds for political sovereignty is very much stronger than that of Palestinians. In contrast to the Palestinians, the Kurds, who do not regard Jews as enemies, have few friends in the international community. Kurdish nationalism emerged a century earlier than did Palestinian nationalism. Collectively, the Kurds—who are not Arabs— live in an area usually referred to as Kurdistan, despite the fact that the borders are unclear. As a significant ethnic group that speaks its own language, part of the Indo-European language group, they now number thirty-five to forty million.

During the late nineteenth century the Kurds made demands, mounted uprisings, and pressed for political autonomy in the areas in which they lived or independence free of any control by the Ottoman Empire or Persian authorities, each of which ruled the areas. The uprisings for an independent state in 1880 were particularly fierce, but the Ottomans and the armies of Qajar Persia suppressed them.

After World War I, the Treaty of Sèvres in August 1920—the peace treaty between the Ottoman Empire and the victorious Allies— dissolved the Empire and replaced it with a number of new nation-states: Iraq, Syria, Kuwait, and Turkey, but not a Kurdish state. The victorious European powers created political structures with less than full regard to their ethnic composition.

The newly created Turkey renounced all rights over Arab Asia and North Africa. Two Articles in the 1920 Treaty were relevant to the issue of the Kurds. Article 62 of the Treaty suggested the creation of an autonomous region for Kurds in the new Turkey. Article 64 proposed the later possibility of an independent Kurdish state "inhabiting that part of Kurdistan which has hitherto been included in the Mosul *vilayet* [of the Ottoman Empire]."

However, the Treaty of Lausanne, signed in July 1923 and put into effect in August 1924, ended the continuing state of war between Turkey and a number of the victorious Allies. Between the two treaties, the monarchy in Turkey had been overthrown, and a republic under Kemal Ataturk had been established. The new Treaty defined the borders of the modern Turkish state and ignored the earlier proposal for a Kurdish state. Political machinations, particularly by the British, who were concerned with the threat of Communist Russia, led to decisions by which the territorial integrity of Iran, Iraq, and Turkey were heightened to counteract the threat.

The Treaty of Lausanne made no mention of Kurdish independence. Instead, the Kurdish population was divided into different areas of Northern Iraq, Southeastern Turkey, and parts of Iran and Syria. Exact figures are difficult to calculate and are disputed, but it is clear that Kurds now constitute large minorities in the different countries; in Iraq they constitute 17 percent of the population, in Turkey 18 percent, in Syria 10 percent, and in Iran 7 percent. In all these countries they have suffered from oppression. In 1962 about 120,000 Kurds were denied citizenship in Syria on the argument that they were not born in the country. Kurdish land in northern Syria in 1973 was confiscated and given to Arabs. Their language and books were banned from schools, and their traditional celebrations were prohibited.

Kurds challenged the state of Turkey by an armed insurgency in the 1980s but were suppressed. Turkey had outlawed the Kurdish language and forbad Kurds to wear their traditional dress in the cities. It encouraged the Kurds to move from their mountain base to the cities to dilute their identity. Kurds see as disparaging the clause in the Turkish Constitution characterizing citizens as "members of the Turkish nation."

Aggression against the Kurds has been physical as well as political and constitutional. In the armed fighting between Turkey and the outlawed Kurdistan Workers' Party (PKK), formed in 1984 and whose leader has long been imprisoned, about forty thousand people were killed, many of whom were PKK fighters. In the 1990s, more than three thousand Kurdish villages, close to the border with Iraq, were destroyed by Turkey. Turkish planes on many occasions have in the last few years attacked PKK bases and killed civilians in northern Iraq. In March 2012 Kurds in a number of Turkish towns including Istanbul, while celebrating the Kurdish New Year (Nowruz) were arrested or wounded by riot police.

In 1988, Iraq used chemical weapons against the Kurds, whose villages were burned, resulting in thousands killed. The attempted Kurdish rebellion after the Gulf War of 1991 was crushed by Iraqi troops. Saddam Hussein destroyed more than four thousand Kurdish villages and killed many thousands of civilians, perhaps as many as one hundred eighty thousand. Only after the brutal regime of Saddam Hussein had ended did Iraqi Kurdistan become an autonomous but not fully independent, regime, an area that was extended after the US invasion of 2003. The alternative still exists for Kurds: either greater autonomy in the individual countries in which they live, or an independent state of their own.

The international community and the world media have argued fervently for a Palestinian state. No such attention or concern has been accorded the Kurds, nor has there been condemnation of the brutality toward and oppression of the Kurds. That oppression and the brutality Kurds have suffered is very much greater than anything experienced by the Palestinians.

The double standard was recently illustrated by an event in Gaza. The Turkish government donated the funds for the seventy-feet-tall monument erected in Gaza City Port dedicated to "international activists." The monument bears the names of the nine "martyrs" killed by Israel commandos in May 2010 when they were on the Mavi Marmara, one of the vessels that tried to break the Israeli blockade of Gaza. The Turkish Foreign Minister, who referred to the "oppressed" Arabs in Gaza, ignores with a mote in his own eye the oppression of the Kurds in his own country. Those purportedly concerned with human rights and self-determination have rarely, if ever, expressed support or paraded for an independent Kurdish state. If a Kurdish state is unthinkable, as Arabs argue, so logically is a Palestinian one. Surely the conclusion should be clear. If a Palestinian state is justified and endorsed by the international community, similar approval and endorsement should be given simultaneously to the creation of a Kurdish state. Why a Palestinian state if no Kurdish state?

14. Secretary-General Ban Goes to Teheran

On February 17, 2012, the United Nations General Assembly adopted Resolution 66/175 on the "Situation of Human Rights in the Islamic Republic of Iran." It expressed deep concern at the ongoing and recurring human rights violations in Iran related to, among many things, torture and cruel, inhuman, or degrading treatment or punishment, including flogging and amputations. The Resolution called on the government of Iran to address the substantive concerns expressed and to respect fully its human rights obligations.

Few could seriously believe that Iran was likely to do what the Resolution requested, but at least the international community had publicly expressed concern about the misdeeds of the country. It therefore came as a surprise that Ban Ki-moon, UN Secretary-General, attended the sixteenth summit meeting of the Non-Aligned nations in Teheran, Iran on August 29–31, 2012.

The Non-Aligned group consists of 120 member states and 21 observer countries, though only thirty-one heads of state and ten foreign ministers were scheduled to attend the conference. Curiously, Ban Ki-moon, the diplomatically experienced South Korean national, partly educated at the Kennedy School of Government at Harvard University, comes from a country that is not a member state of the Non-Aligned group. In Teheran he might have met the head of state of North Korea, who attended the conference.

No one can doubt the good intentions of the secretary-general. It is his judgment on the issue of his presence in Teheran that is questionable. He believed, although Resolution 66/175 was clear on the matter, that his attendance would be an opportunity to convey the concerns and expectations of the international community. These would include issues such as the nuclear program of Iran, terrorism, human rights, and the crisis in Syria. The secretary-general encountered and planned to have "meaningful and fruitful discussions" with Iranian Supreme Leader Ayatollah Ali Khamenei and President Mahmoud Ahmadinejad.

The secretary-general has expressed varying opinions on Middle East issues. During his visit to Israel in January 2012 he urged Israel to stop building settlement construction and to offer good will gestures to the Palestinians, without similar advice about gestures to be made by the Palestinians. However, more recently he expressed disappointment at the decision of the United Nations Human Rights Council to "single out only specific regional item [concerning Israel] given the range and scope of allegations of human rights violations throughout the world." Considering the relentless hostility and animosity of the UNHRC for many years toward Israel and its pathological obsession with Israel without paying more than minimal heed to other countries, his remarks might be deemed a diplomatic understatement.

Mr. Ban, after the ignominious withdrawal of the UN observer mission on Syria in August 2012, urged a "flexible UN presence in Syria." With television cameras daily portraying the slaughter in Syria, it is difficult to take seriously his belief that a presence of this kind, whatever it entails, will provide the UN impartial means to assess the situation on the ground. The secretary-general must be aware that Syria is being supplied with weapons by Iran. He was also aware in his speech in Teheran on August 30, 2012, that "The bloodshed in Syria is the responsibility of all of us and will not stop until there is real intervention to stop it."

The great French diplomat Talleyrand might have said of Ban Ki-moon's visit to Teheran, "It is worse than a crime, it is a mistake." It was a mistake for two reasons: the sponsorship of the organization group of Non-Aligned nations, and the unacceptability of Iran's leaders as hosts of the meeting.

The Non-Aligned movement was founded in Belgrade in September 1961, during the Cold War. Its initial members argued that they were independent of the rival powers, the United States and the Soviet Union. In fact, their policies and actions were more partial to the Russians than to the Americans, frequently criticizing the US as colonialist and aggressive. In 2012 Iran held the presidency of the Non-Aligned Movement.

Now that the Cold War has been over for twenty years, there is no rational raison d'être for a Non-Aligned movement, but it persists as a group with constant criticism of Western democracies. In particular, almost all of its members have voted in international bodies, in which they comprise two–thirds of the membership, for resolutions critical of the US and of the State of Israel. This was not the appropriate venue for an even-handed UN Secretary–General or for genuine nonpartisan discussion.

More important is the fact that Mr. Ban lent legitimacy to the regime of Iran and its leaders, individuals who have violated UN obligations and been a destabilizing force in the Middle East. He did say in his speech in Teheran, "I strongly reject threats by any member state to destroy another [state] or outrageous attempts to deny historical facts such as the Holocaust." However, it was unlikely that his diplomatic efforts could persuade the Iranian leaders to halt their nuclear program and their ambition to develop atomic weapons. The country had already refused on a number of occasions to halt its nuclear enrichment program. Indeed, Iran took advantage of the conference not only to justify its policies in aiding the Assad Syrian regime but also to defend its nuclear program.

Mr. Ban was aware of offensive verbal criticisms of Israel by the Iranian leaders. He could appreciate the full extent of those verbal remarks made by both the Ayatollah Ali Khamenei and President Ahmedinejad. The president stated, "the very existence of the Zionist regime is an insult to humankind and an affront to all nations in the world." His threat is clear. He is not a surgeon, but his diagnosis is that the "Zionist regime and the Zionists are a cancerous tumor" and must be wiped out. Thus there will be no Zionist regime and no domination by the United States in his new map of the Middle East.

Secretary-General Ban, Teheran was no place for you to visit.

15. International Dithering over Syria

Except for the persistent animosity toward Israel, which they continuously express and which remains unabated, the functioning of the agencies of the United Nations and of the international community is reminiscent of the character of Oblomov in the novel by Ivan Goncharov. Oblomov is the personification of the individual who is incapable of making any important decisions or undertaking any significant action. International organizations, moving by consensus and making little demands on their members, have similarly been incapable or ineffective in solving security and political issues.

The most recent illustration of this is the international inability to deal with and end the daily slaughter in Syria. After many thousand Syrians had been killed, mostly by government forces, in the fighting in the country, the UN Security Council on April 21, 2012, unanimously authorized an "observer mission" for an initial period of ninety days, which was renewed, to monitor the end of violence in the country and to implement a peace plan.

The mission, to consist of up to three hundred unarmed military observers and an appropriate civilian component, was given the thankless job of attending to the urgent, comprehensive, and immediate implementation of a six-point plan put forward jointly by Kofi Annan—the former secretary-general of the UN who on February 23, 2012, had been appointed joint special envoy—and the League of Arab States.

In reality, all this was in vain. The cease-fire never took effect, and so far about seventy thousand have died since the revolt against Bashar al-Assad's regime began in March 2011. No truce ever occurred. When the observer team—originally three hundred strong and headed by the Norwegian General Robert Mood—tried to become involved, it came under attack and was forced to withdraw most of its personnel. From mid-June, the members of the team were largely confined to their hotels. That mission has now been withdrawn. The Arab League's monitoring mission of 165 members had already been withdrawn in January 2012.

The bloodshed continued, with escalation of violence. The Syrian government was intransigent and refused to implement the six-point plan that was supposed to have the support of the Security Council, the Syrian regime, and the rebels in order to be activated.

The crucial factor is that the five permanent members of the Security Council have been divided: the United States, Britain, and France want Assad to leave office, while Russia and China support the regime and have vetoed three meaningful draft resolutions to exert pressure on Assad and make him accountable. Moreover, Russia has established a naval base on the Syrian coast at Tartus and continues to sell arms to Syria. This lack of unity has meant that the Security Council will not act to compel the Assad government to agree to a peaceful resolution.

As a result, on August 2, 2012, Kofi Annan resigned as joint special envoy, criticizing the Security Council for its indecision—in reality the obstruction of Russia and China. He declared that rather than action, there is only "finger pointing and name calling in the Security Council." He said that as an envoy he could not want peace more than the protagonists or the Security Council did. His honest appraisal of the reasons for his failure after five months does him credit, but one can ask why Annan was not cognizant of the true reality of the United Nations given the fact that for nine years he was secretary-general. The wonder is that he endured so long.

Others in the international arena have contributed to the farce concerning Syria. The British foreign minister, William Hague, offered £5 million of nonlethal aid to the Syrian armed opposition groups to buy communication equipment and medical supplies. This proposal might be compared to offering sunglasses to a person who was dying.

NATO may have supplied the Syrian rebels with some weapons and helped in training but has not taken any direct action against the regime. On July 5, 2012, the head of NATO, Anders Fogh Rasmussen, instructed Syria to find a political solution to its crisis, after it had shot down a Turkish plane on June 22. Though its Charter, in Article 5, allows the use of force if a member nation has come under attack, NATO refused to use force, though Turkey has been a member of NATO since 1952. Instead, Mr. Rasmussen found the action "unacceptable."

Perhaps most intriguing and telling has been the criticism by François Loncle, a Socialist member of the foreign affairs committee in the French parliament, of the poor performance of Catherine Ashton, the high representative on foreign affairs of the European Union. He spoke of the feebleness of European diplomacy concerning Syria and of "the uselessness of Madame Ashton who never says anything and does absolutely nothing." Catherine Ashton—a British Labour party politician who has occupied her post since 2009 and is said to be the second-highest-paid female politician, after IMF head Christine Lagarde—is by now a figure of fun.

But M. Loncle is not entirely accurate. Ashton did say something, of which he and the EU might be reminded, in March 2012 when she compared the murders of Jewish children in Toulouse to "what is happening in Gaza." The international community ought to be conscious of her comparison of the targeted massacre of Jewish children with the defensive measures of Israeli authorities against terrorists.

Curiously, it is the Arab and Muslim countries that have taken some action. The Arab League, normally regarded as a club of dictators, in November 2011 suspended Syria's membership. Similarly, the fifty-seven-member Organization of Islamic Cooperation, representing 1.5 billion Muslims, suspended Syria in August 2012.

UN Secretary-General Ban Ki-moon has appreciated that "violence and suffering must come to an end." Diplomacy about Syria was entrusted to a new special envoy, Lakhdar Brahimi, the seventy-eight-year-old former foreign minister of Algeria. He can only be wished well in the effort to resolve the ethnic and sectarian complexities of Syria. It is not part of his present function, but he might help achieve a peaceful settlement not only within Syria but also between Syria and Israel. The world might be reminded that Syria has no formal relationship with Israel and has technically been at war since 1948. The international community could be reminded of the Arab proverb, "You cannot turn the wind, so turn the sail."

16. The New Potemkin Village: Syria Disguised

Whether true or myth, the story persists of Potemkin villages, built by Russian minister Grigory Potemkin in 1787: fake settlements presenting the residents as prosperous in order to fool and impress Empress Catherine II during her visit to the Crimea. In the twentieth century, visitors to the Soviet Union, including George Bernard Shaw and the left-wing author Doris Lessing, were taken to the communist equivalent of a Potemkin village. Blinded by their desire to find the USSR the Utopia they wanted it to be, they accepted the illusion as genuine. Like-minded believers still feel nostalgic about that lost paradise.

In similar fashion, Western intellectuals in the past and the present, true believers in the utopia to be built, have refused to believe the evil facts of the reality of the Great Leap Forward (1958–61) in China. The notable writer Edgar Snow accepted the report of Mao that "the situation in the country is excellent" and himself reported that "I saw no starving people in China," when more than forty million people are said to have starved to death.

Our era has witnessed and suffered from a similar acceptance by many commentators in democratic countries of the illusion of the nature of the regimes and conditions of life in Arab societies. For whatever reason, whether because of postmodern belief in moral relativism, adherence to political correctness, or simply mercenary expectations, these commentators have spurned a rational analysis of the true nature of those societies.

Though the events stemming from the Arab Spring have revealed the deficiencies, corruption, and brutality of Arab systems, they have not totally dispelled the illusion accepted by so many Westerners. Nor have these events sufficiently affected the policy-makers in democratic countries, who are still hesitant to condemn the human rights abuses in Arab societies or to mete out punishment for the dictators of those countries.

Nowhere is this truer than in the case of Syria, ironically for some years a member of the United Nations Human Rights Council. Over the last two years Syria has butchered at least seventy thousand of its own people in full view of the eyes of the world. The late dictator Hafez al-Assad had ruled as president from 1971, when he seized power in a coup, until his death in June 2000. The first Syrian ruler who was not a Sunni, he governed ruthlessly through a web of security agencies and intelligence operatives. His regime was a corrupt and economically inefficient system that was virtually a family business of fellow Alawites, a sect regarded as heretics by Sunni Muslims that accounts for about 10 percent of the Syrian population.

The Alawites control the key political and military institutions of the state, though they get some support from other minorities, Christians and Druze. Business was essentially left to the merchant class. Assad delivered his primary contribution to human rights in February 1982, when he authorized the Syrian army commanded by his younger brother to engage in heavy shelling and poisonous gas to massacre thirty thousand of his subjects living in the city of Hama. His major contribution to political philosophy was pan-Arabism and anti-Zionism.

His son, Bashar al-Assad, was an accidental successor because of the death of his older brother in a car accident in 1994. Lulled by the fact that he was a physician trained in ophthalmology at the Western Eye Hospital in London—and because of his well-educated elegant, former banker wife, who grew up the daughter of a wealthy family living in London—Bashar was optimistically viewed by some in the West as having the potential to be a more benign, modern leader than his father. Wealthy expatriate Syrians were invited back to their country, and naive Americans and Europeans, politicians and academics, were wooed to meet with him and other leaders of the regime.

For the sake of reassuring easily convinced Westerners, Bashar immediately engaged in setting up his own version of a Potemkin village. He released some political prisoners, permitted some forms of free speech, tolerated the so-called Damascus Spring, and brought some technocrats into the administration. But few long-lasting reforms were implemented, and free speakers soon re-entered prison. Bashar may not have the suavity or personality of his father, but he has shown himself equally ruthless, duplicitous, and impervious to good sense. The man who many believed might become a reformer in the Arab world turned into a corrupt manipulator who regarded himself as a man of destiny.

His inner power group, all ruthless individuals, has included his cousin, Atif Najjib, as head of security; his uncle, Maher al-Assad, as commander of the elite Republican Guard and the 4th division of the army; and his brother-in-law, Assef Chawkat, as former head of intelligence and deputy chief-of-staff of the army.

Long before the current internal situation, the ruthlessness of Bashar was displayed externally. He sent thirty thousand Syrian troops to Lebanon to control the country. He helped the insurgents against

Saddam Hussein in 2003. He was involved in the assassination in 2005 of Rafiq Hariri, the former prime minister of Lebanon. He became friendly with theocratic Iran.

Catherine Ashton, the European Union high representative for foreign affairs and security policy, in her speech of June 12, 2012, to the European Parliament, is still blinded by a Potemkin village. In that speech, in which she addressed both the situation in Syria and the settlements in Israel, she charged Israel rather than Syria with serious violations of international and humanitarian law. While she expressed how she was appalled "by the sickening violence" in Syria, she suggested little more than a "contact group," an idea already suggested by UN Special Envoy Kofi Annan, to pressure and exert influence on the regime, and called for the Syrian government to implement a humanitarian response plan for which the EU has contributed EUR 28 million.

This fatuous attitude to a brutal regime slaughtering its own people can be compared with her stronger language in the same speech concerning Israel: that Israeli settlements remain the "key and most serious concern." She condemned settlement expansion as illegal under international law. The need to respect international and humanitarian law, which must be observed by Israel, was less pronounced by her in the case of Syria.

Is there some hope that leaders of democratic and other nations will perceive and act on the Syrian deception of a Potemkin village? Turkey began protesting about the continuing harsh treatment by Bashar al-Assad against the domestic opponents of his regime, presumably because it has been overwhelmed by thousands of refugees fleeing Syria. Jordan had taken in about 125,000 Syrian refugees, including military and police defectors. Norwegian General Robert Mood pulled back the three hundred unarmed observer force he led in Syria to its headquarters, and cancelled patrols because it was too dangerous. Yet at the same time, European countries in mid-June 2012 gave up their proposal to stop and search arms shipments to Syria, ostensibly for legal reasons.

Meanwhile, Russia has been providing Syria with arms shipments, above all with attack helicopters. The increase in weapons and ammunition supplied to Syria, which already has an arsenal of five hundred planes and two hundred helicopters, has allowed it to be more aggressive in air and artillery assaults. Syria has other deadly weapons—surface-to-surface missiles, a ballistic missile capability, and a chemical program, in existence for forty years, that includes mustard gas, and

Sarin and VX nerve agents. The sophisticated chemical weapons facilities, deployed on thousands of bombs and warheads installed on Scud missiles, now pose a threat to the whole Middle East.

It is openly acknowledged that some countries, including Saudi Arabia, Turkey, Qatar, and the United States, are helping supply Syrian opposition fighters with medical supplies, communications equipment, and a variety of weapons, but that supply is limited, and they have done little to act aggressively against the regime. Instead, more focus has been on diplomacy. That diplomacy, however, lacks muscle and candor. Secretary of State Hillary Clinton expressed concern about Russian aid to Syria. Yet, both the United States and France continued to have business dealings with Rosoboronexport, the Russian arms firm that was supplying the Assad regime with weapons.

Is it not time for the international community to realize that the starting point of diplomacy is to bring Bashar al-Assad to justice?

17. Multiculturalism Revisited

The brutal murders in and around Oslo on July 22, 2011, by Anders Behring Breivik, the self-declared commander for the Knights Templar of Europe, are to be rightfully condemned, and due punishment must be accorded for his horrible crime. But his massacre of seventy-six innocent people and his 1,500-page polemical diatribe—his European Declaration of Independence, with its obsession with multiculturalism and the threat caused by the Islamic presence in Europe—must not be allowed to prevent a genuine, rational discussion of a complex contemporary problem.

Western countries are perplexed by the problem of the current immigration of large numbers of individuals coming from different cultures, and the tension caused by their reluctance to assimilate and integrate into the larger society. To debate the issues of immigration and the likelihood of groups becoming participants in the larger society is not racist behavior, but rather a necessary consequence of real problems.

Aware of the potential positive value of immigrants, governments along with other agencies have subscribed to a set of policies and values that has become known as multiculturalism. They seek to diminish the difficulties the newcomers face: lack of respect, verbal abuse, and discrimination in general (and especially in housing and employment). However desirable some of the efforts have been, both for immigrants and for their new society, it is evident that Western policies of multiculturalism have drawbacks as well as benefits.

Those policies encounter a number of intellectual and political problems. They aim at accommodating different religious, cultural, and ethnic traditions within a society, but societies require a common culture. The great fourteenth-century Arab historian, Ibn Khaldun, was aware of this when he wrote that civilization arose only when there was solidarity. Today, this idea of solidarity—and commitment to the common culture and to the basic structures and values of democratic countries—is being challenged by identity politics and by advocacy of diversity.

Multiculturalism in Western societies confers benefits on an ethnic or racial minority, enabling it to maintain its own culture. This may lead to friction and to both physical and cultural separation from the majority of the society. It also disparages individual rights, fragments society, and supports the politicization of group identities. The French writer Pascal Bruckner has defined multiculturalism as racism of the antiracists. It tends to chain people to their roots and to imprison them in an ethnic or racial definition of their group. It may not only undermine individuality and self-reliance, but also may prevent people from liberating themselves from their own group traditions. Celebrating differences among people has become a means of enforcing group identity. In recent practice, multiculturalism has led to restriction rather than protection of free speech. Some laws make it a criminal offense to make critical remarks about some religious, ethnic, or national groups. It has led in the West to tolerating minorities that are themselves intolerant.

Contemporary European politicians have understood the political problem. Chancellor Angela Merkel of Germany in October 2010 declared that multiculturalism had failed in her country. She declared that it was not a humane formula to respect other cultures, but a device to deal with immigrant workers who were still committed to the culture of their homeland, not to that of Germany. The German state had accommodated the demands of immigrants, rather than promoting German values, and it would be difficult to integrate the immigrant Muslim population. German scholars have argued that, though differences may exist, European countries need a *leitkultur*, a core or guiding culture necessary for a democratic community concerned with modernity, secularism, and human rights.

Political leaders in both Britain and France have been similarly troubled by recent occurrences. British Prime Minister David Cameron made it clear, in a speech of February 5, 2011, that "under the doctrine of state multiculturalism we have encouraged different cultures to live separate lives, apart from each other and apart from the mainstream." Britain had tolerated those segregated communities behaving in ways completely counter to British values. In France, former President Nicholas Sarkozy similarly declared that multiculturalism is a failure and had fostered extremism. France, he believed, has been too concerned about the identity of the new arrivals and not enough about preserving the identity of the country receiving them.

Sarkozy since 2003 had been responsible for two bills restricting immigration into France. His belief was that Muslims in France must practice French Islam, not just Islam in France. However, it is still an open question whether Muslims want to be part of French society or prefer Sharia law and traditional Islamic behavior.

This problem has arisen in France and in other European countries as a result of Muslim immigration, now amounting to about forty million, more than 5 percent of the population of the continent. Predictions are uncertain because of recent changes and the decrease in the Muslim birthrate in European countries, but one objective calculation is that by 2050 Muslims would account for more than 20 percent of the population. In Germany today about three to four million Turks, about 5 percent of the total population, reside. A recent survey of their life and values showed that they hoped that Germany in the future would have more Muslims than Christians, that Islam was the only true religion, and that Germany should be more considerate of the customs and traditions of Turkish immigrants.

Douglas Johnston in his book *Religion, Terror, and Error* has pointed out that some Europeans discussing the concessions their countries have made to Muslim communities think they are undermining Western values. Among these concessions are the adoption of parts of Sharia law in some areas, the silence about polygamy, the alteration of Western cultural symbols and behavior in order not to offend Muslims (one of which is the removal of the English flag from Heathrow Airport because it contains the cross of Saint George, which Muslims consider offensive), and changes in the educational system to provide for including an Islamic curriculum in the teaching program.

The contemporary belief that all cultural groups and religions should be tolerated and have a right to self-determination or autonomy may be salutary as a general proposition, but the degree of that tolerance should be relevant both to democratic values, whether or not the principles of human rights are being observed by those groups, and also to demographic changes. The monstrous action of Breivik may make it more difficult to criticize the multicultural practices that are promoting racism rather than eliminating it. Yet objective observers should not be too cautious or reluctant to criticize actions or non-actions of Europeans. There is no easy balance for democratic countries today between protecting their cultural values and protecting minority rights.

18. An End to Appeasement

Of course George Orwell said it perfectly: "So much of left-wing thought is a kind of playing with fire by people who don't even know that fire is hot." He was familiar with the "fellow travelers" of the Soviet Communist regime who, in their irresponsible fashion, supported or excused that regime despite its tyranny and brutality, and at no cost to themselves. Intellectual support of or acquiescence in tyrannical regimes or unjust rulers is familiar in history, going back to the beginning. It runs from Plato supporting the tyrant of Syracuse, Seneca praising Nero, Aristotle advising Alexander the Great, and extends to modern times, with individuals such as the philosophers Martin Heidegger approving Hitler for a time and Maurice Merleau-Ponty in 1947 justifying the shameful fraudulent Moscow Trials that condemned the Russian critics of Stalin.

A recent biography of Hewlett Johnson, dean of Canterbury in Britain for over thirty years, provides an illuminating portrait of the deluded, fanatical mind at work. Johnson, safe in his ecclesiastical position and suffering no penalties for his utterances and actions, was a lifelong admirer of both Communism in theory and the Soviet Union in action. He defended the Nazi-Soviet Pact of September 1939, the prelude for Hitler to start World War II. His undying admiration for Communism led him to defend both the arrest in 1949 of Cardinal Mindzenty on false charges by the Hungarian secret police and the Soviet invasion of Hungary. The Red Dean, as Johnson was called, was awarded the Lenin Peace Prize in 1950 and the Stalin International Peace Prize in 1951.

Similar support by Western critics of their own democratic societies has been present in modern times for rulers, such as Gaddafi or Idi Amin, whose grasp on sanity was not immediately obvious, or whose brutality and tyranny was evident, such as Mao. This mindset is now all too apparent among many Western intellectuals, academics, the media, international organizations, and religious groups in their refusal to challenge the many cases of injustice, particularly in Muslim countries, but rather to criticize and condemn the State of Israel at every turn, in spite of the continuing physical and rhetorical aggression against it. These critics, consciously or not, ally with those groups and states whose ultimate objective is the destruction of the State of Israel. Individuals with this mindset in recent years have of course supported worthy causes, such as sanctions against the infamous apartheid state of South Africa and calls for its abolition. These, however, were hardly courageous acts, for they paid no price for such support, but benefited either for ideological reasons or for more personal reasons of self-esteem or glory in success.

What is important is that the compassion shown by these individuals has not been equally present in the face of gratuitous attacks on democratic values, and aggression—physical and rhetorical—against the State of Israel. Nor have they, at least Western Europeans, been willing to face the real current problems in their societies, such as the mass immigration of people from other cultures, individuals who have not been successfully integrated into Western societies, and the rise of Islamism. They rarely discuss the real difficulties in the changing nature, demographically and politically, of the multicultural societies of Britain and France, or the meaningfulness of the reality that over half the Muslims living in Britain believe that the CIA or the Israeli Mossad were responsible for the 9/11 attacks in New York City.

What can explain this spinelessness by self-proclaimed high-minded people in not responding, not only against physical violence but also against attacks on free speech or attempts to prevent criticism of some activity supposedly based on religious principles? Part of the explanation, at least regarding Europeans, may be due to what Walter Laqueur in his book *After the Fall* has called a "crisis of lack of will, inertia, tiredness, self-doubt, a lack of self-confidence." Others, perhaps seeking fame, or acceptance as politically correct, or material rewards, or simply out of ignorance of political reality, pay no price for their appeasement of the actions or language of countries and groups that are critical of democratic values.

Some Western radicals may be deluded by feelings of guilt for the actions of democratic countries in the past; no one wants to be accused of racism or intolerance toward minority groups, or support of Western imperialism. They often express concern about abuses of power in their own countries, but are more quiescent about much greater abuses in non-Western countries. Rarely do they protest about the violations of human rights in Arab and Muslim countries or the honor killings or genital mutilation of Muslim women.

One specious explanation of this quiescence of radicals is that discussion of the issue of Islamist actions—such as the murder in November 2004 of the Dutch filmmaker Theo van Gogh or the death threats against writers such as Salman Rushdie; Ibn Warraq, author of *Leaving Islam*; and Ayaan Hirsi Ali, or condemnation of the Danish journalists, especially the courageous editor Flemming Rose, responsible in 2005 for the controversial cartoons of the Prophet Muhammad—would lead to greater support for right-wing parties who would then call for restrictions on immigration, or mass deportation, or economic and educational discrimination against Muslims. This can hardly explain the refusal of well-known fellow writers John Le Carré, Hugh Trevor-Roper, and Roald Dahl to defend Rushdie after his famous book *The Satanic Verses* was condemned by the Ayatollah Khomeini, who in February 1989 issued a fatwa against Rushdie, a call for the faithful to kill him and his publishers. In his memoir, *Joseph Anton*, Rushdie—who was forced to live a secret life and needed police protection—expresses his disappointment regarding that refusal of British and American publishers and writers to support him and the principles of free speech and free religion.

Why would these supposed upholders of the principle of free speech not protest the decision of the UN Human Rights Council to punish criticism of Islam? Why would they not challenge the Cairo Declaration on Human Rights in Islam of August 1990, which states that Sharia law is "the only source of reference "for the protection of human rights in Islamic countries, a statement that is contrary to the UN Declaration of Human Rights of December 1948? Why do the high-minded progressives acquiesce in the attacks on Enlightenment principles?

A more probable explanation for such behavior is an attitude of appeasement, reminiscent of the refusal by some in the 1930s to recognize and to counter the reality of Hitlerism, or Stalin's rule in the Soviet Union, or Mao's regime in China. In the present, this entails a politically correct acceptance of the cultural relativist position that the demands of Muslim authorities and Muslim habits, values, and customs are appropriate. This view disregards the reality that not all cultures and religious expressions are equal. It is a toleration of the intolerable.

The most plausible explanation for silence in democratic countries is fear. Westerners fear being accused of racial prejudice or Islamophobia. Publishing houses have been wary, for fear of physical violence and economic boycott, of issuing books, such as the novel *The Jewel of Medina* by Sherry Jones, that might offend some in the Muslim community. The behavior of Random House on this issue was not a profile in courage. Nor was the Yale University Press any more courageous. It did publish the book of the Danish cartoons of Muhammad, *The Cartoons that Shook the World*, but yielded to pressure and removed the illustrations of the cartoons.

Both the media and many in the academic and entertainment world have engaged in self-censorship; upholders of the principle of free speech have been unwilling or reluctant to discuss some of those topics, such as jihad or the impact of Sharia law, that might be considered offensive to Muslims or to developing countries. Silence, as Ayaan Hirsi Ali said in a speech in Berlin on May 11, 2012, becomes an accomplice to injustice. She might have added that silence tends to embolden Islamic extremists.

An increasingly important development is the fear of Western commentators who refrain from criticism of or even justify hatred and injustice in the assumption that they may be physically attacked, as was Theo van Gogh, or suffer material loss, or even be accused of the charges so frequently propounded in international gatherings of racism, Islamophobia, or orientalism.

We have been through this before when a policy of appeasement, circumspect if not indifferent, toward the evils of nondemocracies in the 1930s was an inadequate response to the reality of Hitlerism. It is time to apply lessons from this disastrous policy to the present nature of the attacks on Israel by nondemocratic forces. Genuine believers in political and intellectual freedom must not be hesitant to denounce attempts to stifle such freedoms and must not appease those countries and groups who make such attempts.

Notes

1. Elizabeth Samson, "Warfare through Misuse of International Law," *BESA Center Perspectives Papers No. 73* (March 23, 2009).
2. Ruth Gavison, "The Jews' Right to Statehood: a Defense," *Azure* 15 (Summer 2003): 96.
3. Henry Kissinger, *The White House Years* (Boston: Little Brown, 1979), p. 344; William Quandt, *Decade of Decision* (Berkeley: University of California Press, 1977), p. 65.
4. United Nations War Crimes Commission, Law Reports of Trials of War Criminals, vol. VIII, 1949.

2

The Surprising and Disturbing Rise of Contemporary Antisemitism

1. The Devil's Advocate and Free Speech

In October 2011, anti-Israeli activists attempted to get a warrant issued for the arrest of Tzipi Livni, former Israeli foreign minister and leader of the Kadima party, who was visiting London to meet with William Hague, the British foreign minister, to discuss negotiations for ending the conflict between Israel and Palestinians. The warrant was to be based on alleged involvement by Livni in Operation Cast Lead, December 2008 to January 2009, the Israeli response to incessant shelling from Gaza. The intended warrant was part of the continuing campaign to demonize the State of Israel.

These activists, as well as those in Britain genuinely concerned with human rights, had to face the problem of how to react to a visit to London of an individual associated with real demons. No protest was registered by any activist concerning the invitation to the French-Vietnamese lawyer Jacques Vergès to take part in a debate with Martii Koskenniemi, a distinguished Finnish professor of international law, on "International justice: between impunity and show trials," held on February 3, 2012, at the School of Oriental and Asian Studies in London.

In his great book *On Liberty*, John Stuart Mill recognized "the necessity to the mental well-being of mankind (on which all their other well-being depends) of freedom of opinion and freedom of the expression of opinion." The conversation between Livni and Hague can be seen to exemplify Mill's axiom. It is difficult to envisage how any "mental well-being" could ensue from the utterances of Vergès at a serious academic debate at SOAS, a college that was once graced by the teaching of Bernard Lewis.

Vergès is an eighty-six-year-old celebrated, flamboyant Parisian lawyer, an outrageous provocateur, a showman popularly known as The Devil's Advocate. This nickname stems from his well-publicized career of defending Nazi war criminals, terrorists, and Holocaust deniers. Among his clients have been the following: Klaus Barbie, the Butcher of Lyon who was responsible for over 4,000 deaths and 7,500 deportations in France, including the rounding up in Izieu, near Lyon, of forty-four Jewish children who were sent to their death, and the torture to death of the French resistance leader Jean Moulin in 1943; Roger Garaudy, the ex-leftist who converted to Islam, became a Holocaust denier, and was sentenced in a French court for denying crimes against humanity and for racial defamation; the murderous Venezuelan terrorist Carlos the Jackal; Tariq Aziz, Saddam Hussein's deputy prime minister; Khiue Samphan, former head of the Communist regime in Cambodia who is alleged to have been responsible for the killing of two million in the Killing Fields between 1975 and 1979; Georges Ibrahim Abdallah, the former leader of the Lebanese Armed Revolutionary Faction who was involved in the murders of Colonel Charles Ray, the US military attaché, and an Israeli diplomat in Paris in 1982 and the assassination attempt on the US consul in Strasbourg; and Laurant Gbagbo, former president of the Ivory Coast, who since November 2011 has been in the custody of the International Criminal Court on charges of murder, rape, and other forms of sexual violence, corruption, and responsibility for death squads and mass graves. Vergès in the past offered to represent Saddam Hussein and Slobodan Milosevic, and more recently offered his services to Saif Gaddafi, son of the Libyan dictator. In addition, he planned to sue former French President Nicolas Sarkozy for crimes against humanity because of French intervention in Libya in April and May 2011.

Vergès has been the mouthpiece of the Popular Front for the Liberation of Palestine, which hijacked an El Al plane in 1969. He minimized the nature of the genocide by the Khmer Rouge in Cambodia, 1970–75; instead, he argued, people died of starvation and disease caused by the embargo policy of the United States. He spoke of his friendship with Saloth Sar (Pol Pot), as well as with the Red Army Faction in Germany, and particularly with the enigmatic François Genoud, a Swiss banker. Genoud had financial and organizational links with the Nazi leadership during World War II; helped the Nazis steal gold from Jewish victims, which he stored in Swiss banks; and was a confidant of the grand mufti of Jerusalem, the pro-Nazi leader of Palestinian Muslims. After the war,

Genoud helped raise millions of dollars for the Palestine Liberation Organization (PLO); helped finance the FLN, the Algerian Liberation Movement; paid for the defense of the Nazis Adolf Eichmann and Klaus Barbie; published the writings of Adolf Hitler, Joseph Goebbels, and Martin Bormann; financed Arab terrorist groups; and befriended David Irving, the British Holocaust denier.

Vergès claims not to be antisemitic, nor to favor terrorist acts, but his associations with real demonic figures and his own utterances make this questionable. In what was perhaps a playful interview *in Der Spiegel* on November 21, 2008, he said, among other things, that "Monsters do not exist, just as there is no such thing as absolute evil. . . . What was so shocking about Hitler the 'monster' was that he loved his dog so much and kissed the hand of his secretaries." In rendering a judgment on him, one might consider the extent of his sagacity by another of his utterances: "One of my principles is to have no principles."

Vergès has always craved the spotlight. One can recognize that the committing of a criminal offence and the right to legal representation are exclusive. One can also admit that defense lawyers may have values different from those of a defendant. Yet the nature of Vergès's activities suggests he may share, or at the very least look benignly on, the values of those he has defended. His defense of Abdallah in 1982 concentrated on denouncing American and Israeli policies in the Middle East. Later, in 2007, he castigated the US for alleged pressure on the French court that had decided not to release Abdallah from prison; he urged the court "to show our condescending American friends that France is not a submissive girl."

In his denunciation of democratic societies, particularly the United States and Israel, Vergès unwittingly illustrates the wisdom of Edward Gibbon's remark in *The Decline and Fall of the Roman Empire* that in human nature there is a "strong propensity to depreciate the advantages, and to magnify the evils, of the present times."

2. The Blood Libel Charge in Hungary

The list of distinguished Jews, past and present, who were born in or originated from territory controlled by Hungary and made important contributions to science, mathematics, scholarship, political and economic activity, and culture is endless. Among them are Theodor Herzl, John von Neumann, Milton Friedman, Tony Curtis, Leslie Howard, George Szell, Elie Wiesel, Arthur Koestler, Robert Capa, and George Soros.

In spite of that contribution to Hungarian culture, the story of the Hungarian Jewish community has not been a happy one. The Wannsee Conference of German leaders in January 1942 outlined plans for the deportation and extermination of all Jews in German-occupied territory. Its chairman, Reinhard Heydrich, head of the German Main Security Office including the Gestapo, calculated there were 742,800 Jews in the territory controlled by Hungary. Of these, 568,000 were killed by Nazi Germany and by the pro-Nazi party the Hungarian Arrow Cross, whose members killed thousands of Jews and dumped their bodies into the Danube.

Hungary from 1938 on had introduced a number of anti-Jewish laws, so-called race protective orders, according to which Jews, as in Nazi Germany, were essentially removed from the economy, preventing them from employment in law, press, films, theater, and from travelling except in street cars. With the stricter anti-Jewish laws of 1940–41, Jews were not allowed to dress in army uniforms or carry arms and were conscripted into labor battalions, where they wore their own civilian clothing. Few of their members survived the Holocaust.

In the months of July and August 1941, over sixteen thousand Jews were deported from Hungary, which was an ally of Germany at the beginning of the war, to Galicia, then under German rule; all of them were killed. In January 1942, the Hungarian police murdered 3,500 people, of whom 800 were Jews, throwing most of their bodies into the river Danube; others were publicly hanged. Victims had to remove their shoes before being thrown into the river. This is now memorialized by a set of iron shoes along the bank of the river.

The main malfeasance committed in the country came after March 1944, when Hungary was occupied by German forces. The regent of Hungary who ruled the country, the conservative Admiral Miklos Horthy, had not stood up to Hitler, but he had not totally succumbed to or supported German demands. With the German invasion, ghettos were established for seventy thousand people, and Jews were obliged to wear the Star of David. The main criminal in charge of the Holocaust in Hungary was Adolph Eichmann, who did not exemplify the banality of evil but was the energetic and ruthless head of a special unit to deport Jews. In this activity, Eichmann was aided by Hungarian soldiers, police, and government officials. In two months in the summer of 1944, 437,000 Jews were deported to their death.

The deportations ended on July 6, 1944, partly as a result of the impact of D Day and partly because of Horthy's awareness of the advance of the Russian forces into Hungary. The Germans replaced Horthy, who would no longer be a partner of the Nazis, by Ferenc Szalasi, the leader of the antisemitic Arrow Cross party, which was responsible for killing over eighty thousand Jews, some of whom were sent on death marches. Some of these killers were tried as war criminals in Soviet Union courts after the war, but many went unpunished.

Budapest, which once had a Jewish population of 825,000, today has less than 70,000. Prejudice against them remains. A recent survey of Hungarians showed that 75 percent believe that Jews have too much power in the business world.

Two issues have recently occurred as reminders of the unpleasant past. One is the coming into force on January 1, 2012, of the new constitution, The Fundamental Law of Hungary, passed on April 25, 2011. A paragraph in the Prologue can be read to deny any Hungarian responsibility for wartime actions in the country: "We do not recognize the suspension of our historical constitution due to foreign occupations. We deny any statute of limitations for the inhumane crimes committed against the Hungarian nation and its citizens under the national socialist and communist dictatorships." The implication, though not overtly stated, was that since Hungary was invaded and occupied by the Nazis in March 1944, and then later by the Red Army, its government and citizens could not be held responsible for the deportation of Jews to extermination camps. In more venal fashion, this disclaimer could also limit payment of restitution claims by Jews against the state.

Even more disturbing has been the revival of the infamous blood libel accusation against Jews, the accusation that goes back to the first major one in 1144 in Norwich, England that Jews murder Christians—especially children—to use their blood to bake matzos for Passover. In the last few years this has been echoed by people in Russia and Poland; by the Palestinian Hamas group; by the Syrian Minister of Defense, Mustafa Tiass, in a book in 1986; by King Faisal of Saudi Arabia in 1972; and by the leader of the branch of the Islamic Movement in Israel. The blood libel charge was even featured in 2009 in the Swedish tabloid *Aftonbladet,* which published a story that members of the Israel Defense Forces had stolen the organs of more than sixty Palestinians who died in their custody.

The accusation was echoed in a public space in Budapest. Zsolt Barath, one of the leaders of Jobbik (Movement for a Better Hungary), the neo-Nazi party which in 2010 won 47 of the 386 seats in the Hungarian National Assembly, is known as a Holocaust denier. On April 3, 2012, in a speech in the parliament, he referred to the Tiszaeszlar case, 1882–83, in which fifteen Jews were accused of murdering a fourteen-year-old Christian domestic servant for her blood. They were acquitted, but the case was followed by pogroms against Hungarian Jews. The town of Tiszaeszlar has become a pilgrimage site for antisemites. Barath argued that the acquittal was due to outside pressure, in effect Jewish international financers. Hungary, in the views of this Nazi, was again 130 years later facing similar pressure of Jewish finance.

It is not unusual for the malicious, the ignorant, or the misguided to use the blood libel accusation. It is devastating that it should be used in a European parliament. How unfortunate that Raoul Wallenberg, the Swedish diplomat who saved so many Jews in Budapest, and Tom Landos, the Congressman who was a refugee from Hungary, are not alive to pour scorn on recent developments in Hungary.

3. Antisemitism on the Rise in Europe

The European Union in the 1997 Treaty of Amsterdam called for joint efforts to combat prejudice and discrimination experienced by individuals and groups on the basis of their ethnic features, cultural background, religion, gender, sexual orientation, age, or disability. Analysis with comprehensive data about the issue has recently become available in an important report.

This study, *Intolerance, Prejudice and Discrimination: a European Report*, issued by the Ebert Foundation in Berlin, was based on interviews with samples of one thousand people in eight European countries. It examined negative attitudes and prejudices against groups defined as "other," "foreign," or "abnormal." The overall result—showing widespread expressions of intolerance, racism, sexism, dislike of Muslims, concern about immigrants, opposition to homosexuals and gay marriage, and existing antisemitism—is dispiriting.

Though the prejudices against the various groups are of different kinds, the study suggests that they are interconnected, that the people who denigrate one group are very likely to target other groups also. Prejudices against the different target groups are linked and share a common ideology, one that endangers democracy and leads to violence and conflicts. The problem that democratic countries and well-meaning people now face is how to confront and overcome these prejudices that are so empirically observable.

The overall saddening conclusion of the Report, which deals with a number of issues, is that group-focused enmity toward immigrants, blacks, Muslims, and Jews is widespread in Europe. Antisemitism is an important component of this enmity. The Report defines antisemitism as social prejudice directed against Jews simply because they are Jews: categorizing people negatively as Jews. It goes on to say that antisemitism takes many forms: political (Jewish world conspiracy); secular (usury); religious (responsible for the death of Jesus); and racist (Jewish character). A recent shift appears to have occurred moving from traditional antisemitism to secondary antisemitism with refusal to acknowledge the crimes of the Holocaust. Ominously, a reversal of perpetrator and victim has taken place; Jews are seen as taking advantage of having been Nazi victims.

The Report focused on the responses of people to four particular statements concerning Jews; Jews have too much influence; Jews try to take advantage of having been victims during the Nazi era; Jews in general do not care about anything or anybody but their own kind; Jews do or do not enrich the culture of the country. To these were added two other statements: one can understand why people do not like Jews when one considers Israel's policy; and Israel is conducting a war of extermination against the Palestinians. Even though the study deals with a limited number of individuals and European countries, its findings are significant.

The study shows that animosity against Jews is strongest in the Eastern European countries (Poland and Hungary) and in Germany; moderate in France, Italy, and Portugal; and weakest in the Netherlands and Britain. The details are a warning of possible future danger. Auschwitz was liberated on January 27, 1945, but the evil of the extermination camps seems to have been forgotten, if this survey of the views of European citizens is correct. The study shows that 72 percent of Poles, 68 percent of Hungarians, and 49 percent of Germans believe, strongly or somewhat, that the Jews today are benefitting from the memory of the camp and exploit the Holocaust. The figure for the Netherlands is 17 percent and Britain 21 percent.

The most frequently expressed antisemitic view is that Jews have too much influence in the particular country in which they live. Nearly 70 percent of Hungarians hold this view. In Poland, now the home of few Jews, some 50 percent believe this. The lowest figures are in the Netherlands, where is this view is held strongly by only 6 percent and in Britain, where 13.9 percent believe this. The other four countries cluster around 20 percent in agreeing with this statement.

On the question of Jews caring only about themselves, the range of views is somewhat different. Portugal joins Hungary and Poland in agreeing, 51 to 57 percent, while the other six countries vary between 20 and 30 percent. Somewhat surprisingly, a majority in all eight countries believe that Jews have enriched the culture of their country; the highest figures are in the Netherlands, (72 percent), Britain (71 percent), and Germany (69 percent).

Not unexpectedly, the animosity toward Jews extends to the State of Israel. Nearly 40 percent of the Europeans believe that Israel is waging a war of extermination against the Palestinians; the Polish figure is 63 percent. The other countries range from Portugal (48 percent) to Italy (37 percent). A similar range was found in the accompanying question; nearly half in some of the countries think that attitudes of antisemitism result from disapproval of Israel's activities, from Poland (55 percent) to Germany and Britain (35 percent). Ironically, their perceptions of Israel are colored by antisemitism, rather than the reverse.

The Report suggests that it is the task of political education to overcome those factors that favor prejudiced attitudes. These include the low level of education, low income, and a culture, especially in Eastern Europe, where prejudice is more widespread than in Western Europe. For this purpose, some generalizations are pertinent. Antisemitism is most prevalent among people in age group 50–65, and disappointingly in the 16–21 group, and lowest among the 22–34 group. Hostility is shown to increase with age, but the high level in the16–21 age group is worrisome. Though European educational systems are diverse, it appears that those with a medium level of education are not significantly different from those at a low level, and are more antisemitic than well-educated people. Gender plays a minor role; women, though more likely to be prejudiced than men regarding immigrants and Muslims, are not more antisemitic than men.

The Report was restricted to attitudes and beliefs. It therefore did not include statistics on overt acts of antisemitism; the harassment of Jews; the threats; attacks both physical and verbal; the vandalism of Jewish property, institutions, and memorial sites; the use of cyberspace to convey hostile messages; the revival of blood libel charges; the widespread allegation of Jewish conspiracy; the rise of openly antisemitic parties; the success of Islamist parties and groups. Neither does the Report deal with the newest form of antisemitism, that exhibited by Muslim extremists against Jews.

The Ebert Foundation is sympathetic to the opinions of the German Social Democratic party. Not surprisingly, its Report is mainly concerned with right-wing or populist political attitudes, not with those of the political left. It finds that individuals who define themselves as supporters of the political right are more likely than other people to hold prejudicial views. However it did also make mention of the fact that extreme left groups and individuals, probably because of their authoritarian attitudes, are more prejudiced than those of the moderate left.

Yet it does not belittle the importance of the Report to comment that it minimizes the degree of antisemitism displayed by some segments of the well-educated groups, as pointed out in the introduction above, and by the media and the academic community. These last groups are articulate in their constant international condemnations against Israel with their calls for boycott, divestment, and sanctions against Israel and their attempts to delegitimize the State of Israel. These can be explained in a number of ways, but certainly a major one would be an implicit antisemitism. A warning for these groups: "Teacher, heal thyself. Your prejudice and discrimination are on display."

4. Antisemitism Is Alive and Well in Romania

The virus of antisemitism is alive and well in Eastern Europe, and so is the denial of the Holocaust. It is disconcerting that a younger generation in Romania, as elsewhere, should be infected with the virus, and is, or claims to be, ignorant of the reality of the treatment of Jews in the twentieth century.

A recent telling example of the continuation of animosity toward Jews is the case of Dan Sova, the thirty-nine-year-old Romanian lawyer and Social Democrat who has been a Senator in the Parliament since 2008. On August 6, 2012, Prime Minister Victor Ponta promoted him to the position of minister for parliamentary relations.

The promotion was surprising because of a recent incident involving Sova. In a television broadcast on March 5, 2012, he declared, "No Jew suffered on Romanian territory [during the Holocaust] thanks to Marshal Anonescu." Two days later, Sova was removed, supposedly temporarily, from office as speaker of his political party. He has also said "only twenty-four Jews were killed during the Iasi pogrom [of June 28–29, 1941] by the German army."

Both statements by Sova were false and malicious. Ion Anonescu, the pro-Nazi dictator of Romania during World War II, was leader of the state, prime minister, foreign minister, defense minister, and self-appointed marshal. He joined the Tripartite Pact of Germany, Italy, and Japan against the Allies in November 1940, two months after it had been signed. He also established close personal contact with Hitler. It was Anonescu who on June 27, 1941, ordered the commander of the military garrison of the town of Iasi, in northeast Romania, to "cleanse" the city of its Jewish population. The action was not instigated by the Nazis but by the Romanian authorities and the Romanian army on their own initiative.

It is calculated that during the two days of the pogrom in Iasi between thirteen and fifteen thousand Jews were massacred in the streets or died in the death trains, on which over one hundred Jews were horded in each car and most died of thirst, starvation, or suffocation. The actions of the Romanian regime in the Holocaust led to the deaths, not of twenty-four Jews, but of a number that has been calculated between two hundred eighty thousand and three hundred eighty thousand Jews, and is most likely to be the larger number, in the territories under its control. What is significant in this is that it was not Nazi policy that triggered the massacre of Jews but the Romanian government itself with the enthusiastic participation of the military, and the endorsement of the broader society. The self-motivation of the Romanians on their own initiative is reminiscent of the more well-known participation of the French Vichy regime and French authorities in the Holocaust during the war.

In the period after World War II from 1945 to 1989, Romania was under Communist control, first that of the Soviet Union and then as an independent country, and information about the country's actions during the war was largely suppressed. Few Romanians were aware of the involvement of their country in the Holocaust. Perhaps the kindest thing to be said of Dan Sova is that his schooling did not include true or any information about the Holocaust. However, it is difficult to believe that a young lawyer educated at the University of Bucharest could be so ignorant. When criticism arose of his promotion on August 6, he did, four days later, confess that his remarks on the Holocaust were "completely wrong." It would be nice to take at face value his plans to take concrete actions on the matter, one of which will be a course of lectures on the Holocaust.

No matter the degree of sincerity or cynicism in Sova's apologies and regrets, important lessons can be drawn from his case. One is the need to discredit Holocaust deniers, ranging from Mahmoud Ahmadinejad in Iran to Ernst Zundel, a German living in Canada. Education, especially of the young, about the Holocaust is essential to put an end to the falsehoods of distortions of history, as pronounced by individuals such as David Irving in Britain, Robert Faurisson in France, or Louis Farrakhan in the US. Young and old should be informed of the assertions of the deniers so they can ridicule the allegations that the *Diary of Anne Frank* was a hoax because parts of it were written with a ball-point pen, or that Auschwitz was too small to have been an extermination camp.

The ignorance of Dan Sova shows how important it is to reject the argument that too much attention has been given to the Holocaust, and that twentieth-century historians have over-emphasized Jewish suffering. An example of that argument is an article in the *New York Post* of March 17, 1990, in which Pat Buchanan wrote about what he called "so-called Holocaust survivor syndrome," which he said involved group fantasies of martyrdom and heroics. It is painful that some Holocaust deniers, concerned to make the case against the existence of Israel, have argued that Jews should be regarded not as victims but as victimizers. The Catholic Bishop Richard Williamson, who in November 2008 denied the existence of Nazi gas chambers—though he did say between two to three hundred thousand Jews perished in Nazi concentration camps—also declared that the Holocaust was a Jewish invention so that "we would prostrate ourselves on our knees before them and approve their new State of Israel." Deborah Lipstadt has written that these people accuse Jews of using "the world's sympathy to displace another people so that Israel could be created."

One can admit that Nazi Germany was not the only perpetrator of villainous and criminal behavior. The twentieth century abounds with criminal acts. One should acknowledge and deplore—whether one wants to term them genocide or not—the treatments of Armenians and people in Cambodia, the Balkans, Sudan, and the Congo. Yet the Holocaust was unique in its scope and number of casualties. It remains unique in spite of the cavalier denial or minimization of it by ignorant and bigoted people like Dan Sova.

5. Aimez-Vous Wagner?

Should the music of Wagner be played in Israel? There is an Israeli Wagnerian Society, but attempts to play the music, by Zubin Mehta in 1981, by Daniel Barenboim in 2001, and most recently in June 2012 at Tel Aviv University, have been opposed by groups in Israel. The TAU president stopped the private concert on his campus, arguing it would offend the public, especially Holocaust survivors, of whom two hundred thousand remain alive in Israel.

Wagner was an unremitting antisemite, as shown both in his prose and in his music expression. His article "Das Judenthum in der Musik" (Jewishness in Music), written in 1850 under a pseudonym, is a strong criticism of the role of Jews in German culture and society in general, and a more personal attack on the composers of Jewish origin, Giacomo Meyerbeer and Felix Mendelssohn, of whose success he was jealous.

More pertinent to the issue than his antisemitic writings is the fact that the music of Wagner and the persona of Wagner became linked with and embedded in Nazi propaganda. Hitler, at least in official pronouncements, spoke of the Wagnerian opus as the best expression of the German soul, and in his *Table Talk* expressed admiration for Wagner. Indeed, the composer became a symbolic and even mythological figure in the Nazi regime, with its racial and genocidal antisemitism. Hitler had a special seat at the opera house in Bayreuth that Wagner built. Recordings of Wagner's opera *Rienzi* usually opened the Nazi Party conferences.

The case of Wagner is unique. No one objects to hearing the music of Chopin, who disliked Jews and also made antisemitic utterances, though they were casual rather than likely to lead to action. The piece *Carmina Burana* by Carl Orff has been played in Israel, though Orff was close to the Nazi Party and obliged the Party by writing new incidental music for *A Midsummer Night's Dream* to replace the original music of Felix Mendelssohn, banned as a Jewish composer. More difficult to assess politically was the pragmatic Richard Strauss, who was not a Nazi but who was president of the Reichsmusikkammer (German State Music Chamber) from 1933–35, a period during which Jews were prevented from performing, and then president of the Nazi-controlled Permanent Council for the International Cooperation of Composers.

The difference between these other composers and Wagner was not only the prominent use made of him in Nazi ideology but also the claim, which may be unfounded, that his music was played in Dachau and in the death camps to accompany the murders. He is thus regarded, if indirectly, as a key player in the Holocaust. In his famous 1850 article, Wagner wrote that the German people disliked the alien appearance and behavior of Jews and were repelled by actual contact with them.

It is the conclusion of his article that is most disconcerting. He wrote about Jews that the "only thing that can redeem you from the burden of your curse, the redemption of Ahasuerus, going under." Presumably Wagner referred to the Wandering Jew. The crucial question is how to interpret this. Did he mean that what he thought was Jewish separateness should be ended, and that Jews should be assimilated into the mainstream, or that Jews should be physically eliminated? Wagner's last words in the article referring to *Untergang* for the Jews may mean "decline" or "going to one's doom" or "destruction."

The music of Wagner was originally part of the repertoire of the Palestine Symphony Orchestra (now the Israel Philharmonic Orchestra). On November 12, 1938, the overture to Wagner's opera *Lohengrin* was deleted from its program as a protest against the pogrom of Kristallnacht, which had occurred three days earlier in Germany. Since then, Wagner's works have not been performed in public places during the Jewish settlement in Palestine or after the establishment of the State of Israel, though there is no governmental coercion or prohibition, nor is it illegal to play his music in private. Not performing Wagner is a matter of custom.

The essential question is whether playing Wagner's music will be offensive, particularly to Holocaust survivors in Israel. Two separate problems arise from this. One is the conflict between freedom of expression along with artistic freedom on one hand and acute emotional impact and moral principles on the other. The difficulty lies in balancing the memories of the Holocaust with which, because of the Nazis, Wagner is now linked, with freedom of expression. The opposition to Wagner in Israel is not an official or legal boycott, but for some it provokes reminders of the Nazi boycott of Jews and the present-day calls for boycotts of Israel and its citizens by groups in various countries in the world.

However, any equivalence must be challenged. Not performing Wagner's music in public, due to understandable sensitivities of Israelis, is totally different from the unjustified boycotts of Israel and its citizens. The Holocaust survivors may think of Wagner as proto-Nazi with his views on racial purity and his belief that Jews were contaminating German blood, but they are not seeking action against the state of Germany because of him. In contrast, the present-day advocates of boycott, divestment, and sanctions against Israel and its citizens often express a hatred of Jews and aim ultimately at the elimination of the State of Israel.

A second difficult issue that is pertinent is whether or not the individual can be separated from his or her artistic expression, in this case music. Should Israelis enjoy the music and forget the man? Wagner's influence on nineteenth-and twentieth-century culture was enormous, not only on music, perhaps best heard in the works of Bruckner, Mahler and Schonberg, but also on literature, as seen in the works of Thomas Mann, in James Joyce's *Ulysses* and in T. S. Eliot's *The Wasteland*. However, the aura of Wagner's antisemitism continues to be attached to his accomplishments. Woody Allen once remarked, "I can't listen to that much Wagner. I start getting the urge to conquer Poland."

It's a complex problem. We all can feel repulsed by the virulent antisemitism of Wagner and recognize him as a preacher of hate, even while the music may be admired. Some Israelis are justified in being distressed on hearing his music, with its symbolic association with the Nazi regime and the praise of Wagner by Hitler himself. But should the music be banned? The controversy understandingly remains bitter and fierce. Does banning Wagner's music from performance help heal the wounds of the past? It may be more meaningful for Israelis to honor Holocaust survivors by making a gesture against censorship. Allow the music to be played; those who feel differently should absent themselves. Music, an international form of communication, should be accessible to all who want to hear it.

6. Charles de Gaulle, Raymond Aron, and Israel

The lives of Raymond Aron and Charles de Gaulle intersected at significant moments in twentieth-century history—cooperatively in London during World War II, and antagonistically in Paris as a result of President de Gaulle's press conference on November 27, 1967. The two Frenchman formed an incongruous duo. General de Gaulle, the heroic man of June 18, 1940, the symbol of French resistance to Nazi Germany, the founder and first president of the French Fifth Republic, was the quintessential exponent of the grandeur and national sovereignty of France. Aron, the brilliant scholar and journalist, the intellectually courageous critic of the prevailing, fashionable, politically correct attitude of sympathy and tolerance among the French intellectual and cultural elite toward the actions and behavior of the Soviet Union, was the "dejudaised" Jew who had rallied to the Free French movement in London in 1940 but was not an unqualified admirer of Charles de Gaulle during or after World War II.

Raymond Aron early showed his brilliance by being placed first in the agrégation in 1928, after four years at the Ecole Normale Supérieure, in a class that included Jean-Paul Sartre, Paul Nizan, and Georges Canguilhem. His experience while studying in Germany, in Cologne and Berlin, from 1930 to 1933 made him acutely aware of the threat and violence of Nazism. In London during the war, he was the acting editor, together with André Lebarthe as manager, of *La France libre*, the monthly review of the Free French movement that first appeared to there in November 1940 and for which Aron wrote in fifty-seven of the fifty-nine issues.

Aron had taught philosophy at Le Havre before the war, worked at the Centre de Documentation Sociale de l'Ecole Normale Supérieure, and was to have a distinguished academic career: at the Sorbonne (1955), at the Ecole practique des Hautes Etudes in 1960, at the Collège de France, as professor of European civilization, from 1970 to 1979. During that career as philosopher, historian, sociologist, and political scientist, he published over forty books. Important as was his scholarship, more influential for the general public, were Aron's journalism and editorial writing for *Combat* (April 1946 to June 1947), for *Le Figaro* (1947 to 1977), for *L'Express* (1977 to 1983), and for the monthly *Preuves, Commentaire*, and *Encounter*. Addressing almost daily both domestic and international issues, Aron in his thousands of articles was the model of polite but frank discourse and reasoned argument and analysis.

Aron's writings, both scholarly and journalistic, spanned an extraordinary range of subjects, including international relations, sociology, economics, ethics, liberalism and the crisis of democracy, intellectual history, war and peace, the concepts and implications of industrial society, and current ideologies. Aron concentrated on concrete issues rather than on formal or epistemological problems. Because of his independent, nonpartisan judgments and objective analysis, people found it difficult to place him in any particular political category. That objective analysis was grounded in a realistic assessment of political behavior. In his inaugural lecture on December 1, 1970, he explained that his experience in Germany in the early 1930s had marked him and inclined him to an active pessimism; "I lost faith and held on, not without effort, to hope." His objective as a historian was, by retrospective analysis of possibilities, to reveal the articulations of the historical process.[1]

He was also a committed observer, prepared to take a position on historical and contemporary events. As active citizen, Aron, a man with good connections in French society unattached to any political party, participated in the work of some anticommunist groups in France and was a member in 1950 of the executive committee of the Congress for Cultural Freedom. As advocate of reasoned discussion he was particularly critical of the violence and "psychodrama" exhibited by Parisian intellectuals and students in the university riots in 1968.

Aron's writings, like his life, were unostentatious. They were clear, precise, sober, and moderate in tone, critical of ideologies he considered false or embodying fanaticism. They had the cool, urbane tone of classical French expression, free from Teutonic obscurity or turgidity. Aron was particularly critical of those literateurs, such as his former classmate Sartre and companion Simone de Beauvoir, whose writings he viewed as justifying deprivation of liberty of other people at the hands of totalitarianism and terror. In his most well-known work, *The Opium of the Intellectuals*, published in 1955, Aron sought to reduce the "poetry of ideology" to the level of the "prose of reality." Why, he asked, are some intellectuals ready to accept the worst crimes as long as they are committed in the name of the supposedly proper doctrines? His criticism was particularly applicable to Sartre, Merleau-Ponty, and their disciples, with their abstract theories of "the left" and "the Revolution," their moralizing, their disregard of contemporary political reality, their hatred of "the bourgeoisie," their existentialist theory of pure freedom in a "different society, boundless, universal."

By contrast, Aron, the unfashionable intellectual loner, emphasized that political reflection could not ignore reality or the desirable European values, embodied if imperfectly in a liberal, free, efficient, secular, pluralistic, and democratic society.[2] In a striking critique, Aron in his article on "Alexander Solzhenitsyn and European 'Leftism'" (1976), contrasted Sartre, enjoying privileges and fame and the ability to travel the world unhindered, with the Russian writer hounded by the Soviet system. Parisian intellectuals, ever ready to accept and uphold the myth of the Revolution, never forgave Aron for his accurate analysis and condemnation of the actions of the Soviet Union and Communist behavior, or for his advocacy of NATO and an Atlantic Community in which the United States would be a pillar.

Descended from solid, bourgeois Jewish families in Eastern and Northern France, which could be traced back to Lorraine at least since the eighteenth century, and which had been successful in the textile business, Aron was a characteristic member of those secularized, old established French Jews who were nonbelievers and nonpracticing and who as citizens considered their culture to be French. Those assimilated Jews, linked by social relations, family ties, and ideological affinities, the universalistic values of the Republic embodying freedom and justice, did not perceive antisemitism as a general, major problem.[3] These Jewish citizens, emancipated since 1791, with full political and civil rights and ability to practice religion, had these rights as individuals, but not as part of a Jewish people. As French citizens of the Jewish faith or mosaic persuasion, they were sometimes designated and self-styled as Israélites rather than termed Jews, keeping distance from those Jews, particularly nonnatives, who continued to observe religious rituals, had separate organizational ties, and who were more apt to lean toward socialism or Zionism.

The assimilated Jews played a considerable role in French life and culture. Some, such as the "state Jews" discussed by Pierre Birnbaum, served the Republic in public official positions as prefects, judges, counselors of state, ministers, deputies, and generals.[4] Others were part of the intellectual contribution of Jews to French culture, such as Emile Durkheim, Marcel Mauss, Léon Brunschveig, and Aron himself, patriotic and politically integrated. Yet those Israélites who gained political, economic, or social prominence were sometimes accused of double loyalty. Among the best known individuals charged in this fashion were Léon Blum, through most of his political career, and Pierre Mendès-France, both barmitzved, both acknowledging they were Jews, and both insistent on and proud of their French culture and roots. Aron too always insisted he was French, and that Jewish values constituted only a small part of what framed his person and outlook.

Aron never entered into a full discussion of his Jewishness and rarely expressed himself strongly or emotionally on Jewish questions until de Gaulle's press conference of November 27, 1967, when "a burst of Jewishness exploded within my French consciousness." In his speech to the French Bnai Brith on February 21, 1951, he used the usual formula: "I am a Frenchman of Jewish origin or tradition." In a conversation in 1983 he commented, "I am incapable of defining the specificity of what is Jewish for me.[5] I am a French citizen but I do not want to break links with the other Jews in the world or with Israelis." Aron pondered his refusal to break links. Perhaps it was fidelity to his roots or to his ancestors. But this was too abstract and was rather an intellectual justification for an existential choice.[6] Certainly, he was not determined by his Jewish origins but was the product of the French language and literature to which he was attached.

A similar ambiguity related to his support for the State of Israel. Was his solidarity, he the French patriot, with the Jewish people and with Israel more intellectual or more organic? Perhaps some of both, but that solidarity did not suggest a "sacred history" of the Jewish people, the definition of whose identity did not fall into the usual categories of social or historical analysis. Aron could not easily define a people scattered in diasporas in the world but who nevertheless maintained some kind of unity or solidarity. Jews for Aron were not, for the most part, biological descendants of the Semitic tribes of the Bible, yet the historical singularity of Jews shaped their character.

The Diaspora communities had none of the characteristics that ordinarily make up a people: neither a land, nor a language, nor a political organization. Their unity was based on their Book, their faith, and certain practices. Jews of the Diaspora for Aron are not a people; they are minorities who profess the same religion, who continue to have a certain feeling of solidarity toward each other. Aron saw the dilemma that Jews simultaneously claim all the rights allowed citizens in their state of residence and the rights implied by the fact of belonging to a group distinct from that of the state.

Aron held that a Jew imbued with French culture, coming from a family that had been French citizens for several generations, is not required to consider himself a Jew.[7] He has a free choice. Moreover, a secularized Jew who rejects all ties with other Jews is not repudiating any part of himself, though he remains a Jew in the eyes of others. Aron accepted his destiny as a Jew, viewing it with neither pride nor shame.[8] However, he never believed in the idea of a covenant between Jews and God, nor in that of the chosenness of an elect Jewish people.[9] Judaism, as he stated in his article of February 24, 1962, included both nationalism and universalism, and it was the latter which was the genuine vocation of Judaism.

He explained at the end of his life, in L'Arche, September–October 1983, that in his family upbringing only a small number of Jewish rites, practices, or symbols were present, while religion and faith were absent. He had no religious education, and though he was conscious as a youngster of antisemitic remarks, they had no effect on him. Embracing the universal values of liberty and equality, Aron took no active part in Jewish political activities. Awareness of his Jewish identity was imposed upon him by Hitler and Nazi Germany in 1933. Aron could never fully resolve the antinomy between universalism and nationalism. Imbued as he was with French culture and universal values, his outlook was modified by Hitler, the Holocaust, and finally de Gaulle's press conference. Lecturing at the Ecole Normale, he referred to his Jewish origins. Nazi antisemitism led him to assert those Jewish origins without ostentation or humility or compensatory pride.[10]

Aron in his youth had challenged his teacher, an adherent of Action Française, who expounded an anti-Dreyfus position. For Aron, the

Dreyfus Affair, which held his interest throughout his life, was a simple matter of truth and falsehood. He was critical of Hannah Arendt, "who affects a tone of haughty superiority regarding things and men" and whose factual errors about and interpretation of the Affair he felt did not conform to reality and left an equivocal impression on the French reader.[11] Near the end of his life he wrote that the Dreyfus Affair provided evidence of the resistance of French society to antisemitism as well as to the virulence of the evil.[12]

Two interrelated aspects of his remarks on Jews and the State of Israel are worth noting. Aron was always conscious of the allegation that Jews were culpable of double loyalty and discussed it on a number of occasions. Each person, he held, could have a country and a religion, but one could not have two countries (*patries*). Loyalty to Israel entailed emigration to it. Yet, though his fatherland was France, Aron confessed he was attached to Israel for which he had a "*particulière dilection*" (special affection). Aron was a friend of Israel but not a Zionist. He had not experienced any great emotion on the creation of the State of Israel in 1948, which he did not regard at the time as a world-historical event, nor did he identify with the pioneers preparing and building the state, a lack of emotional involvement he later regretted as he became aware of the tragic events of World War II.[13] After his first visit to Israel in 1956 he wrote of his admiration for its army and fighting pioneers.

Aron also regretted, late in his life, the restraint of his articles in 1933 on Nazi Germany and its antisemitism.[14] The fact was that Aron, who wrote on such an extraordinary variety of subjects, rarely wrote on the Jewish question, even in the face of Nazism. Nor did he write on the discrimination and persecution of Jews by Vichy France while in London, where the Free French group around de Gaulle by convention mentioned Jews as little as possible.[15] The given reason was to emphasize that the war was being fought to end totalitarianism and free France from the Nazis, not to liberate the Jews. Aron confessed he exercised a kind of "emotional precaution" or self-restraint in thinking as little as possible about the fate of Jews during the war, and what some Frenchmen were doing to the Jews.

Later in life Aron, who had used the pseudonym René Avord, tried to explain why *La France libre*, in London during the war years, for which he wrote a monthly article "Chronique de France," barely mentioned the plight of the Jews in Europe. Only three paragraphs in four years were devoted to the status of the Jews or to the notorious Vel d'Hiv roundup, when 13,152 Jews were arrested in Paris by the Vichy police and soon deported to their deaths in Auschwitz. Aron acknowledged in his *Mémoires* he should have discussed antisemitism in his *Chroniques*, commenting that he was more concerned with pro- or anti-German feelings of people in France than with their opinions on domestic politics. He was also conscious of antisemites among the Gaullists in London. He confessed that though he was aware of the cruel Nazi concentration camps,he could not imagine the gas chambers or the program of genocide, and thus could not write about it in *La France libre*.

Aron tried to explain his *particulière dilection* for Israel. Discussing in January 1980 the relationship between Israel and the Jewish Diaspora, Aron argued that the latter should feel free to criticize the policies and opinions of the Israeli leaders, just as he might criticize the policies of France. Already in February 1962 in *Le Figaro littéraire*, he had differed from Ben Gurion's contention that to be a Jew today meant to live in the State of Israel. Concerning policies, he was critical of the Suez adventure in 1956 and the British-French-Israeli attack. While aware that Israel was surrounded by hostile Arab states denying its right to exist, Aron criticized the idea of a Greater Israel based on annexations and occupation as being unacceptable to those states.[16] He also spoke of the political and military error of the Bar Lev line, the Israeli defense position in the Canal zone, which was located too far from the Israeli military bases.

The main thrust of Aron's argument on this general issue was that the State of Israel had a right to exist but that its creation had offended the Arab world. He commented independently on Middle East events: criticizing the French and the British more harshly than Israel in the Suez 1956 adventure; blaming Egypt for causing the 1967 war; criticizing Israel for occupation policies from 1967 to 1973; understanding the reason for the Egyptian-Syrian attack on Israel in October 1973; generally supporting the Camp David peace process without illusions.

Aron celebrated Israel, but not its military victories, about which he became more concerned as time passed. He even warned of the new myth of Israel as the Prussia of the Middle East.[17] Aron also had reservations about the Franco-Israeli alliance that had developed in the 1950s and was especially troubled by the Suez expedition and the joining of the two countries and Britain. Aron regarded the alliance as precarious and incongruous, the result of the historical accident that France and Israel were both engaged in hostilities with countries in the Arab world. He correctly recognized that when the Algerian war ended, the Franco-Israeli relationship was bound to change.

Aron's method of analysis and his growing understanding of changing events in 1967 and of the threat to Israel are well illustrated in his articles. The article of May 21, 1967, suggests that no party wanted war; that of May 25 realizes a dangerous diplomatic game is being played; that of May 28 asserts that Nasser's actions posed a challenge to both the United States and Israel; and then on June 4 realizes that Nasser wanted to destroy the State of Israel.

Raymond Aron rallied to the Free French cause in London in 1940, but he was never an uncritical Gaullist or a trusty vassal. He differed from de Gaulle on some significant issues during the war. In a 1941 article, "Le Gouvernment des Notables," he differentiated between the attitude and responsibility of the Vichy government and the French Nazi collaborators in Paris, unlike de Gaulle, who regarded anyone who obeyed Marshal Pétain as a traitor.

More important, Aron expressed his concern about the personality of de Gaulle, as well as about a number of his policies. He refused to regard de Gaulle as the incarnation of French national legitimacy. He expressed his concern in two important articles in *La France libre*: *Vive la République* in June 1943, and *L'Ombre des Bonaparte* in August 1943. In the first, Aron called for a duumvirate to head the Free French movement and for a liberal, democratic French system, not one based on personal adventure.[18]

In the latter, brilliantly argued article, he compared Bonapartism with fascism: he saw French Bonapartism, exemplified by Louis Napoleon's ascent to power, as both the anticipation and the French version of fascism. The implied reference to Charles de Gaulle was clear. Bonapartism, the result of political instability, patriotic humiliation, and concern for social improvement, was characterized by the popularity of one man, or a name, the rallying of the bourgeois classes to that man, the myth of a national hero, appeal to all sections of the people, disparagement of parliament and political parties, use of plebiscites and referendums, heightened patriotism, and strong authority. The French version of fascism inevitably referred back to the great French Revolution, paid a verbal tribute to the national will, and embraced the adoption of a left-wing vocabulary with passionate groups crystallizing around one person, a leader who tries to address the whole people over the heads of political parties.

In the postwar period, Aron differed from de Gaulle on a number of issues, including Algeria. In his article "Adieu au Gaullism," in *Preuves*, October 1961, which he later regretted, Aron, who had supported de

Gaulle in 1940, 1947, and 1958, criticized the Algerian policy. Later, he acknowledged that the president had transformed abandonment and defeat in Algeria into victory and had persuaded the nation that Algerian independence was good for France. He also acknowledged that while de Gaulle had attributed to himself an inalienable legitimacy, had detested political parties and factions, and had used the device of a plebiscite (as had Louis Napoleon), the president, on his return to power in 1958, had limited his power in advance out of democratic conviction.

Aron also differed on other issues: on nuclear policy, on NATO and the Atlantic community, on France as a third force between the US and the Soviet Union, on Quebec independence, and on the real cause and nature of the threat from the Soviet Union. In a sweeping statement, Aron accused de Gaulle of having legitimated anti-Americanism and of having sometimes suggested that France was threatened equally by the two super-powers.[19] French diplomacy was thus paralyzed by a vision of the world that Aron considered contrary to reality. In spite of their differences, Aron never thought of de Gaulle as a tyrant or as an advocate of unlimited rule, but rather as a "paternal monarch."

For his part, de Gaulle was conscious of his differences with Aron, as he politely indicated in letters to Aron, who sent him copies of some of his books. On August 7, 1962, de Gaulle complimented and admired "Paix et guerre entre les nations" but was not convinced by the argument of Aron, who "rarely approves of what I do." On December 9, 1963, he wrote he had read "Le Grand Débat," "as I often read what you have written on the same subject . . . you return to it incessantly . . . maybe because the line you have adopted does not fully satisfy even you." For de Gaulle, France must be France, whereas Aron kept examining the questions of the Atlantic Community, NATO, and arms.[20]

The strongest direct criticism by Aron of de Gaulle's language and policy resulted from the famous press conference of November 27, 1967, and the president's reference to Jews as "an elite people, self-assured and domineering." Aron saw de Gaulle confusing the issue of Israel and that of French Jews, the question of Israeli policy in 1967 and other times and that of a Jewish people. Again, Aron stressed the right of individuals to be, at the same time, French and Jews. Aron raised the questions of whether de Gaulle wanted to deliver a message to the Jews in the Diaspora, not simply attack those in Israel. He was not alone in being disturbed by de Gaulle's cryptic remarks about a Jewish people which provoked or rather aroused waves of ill feeling in certain countries and at certain times.

Aron did not accuse de Gaulle of antisemitism, but felt that for the first time in postwar Europe a major leader used language and ideas that lent respectability to antisemitism and made it legitimate. The language and style was reminiscent of former French antisemites Charles Maurras, Edouard Drumont, and Xavier Vallat, first commissioner for Jewish questions in Vichy. Indeed, Vallat, in an immediate comment, "De Gaulle and the wandering Jew" in the weekly *Aspects de la France*, wrote of the press conference, "Why should I hide that the passage on the Middle East gave me the greatest satisfaction."

Though Aron did not make the point, de Gaulle's language also resembled that of André Gide in his diary entry of January 24, 1914. Reflecting on the character of Léon Blum, whom he had not met, Gide wrote of Blum's "apparent resolve always to show a preference for the Jews," of Blum's particular sensitivity to Jewish virtues, and of Blum's considering the Jewish race as superior. Gide contended that Blum believed that the Jewish race was called on to "dominate after having been long dominated, and thinks it his duty to work towards its triumph with all his strength. Perhaps he glimpses the possible dominance of that race."[21]

Aron did criticize de Gaulle for condemning Israel alone and for his anger both that Israel had not followed his advice in June 1967 and that Jews in France had demonstrated their joy at Israel's victory in the Six-Day War. Aron claimed the right as a French citizen to combine allegiance to the French state with sympathy for and support of Israel's right to defend itself.

De Gaulle's remarks about Jews were offensive to others besides Aron. Former Prime Minister David Ben Gurion, whom de Gaulle had welcomed on a number of occasions in 1958, 1960, 1961, and 1964 as leader of Israel, "our friend and ally," and who flattered him as "one of the great men of the century," took exception to the unjust remarks in the press conference and wrote de Gaulle a long letter on December 6, 1967. The Israeli provided the French president a concise version of the 2,500-year history of the Jews in the Middle East and reminded him that the first step in the nineteenth century toward establishing a Jewish state was the founding of Mikveh Israel, the first Jewish agricultural school, by the French Jews of the Alliance Israélite Universelle under Adolphe Crémieux, then minister of justice, an action that fostered Jewish immigration and settlement in Palestine.

Ben Gurion explained that Jews were not a "dominating people," that Israel had a strong desire for peace with its neighbors, that Israel had no expansionist ambitions, and that "the chosen people" to whom de Gaulle had referred did not consider itself superior to other people. He informed de Gaulle that in his statement before the 1936 Peel Commission on the future of the British Mandate of Palestine he had said "Our mandate is the Bible"; no one suggested conquering additional territory. Conflict with the Arabs had not broken out as a result of Israel's expansionist ambitions.

In his much shorter reply of December 30, 1967, de Gaulle dealt with Israeli policy, not with the Jewish question as such. He reminded Ben Gurion that he would have been opposed to the annihilation of Israel, which he had publicly called a "friendly state and ally." However, Israel must show strict moderation in its relations with its neighbors and in its territorial ambitions. Israel must remember that the "lands initially recognized" to it by the powers are considered by the Arabs as their property, and that France has had old and natural friendship with the Arab countries. Israel, he argued, had exceeded the limits of the requisite moderation in a number of ways.

De Gaulle told Ben Gurion and others that Israel had disregarded his warning not to start hostilities in 1967. He argued that Israel had taken possession of Jerusalem and many Jordanian, Egyptian, and Syrian territories by force of arms, practiced repression, and expulsion, which were the consequences of an occupation that was tending to annexation. In typical oracular fashion he warned Ben Gurion that Israel's policy "is valid only on condition of being adapted to the realities." In a single reference, de Gaulle defended his remarks about the "elite" Jewish people and stressed its qualities "thanks to which this strong people was able to survive and remain itself after nineteen centuries spent in unimaginable conditions." In a separate exchange, on January 1968 at the Elysée Palace with Chief Rabbi Jacob Kaplan, de Gaulle argued that his words were, in a sense, a compliment to Jews. Moreover, he admitted that the sympathy of French Jews for the people and the land of Israel was quite natural and was not incompatible with their obligations as French people.[22]

Raymond Aron's book *De Gaulle, Israel, and the Jews* allows an opportunity to raise questions about de Gaulle and his policy in the Middle East: was he antisemitic, what were his real attitudes and policies toward Israel, and how did they relate to his policies on the Middle East and on international affairs?

Nothing in de Gaulle's career, his words or actions, suggests antisemitic prejudices.[23] Rather, his life was marked by indifference or lack of attention to issues concerning Jews, to which he gave little thought. He was almost silent on the Holocaust in general and on the plight of Jews under Vichy. He did, however, in 1943 after the Allied forces had liberated North Africa, restore to Algerian Jews the French citizenship that Vichy had taken away in 1940.

De Gaulle's lack of attention to Nazi atrocities or to Jewish issues did not prevent him from friendship with individual Jews or understanding of those issues. He had, after all, grown up in a household where his father, a Catholic monarchist, teacher of philosophy and literature, was convinced of the innocence of Dreyfus.[24] De Gaulle himself rarely referred to the Dreyfus Affair. It was for him a "lamentable trial. . . . it divided the French people." His interesting comment at the time of the general coup in Algeria in 1961 was that "the French army has always been wrong. It was against Dreyfus, for Pétain, and now it is for a French Algeria."[25] An equally telling incident occurred when de Gaulle was considering the appointment of a person as ambassador to an Arab state. Reminded that the individual had a Jewish wife, the granddaughter of Captain Dreyfus, de Gaulle replied, "She is the granddaughter of a French officer."[26]

In his early career he was influenced and encouraged by Colonel Emile Mayer, a Jewish graduate of the Ecole Polytechnique who himself had been discriminated against largely because of his articles on the falsehoods of some generals during the Dreyfus Affair, and on the needed administrative reforms of the army. Mayer, his senior by thirty years, influenced de Gaulle's thinking on military matters, on strategies and new styles of weapons and mechanized warfare. Mayer encouraged his friends to read de Gaulle's *Vers l'Armée de Métier*, and helped in the 1938 revision and expansion of de Gaulle's *La France et son Armée.*

Mayer also introduced de Gaulle into a group that met weekly in the apartment of his son-in-law between 1932 and 1937, where de Gaulle met not only Léon Blum but also the lawyer and writer Jean Auburtin and his friend Paul Reynaud in 1934, who sponsored the idea of a professional mechanized army in the French Parliament and who told the head of his cabinet, Gaston Palewski, to work on it with de Gaulle. Among other Jews with whom de Gaulle was friendly was Dr. Edmond Lévy-Solal, grandson of a rabbi, who delivered de Gaulle's children in 1921 and 1924.

In London as leader of the Free French, de Gaulle was accompanied by talented and prestigious Jews including Raymond Aron. The most important of this group was probably René Cassin, the first civilian to leave Bordeaux to join de Gaulle in London, the person who drafted all the legal texts of the Free French, who conducted negotiations with the British, and the man who after the war was to be vice president, the real head, of the Conseil d'Etat, president of the Higher Court of Arbitration, member of the Constitutional Council, and winner of the Nobel Peace Prize in 1968.

France in London during the war, it has been said, was the France of the metro and the synagogue.[27] It was also rumored that de Gaulle offered the position of advisor on foreign affairs to the popular novelist André Maurois (the Jewish Emile Herzog), who declined it and left for the United States. Other Jews were available for other tasks: Georges Boris, Léo Hamon, Pierre Mendès-France. The Vichy authorities even called de Gaulle "the docile servant of the Jews."[28]

De Gaulle was no such servant, but he maintained cordial relations with Jewish leaders and was conscious of the help given by the Jews to the Free French in Palestine during the war, contrasting that with the opposition of the Arabs who were on the other side.[29] In London he met in August 1940 with Albert Cohen, local representative of the Jewish Agency in Jerusalem and of the American branch of the World Jewish Congress, commenting that antisemitism resulted from Jews being made the scapegoats for economic and social problems. He also spoke of Zionism with sympathy and admiration. In its turn, the Jewish Agency was one of the first international organizations to give official recognition to Free France.[30]

De Gaulle promised Cohen, in a letter of August 22, 1940, that, when France regained its liberty, all French citizens, whatever their religion, would enjoy equal rights. Writing from Brazzaville on November 11, 1940, to Stephen Wise, president of the World Jewish Congress, de Gaulle considered the Vichy legislation as null and void and as an injustice with regard to Jewish citizens. On a number of occasions he stated his intention to abolish that shameful legislation after liberation. On February 20, 1943, de Gaulle declared that the laws of the French Republic must be immediately reestablished in Africa, and in a letter to Stephen Wise of September 27, 1943, wrote of the need for reparations in Algeria and the restoration of nationality for Jews there. After the defeat of the Vichy forces in Syria and Lebanon by the Free French, antisemitic decrees were annulled there on August 2, 1941.

On the general question of Zionism, de Gaulle gave no clear answers to his views in conversations with Chaim Weizmann in 1942 and 1943. He took no official position, preserving options for France in Syria and

Lebanon and being careful in his delicate wartime relationship with Britain—to which, as Winston Churchill wrote, he was rude but which held the League of Nations mandate for Palestine. He recognized that relations between the Jews in Palestine and Free French forces and officials during the war were cordial and cooperative in a number of ways, since they shared similar objectives. Early on, from September 1940 to June 1941, a radio station, Radio Levant France Libre, headed by de Gaulle's advisor, François Coulet, and protected by the Haganah, functioned in Haifa at the home of David Hacohen, future politician in Israel. With its strong signals, the station challenged the Vichy radio station in Beirut.

A Free French consulate was set up in Tel Aviv in 1941, and in early 1942 a Jewish Association for the Free French was established, providing for daily contact between the two sides. An energetic engineer and businessman, Paul Repiton, was appointed in August 1941 as representative of the Free French in Jerusalem, where he benefited from information from Jewish sources. Palestinian Jews encouraged the teaching of French in high schools and organized an exhibition of French painting in Tel Aviv in May 1942, while the Free French provided a subsidy for a chair in the French language and civilization at the Hebrew University. Politically, the Jewish press supported de Gaulle in the conflict with General Giraud at the end of 1942.

Though General Georges Catroux, head of the Free French in the Levant, and some officers in his headquarters in Cairo, and others such as the antisemitic Captain Jean-Louis Montezer, author of *La France et L'Islam*, objected to and spurned the Jewish offer to help, nevertheless Jewish Palestinians fought together with Allied Forces, including the Free French contingent under Colonel Collet against Vichy France, which was aiding the Germans in Lebanon and Syria. In one such action Moshe Dayan lost his left eye in June 1941. The Free French forces, about six thousand, were transported from Palestine to the Syrian border in Haganah trucks.

Outside of Palestine, a Jewish unit of five hundred men, attached to the King's West African Rifles, linked up with General Koenig, victor of Bir Hakeim: almost all perished in the fight against Rommel's tanks and planes.[31] In his conversation with Jean-Claude Servan-Schreiber on July 5, 1968, de Gaulle recalled that "the young Jews in Palestine in 1941 were marvelous; they fought on our side while the Arabs were on the other side." Jacques Soustelle even spoke with exaggeration of 150,000 Jewish volunteers, including 50,000 women, some of whom fought in Flanders and St.-Malo.[32]

De Gaulle, who had been stationed in Beirut between 1929 and 1931, was aware of the complex political factions in the Middle East. At one point, in March 1941, he proposed a Jewish military unit as part of the Free French contingent but gave up the idea because of British opposition and concern of Catroux, who argued that such a unit and Jewish mobilization would be a danger to peace in the area. On one side were supporters of a Jewish active role, such as Colonel Collet in Palestine and General Koenig. On the other side were those arguing that Free France should limit its relations with the Jews, that it should link up with Arabs, and that it should reduce tension with Britain over the future of the Levant. If de Gaulle appreciated the value of the Jewish contribution to his cause, he was also aware of the problem of pan-Arabism and interested in the maintenance of the French mandate in Syria and Lebanon.[33] That mandate had after 1920 tried to delineate the border between the two countries, but the exact division was never completed and no formal international boundary has been recognized.

After the war, France did not openly aid the Zionist cause, though some French people, especially Jacques Soustelle, helped leaders of Jewish Palestinian resistance groups, assisted some members of the Irgun Zvai Leumi, led by Menachem Begin, and Stern, LEHI, gangs who had escaped British prisons in Palestine, and provided some arms supplies. De Gaulle broke his silence on the question of Palestine with a declaration in *The Times* in September 1945 that Middle East issues, including that of Jewish immigration into the country, should be regulated by cooperation of Britain and France. Shortly after, in his desire to reduce British influence, de Gaulle called for internationalization of the Palestinian problem.

According to Jacob Tsur, Israeli ambassador to France, who visited him on April 28, 1955, de Gaulle considered the creation of the Jewish state as a historic necessity, appreciated the talents and energies of Jews, and was particularly surprised by Israeli success in agriculture.[34] The presence of Israel in the Middle East was a reality that could not be ignored. The great powers, he felt, must assure the existence of the state. But Israel had to correct its boundaries, including Jerusalem.

De Gaulle was not always consistent or clear about those boundaries of Israel. Tsur reported his remarks in a conversation on November 16, 1956, after the Suez adventure, that though Israel must withdraw from Sinai, its international position had completely changed because of its brilliant military victory. Yet de Gaulle also regretted that the Suez offensive in October 1956 had not been carried to Cairo, and in conversation with Menachem Begin in February 1957 remarked that he admired the courage of Israeli soldiers and instructed the Israeli, "Do not leave Gaza."[35]

De Gaulle approved the UN Resolution of November 29, 1947, calling for the partition of Palestine, though he later complained that France had not been consulted on the borders of the two states: he was out of power at that time. He also approved the UN General Assembly plan of September 1948 that allocated the Galilee and the Negev to Israel. His attitude was influenced by various factors: humanitarian sentiment, seeing the creation of the State of Israel as just reparation for the suffering of the Jewish people; concern to protect minorities in the Middle East against Pan-Arabism; desire to see British influence in the region limited.[36]

In the postwar period, France was not a major player in Middle East affairs. It had conceded independence of Syria and Lebanon in 1946 and was excluded from participation in the Northern Tier agreements, the Baghdad pact of 1955 and CENTO in 1958, attempts to create a buffer zone between the Soviet Union and the Middle East. Concerned about its position in North Africa and by the uncertain ramifications of the Arab-Israeli dispute, France joined with the US and Britain in signing the 1950 Tripartite Agreement to monitor the flow of weapons into the Middle East and to take action "both within and outside the United Nations," to prevent violation of boundaries or armistice lines, hoping to prevent further hostilities. It also became concerned about the increasing Soviet influence in Egypt between 1954 and 1955 and by the rise of Gamal Abdul Nasser as the dominant leader in the Arab world and as a potential troublemaker in Algeria.[37]

The nationalization by President Nasser of the Suez Canal in 1956 led to the joint British-French attack on Egypt and to the Israeli capture of the Sinai. A year earlier, Nasser had made an agreement to receive weapons from the Soviet Union, and the arms supply increased. In response to this trend, France not only engaged in cooperative projects in science and technology with Israel and supported it in international forums but also began supplying it, partly as a result of the activity of Israeli military purchasing agents and defense strategists, with modern weapons.[38] They included arms, AMX tanks, and then Mystère IIs and IVs, rockets and rocket-launchers, 75 mm guns, and mobile artillery. As part of the secret Sèvres agreement of October 22, 1956, planning the joint attack on and occupation of the Suez Canal, French pilots were to be sent to Israel.

Ben Gurion, in a speech in the Knesset on April 22, 1956, acknowl-edged that France was Israel's major arms source.[39] Cooperation between the defense establishments and intelligence networks of the two countries was close. Some French people, at a time when France was at war with Algerian rebels, talked of a formal alliance: in November 1956 an organization, the French Committee for an alliance, did emerge, headed at first by Jacques Soustelle and then by General Koenig. Dif-ferences on French policy between politicians and military personnel in the Fourth Republic and diplomats were evident. The first group, especially Maurice Bourgès-Maunoury, minister of defense and former resistance fighter, wanted to assist Israel and to increase supply of arms because of the fear that Nasser—regarded by many as the undisputed leader of the Arab world, not simply as the head of Egypt, where Nazi officers served in the army and administration—would aid the Algerian rebels fighting France, which might mean the end of French Algeria.

Aid to Israel would help check Nasser's activities. The French defense industry, and Gaullists such as Diomède Catroux in the Air Ministry, General Pierre Billotte, Koenig, and Soustelle, advocated sale of arms to Israel. In contrast, the French Foreign Office, especially its Africa and Levant Directorate, was not happy with this aid, which it felt would alienate Arab states, and wanted other European countries to provide arms and tanks. Because of the internal friction, the Quai d'Orsay was virtually excluded from any planning on Suez, and some diplomats were transferred, the most conspicuous being Maurice Couve de Murville, who went from Washington to Bonn.

In addition to military aid and political cooperation, France also entered into a nuclear agreement in 1953 covering heavy water and uranium production co-operation, which increased after the 1956 Suez war. The agreement was said to have provided Israel with a large reactor capable of producing plutonium at Dimona. The nuclear instillation was built with the help of French scientists and equipment.

After Suez, diplomatic relations with Arab states, apart from Lebanon, were limited, while Pierre Etienne Gilbert, French ambas-sador to Israel, remained influential.[40] On return to power in 1958, de Gaulle—who had not taken any public position on the desirability of a Franco-Israeli alliance—reconsidered what he thought was in the best, vital interests of France. He explained, in his *Mémoires,* that the Algerian crisis and the Suez Affair had shut France out of the Arab world: "I naturally intended to reestablish our position in this region."[41]

Politically, those vital interests required a strong, independent France, one of grandeur, which de Gaulle would implement and which could provide for its own defense and participate in Great Power decisions, balancing if possible the two superpowers, and play a greater role in Middle East affairs, cooperating with and assisting the Arab world.[42] At a time when the Algerian insurgence and desire for independence was dominant, de Gaulle meant to end the favored treatment of Israel and to increase closer relations with Arab countries. Relations with Israel were too close. De Gaulle was unhappy with the presence of Israeli officials in French military headquarters. He refused Ben Gurion's request for French assistance for a building to separate isotopes. Israeli research scientists, observing day-to-day operations of the nuclear research center at Saclay, were sent back to Israel. De Gaulle viewed aspects of scientific collaboration with Israel as incompatible with the sovereignty and national interest of France. To Jacques Soustelle, his longtime supporter who would break with de Gaulle over Algeria and who called for accelerating construction of an atomic pile near Dimona, de Gaulle replied that "Your sentiments towards Israel must not interfere with 'la politique' of France."[43]

De Gaulle may not have had similar sentiments, but he did not end friendly relations with Israel. Couve de Murville made this clear in December 1964, when he said to King Hussein of Jordan that "friendship with Israel is deeply rooted in the French people." The flow of arms begun by the Fourth Republic continued: during the last two weeks of May 1967 over $40 million supply of arms were sent, most of it in El Al planes.[44] More planes were delivered: in 1961 de Gaulle approved the sale of seventy-two Mirage IIIs, which could counter the Soviet Mig 21s sold to Egypt. In April 1966 he approved the sale of fifty Mirage Vs and, later, six Super-Frelon helicopters. Some collaboration on rocket research continued.

In welcoming Ben Gurion on June 14, 1960, de Gaulle touched on his admiration, affection, and confidence in Israel and spoke of his guest as a doughty warrior and champion who symbolized "the marvelous resurrection, renaissance, pride, and prosperity of Israel" and who was "one of the great statesmen of the century." A year later, on June 6, 1961, de Gaulle spoke of "our solidarity and friendship to Israel, our friend and ally." De Gaulle's extravagant rhetoric amply justifies the comment of Manès Sperber that de Gaulle was a psychologically adroit and convincing flatterer, an individual of indefatigable cunning.[45]

Yet, signs of the change in the French attitude to the Middle East were unmistakable. The Hebrew-speaking Ambassador Pierre-Etienne Gilbert, the most popular Frenchman in Israel, who forwarded Franco-Israeli friendship, was recalled from Israel in 1959; Jacques Soustelle, the most ardent defender of Israel, left the government in February 1960; the pro-Arab Pierre Guillaumat was appointed minister for arms; Couve de Murville, former Vichy official and Ambassador to Egypt who was anxious to renew ties with the Arabs, headed the Quai d'Orsay which had already favored such renewal; Jean Chauvel was sent to foster the French language in Lebanon and Iran; Arab leaders, not only King Hussein of Jordan but also General Amer of Egypt in 1965, were welcomed; diplomatic relations were resumed with Egypt, while at the UN, French delegates became more reserved toward Israel.[46]

The visits of Ben Gurion and Levi Eshkol to France were kept low-key; French ministers rarely visited Israel; André Malraux's visit was cancelled, though he went to Egypt; the Comte de Paris was sent in spring 1961 to Libya to improve relations; French cultural and economic interests in the Middle East were emphasized, especially increased trade, commercial exports, and oil supply. De Gaulle in a letter to Ben Gurion of May 16, 1961, reminded the Israeli leader they had agreed on June 17, 1960, that the Israeli program for development of atomic energy, which France supported, was for exclusively peaceful, not military ends. De Gaulle ended France's governmental support of Israel's nuclear program, the transformation of uranium into plutonium, from which atomic bombs might emerge, in Dimona, though French companies remained.

To forge stronger links with the Arabs and to help assure oil supplies, a Franco-Algerian agreement on hydrocarbons was signed in July 1965, and another between France and Iran was signed in August 1966. The French government merged gas and oil interests into ERAP (Enterprise de Recherches et d'Activités Pétrolières) giving it, a state-owned corporation, more control over energy. Commercial relations between France and Arab countries increased. The disparity was clear. In 1966 French exports to those countries totaled 4,503 million francs, and imports 9,980 million. Exports to Israel totaled 232 million francs, and imports 84 million. In its desire for oil, France sought to increase services and equipment in Arab capitals.[47]

De Gaulle's attitude to the 1967 Six-Day War was the outcome of policy concerns and personal pique due to Israel's disregarding of his advice. Cutting short the attempt of Israeli Foreign Minister Abba Eban to state the Israeli case on May 24, 1967, de Gaulle abruptly declared, "Do not make war. In any case don't be the first to open hostilities."

By this de Gaulle was not only ignoring fast-moving events, but also denying French commitments. On May 11, 1967, the Soviet Union provided Egypt with false intelligence of Israel's plans for war and intentions to invade Syria. Three days later, Nasser sent two Egyptian divisions into the Sinai. He then, on May 16, requested that UNEF (United Nations Emergency Force) be withdrawn from Sinai. U Thant, the UN secretary-general, immediately complied and even went further, ordering the troops out of Gaza. On May 22, in a crucial step, Nasser announced the blockade of the Tiran Straits, which was a violation of international agreement. De Gaulle did not regard this as an act of aggression, though France at the UN in March 1957 had agreed that obstruction of free passage in the Gulf of Aqaba, was contrary to international law. For de Gaulle, 1967 was not 1957.

France was also bound by the Triple Declaration—of the US, Britain, and France—of May 25, 1950, which sought to guarantee the territorial integrity and sovereignty of all states in the Middle East, by preventing violence to change frontiers. In 1967, Israel did not obtain an unqualified commitment by the international community to lift the blockade nor to uphold Israel's right to self-defense. However, on May 29, 1967, after President Lyndon Johnson declared the United States would take "any and all measures" to reopen the Gulf, de Gaulle reaffirmed the principle of free passage through the Straits.[48]

Yet, de Gaulle did not view the blockade of Aqaba as a *casus belli*, nor did he accept that Egypt had fired the first shot by closing the Straits, nor did he see the reopening of the Straits as "an unconditional and paramount interest," as Abba Eban argued. Israel, de Gaulle was later to say to Jean-Claude Servan Schrieber on July 5, 1968, "exaggerated, it always exaggerates."

De Gaulle did not approve the international Red Sea Regatta proposal, an idea put forward by Britain to send a convoy of ships, one from forty maritime powers, through the Straits, which would have broken the blockade. Instead, he insisted, on June 2, on a Four-Power consultation and initiative, of which the Soviet Union would be a part. For him no settlement in the Middle East was possible without the approval of the Soviet Union, which in turn would aid France in the Maghreb. Equally important, the Four-Power idea, which in fact was rejected by the Soviet Union—a rejection de Gaulle regarded as a personal affront—would allow France to play its due role in significant international affairs. Exercising that role de Gaulle imposed on June 2 an embargo on the supply of weapons of an "offensive nature" to the Middle East. To the remonstration of Israeli Ambassador Walter Eytan that the ban would in reality apply only to Israel, de Gaulle repeated what he earlier had said to Eban: "If you are attacked, your destruction will not be allowed (*on ne vous laissera pas détruire*)." As so often, de Gaulle's language was misleading, perhaps even deceptive. In the press conference of November 22, 1967, and repeated in his *Discours et message*, vol. 5, the formula was less indirect: "If Israel is attacked, we shall not let her be destroyed (*nous ne vous laisserons pas détruire*)."[49] Whatever the correct formula, France condemned the opening of hostilities by Israel in the Six-Day War. De Gaulle did not view the war as a just war in which Israel was justified in acting before it would be attacked by hostile forces on its borders.

After the war, de Gaulle's policy hardened. On July 4, 1967, France voted in favor of a Yugoslav motion, supported by the Soviet Union and the Arab countries, at the United Nations, which demanded that Israeli forces withdraw from occupied territory. The same day, France voted in favor of a motion presented by Pakistan on the issue of Jerusalem, declaring that Israeli actions and votes reunifying the city should be nonvalid and that Israel should refrain from any action that would change the status of the city. At the November 27, 1967, press conference, de Gaulle approved an international statute for Jerusalem. He also said then what he did not say in 1956, that after Suez, "We watched the emergence of a State of Israel that was warlike and set on expansion."

On a number of occasions France made clear its criticism of Israel. At the UN General Assembly on June 22, 1967, Foreign Minister Couve de Murville virtually defended the refusal of the Arabs to meet with Israeli leaders; such a dialog, he held, was difficult to imagine. Again, at the UN on September 28, 1967, Couve de Murville regarded Israeli withdrawal from occupied territories as a prerequisite for any move toward a peaceful settlement of the Arab-Israeli conflict. This issue was heatedly debated in the discussion of UN Security Council 242 of November 22, 1967. The agreement as stated in the English language text is, "Withdrawal of Israeli armed forces from territories occupied in the recent conflict," but ambiguity remained in the French version of the text because of the word *des* which the French might interpret as total, rather than partial, withdrawal. It is ironic that the UN, for which de Gaulle had expressed contempt, was providing France the opportunity to play a major role in the international scene.

De Gaulle's critical stance toward Israel continued. He called on the UN to condemn Israel for its military response in March 21, 1968, on the Jordanian village of Kareme as a result of an Arab attack on Israeli schoolchildren. After Palestinians had attacked Israeli aircraft in Athens on December 26, 1968, and Israel had retaliated two days later by bombing the Beirut airport, de Gaulle denounced Israel's "exaggerated acts of violence on a civil airport of a pacific country, a traditional friend of France." He imposed a total embargo on arms to Israel without consulting his ministers or associates, some of whom—like Soustelle, Gaston Palewski, Jacques Chaban-Delmas, and Michel Debré—remained friendly to Israel. As a consequence, the fifty Mirage Vs for which Israel had paid in summer 1966 were not delivered.

A mixture of motives entered into de Gaulle's change of direction of French policy. Even before the Six-Day War he thought that Israel might be tempted to attack the weaker Arabs.[50] He was not convinced by Ben Gurion's answer in 1960 to his question about the Israeli's dream for the real borders of Israel: "I had larger visions in the past, but am now content with the existing borders." In a letter to Ben Gurion of June 11, 1963, de Gaulle did not "understand your anxiety about the Arabs. We are concerned about an armed conflict."[51] The president was to dwell on this in two phrases in the November 27, 1967, press conference. Referring to Suez in 1956, de Gaulle said, "We watched the emergence of a State of Israel that was warlike and set on expansion." Almost certainly referring to Israel, he continued, "On May 22, the vexatious affair of Aqaba, created by Egypt, was to offer a pretext to those who had been longing to come to blows."

Other factors help explain the change in policy: irritation that Israel had ignored his advice in 1967, and was successful, and that many in France—including newspapers, radio, television, and street demonstrations—had supported a foreign country enthusiastically in that success;[52] a genuine concern about development of Israel's nuclear program; annoyance that Israel had in April 1967 secretly shipped out from Cherbourg two of the twelve missile boats for which Israel had paid and which were being built by the French; an opportunity for France to exhibit grandeur, to counter US influence in the Middle East, to act as a neutral between the US and the Soviet Union, and to be an impartial mediator in the Arab-Israeli dispute.[53] The fact that, after the 1962 Soviet-Egyptian arms deal, the US in 1963 agreed to supply short-range ground-to-air Hawk missiles and in 1965 to sell Skyhawk light bombers, indicated that the virtually exclusive French military ties to Israel had ended. Above all, the end of the war in Algeria provided the opportunity for more cordial relations with Arab countries and for aid in their development. Ties with the Third World, especially the Francophone countries to which French teachers and technicians were sent, could be strengthened. Oil supply could be more assured.

With de Gaulle's resignation in 1968, this particular controversy between him and Aron was ended. For Aron, related issues remained: criticism of Israel, the resurgence of antisemitism in France, and Holocaust denial.

Aron continued supporting Israel, making measured criticisms of some of its policies. But he refused to join in the condemnations of Jewish-born intellectuals like Maxime Rodinson, the left-wing distinguished historian of Islamic societies, who did not support the Israeli position and were more sympathetic to the Arabs in the Arab-Israeli conflict.

Aron was critical of those such as Bernard-Henri Lévy in his book for magnifying the dangers of antisemitism in France: "With his own hysteria he is only going to feed the hysteria of a small part of the Jewish community that is already inclined to wild talk and wild actions."[54] France, Aron argued, had not produced an authentic fascism or Nazism—nor even, except under Vichy, right-wing authoritarianism. In the 1980s, no political party or journal professed antisemitic views, nor did any elected official.

At the same time, Aron did become concerned by the number of antisemitic incidents that were officially ignored. After the bombing outside the synagogue in rue Copernic in Paris, which killed four passers-by, Aron, in his editorial "Antisémitisme et terrorisme," in *L'Express*, October 11–17, 1980, wrote his strongest statement about the increasing number of attacks on Jewish institutions and people and deploring the indifferent attitude of French officials and their reluctance to address the issue. For Aron, President Giscard d'Estaing had not understood that the Copernic attack was not simply a news item but a historic event whose echo would reverberate across the world. If France was not to be seen as the foyer of a new antisemitism, the president had to speak, reassuring Jews who were now threatened and dealing with those who had committed the terrorist attacks.

This blind terrorism had taken Jews as its target, and given this symbolic significance. Aron argued there be a limit in France to the complaisance toward oil producers and buyers of French arms; beyond that limit France risked losing its soul and also its life.

110

Aron also confronted the French Holocaust deniers. He was particularly disturbed that *L'Express*, the journal for which he wrote, published, without consulting him, in October 28–November 4, 1978 an interview with Louis Darquier de Pellepoix, head of the Vichy General Commission on Jewish Questions between 1942 and 1944 who had escaped punishment and was living in Spain. The title of the article reflected Darquier's position: "At Auschwitz only lice were gassed." Together with Jean François Revel, Aron immediately replied in *Le Monde* of November 1, 1978, denouncing Darquier's "untrue and unacceptable" charge. The following week in *L'Express* of November 11–18, 1978, Aron commented that Darquier's interview had revealed the singularity and specificity, not the banality, of Nazism: the Holocaust, the deliberate extermination of a whole people, Jews and Gypsies, the will to kill those it hated and refused to recognize as part of humanity.

Thirty years after his death, Aron's voice, denouncing both self-righteous and oversimplified expressions of hostility to the State of Israel and the disquieting violent antisemitic actions and rhetoric in his country, is sorely missed.

7. The Heroic Italian and the Vel d'Hiv

The past may be a foreign country, but it is pleasant to have the memory of a heroic figure and the record of his deeds recalled in a recent biography of Gino Bartali, the legendary Tuscan Italian cyclist who died in 2000 and is acclaimed in his home country but less well-known internationally.

Bartali's greatest sporting feats as a cyclist were to win the Tour de France twice—in 1938 at the age of twenty-four and in 1948—and the Giro d'Italia three times. His skill as a cyclist was widely admired, especially for his winning three consecutive mountain stages of the Tour in 1948, a feat that remained unequalled until Mario Cipollini's four consecutive sprints in 1999.

However much admired Bartali is for his sporting accomplishments, he is even more worthy of admiration for his heroic wartime activity. More deadly than the Italian cycling rivalry between Bartali and Fausto Coppini with the country divided into "bartalini" and "coppini" adherents was the wartime division between fascists and partisans. Bartoli, an active member of Catholic Action and a tertiary of the Carmelites, kept his distance from Fascist authorities and refused to dedicate his cycling triumphs to Mussolini as was expected.

Bartali was a modest man, and the story of his heroic activity has only recently been revealed, particularly his activities in World War II that helped save eight hundred Italian Jews from death. After Nazi Germany had occupied Italy, in fall 1943 Bartali was asked by two individuals to act in dramatic fashion. The archbishop of Florence, Cardinal Elia Dalla Costa, asked him to help supply local Jews with food, shelter, and false identity papers. Bartali's Jewish friend Giacomo Goldenberg in Fiesole informed him about the Holocaust that was occurring, and the danger to the Jewish community. The Nazis were deporting ten thousand Italian Jews to death camps.

Bartoli, though aware of the danger and having a wife and two-year-old son, responded in remarkable fashion. As a member of the Assissi underground resistance he helped Jewish refugees escape through the Swiss Alps. He helped distribute funds to Jewish families hiding in Florence. Wearing his racing jacket with his name on it he made over forty cycling trips between Florence and Assisi, a trip of 110 miles, and other places including as far as Rome; he carried false documents in the tube of his cycle. He took photos and paper to the resistance clandestine printing presses, which produced the forged documents by which Jews could conceal their identity. It was revealed only in December 2010 that Bartoli had hidden a Jewish family in a cellar in Florence and thus saved their lives.

Though Bartali was often stopped on his trips by the Fascist police force, he managed for some time to avoid arrest. He was, however, questioned by the notorious and brutal Major Mario Carita, head of the Florentine secret police who with his gang of some two hundred fascists pursued Jews and antifascists. Bartali was imprisoned for over a month but was never tried and was released.

For his deeds and courage as a man who dedicated himself to saving others Bartali has been honored by a tree planted in his name in his hometown of Florence. He has now been nominated as one of the Righteous among Nations at the Yad Vashem Holocaust Memorial in Jerusalem. He embodied the criteria of Yad Vashem: to have acted without payment for altruistic motives and without diplomatic immunity.

By contrast, a man who has no claim to be honored is Jacques Goddet, the French sports journalist and director of the Tour de France from 1936 to 1986, years in which Bartali won twice. At best, his record during the Vichy regime in World War II can be viewed as ambiguous. He did protect the Tour de France from collaboration with the Nazis. President Jacques Chirac called him one of the inventors of French sport. At worst, however, he can be seen as a participant in the most despicable event in France as a personal collaborator.

As a journalist, Goddet—at least in the first years of Vichy—expressed strong support for Marshal Pétain. The marshal, he wrote, was giving France a purifying bath. Goddet was more a right-wing traditionalist than a Nazi or Fascist; he claimed to be upholding the true patriotic intentions of the old soldier.

However, Goddet will always be infamous for having handed over the keys to the Vélodrome d'Hiver (Vel d'Hiv), the Parisian cycling stadium, when the Nazis wanted to intern thousands of Jews there. Goddet never clearly explained his behavior on this occasion. This event can be regarded as the single most appalling event in the story of Vichy. On July 16, 1942, the French police, together with French fascists and the Nazi SS, arrested 13,152 Jews in Paris. About eight thousand of them were confined to the Vel d'Hiv before being sent via Drancy to Auschwitz and other camps.

After the war Goddet was charged with collaboration, but through the intervention of friends, especially Emilien Amaury, he was not punished. The bitter end of this story is that on July 16, 2012, the Amaury Sports Organization (ASO)—which now runs the Tour de France—refused to commemorate the event that had discredited France seventy years earlier at the Vel d'Hiv, which had been torn down in 1959.

Gino Bartali would have been appalled at this travesty and at the display of inhumanity. It is good to remember the past and the display by Bartali of courage, the first of human qualities.

8. The New Trojan Horse for Democracies

Political noise in France has long been voiced over diverse and complex issues, both internal and external. The country has been divided by intellectual civil war, by struggles over competing ideas, ideologies, and values. Among the most passionate of these battles has been the so-called Jewish question and the accompanying controversy over acceptance of Jews as part of the French community with equal political and civil rights granted by the emancipation of Jews in 1791.

Antisemitism, or Judeophobia—hatred of Jews—is a virus that still plagues the world. France is not immune from this. Although it is not currently the worst example among European countries, about a third of which exhibit high levels of antisemitism, a recent survey finds that 45 percent of the French think that Jews are more loyal to Israel than to France; 35 percent believe Jews have too much power in the business

113

world, and 35 percent think Jews talk too much about the Holocaust. Some encouragement may be found: 16 percent fewer antisemitic acts (389) occurred in France in 2011 than in the previous year (466), though the incidents of physical aggression remained the same.

The temperature of French antisemitism has varied in recent years, resulting from a variety of factors: positive action by public authorities to prevent or punish it, the impact of Jewish organizations, geopolitical changes in the world, the reaction to Israel's actions to defend itself, and changing sympathy for Palestinians when Hamas and Hezbollah engage in violent actions against Israeli civilians.

It is clear that antisemitism in France, as elsewhere, is interrelated with expressions of hostility to the State of Israel. Although the old hostile stereotypes of Jews remain, France cannot be considered an antisemitic country in the old sense. A recurrence of the Dreyfus Affair and violent outbreaks by French citizens against Jews is improbable. Antisemitism in the past was exhibited by political movements, by racist tracts written by writers like Louis-Ferdinand Céline in the 1930s and 1940s and his call for the death of Jews, and by the participation of the Vichy regime during World War II in the death of seventy-six thousand Jews from France in the Holocaust. It was a sign of change that in early 2012 the French Culture Ministry decided, after some protest had been made, that Céline, whether regarded as great writer or not, was not worthy of being included in the list of cultural personalities to be commemorated that year.

The main manifestation of antisemitism in France today, as elsewhere in the world, comes from Islamic forces, which have been responsible for some of the terrorism over the last thirty years. Among the violent acts have been the desecration in May 1980 of the Jewish cemetery in Carpentras, the site of the oldest surviving synagogue in France; the Palestinian attack on the Goldenberg restaurant in the Marais district in Paris on August 2, 1982, when six were killed and twenty-two wounded; the bombing on October 3, 1980 of the synagogue on Rue Copernic in Paris, where four were killed and forty injured; the kidnapping, torture, and killing of twenty-three-year-old Ilan Halim in January 2006, and continuing assaults on Jewish French citizens, who have also suffered harassment and abuse. Jewish graves have been vandalized in Paris and in Nice.

The picture in France is mixed. It is disturbing that Jean-Luc Godard, a key figure in the French New Wave film movement, should have been so obsessed about Jews, calling a producer "a filthy Jew," defending the Palestinian massacre of eleven Israeli athletes at the Olympic games in

Munich in 1972, implying in his documentary that Hitler and Golda Meir were equivalent tyrants and that Israel was a cancer on the map of the Middle East. It was disquieting that the guilty verdict ruled by the Versailles court of appeal in May 2005 of "racist defamation" of Israel and the Jewish people by three writers and the editor of *Le Monde* who had written of "Israel-Palestine: the Cancer," led to further expressions of antisemitism. Among the more objectionable passages were that Jews are a "contemptuous people taking satisfaction in humiliating others" and that Israel is imposing its unmerciful rule over Palestinians.

By contrast, it was encouraging that none of the major presidential candidates in 2012 uttered any language critical of Jews or Israel. On the contrary a considerable debate centered on immigrants and the place of Islam in France. It is significant that Martine Le Pen, sincerely or for electoral purposes, seemed to have renounced the views of her father, Jean-Marie Le Pen, that the Nazi gas chambers were an "insignificant detail," and the President Jacques Chirac was "owned" by the B'nai B'rith. She immediately condemned the murders in the Jewish school and called for the suspension of the presidential campaigning by all parties.

Similarly, right-wing parties have reduced the level of their rhetoric against Jews. An interesting comparison is that while in 1966 about half the population opposed the possible election of a Jew as president, in 2011 less than 10 percent did so. Antisemitic manifestations by the French extreme right or by neo-Nazis have substantially declined in recent years.

But the large numbers of Muslim immigrants into France, variously calculated at between five and eight million—over 10 percent of the French population, the largest number in any European country—have introduced a new strain of antisemitism coupled with anti-Zionism or hostility against Israel. Since 2000, the year of the second Palestinian intifada, synagogues, and Jewish schools have been attacked, and Jewish graves have been desecrated. Unemployed Arab youths, those living in economically depressed areas around cities, the *banlieues*, intellectuals, and imams have all participated in antisemitic behavior and discourse. In 2011 France made clear who were the perpetrators of antisemitic violence: of the sixty-seven arrested for serious attacks on Jews, forty-five were of North African descent. As a result of Islamic violence, more than eleven thousand Jews left France.

The problem with assessing the actions of Mohammed Merah—the twenty-four-year-old who murdered three off-duty French soldiers on

March 15, 2012, in Montauban, and four French citizens, three Jewish children, and a rabbi in a Jewish school in Toulouse on March 19, 2012—is that he was both a radical Islamist whose parents were Algerian born and who claimed to be a member of al-Qaeda, and also a French citizen living in Toulouse. He murdered individuals in two pillars of France, the army and the school. Was he acting to protest France's ban on the wearing of the burqa, or French involvement in Afghanistan, or on behalf of the Palestinians in their conflict with Israel? Was he simply a deluded individual, or did he act as symbolic identification with the celebration of the fiftieth anniversary of Algerian independence, or as a result of reading the Koran, as he claimed? Was he acting out his personal problems as a lone wolf, or as part of the small but extreme group of Islamic fundamentalists? Was this pathology or ideology?

The United States and the democratic European countries now face a challenge: to respond to terrorism, particularly from home-grown terrorists, without violating individual and group civil rights. Britain faced this as a result of the events of July 7, 2005, when four Islamic suicide bombers, most of whom were born and raised in Britain, denoted bombs in London's transport system, killing fifty-two and injuring over seven hundred. France in March 2012 experienced the brutality of its home–grown terrorist. This incident is the canary's warning of future danger. International problems in the Middle East and in Afghanistan have coalesced with European national and local problems, particularly the alienation of minority groups, the failure to integrate into the larger society, and the continued immigration from Arab and Muslim countries. Decision-making on domestic and international issues has consequently become more difficult in Western countries.

The West might remember the warning of Laocoon: don't accept the Trojan horse from the Greeks; it is a "deadly fraud." The place of Islam in democratic societies must be examined honestly and without prejudice in a general way. Yet even more, those countries must ensure that Islamist extremism or attempts to introduce jihad against innocent individuals or groups is not tolerated. They must ignore the false charges of racism. It is fatuous to excuse or defend the terrorist as a victim of the system, or to claim that society was the cause of his behavior. It is telling that the murderer was applauded by fellow Muslims in the housing estate in which he lived. Postcolonial rhetoric should not excuse violent actions by those taking advantage of democratic systems.

Nor should it excuse the behavior of those desirous of killing Jews as a result of their relentless hatred of the State of Israel. This was understood by French Minister of the Interior Manuel Valls, who in November 2012 expressed concern about the "new breed of anti-semitism in our neighborhoods, in our suburbia, propagated by youth claiming to be Muslims."

It was ungracious, as mentioned earlier, for Catherine Ashton, the European Union's high commissioner for foreign affairs, to appear to equate, in spite of a later "clarification," the murders in Toulouse with "what is happening in Gaza." Her behavior has become typical of the attitude of the European Union. In a demonstration of appeasement in September 2012, the EU refused to classify Hezbollah as a terror-ist group, although it has incited violence against Western interests as well as firing more than 4,200 rockets into Northern Israel, killing forty-four Israeli civilians in the summer of 2006. Moral relativism of this kind may become the Trojan horse of democracy.

9. France Condemns the Holocaust and the Antisemitic Atrocities of the Past

In 2010 the French film *Sarah's Key*, based on the novel by Tatiana de Rosnay, was shown publicly. Film and novel both portrayed accurately the willing participation during World War II of the French Vichy State, its authorities and police in facilitating the Holocaust. They presented a harrowing picture of the single most dramatic incident, the darkest chapter, in the infamous treatment of Jews in France during the war.

This event was *La Rafle* (The Raid), the round-up euphemistically codenamed Operation Spring Breeze (*Opération Vent printanier*), which took place on July 16–17, 1942. During those two days the French police, acting on the authority of René Bousquet, the Vichy secretary general of police and on the basis of lists they themselves had drawn up, arrested over thirteen thousand Jews—men, women, and children—living in Paris. Childless couples and single people were interned in Drancy, a suburb of Paris, which was equipped with watchtowers and barbed wire fences and served during the war as a transit point for the deportation of more than sixty-seven thousand Jews to their death. The first train convey left Drancy on July 19, 1942, for Auschwitz.

Of the others, more than 8,100 of those seized were put in the Vélodrome d'Hiver, the bicycle stadium in the fifteenth arrondissement of Paris, where they suffered from inhuman conditions before they were deported to extermination camps. From the Vel d'Hiv the French gendarmerie escorted the Jews to the internment camps, Beaune-la Rolande and Pithiviers, before the final destination of the gas chambers of Auschwitz-Birkenau. Not a single German soldier was mobilized to take part in this Vel d'Hiv event.

The Jews incarcerated in the Vel d'Hiv were part of the total of seventy-six thousand Jews who were sent to those death camps. It took a considerable number of years for French officials to acknowledge this sad episode in French history. However, Jacques Chirac, then president of the French Republic, on the anniversary of Vel d'Hiv on July 16, 1995, did admit and apologize for "the dark hours which will forever tarnish our history."

Similarly, François Hollande, now president of the Republic, admitted in a moving speech on July 16, 2012, that the Vel d'Hiv roundup and deportation of Jews was "a crime committed in France by France." After laying a wreath at the site of the Vélodrome, which was demolished in 1959, Hollande at that place spoke of "the horror of the crime" and the "dark hours of collaboration" and of France's responsibility. He told his audience, "We are also here to pass on the memory of the Holocaust."

His words should be heeded in view of a recent poll that revealed that 42 percent of French people today did not know of the Vel d'Hiv event, nor did 60 percent of the youth between the ages of eighteen and twenty-four. In view of the availability of the novel *Sarah's Key*, and the film based on it, the forthright speeches of two French presidents, and several TV documentaries on the France during World War II, it is surprising that such a large proportion of the French population confessed to be unaware of the Vel d'Hiv atrocity, which Hollande called "a crime against France, a betrayal of its values."

It is commendable and a sign of change in France that the Jewish victims, along with other victims, particularly gypsies and homosexuals, are being remembered in France in various ways. These memorials include a national Day of Commemoration, the Foundation for the Memory of the Shoah, the Commission for the Compensation of Spoliation resulting from Vichy antisemitic legislation, and a museum at Drancy, among other tributes.

Yet the only true monument to the victims is the retention of the memory of the crime by present and future generations. Clearly, based on the recent polls, schools in France, as in other countries, must instruct pupils about the unique horror of the Holocaust to a greater degree than presently exists. This must be accompanied by refutation of falsification of history, especially the denial or minimalizing of the Holocaust that is present in books, TV programs, and on college campuses.

That refutation of Holocaust denial or revisionism, already attempted by the French historian Pierre Vidal-Naquet in his 1992 book, *Assassins of Memory*, must be sustained, together with the confrontation of antisemitism in all its forms. It is even more necessary in view of the derisive and dangerous comment in February 2006 of Iranian President Ahmadinejad that it is a crime in Europe to ask questions about "the myth of the Holocaust." In his eyes, protest against Holocaust denial is a sign of Zionist power and domination, the incarnation of evil, and support for the State of Israel. In essence, it is an indirect call for the elimination not only of Jews but also of Israel.

The recent death in June 2012 of Roger Garaudy is a reminder of the need for protest. Garaudy, known as an intellectual and a brave resister in World War II, was also an extreme Communist, who became a Catholic and then a fervent Muslim. He became a Holocaust denier and denied that gas chambers were used by the Nazis to kill Jews during the war. A similar argument was made by Pat Buchanan in the *New York Post* on March 17, 1990, where he wrote that it was impossible for Jews to have died in gas chambers of the Treblinka death camp because the diesel engine used did not emit enough carbon monoxide to kill anybody.

It is disconcerting to read the results of a survey by the IPO in March 2012 of the degree of antisemitism in ten European countries. In response to the question that asked if "Jews still talk too much of about happened to them in the Holocaust," the positive answer ranged from 63 percent in Hungary and 53 percent in Poland to 24 percent in Britain.

President Hollande has behaved commendably not only by his strong speech at the Vel d'Hiv site but also by his action in August 2012 depriving John Galliano, formerly of the House of Dior, of the decoration as a Chevalier of the Legion of Honor that he received in 2010. Galliano had been convicted for making racist and antisemitic remarks while drunk in a Paris café.

No one wants the ghosts of the past to overshadow the joys of the present. But the uniqueness of the Holocaust and the evils associated with it must not be forgotten. At the present time, when the leaders of Iran, which is supplying deadly weapons to Israel's neighbors, and some Arab spokespeople threaten to exterminate the State of Israel, one must reject the argument that too much attention to the Holocaust would cause political problems. One should pour scorn on those such as Pat Buchanan who in his article spoke of the "so-called Holocaust survivor syndrome, group fantasies of martyrdom and heroics." François Hollande has shown the right way to deal with absurdities of this kind.

This involves two things. One is to highlight the singularity of the Holocaust, the attempt to eliminate all the Jews on the European continent. Holocaust Remembrance need not take the form it does in Israel, the moment of nationwide silence and halting of commerce and travel. But people everywhere ought to become aware of the facts of the extermination and concentration camps and the ghettoes into which Jews were forced, and draw the appropriate lessons from the information about the wartime horrors. They may appreciate the signification of the words of the antisemitic character in Gotthold Lessing's play *Nathan the Wise*: "Never mind, the Jew is for burning."

Perhaps universal lessons about the need not to be indifferent to the suffering of others may be drawn from information about the Holocaust, or, more modestly, lessons in tolerance might be learned. Those lessons are not likely to be learned by recent developments in British education, as the teaching of the Holocaust is being dropped from history lessons to avoid offending Muslim students. As a minimum, the speech of Cardinal Carlo Maria Martini in Rome in 2004 might be taken to heart: "It is not enough to be against antisemitism. We need to build friendships, recognize our differences, but not allow them to lead to conflict."

Saying "We must have the courage to look at the truth," the prime minister of Belgium, Elio Di Rupo, made an even stronger statement on September 11, 2012. He apologized for the complicity of his country's state authorities in the murder of Belgian Jews during the Holocaust and for the steady participation by them in the persecution of Jews. Symbolically, he made the statement in the town of Mechelen, which was near the army barracks used as a staging post to send twenty-five thousand Jews to Auschwitz in the summer of 1942. Of the 56,000 Jews in the whole of Belgium in 1939, only 1,200 survived.

The other issue is to seek to control the virus of antisemitism, which is still active in France as elsewhere in the world, and to unmask and punish those who manifest the intolerance and fanaticism induced by it. No future political leader fifty years from now will then have to apologize as President Hollande has done for the acts of "blindness, stupidity, lies, and hatred" of the past. They would equally vigorously reject the absurd complaint of Mahmoud Ahmadinejad that "colonial powers threaten anyone who questions the Holocaust."

10. The French Railroad and the Holocaust

Making categorical moral judgments about the motivation, actions, or non-actions of people is a hazardous undertaking. The behavior of people and organizations in wartime France, under the Vichy regime (the French State headed by Marshal Pétain) is an intriguing illustration of a complex mixture, an ambiguity that embraces at one extreme self-abasement before collaboration with Nazi Germany, at the other extreme heroic resistance against the occupiers. But for the most part people behaved in a manner thought necessary for survival.

Now, the issue of legal as well as moral judgment has arisen again in lawsuits involving the actions of the Societé Nationale des Chemins de Fer Français (SNCF), the French railroad system, during World War II. For a long time there was denial and eerie silence on the part of postwar French authorities in general and the SNCF in particular about their participation in the Holocaust. However, on November 4, 2010, Guillaume Pepy, who has been chairman of SNCF since 2008, issued a statement that "The Nazis and their French Vichy collaborators directed these terrible actions" and conveyed "profound sorrow and regret for the consequences" of the acts of SNCF. Those acts were the transport in French trains of seventy-six thousand Jews in France to the death camps.

Pepy again spoke on the issue in January 2011 in Bobigny, a suburb of Paris, the depot and transfer point from which twenty-two thousand Jews who had been interned at Drancy were shipped to Auschwitz and other places. He then said, "In the name of the SNCF I bow down before the victims, the survivors, the children of those deported, and before the suffering that still lives." He pledged that a memorial would be built at Bobigny to commemorate the victims.

Opposition in the United States from Holocaust survivors has arisen because of the fact that SNCF has never made restitution or reparations to the victims. In spite of these recent expressions of regret, the company is still unwilling to provide compensation to survivors for its wartime actions. Those actions have been amply documented. The SNCF in French trains transported seventy-six thousand Jews, in seventy-five convoys from March 27, 1942 to August 17, 1944, from French camps to the death camps. Fewer than three thousand would return.

The participation of SNCF in the deportation of Jews and questions of the payment involved have been controversial issues.

The transports continued into August 1944, two months after the Allied landing on D-Day, and a week before Paris was liberated. The other is that the Germans paid Vichy per head and per kilometer for third-class tickets for the victims, who were transported in about 3,000 cattle wagons, each usually containing fifty people. Vichy in turn paid SNCF, but the method and the amount are unclear. Accounts of those transports indicate that conditions were horrendous: long trips lacking elementary hygiene, and with minimal food and water supplies. The SNCF continued to reclaim payments of bills even after the liberation of France.

Did SNCF have any choice other than to transport the seventy-six thousand Jews to death camps? By an agreement of June 30, 1940, Germany approved the principle of French operation of the French railroads under German supervision. Like other French agencies, SNCF willingly undertook the services required by the Nazis. Although it did in reality have a margin to maneuver and undercut orders, it ran the transport trains without any secrecy on regular schedules, in full knowledge of the ultimate fate of the Jewish passengers. It never tried to delay a train or to prompt sabotage. Except in a few cases, orders were carried out without protest or resistance. The railcars were disinfected after each deportation and prepared for the next shipment. Senior rail officials accompanied the trains to the French border.

Those officials at the time explained their behavior in two ways. One was that SNCF was simply applying the laws and rule of the Vichy government. The other was that they were forced to comply with the Nazi demands. Disregarding the moral controversy surrounding the issue, the French Conseil d'État in February 2009 finally declared that the state was responsible for facilitating the deportation of Jews.

Can the railroad workers be reproached for not sabotaging the rail lines, or for not disobeying orders? Only one SNCF worker, Léon Bronchart, refused on October 31, 1942, to work on a convoy. He was given only a brief suspension for his action; he was honored by Yad Vashem, the Holocaust museum in Jerusalem, as a "righteous gentile." His action showed that acts of courage and refusal to comply with unjust orders were possible without serious punishment.

On the actions of SNCF, the official impartial report by Christian Bachelier is devastating. Bachelier found no record of any official protest by SNCF against the deportations. He concluded that, right from the start, representatives of SNCF were involved in the technical details of transport. The SNCF participated in the events following the roundup of thirteen thousand Jews in Paris on July 16, 1942, eight thousand of whom were held in the Vél d'Hiv cycling stadium. The SNCF managed the transport of these Jews to the camps of the Loiret. It also managed the transport of Jews from the free Vichy area to occupied northern France. The French convoys of these victims, openly and fully listed as part of European railroad scheduling agenda, were formed, routed, and driven by French railroad employees.

The moral case against SNCF is clear. The legal argument is more in question. The SNCF was formed on January 1,1938, by the consolidation of five privately owned rail companies; the French state owned 51 percent and subsidized it. It can therefore be considered government owned. After the war it became totally owned by the French government. On December 31, 1982, all assets of SNCF passed to the state; thus SNCF became a state-owned body. Instead of being a corporation, SNCF became a division of the French government, technically an *Enterprise Publique Industrielle et Commerciale.*

Up to 2001, the French government and its agencies were immune from prosecution because they, including SNCF, claimed sovereign immunity. This immunity was lifted in 2001, and therefore agencies could be sued. Furthermore, the SNCF has claimed protection under the US 1976 Foreign Sovereign Immunity Act. The legal problem is complex. Under French law, reparations are the exclusive domain of the French state; consequently, the SNCF claims it cannot be responsible for reparations.

However, Holocaust survivors and descendants of those transported have in recent years in France and in the US sought financial compensation as well as SNCF acknowledgment of guilt. In France a suit was brought by Alain Lipietz on behalf of his uncle and his half-brother who had been transported in 1944 from Toulouse to Drancy, the French antechamber of Auschwitz. In June 2006, the court in Toulouse found the SNCF guilty of collaborating with the Nazis in deporting the two men. The SNCF was fined EUR 61,000 for this act, though both men survived the war. However, in the Court of Appeals in Bordeaux the case was dismissed in March 2007. The case went to the Conseil d'État, the French administrative court of last resort, which without commenting on the substantive issues concluded on December 21, 2007, that it lacked jurisdiction in the matter since it was not a French state issue. Its rationale was that the SNCF during the war was a mixed enterprise but essentially a private company.

Following the Lipietz trial, hundreds of other survivors filed similar claims. Since France has no class action suits, the SNCF has to answer each claim, which may lead to individual lawsuits. But since the decision of the Conseil d'État, the French courts are closed to individual suits against SNCF.

In the US a class action (*Abrams v. SNCF*) was brought on behalf of over three hundred survivors. The court held in December 2001 that it lacked jurisdiction because SNCF was an agency or instrumentality of a foreign state protected under the US 1976 law. The plaintiffs appealed, arguing that at the time the actions occurred SNCF was not a state agency. But the charges that SNCF had committed war crimes and crimes against humanity were dismissed by the US Court of Appeals for lack of jurisdiction. It held that the "evil actions" of SNCF were not "susceptible to legal redress in US federal court today."

Another lawsuit (*Freund v. SNCF*) was filed in March 2006, by twenty-six persons who were then joined by four hundred other people. It charged that the SNCF collaborated with the occupation authorities, complied with their instructions, and profited from its actions. The main lawyer for the plaintiffs contended that SNCF was an independent commercial and economic entity and therefore can be sued. The lawsuit therefore was not against the government but against a privately owned French company alleged to have been involved in war crimes and crimes against humanity. However, the Second Circuit Court of Appeals in September 2010 held that immunity still applied to SNCF.

In all these legal encounters the SNCF has used different arguments. In the French case it argued that the court had no jurisdiction over it because it was a private corporate body. In the US it argues that courts have no jurisdiction over it because it is an arm of the French government, not a private company.

To overcome the obstacles, a bill called the Holocaust Rail Victims Justice Act was introduced in the US Congress in March 2011 to allow US citizens and others to make claims and to take action against railroad companies that had deported them or their relatives to Nazi concentration camps on trains owned or operated by those companies. The bill would waive the claim of SNCF that it is shielded by foreign sovereignty protection. At this point, the bill has not passed.

Some French historians and official Jewish community leaders, including Roger Cukierman, head of CRIF (the official organization of French Jews), and Serge Klarsfeld and his son Arno, have opposed or been neutral to the claims against SNCF on the argument that it was acting under duress, under orders, and that it has been more forthright than other French bodies in explaining its wartime activities. The historical record lends some support to what is a complex and contentious issue.

The Armistice agreement (Article 13) between Germany and the French government placed all French rail under the authority of the German Ministry of Transport. Proclamations by the Nazi authorities detailed the procedures and the manner in which Jews would be deported. Posters warned that death would be the outcome of any employee of SNCF who resisted German orders. It was not these SNCF employees but Vichy and German authorities who loaded Jewish passengers into the freight trains. The controversy over the activities of SNCF continues.

11. A Convenient Hatred

A Convenient Hatred: the History of Antisemitism by Phyllis Goldstein is a welcome addition to the literature on the subject. Goldstein traces the history of antisemitism throughout history, using certain historical events and episodes to illustrate the diverse nature of antisemitism and to link the past events to moral questions we face today. She acknowledges that others may differ in the choice of events to illustrate antisemitic behavior.

Goldstein writes in a clear, precise manner, in a tone that is devoid of polemics, ideology, or exhortation. She does however hope, perhaps idealistically, that the presentation of information about antisemitism and other hatreds and the way in which these hatreds are transmitted may help overcome them. She understands that myths and stereotypes become embodied in individuals, institutions, and classrooms, and then infect political and social leaders and action. She indicates the way in which antisemitism has ranged from rhetorical and polemical utterances and writings to discriminatory and punitive actions.

In the book, the widespread globalization of hateful antisemitism is regarded as a mental condition conducive to paranoia, impervious to truth, a very peculiar pathology that recognizes no national borders. Goldstein, starting with the antisemitism displayed over 2,500 years ago in Elephantine, an island in the Nile in southern Egypt, puts this mental condition on display. Prejudice against Jews goes back to early history and is found in Egyptian, Greek, and Roman writings and actions, and in early Christianity.

Behavior patterns that have become familiar through two thousand years were present in this early period: in the burning of the Jewish temple and the use of Jews as scapegoats in the struggle between the rival Persian and Roman powers in Egypt; in Alexandria, in which Jews constituted 40 percent of the population, there was in AD 38 mob violence against Jews fed by false accusations, and the categorization of Jews as a "diseased race of lepers" by Apion, a Greek lawyer resident there. It was realized early that antisemitism was a convenient device for a leader or a group to unite adherents against a supposed enemy, a way of diverting attention from problems and the real causes of them.

Goldstein provides some interesting details while telling her stories. One of particular interest, in the light of events that would occur shortly thereafter, with blame for the crucifixion of Jesus falling on the Jews, was the Roman action in erecting two thousand crosses outside Jerusalem on which to hang Jews, a few years before Jesus was born. She does not claim to be a deep specialized scholar, in the sense of Anthony Julius in his book on antisemitism in Britain, nor is she an expert in the many languages in which antisemitism has been expressed, but she has mastered the existing literature in English on the subject. She presents her thoughts in a readable style and systematic manner and brings the subject up to date by relating the distortions of present-day Holocaust deniers and the unpleasant fulminations of Mahmoud Ahmadinejad, president of Iran. Goldstein might have dealt more fully with the sordid record of the mufti of Jerusalem and with the present complicated interaction of antisemitism and anti-Zionism.

In this historical tour we witness the manifestations of antisemitism during the emergence of Christianity from the followers of the Jewish Jesus, the anti-Jewish laws issued by Emperor Constantine in 314 after his conversion to Christianity, the accusations of Jews as "Christ killers," the impact of Islam and its empires, the episode of the Crusades, the struggle between the new Protestantism and Catholicism, the mixed fruits of the Enlightenment, the false conspiracy theories of Jewish power, the distortion of race theories, the machinations of the Soviet Union, the abuse of international organizations, and the Arab-Israeli conflict.

Throughout two thousand years, demonization, dehumanization, and discrimination against Jews have occurred. This behavior has been illustrated on many occasions: included are those in AD 167 on the charge of deicide, or the murder of God; the burning of synagogues in Iraq in 388; the slaughter of Jews in the Rhineland during the first

Crusade in 1096; the even greater slaughter by the leader of the Crusade of Jews in Jerusalem in 1099; the attacks on Jews by individuals and groups during the second Crusade in 1146–7; the imposition of special taxes on Jews and attempts to remove them from international trade; the incitements by John Chrysostom in Antioch in the late fourteenth century; the expulsion of Jews from England in 1290 and later from other countries, including Spain in 1492; the charge in 1144 of ritual murder of Christians to obtain their blood; alleged responsibility for poisoning wells and the Black Death in the fourteenth and fifteenth centuries; the desecration of the host in the late thirteenth century; the insistence by the Church from the thirteenth century on that Jews wear clothing or head covering that distinguished them from Christians; the attacks on the Talmud and the burning of Jewish books in 1242 in Paris; the expulsion of Jews from Spain in 1492; forced conversions; the Inquisition in Spain in 1480 to deal with alleged false conversos by burning or torture (the notorious auto-da-fe, the burning of Jews at a public event); the insistence in Spain on purity of blood (*la limpieza de sangre*), which made race a major rationale for antisemitism; the assault of Martin Luther on the "damned, rejected race of Jews"; the prejudice of the Jesuits that lasted until 1946; the teaching of contempt of the Jews in church documents, a practice that was not disavowed until 1947; the inclusion of Jewish books in the Vatican Index of Forbidden Books in 1549; the confinements of Jews to ghettoes starting in Venice in 1516; the belief of Voltaire during the Enlightenment period that Jews "were ignorant and barbarous people"; the special clothing, hats, and even shoes Jews were obliged to wear in the Ottoman Empire; the massacres in the Ukraine in 1648; the second class status, *dhimmis*, of Jews under Muslim rule; the political use of anti-Jewish rhetoric by Tories against Whigs in the 1754 British election; the murder in 1840 of innocent Jews for the disappearance of a monk in Damascus; the racial doctrines of Richard Wagner; the anticapitalist and anti-Jewish argument of Karl Marx; the refusal of many European countries to allow Jews to become citizens; the well-known Dreyfus Affair in France in the 1890s; the pamphlet in 1879 by William Marr that coined the word "antisemitism"; the racial theories of Ernst Haeckel; the forged *Protocols of the Elders of Zion,* a document purporting to be the minutes of secret meetings by a cabal of Jews, which was produced by the Okhrana, the Russian secret police, cited by Adolf Hitler, and later publicized by Henry Ford in his *Dearborn Independent* newspaper and a book form, by Saudi Arabia which gave copies to state visitors, by a forty-one part television series in Egypt based on it, and by Hamas in Gaza; the confinement of Jews to the Pale of Settlement in Western Russia and attempts to convert Jews to the Russian Orthodox faith; the pogroms (thunder) beginning in 1881 in Russia and continuing for over two decades and then resuming in 1917–9 in the Ukraine; the lynching of Leo Frank in Atlanta in 1913 for the murder of a thirteen-year-old girl; the allegation of responsibility for the Russian Revolution and two World Wars; the Holocaust by Nazi Germany and its associates; the massacre in Kielce, Poland in July 1946; the ritual murder of Daniel Pearl in Pakistan in 2002; and the incessant condemnations of Israel since its establishment.

It is still difficult to provide a rational, unprejudiced explanation— economic, social, religious, or political—for the persistence of anti-semitism which has appeared in such an extraordinary variety of guises throughout the years up to the present. Why, for example, is antisemitism so deeply embedded in the culture of Spain, since it is over five hundred years since Jews were expelled from the country? Why did General George S. Patton in his diary on September 15, 1945, refer to Jewish DPs in the camps in Europe as "lower than animals?"

The danger of antisemitism remains—in governmental actions and in international bodies, especially those related to the United Nations, the Durban Conferences, and among those opposed to the existence of Israel. After centuries of animosity toward Jews displayed by Christian churches it is saddening that Arab and Islamic organizations, influenced by the example of the mufti of Jerusalem, who called for the removal of Jews from Palestine, have now made antisemitic rhetoric and calls for action against Jews a significant part of their activity. Radical Islamicists have linked antisemitism, or Judeophobia, to their disproportionate criticism and hostility to the State of Israel.

One must ask why international organizations, supposedly promot-ing and protecting human rights around the world, have been obsessed with condemning and demonizing the State of Israel for fifty years through one-sided resolutions and disproportionate criticism. The fantasy of Jewish and Israeli power and conspiracy reached an absurd climax when some declared that Jews were responsible for the destruc-tion of the World Trade Center in New York on September 11, 2001.

Though Zionist theorists hoped that antisemitism would end, or considerably diminish, with the creation of a Jewish state, this has not happened. New facets have appeared in the present age. The virus of antisemitism has been linked with hostility to the United States and to

American support of Israel. Even some academics have argued that the Jewish or the Israeli lobby dominates American foreign policy. Critics have asserted the two countries are bound together, both exercising power over the world. Wall Street has symbolized American greed and Jewish speculation and economic power. Moreover, the reality today is that antisemitism emanates from Muslim sources to an even more considerable degree than from Christian ones, and that is pronounced as much by the political Left as by the Right.

12. The Hilsner Case and Ritual Murder

On April 1, 1899, the day before Easter, the body of Anezka Hruzova or Agnes Hruza—a nineteen-year-old Christian seamstress who had disappeared on her way home on March 29, Ash Wednesday—was found in the Brezina Forest near Polna. This city was a German-speaking town of about 5,000 people, including 212 Jews, in eastern Bohemia, about sixty miles from Prague and close to the Bohemian-Moravian border in the Austro-Hungarian Empire. Hruza's throat appeared to have been cut and her head partially severed. A small pool of blood and some stained stones were found, as were torn clothes and a rope near the body.

At once the rumor spread among the general public, fostered by the antisemitic press, that the victim had been murdered by Jews, raising the age-old blood libel, the accusation that the Jews murdered Christians in order to obtain their blood for ritual purposes, the baking of unleavened bread or Passover matzos. Articles in the press and brochures repeated the occurrence and denunciation of ritual murder. Within a few days, on April 5, the day after the girl was given a martyr's funeral, a twenty-two-year-old Jew, Leopold Hilsner—a weak-minded, lazy, unemployed shoemaker who lived with his mother and who often walked in the area where the body was found—was arrested.

One woman witness had told the legal committee, set up by the local authorities to investigate the crime and which paid for testimonies, that she had seen Hilsner and two other Jews at the scene of the crime on the day of the murder, March 29. When later confronted with Hilsner at his trial, she conceded she could not be certain he was the same man she saw. Two other persons asserted they had seen Hilsner and the two other men running toward the murder scene on the afternoon of March 29 and then walking away from it. Hilsner was charged with Hruza's murder; his arrest and the charge triggered antisemitic riots and the destruction of property in the Jewish part of town.

The original examination of the body stated that Hruza sustained a number of wounds on the head, which was covered with blood, through the use of stones or sticks; her skin was lacerated, and she had suffered bruises on her arms. Her clothes were torn off with violence, and she had been dragged a distance into the hollow. A tremendous wound was found on her throat, which had been cut by a long, sharp instrument struck with great force. In the center of the throat was a strangulation mark. The throat wound was fatal, the strangulation mark danger-ous. It suggested that a noose, part of which was found on the crime scene, had been thrown over the head of the victim, and that she had been dragged from the place of the murder into the forest. To do this, several people must have participated in the crime.[55] The postmortem examination reported that no signs of indecent assault or traces of a sexual crime were found. Its crucial point was that only an insignificant amount of blood was found in the body and only a few blood spots nearby, far less than might be expected after a murder of this kind. No other bloodstains or caked blood were found.

The police and judicial investigations outlined allegations of Hil-sner's character and behavior. He often carried a large, sharp knife; he never held a job for long and evidently disliked work; he lived off his poor mother; he had loose morals; he had threatened to kill a former girlfriend; he was mentally below normal; he had followed Hruza in the past and he knew her daily routine; he had changed his clothes several times on the day of the crime; he had no alibi for the time the crime was committed; he had a shabby past. In contrast to the conclusions of the postmortem examination, the assizes judge, Dr. Baudys, who in April 1899 investigated the crime, thought it was committed by a sex maniac and recommended that the police act on this assumption, but the trial turned out otherwise.[56] Though the crime was not legally treated as a ritual murder, and official documents did not use the term, in effect the arguments of the prosecutors and outside pressure sug-gested that it was.

Blood libel accusations have a long history in Central and Southern Europe, from those in Fulda, Germany in 1235, and Trent, Italy in 1475 and continuing through the twentieth century, though no case was ever proved. In the years before Hilsner, a number of other cases in the general European area had implied ritual murder: the most prominent were in Tisza-Eszlar in Hungary in 1882; in Corfu in 1891, which resulted in the antisemitic editor of a Prague paper, Jaromir Husek, being charged with "incitement against a religious community";

in Xanten in the Rhineland in 1891–2; in Novy-Benatach in 1892; in the Moravian town of Kojetin in 1892; in Kolin in Bohemia in 1893–4. Some of these allegations, many of which concerned Christian servant girls employed by Jewish families, were provoked by rhetoric of a Viennese priest, Joseph Deckert, whose 1893 brochure *Ein Ritualmord* was widely distributed and influential in Bohemia and who claimed irrefutable evidence existed of ritual murder crimes, going back to Simon of Trent, murdered in 1475. [57] Between 1864 and 1914, twelve ritual murder trials were held in Germany and German-Austria; all except that of Hilsner collapsed. [58]

This increase in antisemitic ritual murder accusations, if not caused by, coincided with increased expressions of Czech nationalism in the 1890s, by hatred of Jews who were regarded by Czechs as Germans, by anti-German and mainly anti-Jewish boycotts, by political activity to obtain linguistic parity for the Czech language with German in Bohemia, and by pressure by Czech nationalists to close the Jewish schools that used German in Bohemia. Economic nationalism interrelated with provincial interests.[59] Antisemitic sentiment and utterances were manifested by diverse groups and individuals: the populist politics of the Young Czech Party in 1897; the violent diatribes by August Rohling, religious and racially expressed antisemitism; the economic arguments of the National Liberal Party, secular and national, for whom Jaroslava Prochazkova wrote, which saw Jews as in control of the banks and the economy; liberals like Karel Adamek, who saw the Jews as spreading German culture in the Czech regions of the country.[60]

The Hilsner trial for willful murder took place in the district court in Kuttenberg (Kutna Hora), about thirty-five miles east of Prague.[61] The twelve members of the jury heard thirty-two witnesses. Lasting five days, September 12–16, 1899, the trial ended with Hilsner being sentenced to death for complicity in the murder of Hruza, and ordered to pay court fees and funeral expenses. In his own testimony at the trial, Hilsner pointed out that the chief witness against him, a man named Pesak, claimed to have seen him at a distance that turned out to be 890 paces or 676 meters. He denied having a knife other than a penknife.

The official prosecutor, Dr. Schneider-Svoboda, supreme counselor of the provincial court, noting the great press and public interest in the case, alluded to it as the Austrian Dreyfus affair. Presenting the evidence of the self-declared witnesses and the conclusions of the medical group, he argued that Hilsner had approached the scene of the murder, committed the crime, and left the area immediately.

He acknowledged that Hilsner had no criminal record, but held that Hilsner was an unsavory individual who was on the verge of crime on a number of occasions and who had threatened a girlfriend with death. The prosecutor thought the motive was of minor importance, though he acknowledged the press had discussed it at length.

A more aggressive approach was taken by Dr. Karel Baxa, a Prague attorney and nationalist politician who in 1923 became mayor of Prague, who was financed by a German-Czech committee and who acted on behalf of the victim's family. It was Baxa who, in stressing the importance of the motivation for the crime, made ritual murder central to the trial. His argument was that Hruza, the virtuous Christian virgin, had no enemies and could not have been killed out of revenge, or jealousy, or for sexual reasons. The murderers were not concerned simply with her death but with other factors. Since there were people who desire to kill their neighbors in order to get hold of their blood, the real motive in the Hilsner case was clear. Like the first murder in the world, the blood of the victim cried out aloud for revenge.

No blood, Baxa argued, was found in the victim's body, and little was found near it. She had been slaughtered with a large, sharp knife. This sacrificial lamb was a martyr, a Christian innocent murdered by attackers of a different race, eager to get her blood. Hilsner had acted with other Galician Jews living around Polna to collect as much blood as possible. Though the words "ritual murder" were not uttered by Baxa, and not by the official prosecutor, the argument was made that the crime was committed for religious reasons. Hruza was a martyr in the true sense of the word. The purpose of the murder was to get her blood.

It was the defense counsel, Dr. Zdenmko Aurednicek, a local Kuttenberg lawyer, openly related the history of ritual murder accusations starting with the twelfth century. He reminded the court that popes, including Gregory X in 1272, Innocent IV, Martin V, Paul VII, and Clemens XIV, had condemned such accusations as stemming from Christian enmity toward Jews. The Hilsner case, he argued, was perhaps one of sadism or sexual perversity satisfied by the sight of the blood, not one of ritual murder, as the antisemitic press had declared and Baxa had implied.

By implying that Hilsner as a Jew had committed a murder for religious purposes, Baxa was accusing not only this individual but a whole people, of which Hilsner was a member, of ritual murder. Baxa's citing religious fanaticism as the motive for the crime was applauded by the antisemitic press, which was inciting race hatred.

Aurednicek sought to discredit Dr. August Rohling, professor of theology at the German University in Prague, on whose work Baxa had relied for theological argument and whose fanatical hatred of all religions other than his own Catholic religion, especially Judaism, had influenced antisemitic writers in general. Rohling had plagiarized much of his diatribe from Johann Andreas Eisenmenger (1654–1704), whose 2,100-page book, *Entdecktes Judenthum*, printed in 1700 and published in 1710, had been immensely influential in presenting a negative picture of Judaism.[62]

Eisenmenger, professor of Oriental languages at Heidelberg, erudite and polyglot scholar who had explored the literature on Jews and aimed to expose its supposedly hidden secrets in the Talmud and in Jewish traditions and legends, wrote of the foolish beliefs and wicked laws of Jews and of their mocking of the Christian religion and blasphemy and dishonoring of it. He asserted that Jews had continually robbed and murdered Christians, including ritual murder, and that many Christian children had died because Jews wanted to satisfy ritual needs.

Rohling's work *Der Talmudjude,* published in Munster in 1871 and which became the accepted text of antisemitism though its author could not read either Hebrew or Aramaic, argued that the Talmud ordered the Jews to practice deceit and fraud and to show contempt for gentiles. He was challenged by knowledgeable theologians, Christian as well as Jewish. Dr. Theodor Kroner, principal of the Jewish Teacher's Seminary in Munster, argued he had misrepresented the sources of the Jewish religion. Herman L. Strack, a prominent Protestant theologian at Berlin University, in his book *The Jew and Human Sacrifice* (1892) accused Rohling of perjury and gross forgeries.[63] When Rabbi Josef Bloch accused him of fabricating data and called him a liar for stating that Jews require Christian blood for the Passover ritual, Rohling brought a suit against him but was compelled to withdraw the complaint at the Tisza-Eszler trial in 1882 when his ignorance of Hebrew had been revealed.

Emotions stirred by the Hilsner trial led to riots and destruction of Jewish property as well as to antisemitic expressions in newspaper articles, pamphlets, cartoons, picture postcards, letters, and songs. Sometimes these expressions were seen as excessive: August Schreiber, an editor of the *Deutsches Volksblatt,* was sentenced to four months in prison for libeling Jews. The reaction to events was not wholly one-sided. Jewish organizations and other groups protested to the prime minister and other ministries about the injustice of the trial and verdict.

Prague physician Dr. J. A. Bulova pointed out a number of mistakes in the inquiry and in the postmortem examination and in 1900 published a brochure criticizing the trial, and the later second trial.[64]

The trial and consequent developments became a significant historical event, with the emergence of Thomas Garrigue Masaryk, the distinguished academic and rising politician, as the most prominent and unexpected of the non-Jewish critics of the trial and of ritual murder accusations. Born in 1850 of humble origin, with a Slavic coachman father and a Czech domestic servant mother, Masaryk had studied in Vienna, been an instructor in the university there, was appointed in 1882 as a lecturer in philosophy at the Czech University in Prague, and in 1896 became a full professor. As politician, he co-founded the Realist faction in the Young Czech party in 1889 and was selected from a small Bohemian district to Parliament in Vienna in 1891, representing that party. He was also elected in 1892 to the Czech Diet and was part of the delegation at the Reichsrat, the meeting of deputies from the Austrian and Hungarian parts of the empire. He resigned from the parliamentary positions in 1893.[65] In 1900 he established a new party, the Popular (Progressive) party. He was returned to parliament in 1907 and was to become president of the newly established country of Czechoslovakia in 1918.

Masaryk, before the Hilsner case, had shown his courage, dedication to the truth, and sense of moral justice by his stand in the celebrated case of the disputed Königinhofer manuscripts in 1886. These documents purported to be historical manuscripts, poems, and stories about a legendary founder of the Czech Kingdom and other early Czech rulers. Some of them were said to be from the ninth or tenth century, thus indicating that Czech culture and political institutions had existed considerably earlier than previously believed, a fact that propelled Czech pride and national consciousness. Masaryk supported the philologist who questioned the authenticity of the manuscripts, which after heated dispute were seen to be forgeries. Czech nationalists attacked Masaryk as being unpatriotic and a national traitor. For his part, Masaryk explained the matter was mainly a moral one, that Czech pride and culture must not be based on a lie, that forgeries ought to be admitted, and that the manuscripts could not have originated in the Middle Ages. The disputes about the manuscripts gave him an insight into Czech political problems.

Masaryk had at first paid little attention to the Hilsner case and apparently did not know where Polna was. He read nothing about it.

He was drawn in unwittingly after being approached by his former Viennese student, Siegmund Muenz, editor of the *Neue Freie Presse*, who informed him that all the Czech newspapers were writing of the blood libel. Masaryk's response was a letter published in the paper on September 29, 1899, for which the clerical press bitterly attacked him, in which he referred to the significance of the antisemitic superstition of ritual murder, which was becoming an international and widespread phenomenon, as was shown by the Hilsner and Dreyfus trials, occurring in different countries at almost the same time.

He concluded that the Hilsner trial was a travesty, a miscarriage of justice, later explaining his views in the Austrian Parliament on December 5, 1907. He quickly understood that it was not a case of ritual murder. Significantly, apart from everything else, the murder was committed after, not before, the Jewish festival of Passover, which meant that ritual murder was irrelevant. Equally significant for him in view of his upbringing was his assertion that no one who believed in Jesus could be antisemitic.

Aware of the discrepancies in the testimony of witnesses and in the medical postmortem report, which he regarded as inadequate, and conscious of the undercurrents of antisemitism and ritual murder in the case, Masaryk wrote a brochure, *The Necessity of Reviewing the Polna Trial*, published on November 6, 1899, written not to defend Hilsner for whom he had no personal sympathy but to defend the country against superstition. It was immediately confiscated on the grounds that criticism of the trial proceedings was not permissible for technical reasons. However, it was made public by special permission of the minister of justice after members of Parliament raised the issue.

Masaryk's criticism was both general and detailed. The trial had taken place under the pressure of antisemitism and the superstition of ritual murder. He was concerned that the antisemitic superstition of ritual murder was acquiring more significance, and emphasized the growing danger of "spiritual and physical" violence against the Jewish people. In addition to the misrepresentations and untruths in the case, the lack of judgment and the inhumanity displayed made it comparable to the Dreyfus Affair.[66] Not surprisingly, Masaryk was seen by sympathetic admirers as the Zola of the Hilsner case, defending the truth and seeking justice, acting as a private citizen with no ties to the defense, expending time and energy and provoking political enemies, as the French writer had done in the Dreyfus Affair. He was caustic about the attitude of the press of the political parties, and their antisemitic expressions, and also about his fellow academics and professionals who remained silent and who had not condemned the student demonstrations against him.

Masaryk objected to the slipshod police investigation, the failure to perform a complete autopsy, the refusal to follow up certain clues. He discussed some of the technical details, on which he would later elaborate, concerning the condition of the body: the bent legs resulting from rigor mortis; his belief was that the body had been moved from the place of the murder to where it was found in a more conspicuous place. Bloodstains he thought must have been present where the murder was committed. The throat of the victim was not cut; she was stabbed. Referring to Baxa, Masaryk said it was blasphemy for a Christian to state that ritual murder comes from the spirit of the Jewish religion. No statement in the Talmud could serve as a basis for the idea of ritual murder.

Response to Masaryk's brochure was immediate, with criticism from the papers of the nationalist and clerical press in Prague and Vienna, from part of the political world from which he suffered to some extent in his career, and from Czech university students who prevented him from lecturing on November 13 and whose entrance into demonstrations bringing in clerical students, radicals, and the National Labor Party led to cancellation of his lectures for about two weeks. A hostile brochure, attempting to refute Masaryk's detailed arguments, ended with an allusion to rumors that he had been paid by Jews to defend Hilsner, though more critics argued that megalomania or inflated ego explained his behavior.

Undeterred by hostile response, Masaryk continued his criticism of the case in political and literary forums. In the Reichsrat (parliament) in Vienna, a Christian-Socialist deputy, Ernst Schneider on November 10, 1899, defended the ritual murder accusation, relying to a large extent on the supposed expertise of August Rohling who had been appointed a canon by church authorities. Masaryk responded to Schneider and also to Baxa's role in the Hilsner case by pointing out the inaccuracies in Rohling's work that had fostered belief in ritual murder accusations as well as expounding extreme forms of anti-Jewish prejudice.[67] Generalizing from Rohling's work and his influence, and specifically criticizing Baxa, Masaryk reproached people who pretend to save the Czech nation from the Jewish threat—especially from their supposed control of industry, banks, and the press—but who actually poison it with base incongruent lies and ignorance. Antisemites regarded every murder committed by a Jew as a ritual murder, and this was fraud, deceit, dishonesty, and superstition in the worst or fullest sense of the word.[68]

Masaryk repeated some of this in literary form. After the article "The nature and origin of the ritual superstition" in *Die Zeit* on March 24, 1900, he issued a second pamphlet, *The Significance of the Polna crime to the Ritual Murder Libel*, arguing that this crime was not one of ritual murder, but perhaps one of passion. Many details of the case were not solved, and a new examination was needed. To write the pamphlet and to provide a detailed analysis of the case, Masaryk studied medical and legal literature, criminology, and physiology; consulted experts; and even employed a detective agency. In a severe indictment of the trial and the evidence provided, he was critical of both the prosecution and the postmortem examination. He disputed the prosecution's conclusions about the time and place of the murder, giving detailed reasons for his own analysis, including the time of day, the technique of strangulation, the numerous head wounds, the rainy state of the ground, the openness of the spot where the body was found.

Some of the points in the detailed analysis were telling. The body of the victim was not hidden; it was moved to the spot where it was found, several hours after death. Bloodstains must have been present where the murder had been committed. The small amount of blood found in the body was explained by the removal of the body from the place of the crime. The throat of the victim was not cut by a slash, a horizontal incision by a butchering knife; she died because she was stabbed. The case therefore could not be one of ritual murder; in any event, Hilsner's knife, mentioned in the trial, was rounded and did not have a point. Moreover, by March 29 the Jewish festival of Passover had ended.

For Masaryk, the motive for the crime was of primary importance. On the basis of the scientific findings alone, no composite psychological picture of the motivation could be found, but on the basis of the evidence, no case for ritual murder existed. He did cautiously suggest that the mother and younger brother of the victim had not been adequately considered, since the inquiry about the latter had stopped in 1899. Masaryk was possibly right on this point. According to one analyst, though not legally accepted or generally agreed, Hruza's dying brother confessed in 1969 that he had murdered his sister.[69] However, though Jan Hruza was regarded by some as a suspect, no conclusive evidence was ever presented. Irrespective of conjecture about the identity of the true murderer, the main point for Masaryk was that suggestions of the ritual murder legends "are the disgrace of our times; a fiery accusation against official Christianity." The legend, which had to be refuted, was false, a superstition that abused both religion and nationality. It had been fostered by clericalism, his main enemy, consisting of priests, the Catholic press, and people like Rohling, but also by nationalists, including professionals and university people.

Masaryk challenged the validity of the testimony of the witnesses and castigated the prosecuting lawyers and medical experts for their incompetence, inexact observations, and wrong conclusions. Only an objective review of the trial could overcome the mistakes—religious, medical and judicial—of the Kuttenberg trial. The Polna case for him was "a horrible symbol of decay of our Bohemian and Austrian culture" and was a disgrace for the Bohemian people. He saw the Jews of Bohemia as belonging to the elite of Jews, not only of Austrian Jewry but also of Jewry as a whole. How could they be accused of barbaric ritual murder? Because of the inexact observations, premature conclusions, and discriminatory behavior shown during the case, he suggested that the Dreyfus trial "has found a psychological sequel" in the Polna case.[70]

Masaryk's intervention in the case and criticism of the nature of the proceedings and of the legal and medical authorities was courageous not only in itself but also in light of his own past beliefs and prejudices. In an autobiographical memoir of February 1914 he confessed that, coming from a poor peasant family in the city of Hodonin, in southern Moravia near the Slovak border, he was infected in his youth in the 1850s by the virus of antisemitism in his environment, in his family (especially his mother), school, parish priest, and society in general. He told Karel Capek that in his youth he was afraid of Jews.[71] The mistreatment of a Jewish boy in his school shocked him but did not end his antisemitic prejudices.

Those prejudices, and to some extent the ritual murder myth, remained until he was a student, when he met Jewish boys of his own age and tutored sons of a Jewish bank director in Vienna. He maintained cordial relations with Jewish colleagues at the Czech University in Prague. In 1883 Masaryk referred to antisemitism as a "hateful disease which has put our organism in a fever" and suggested that Jews and non-Jews should get to know each other better.[72] Yet he confessed later that he had never got over the folk antisemitism of his youth on an emotional as distinct from a rational level.[73]

Masaryk spoke out against all discrimination based on religious, ethnic, or racial grounds. Antisemitism, as he explained in a speech in the Vienna Parliament in 1907, was immoral, crude, and vulgar: a Christian could not be an antisemite. The program of his People's Party in 1900 condemned antisemitism of all kinds, demanding tolerance toward Jews and decisively rejected the ritual murder superstition exploited for their own means by clericalism and then by radicals. As for him personally, Masaryk explained in March 1914 that of all his struggles, that against antisemitism cost him the greatest amount of effort and time, of intellectual concentration and emotional strain.

Masaryk also acknowledged that if in adult life he was not antisemitic, he was also not philosemitic. He acted in the Hilsner case not out of love for Jews but because he regarded the ritual murder accusation as a disgrace and because the issue was one of human rights. He did recognize that, if he suffered a brief professional check to his career, he was praised by Jews, particularly in the United States. Among the orthodox and Zionist Jews who befriended him were Justice Brandeis, himself of Bohemian descent, Julian Mack, and Nahum Sokolow. Acknowledgment of Masaryk's helpful role was shown by the dedication in 1930 of the planting of Masaryk Forest of twelve thousand trees in the valley of Emek Jesreel in Palestine with money raised by the Jewish National Fund.

At the Kuttenberg trial, Hilsner was sentenced to death, but because of criticism of it, especially by Masaryk, the Supreme Court in Vienna ordered a new trial by jury in Pisek, in southern Bohemia, which the court believed would provide a more neutral and less passionate setting than the Polna environment. It also called for experts in the medical faculty of the Czech University in Prague to examine the report of the medical officials in the first trial. These new experts found that report contained substantial errors: it was not true that insufficient blood was found in the body, nor was there any evidence that blood had been removed from it. They suggested that the crime was sexual in character.

For a time the legal proceedings were slightly confused. Hilsner, frightened of his potential fate as he saw the gallows—and promised immunity if he did so—confessed he had carried out the crime and was helped by two Jews whose names he mentioned. After it was clear that one of these men was in prison on the day of the murder and the other was miles away in Moravia, Hilsner recanted the confession. At the Pisek trial in October–November 1900, the implication of ritual murder was absent, though a continuing undercurrent remained.[74] This became evident when the prosecution held that the knife that had been mentioned in the first trial as being in Hilsner's possession was now said to be the kind of knife used for ritual slaughter. Hilsner was now charged with a second murder, that of Maria Klima or Klimova, a servant girl who had disappeared on July 17, 1898. A body had been found on October 27, 1898, in the same forest where Hruza had been discovered, but it was severely decomposed. Nevertheless, it was assumed to be that of the servant girl, and Hilsner was charged with her murder as well as that of Hruza.

In spite of the new medical report and the absence of any new evidence, Hilsner was again found guilty of complicity in murder and sentenced to death. This was commuted to life imprisonment in July 1901. After being in prison for nineteen years, he was pardoned by Emperor Charles I in March 1918. He changed his name and spent the rest of his life in poverty until his death in Vienna in January 1928 at the age of fifty-two. By this time Masaryk was president of the new Czechoslovakia. Hilsner's lawyer, Dr. Aurednicek, was less successful. He lost his clients in Kuttenberg as a result of his acting for the defense and was obliged to move to Vienna to practice.

The Hilsner case—and responses to it that included heightened antisemitism displayed in pamphlets, cartoons, picture postcards, leaflets, letters, songs, and parliamentary speeches—has to be put in the context of the position of the Jews in the Czech territories of the Austro-Hungarian Empire. Various forces contributed to antisemitic beliefs and behavior: the influence of clericalism and nationalism in Austria; the pan-German nationalists, led by Georg Schönerer, and the Christian-Socialists, led by Karl Lueger, who was elected mayor of Vienna in 1895 and assumed the position in 1897; the struggle between the Czechs and the Germans over linguistic and cultural equality in parts of the Austro-Hungarian Empire, particularly Bohemia, with demagogues trying to influence people on this question by resorting to antisemitic rhetoric. The Czech political parties, in spite of theoretical belief in racial equality, displayed intolerance, prejudice, and antisemitism; extremists of the Young Czechs and of the Nationalist Socialist party expressed these prejudicial views as the rise of radical nationalism was accompanied by antisemitism.

Czech nationalists saw as pro-German behavior the fact that most Jews, though often speaking Czech as their language of daily life, attended German-language schools. Czech business people, especially in small trade, saw Jews as economic rivals. These linguistic and economic concerns occasioned demonstrations, riots, destruction of Jewish property, economic boycott against Germans and Jews, as well as the rumors of ritual murder.

In the Austro-Hungarian Empire the position of Jews was complicated, especially in those areas where the Czechs claimed recognition and implementation of the historic identity and rights of Bohemia. Though many Jews tried to be neutral between Czechs and Germans, and though Jews in rural areas of Bohemia were more likely than those in urban areas to be bilingual, in general Jews living in Czech areas were part of the Germanic world from a linguistic and cultural point of view.[75] Those in Prague were essentially loyal to Emperor Franz Josef in Vienna.

According to the Austrian census of 1900, the Jewish population of Bohemia was 92,746: of this number 50,080 or 53.9 percent declared Czech as their language of daily use, 43.6 percent declared German, and 2,145 spoke other languages.[76] However, these figures must be treated with caution. In a similar census in 1890, about two-thirds of Bohemian Jewry, and three-quarters of Jews in Prague said their daily language was German. The apparent shift to Czech may have resulted from Jewish caution and political expediency and reluctance to offend Czech nationalism. Yet if some Jews showed increasing interest in Czech culture, most recognized that advancement lay through mastery of the German language and culture. Only a very small number of Jewish children attended Czech schools in Prague. Most Jews in higher education chose German rather than Czech institutions, and Jews in the main continued their cultural assimilation with German culture.[77]

Fourteen years after the Hilsner case, another ritual murder trial, notorious and well-known, took place in Kiev in October 1913. Lasting three weeks, it ended with the Jewish bricklayer Mendl Bejlis being found innocent. Again, Masaryk disputed the testimony of the expert witnesses at the trial and the prosecution's indirect reliance on the discredited August Rohling. Masaryk took the opportunity to call for a reexamination of the Hilsner case but was unsuccessful. Others were also conscious of the possible connection of the two cases. On the arrest of Bejlis, the Association of Progressive Czech Jews, protesting against the superstition of ritual murder, proclaimed on September 26, 1913, "The Polna affair, which evoked such great excitement among the Czech people, is still a fresh memory."

The Hilsner case still arouses emotion on both sides. During the Nazi occupation of Czechoslovakia in World War II, memories of the case were revived by the Czech Nazi-sponsored Fascist organization, which opened an appeal for funds to erect a monument on the site where Hruza was found, while a Czech antisemitic paper published a history of ritual murder cases.

In 1999, commemoration ceremonies took place in Polna, remembering Hilsner with a declaration criticizing the behavior of the authorities in the town a century earlier, and the Jewish museum in Prague organized a special exhibition and conference about him. Yet at the same time a pamphlet was published proclaiming the guilt of Hilsner with a photo of Masaryk wearing a yellow star of David on which were the words "Perish, deport, shame."

Letters in 1999 and 2001 to President Thomas Klestil of Austria and President Vaclav Havel of the Czech Republic called on them to condemn what happened to Hilsner and thus perform a symbolic act that would not only commemorate the victim of Czech nationalism and Austrian antisemitism but would also celebrate President Masaryk, who was engaged in the case and symbolized a link between Prague and Vienna. In June 2000, a number of Austrian citizens attended the unveiling in a cemetery in Vienna of a tombstone for Hilsner that proclaimed his innocence. Since problems still remain regarding a judicial approach to the case, this was a fitting tribute. Hilsner was not a heroic or even an admirable figure, but he was certainly innocent of the charge of ritual murder.

13. Against All Odds: A Profile of Jewish Survival

A welcome response to those who argue that Jews have made too much of the Holocaust and still benefit from it comes from a film that had its premiere at the Toronto Film Festival in August/September 2012. This is *No Place on Earth,* an eighty-one-minute film about a number of Ukrainian Jews who survived the Holocaust by living in two underground caves during World War II.

Like some other people in the media today, Janet Tobias, the American television journalist who was the director of the film and who had been a producer for CBS's *60 Minutes, Date Line,* and *Nightline,* was reluctant to add to the stories about the Holocaust. She changed her mind after reading a captivating story in an article in *National Geographic.*

This tale, untold for decades, was about the thirty-eight Jews from five extended families, the members of which ranged from a one-year-old to a seventy-six-year-old, who spent 511 days in two gypsum caves in Western Ukraine during World War II to escape murder by the Nazis. All survived the remarkable ordeal in the caves, but after the

Nazis retreated from the area and the Jews emerged from the caves, five of them were killed by Ukrainians.

The leader of the group was the intrepid Esther Stermer, an erudite woman who could read papers in a number of languages. She suggested survival through living in the caves. She was shrewd enough, before the flight to the caves, to tell her family in Korolowka, near Lvov, to disobey the local town order for Jews to register. That very day the Germans rounded up the thousands of Jews in five towns who had registered, and sent them to their deaths.

The story came to light when Chris Nicola, an American caver of Ukrainian ancestry, had found one of the caves and saw household and personal objects in it. After a long search of about nine years, he located a man named Sol Wexler and five other survivors of the cave, one of whom was only four years old when she was in the caves. The survivors were mostly members of the extended Stermer family. The cave survivors had emigrated mostly to Canada, to where they had previously had permits, and to the United States, where they had been initially silent about their story and then disbelieved when they tried to tell it.

The Jews in the caves lived mostly in the dark and survived by drinking water that dripped from the rocks and by food stolen in foraging raids during the night from local peasants. The families had been in the first cave, a tourist cave named Verteba, for eight months when in May 1943 a Nazi patrol found them. Five people were detained and two were shot. Most were able to escape into the woods, leaving all their personal belongings in the cave. They then hid in a second, unexplored cave known as Popowa Yama, the priest's grotto cave, seventy-seven mile long, one of the longest caves in the world, until the Russian Army conquered the area in April 1944.

The story is remarkable in many ways. It takes place in the context of the genocide of Jews; about 95 percent of the Jews in the region of Ukraine were killed in the Holocaust. The families lived in caves and survived for a longer period than anyone else in recorded history. They did not live communally but as five families. Most important, it is a story of heroism and courage, ingenuity and willpower, facing problems such as bodies in a hypothermic state due to hard work, overcoming bats, becoming accustomed to smoke from cooking fires, and trying to avoid getting lost in the dark since candles were limited to three short periods a day. They never saw the sun for a year and a half.

In the second cave the inhabitants had no personal effects. The families not only had to find food and water, but they also cut wood, leveled the ground, and built secret escape routes to avoid capture. They used a millstone, which one individual had carried on his back for three or four miles, to grind grain to make bread. They devised a passport system to allow safety for those who left the cave to forage for food.

The film, which was mainly made in Hungary, not the Ukraine, is told through on-camera interviews, wartime footage, and reenactments. It features emotional moments, when some of the survivors and their children and grandchildren were brought on a journey of remembrance to the Verteba cave.

It is encouraging that Magnolia Pictures has acquired the US film rights to *No Place on Earth* and that the film will be shown in the United States and elsewhere. If Jewish history has often been a lachrymose one, the story of the Ukrainian caves is an upbeat, optimistic one with emphasis on family, mutual help, courage, and resourcefulness. For Holocaust deniers it is essential.

14. Where Is the Art?

Binding up the nation's wounds to achieve a just and lasting peace was not easy for Abraham Lincoln, nor is a just and lasting settlement for those who suffered from the Holocaust immune from problems. Such a settlement has been a complex undertaking, both general and individual in character. Claims for assets deposited in bank accounts or for unpaid insurance policies have been handled by centralized settlements. On other matters, such as art works of various kinds and Judaica, claims are resolved on an individual basis and on specific objects of art with museums and private collectors.

In both cases, the Holocaust Claims Processing Office (HCPO) of New York State Banking Department, created in June 1997, has been helpful in providing assistance to individuals seeking to recover assets lost because of Nazi persecution, since the processes for filing claims can be difficult to undertake. The HCPO has helped claimants to collect as much detailed and accurate information as possible.

In contrast, a disquieting problem concerning justice for Holocaust survivors or their heirs remains unresolved, as does the question of the moral compass of a major organization founded to deal with the consequences of the Nazi regime. The controversy concerns the activities and non-activities of the Claims Conference (Conference on Jewish Material Claims against Germany), CC, founded in October1951 largely at the urging of Israeli Prime Minister David Ben Gurion, with twenty-three Jewish organizations as members, to negotiate with the

German government for compensation for Jewish victims of Nazi persecution.

In August 1990 the CC negotiated with the German government, after reunification of the country, for Jewish owners and their heirs to file claims for unresolved property in the former East Germany, and to recover unclaimed formerly Jewish properties in that area. The CC obtained nearly EUR 2 billion from the sale of properties and other assets in East Germany looted by the Nazi regime. The funds were distributed, not to the families of the victims or their heirs, but to relieve poverty and hardship, and to fund other projects, including education.

The critical problem arose as a result of the agreement by the German government to transfer unclaimed properties to the CC in the belief that it was acting on behalf of the heirs of the victims. These unclaimed assets, about $2.5 billion, were sold by the CC, which gave the money to Holocaust survivors and for Holocaust education, documentation, and research. However, the German government had set deadlines for potential heirs to claim properties; deadlines were December 31, 1992, for real estate and June 20, 1993, for moveable assets. After 1992, properties where no heir was found went to the CC.

The German government did not object to the CC transferring property to heirs who had missed the filing deadlines. In 1994 the CC set up the Goodwill Fund to help heirs who missed the deadlines to make claims. It set its own deadline of December 31, 1997, then extended it to December 31, 1998. The Fund therefore operated for five years, and then again for a period of six months, from October 2003 to March 2004 when it was closed. A major criticism resulted from the short term of the Fund, and another over the distribution of the money held by the CC.

The various concerns about the CC led the Board of Deputies of British Jews, which since 1760 is the body promoting and defending the religious and civil liberties of British Jewry, and which consists of deputies elected by synagogue congregations and communal organizations, to inquire into the persistent complaints about the activities of the CC. As a result it commissioned a report on the issue of the properties and businesses formerly owned by Jews in East Germany. The report, which was presented on December 2, 2010, was written by a highly respected barrister, Jeffrey Gruder, QC.

The report was critical of the CC on a number of counts. There were no allegations of corruption or malfeasance on the part of the directors of CC, but there was concern about competence, lack of transparency and accountability, and misplaced priorities in the distribution of resources and money. It concluded that the CC had not done enough to help heirs of victims recover their property. A major shortcoming was that the CC had possessed information that might have been helpful to owners and heirs in making a claim but did not publicize the information, at least until October 2003, and then the information remained accessible only for six months. The list, which the CC provided, of Jewish property in East Germany without heirs was incomplete: it lacked information on names, addresses, and amount of compensation, and details of properties.

The CC appeared to lack commitment to the restitution of expropriated property, and had not done enough to help potential heirs locate their assets. It felt it had no obligation to owners or heirs. The Gruder Report found that the CC rejected any obligation to assist owners and heirs in making a claim within the relevant time limit, and that it disclaimed any duty to provide information to help claimants to take advantage of the Goodwill Fund. It argued that the Fund should be reopened for new claims. The Gruder Report argued that the CC had a moral duty to publish the information it had, and to assist and identify any heirs who were rightful claimants.

An equally important moral and ethical problem arose over the use of funds held by the CC. On one hand, some of the funds have been used for Holocaust education and Jewish cultural activity, which all agree is beneficial. On the other hand, allegations have been made that insufficient resources go to help Holocaust survivors who are living in poverty and lacking in indignity. The moral compass of the CC depends on its answer to this problem.

Notes

1. Raymond Aron, *Introduction à la philosophie de l'histoire* (Paris: Gallimard, 1967) p. 204.
2. Raymond Aron, *In Defense of Decadent Europe* trans. Stephen Cox (South Bend: Regnery Gateway, 1977) p. xviii.
3. Dominique Schnapper, *Jewish Identities in France: an analysis of contemporary French Jewry* (Chicago: U. of Chicago Press, 1983) p. 107.
4. Pierre Birnbaum, *Les Fous de la République: histoire politique des juifs d'Etat de Gambetta à Vichy* (Paris: Fayard, 1992).
5. Raymond Aron, *Essais sur la condition juive contemporaine,* ed. Perrine Simon-Nathan (Paris: Fallois, 1989) p. 272.
6. *L'Arche,* September–October 1983, in Aron, *Essais,* pp. 267–280.
7. Raymond Aron, *Memoirs: fifty years of political thought* (New York: Holmes and Meier, 1990) p. 337–8.

8. Raymond Aron, *Thinking Critically: a liberal in the age of ideology* (New Brunswick: Transaction, 1997) p. 33.
9. Raymond Aron, Mémoires (Paris: Juillard, 1983) p. 525.
10. *Mémoires*, pg 57.
11. *In Defense*, p. 98; *Commentaire*, February 1985, pp. 416–417.
12. *Mémoires*, p. 708; *Mémoires*, 445.
13. *Thinking Critically*, p. 87.
14. Serge Quadruppani, *Les Infortunes de la Verité* (Paris: Orban, 1981).
15. Raymond Aron, *The Committed Observer*, trans. James and Marie McIntosh (Chicago: Regnery Gateway, 1983) pp. 87–8, 101.
16. *Mémoires*, p. 525.
17. *L'Arche*, Sept.–Oct. 1983.
18. Robert Colquhoun, *Raymond Aron, vol. I* (Beverley Hills: Sage, 1986), p. 234.
19. *Mémoires*, p. 289.
20. Charles de Gaulle, *Lettres, Notes et Carnets, Jan, 1961–Dec. 1963* (Paris: Plon, 1986) p. 400.
21. André Gide, *Journal I, 1887–1925*
22. J. R. Tournoux, *Le Tourment et la fatalité* (Paris: Plon, 1974) p. 206.
23. *Memoires*, p. 135.
24. Paul-Marie de La Gorce, *De Gaulle* (Paris, Perrin, 1999) p. 24.
25. Pierre Accoce, *Les Français à Londres, 1940–1941* (Paris: Balland, 1989).
26. Pierre Lefranc, *De Gaulle, un portrait* (Paris: Flammarion, 1989) p. 13.
27. J. R. Tournoux, *Pétain and de Gaulle*, trans. Oliver Coburn (London: Heinemann, 1966) p. 207; Pierre-Louis Blanc, *Charles de Gaulle: au soir de vie* (Paris: Fayard, 1990).
28. Georges Catroux, *Dans la bataille de Méditérranée: Égypt, Levant, Afrique du Nord, 1940–1944 (*Paris: Juillard, 1949) p. 49.
29. Conversation of Jean-Claude Servon-Schreiber with de Gaulle, July 5, 1968.
30. Henri Lerner, "Avec de Gaulle, en Palestine," in *Revue d'Histoire Moderne et Contemporaine*, 39, October–December 1992, p. 605.
31. Samy Cohen, *De Gaulle: les Gaullistes et Israel* (Paris: Moreau, 1974) p. 29.
32. Jacques Soustelle, *La longue marche d'Israel* (Paris: Fayard, 1968) p. 123.
33. David Lazar, *L'Opinion française et la naissance de l'Etat d' Israel* (Paris: Calmann-Lévy, 1972) p. 230.
34. Jacob Tsur, *Prélude à Suez: Journal d'une ambassade, 1953–1956* (Paris: Presses de la Cité, 1968) pp. 200–201.
35. Soustelle, p. 318.
36. J. R. Tournoux, *La Tragédie du Général* (Paris: Plon, 1967) pp. 211; De Gaulle, *Memoires d'Espoir I*, p. 280.
37. Sylvia K. Crosbie, *A Tacit Alliance: France and Israel from Suez to the Six Day War* (Princeton: Princeton U. P., 1974; Michael B. Oren, *Six Days of War: June 1967 and the Making of the Modern Middle East* (New York: OUP, 2002).
38. Crosbie, p. 226.
39. Louis Terrenoire, *De Gaulle Vivant* (Paris: Plon, 1971) p. 133.
40. Gorce, p. 1165.
41. de Gaulle, *Memoirs*, p. 264.
42. Michel Cazenave, *De Gaulle: une certaine idée de la France* (Paris: Criterion, 1990); Max Gallo, *De Gaulle: La Statue du Commandeur* (Paris: Laffout, 1998); Philip G. Cerny, *The Politics of Grandeur (*Cambridge: Cambridge U.P., 1980).

43. Jacques Soustelle, *Vingt-huit ans de gaullisme* (Paris: La Table Ronde, 1968) p. 353.
44. Bernard Ledwidge, *De Gaulle* (London: Weidenfeld and Nicolson, 1982) p. 329.
45. Manès Sperber, *Man and His Deeds*, trans. Joachim Neugroschel (New York: McGraw Hill, 1970) p. 98.
46. Daniel Amson, *De Gaulle et Israël* (Paris: Presses Universitaires de France, 1991); Maurice Couve de Murville, *Une Politique Etrangère, 1958–1969* (Paris: Plon, 1971).
47. Paul Balta and Claudine Rulleau, *La Politique Arabe de la France de De Gaulle à Pompidou* (Paris: Sindbad, 1973).
48. Oren, pp. 13, 26.
49. de Gaulle, *Discours et messages, vol. 5* (Paris: Plon, 1970–1971) p. 234.
50. Ledwidge, p. 328.
51. de Gaulle, *Lettres, notes et carnets* (Paris: Plon, 1980–1988).
52. Gallo, p. 210.
53. Crosbie, p. 24.
54. Raymond Aron, "Antisémitisme et terrorisme", *L'Express*, October 18, 1980.
55. Ernest Rychnowsky,"The Struggle against the Ritual Murder Superstition" in Benjamin R. Epstein, ed. *Thomas G. Masaryk and the Jews* (New York: Pollak, 1941), pp. 154–155; other works in English which touch on the Hilsner case are Stanley B. Winters, ed. *T. G.Masaryk (1850–1937), vol 1, Thinker and Politician* (London: Macmillan, 1990); Hanus J. Hajek, *T. G. Masaryk Revisited: a Critical Assessment* (New York: Columbia University Press, 1983); Robert B. Pynsent, ed. *T. G. Masaryk, vol. 2 Thinker and Critic* (New York: Macmillan, 1989; Edward P. Newman, *Masaryk* (London: Camion, 1960).
56. Paul Selver, *Masaryk* (Westport: Greenwood, 1975), p. 175.
57. Hillel J. Kieval, *The Making of Czech Jewry: National Conflict and Jewish Society in Bohemia, 1870–1918* (New York: Oxford University Press, 1988); Kieval, "Death and the Nation: Ritual Murder as Political Discourse in the Czech Lands," *Jewish History*, 1996, 10 (1), pp. 75–91.
58. Peter Pulzer, *The Rise of Political Antisemitism in Germany and Austria* (London: Halban, 1988), p. 69.
59. Kieval, *Jewish History*, p 77.
60. Steven Beller, "The Hilsner Affair: nationalism, antisemitism, and the individual at the turn of the century," in R. J. Pynsent, pp. 52–76.
61. Arthur Nussbaum, "The 'Ritual Murder' Trial of Polna," *Historia Judaica*, 1X, no. 1 (April 1947), and Nussbaum, *Der Polnaer Ritualmordprocess: Eine Kriminal-psychologische Untersuchung* (Berlin, 1906); Frantisek Cervinka, "The Hilsner Affair," *The Leo Baeck Institute Year Book*, X111 (1968), pp. 145–148.
62. Jacob Katz, *From Prejudice to Destruction:Antisemitism, 1700–1933* (Cambridge: Harvard University Press, 1980), p. 15.
63. Frantisek Cervinka "The Hilsner Affair," in Alan Dundes, ed. *The Blood Libel Legend: a Casebook in Antisemitic Folklore* (Madison: University of Wisconsin Press, 1991), pp. 135–161.
64. Cervinka, p. 148.
65. Z.A.B. Zeman, *The Masaryks: the Making of Czechoslovakia* (London:Weidenfeld and Nicolson, 1976), p. 49.

66. H. Gordon Skilling, *T. G. Masaryk, against the current, 1882–1914* (University Park: Penn State University Press, 1994), p. 146; Skilling, "Masaryk: Permanent Dissenter: the Hilsner Case and Antisemitism," *Cross Currents* 1989, 8: pp. 243–260.

67. Kieval, p. 69.

68. Selver, p. 180.

69. Roman Szporluk, *The Political Thought of Thomas G. Masaryk* (New York: Columbia University Press, 1981), p. 204.

70. Rychnowsky, p. 233.

71. Karel Capek, *Talks with T. G. Masaryk* (North Haven, Catbird, 1995), p. 49.

72. Skilling, *Cross Currents*, p. 252.

73. Karel Capek, Talks, p. 49, and Capek, *President Masaryk Tells his Story* (New York: Putnam, 1935), p. 29.

74. Skilling, p. 246

75. Szporluk, p. 120.

76. Michael A. Riff, "Czech Antisemitism and the Jewish Response before 1914," *Wiener Library Bulletin*, vol. 29, no. 39–40, pp. 17–18.

77. Gary B. Cohen, "Jews in German Society: Prague, 1860–1914," *Central European History*, vol . X, no. 1, March 1977, pp. 33–34; and Gary B. Cohen, *The Politics of Ethnic Survival:Germans in Prague, 1861–1914* (Princeton:Princeton University Press, 1981); Skilling, T. G. Masaryk, p. 91.

3

The Arab World and the Islamist Threat

1. The Problem of Sharia Law in Britain

James Madison warned of the power of an "ecclesiastical establishment." Britain now is confronted by such a threat. The estimated Muslim population in Britain is now 2.9 million, nearly 5 percent of the total population, and an increase of about 75 percent in a decade. In Britain, which has the third-largest Muslim population in Europe, over twenty-five metropolitan areas have large Muslim populations. The Muslim increase has resulted from a high birthrate, greater immigration, and conversion. Over five thousand people in Britain convert each year. Hundreds of mosques have been built. Islamic primary and secondary schools devote part of the time to religious instruction.

The country is therefore challenged by a number of issues connected with the issue of multiculturalism: the existence of geographical areas with a considerable Muslim population; influence of Islamic religious extremists; the role of religion in society; differences over social issues such as women's rights, marriage, and divorce; and a separate law for Muslims.

Five major problems have ensued from the growing impact of Sharia (*path* in Arabic) law, the divine law of Islam, which comes from a number of sources: the Koran; the teachings (Sunna) of the Prophet Muhammad, and interpretations of them; and fatwas, the ruling of Islamic scholars. In Britain that law is practiced in Sharia councils, Muslim Arbitration tribunals and informal tribunals. Since 1982 Muslims have been resorting to Sharia courts, now eighty-five in number and increasing, which act in accordance with Muslim principles and whose rules are legally binding. About 3,500 Muslims now go each year to these courts for arbitration.

The initial problem is the procedure of these courts. The presiding judges are imams; there is no control over their appointment; there

151

is little or no access to legal representation; the proceedings are not recorded; there is no real right of appeal.

The second problem is that having different legal systems for individuals of different religions promotes division, and some of the rulings of those Sharia courts are both contrary to British common law and are discriminatory against women and non-Muslims. Muslims and non-Muslims would be held to different standards. Sharia courts have tried to ban alcohol, drugs, gambling, smoking, prostitution, pornography, homosexuality, and sexes mixing in public. Extremist Muslim groups, especially Muslims against the Crusades, have even called for the creation of a "Sharia-controlled zone" in three boroughs (Waltham Forest, Tower Hamlets, and Newham) in London, and in others towns including Bradford, Luton, Leicester, and Dewsbury. These would be autonomous entities operating outside British law. Their objective is to defeat "Western decadence" in Britain, and the first step in the creation of an Islamic state.

Sharia law reflects Muslim cultures in which compliance is enforced. Significant problems in this is that there may not be genuine consent by both parties to the arbitration in the hearing, and also that Sharia law treats women as second-class citizens. Already, about seventeen thousand Muslim women in Britain are said to have become victims of forced marriages, have been raped by their husbands, and have been subjected to female genital mutilation.

Surprisingly, Dr. Rowan Williams, then archbishop of Canterbury, in February 2008 argued that the adoption of certain aspects of Sharia law seemed unavoidable, and that such adoption, or "constructive accommodation," would help maintain social cohesion. He held that Muslims should not have to choose between the stark alternatives of cultural loyalty or state loyalty. He sought "constructive accommodation with some aspects of Muslim law." Though the principle that there is only one law for everyone is an important pillar in a Western democracy, Williams held that people also hold other affiliations and loyalties that shape and dictate how they behave in society, and that the law must take account of that reality.

The fundamental question is whether Islamic courts should be forced to acknowledge the primacy of British common law, especially on the issue of discrimination against women. The Sharia courts claim that their verdicts are officially binding in British law in cases involving divorce, financial differences, and domestic violence, which is a criminal—not a civil—offence. Indeed, Lord Phillips, the former lord chief justice, spoke of the "widespread misunderstanding" of Sharia law and approved the use of Islamic courts for cases of family, marital, and financial disputes.

However, many disagree with that view and hold that British law is absolute. Two issues arise. First, should the rulings of those courts be officially enforced rather than simply accepted voluntarily? As a result of the British 1996 Arbitration Act, which allows private disputes to be settled by an independent arbitrator, the rulings of religious bodies have legal force in disputes about inheritance and divorce, and can be enforced by county courts or the High Court, thus making them binding in British law. Second, will Sharia law become the dominant law in Muslim areas? Surveys show that most Muslim students in Britain want Sharia law to be introduced into British law.

At the heart of the problem in this increasingly parallel legal or quasi-legal system is the discrimination against women and the possibility that women will be pressured to accept the ruling of the Sharia court. To this end, Lady Cox in June 2011 introduced a bill in the House of Lords to acknowledge the primacy of British law; the bill was due to be discussed during the 2012 parliamentary year. She and others had deep concerns that Muslim women suffer discrimination in Sharia courts, particularly on cases involving child custody and domestic violence. The custody of children reverts to the father at a set time, usually the age of seven, regardless of the best interest of the children.

The proposed bill would make it an offence to claim that Sharia courts have legal jurisdiction over family or criminal law. It would end the Sharia practice of giving women's testimony less weight than that of men, and overcome the unequal access of women to divorce. A man can divorce his wife by repudiation; a woman must provide justifications. Female evidence is not permissible in a Sharia court in the case of rape. Women cannot become judges in those courts. Critics of Sharia law argue that the general principle should prevail that human rights laws take precedence over religious law. The immediate point is that women be free of coercion, intimidation, and unfairness.

Of course, Sharia law, like all law, has been interpreted in different ways by Muslim judges. Not all would accept the view of one judge, Dr. Suhaib Hasan, that the penal law should provide that women be stoned for adultery and that robbers have their hands amputated. Nor is it clear to what extent women go to Sharia courts voluntarily and accept unfair decisions. It is more probable that they are pressured by families to abide by those decisions, and even more probable that they do not know their rights under British law.

Opponents of Sharia law object to the possibility of law being the result of theocratic rules. Once confined to Saudi Arabia, the idea of enforcing those rules through national laws in democratic countries has become a troubling issue. It is not consonant with true values of democratic systems: rule of law, legal equality, and open justice.

2. Is Sharia Law Compatible with Democracy?

Over sixty years ago we learned from Richard Rodgers and Oscar Hammerstein II that Oklahoma is "where the wind comes sweepin' down the plain." We now know that it also the center of a political storm as a result of the decision of the Tenth Circuit Court of Appeals in Denver on January 10, 2012, upholding the order of the US District Judge Vicki Miles-LaGrange that the implementation of a proposed amendment, State Question 755, to the Oklahoma Constitution be blocked. The amendment stated, "The courts shall not look to the legal precepts of other nations or cultures. Specifically, the courts shall not consider international law or Sharia law."

Proponents of the amendment argue that only the federal and state laws of the US should apply before the courts. Judge Miles-LaGrange, in issuing a preliminary injunction preventing implementation of the amendment, however, said that the amendment conveyed a message that the state favored one religion or belief over others. She argued it singled out Sharia law, thus conveying a message of disapproval of the Muslim faith, and had the effect of inhibiting the Muslim religion. The Federal Court similarly held that the proposed amendment was discriminatory because it twice specifically mentioned Sharia law.

A cardinal principle in democratic systems is that the same law applies to everyone in the society. That law is secular. In European countries and in the United States, concepts of multiculturalism and cultural relativism have many groups in the social fabric to assert their cultural heritage. In some cases, as in the arts and literature, the result has been positive. In the political arena, however, the result has been more problematic, sometimes threatening the rights of freedom of expression and behavior.

Today, the principle of a secular law equally applied to everyone is being challenged, if not yet under assault, by Muslim communities wanting to insert decisions made in Sharia courts and tribunals into the normal legal system and hence make them acceptable. Within the

154

United States, voluntary systems of rabbinical courts and American Indian tribal courts have existed for some time, but they have not intruded into the general legal system. But because of the growth of the Muslim population in European and American communities, the question has arisen of whether legal decisions based on cultural values at odds with democratic principles should in any way and in the name of religious freedom be accepted and incorporated into laws of democratic countries.

The problem remains, as stated in 2008 by the Archbishop of Canterbury, to "what degree of accommodation the laws of the land can and give to minority communities within their strongly entrenched legal and moral codes." The American philosopher John Rawls proposed a "comprehensive doctrine" by which reasonable people accept the existence of different beliefs about life and law and do not impose their own doctrine on others who are equally willing to abide by this situation.

The answer given by the Oklahoma electorate, in preventing the introduction of other systems of law, is that the secular state must have a monopoly of legal authority. Because the proposed amendment refers specifically to Sharia law, it implies that Islamic values and law might be harmful to individual rights and the rule of law.

The Supreme Court will have to face the constitutional question of whether the judicial branch of government can block or veto a decision of the people made in proper legal fashion. The amendment of the Oklahoma Constitution was approved by 70 percent of the electorate in November 2010. But that question should not override the issue, already a significant one in European countries, especially in Britain, of whether Islamic Sharia law is compatible with a democratic legal system, or can be integrated into it. Can the Islamic law applying to Muslims on issues of marriage, divorce, inheritance, and custody of children be accepted as part of the regular civil code?

This problem had already arisen in New Jersey. In August 2010 Judge Joseph Charles, a family court judge, refused to grant a restraining order to a woman who had been sexually abused by her Moroccan husband. The judge held that the man thought he had behaved according to his Muslim beliefs. His argument was that according to the Islamic religion the woman should submit and do anything he asked her to do, which meant having sex whenever he desired. The judge's decision was overruled by the Appellate Court of New Jersey which held that the religious beliefs of the husband were irrelevant to the case and that assault was illegal. This follows the well-known decision of the

Supreme Court in *Reynolds v. United States,* 1878, that the claimed religious duty of a Mormon to engage in bigamy was not a defense against criminal indictment.

No doubt there are some myths and social stereotypes that have been articulated in the West and may not be accurate representations about behavior and relationships in the Islamic world. Nevertheless, the starting point of objective analysis is that Sharia law is not compatible with democratic law. Sharia law, which regulates all aspects of Muslim communal and private life, is discriminatory against women and children, denying them rights that have been won over the last two centuries in democratic countries. Muslim women, treated as inferiors, are often not allowed to take advantage of the protection from discrimination or abuse provided by the secular courts. They are often pressured by their families to go to tribunals where the principles of Sharia law are applied. That law is implemented by councils or arbitration tribunals that operate on religious principles, derived from a number of sources: the Koran, the sayings and actions of Prophet Muhammad, Islamic jurisprudence, and rulings or fatwas issued by scholars.

Can this law be compatible with that of law in states not constructed on a religious basis? Can decisions from those courts be considered part of the ordinary legal system? It is difficult to envisage the compatibility of alternative legal systems with the law in democratic societies, particularly with an Islamic legal system that calls for the death penalty for apostasy, sexual crimes of women including adultery, and homosexuality. Women are handicapped on issues of marriage, divorce, inheritance, and child custody. A Muslim man is permitted to have four wives and can divorce one of them with ease, but women have a more difficult path to obtain a divorce. At the worst, women can be stoned to death for sex outside marriage. Judgment in criminal cases can be harsh; thieves may be punished by amputation.

The cases in Oklahoma and New Jersey have paved the way for an important decision by the US Supreme Court in the near future. Will it allow Muslim law to be used in civil cases relating to their own community? Will the decisions of Sharia tribunals become legally binding if the parties agree? Or will it decide—as did the highest court in Britain, the Law Lords, ruling in a case involving a woman and custody of her child in 2008—that the Sharia law applied in that particular case was discriminatory and a violation of human rights? It is not a manifestation of xenophobia or prejudice that the voters in Oklahoma acted on the belief that Muslim Sharia law is antithetical to democratic values.

The courts and legislators in the United States must be conscious of a real and growing difficulty in our society.

3. Sharia Law, Secular Law, and Rabbinical Courts

The Archbishop of Canterbury, as already suggested, in a speech in February 2008 inaugurated a controversial discussion on the existence and place of religious law and courts in Britain. His challenging premises were that adopting parts of Islamic Sharia law into the British system would help maintain social cohesion, and that Britain should find a "constructive accommodation" with some aspects of Muslim law, as it had already done with some aspects of other religious laws.

In a passing reference to other religious laws, he mentions Jewish rabbinical law. However, the archbishop was imprecise in his casual analysis, seeming to equate Sharia courts and law with the Orthodox Jewish rabbinical courts and Jewish regulations (*halakhah*), stemming from the Bible, oral law, and rabbinical explications in the Talmud and the Mishnah. He did not draw any distinction between the nature of the two sets of courts and law, or their claims for their jurisdiction.

The archbishop raises important questions relevant in the United States to the concept of separation between church and state, enunciated by Thomas Jefferson in a letter of January 1, 1802, and the First Amendment, the Establishment Clause, of the Constitution. One is the meaning of the rule of law in ethnically, culturally, and religiously diverse contemporary plural societies, in which individuals have overlapping identities. Another is whether adherents of religious faiths can or should opt out of national legal provisions where their religion differs from those provisions. These general issues are important in democratic societies.

Some Sharia courts in Britain and Canada have pressed for their decisions to carry legal force in the national law. In contrast, while a complicated and developing relationship exists in the United States between decisions of rabbinical courts and the secular court system, the rabbinical courts have exerted no similar pressure. Unlike the claims of Sharia courts, decisions in Jewish rabbinical courts are limited to the very small number of Jews who resort to them, not to the whole Jewish population.

Both parties going to the rabbinical courts attend voluntarily and both must accept its judgments in order for them to be binding. The rabbinical courts have no coercive power over the Jewish community as a whole, whereas Sharia law is imposed on the entire Muslim population. Furthermore, Sharia law appears inflexible when compared with rabbinical law, the interpretation of which is constantly changing by different authorities. The different branches of Judaism, Orthodox and non-Orthodox, have their own rabbinical authorities and therefore issue pluralistic, different interpretations of *halakhah*. Moreover, the procedures, rules, schedules, and requirements used in rabbinical courts fluctuate at different times and in various places.

Jewish communal judgment and adjudication of disputes in accordance with *halakhah* goes back to Biblical times and operates today in many European countries and in the United States. The rabbinical court performing this function is called a Beth Din (plural, batei din). These Jewish courts, used voluntarily by Jews to settle disputes, have been in use for over two centuries in Britain as arbitration panels.

A Beth Din is generally composed of three observant Jews, usually rabbis, who decide cases on the basis of Jewish law. Its functions have for long focused on divorce and business affairs, but the Beth Din also deals with issues of the Jewish community such as certifying caterers and restaurant businesses as kosher, deciding on medical ethics for Jewish patients, issuing verdicts on breach of contract in disputes between traders as well as in tenancy cases, ruling on who is a Jew, and deciding on the legitimacy of religious conversions. Some of these are decrees on personal issues of faith; these are nonbinding.

In Britain, if a dispute relates to a contract under British law, the Beth Din can incorporate some rules of that civil law into Jewish law. Most arbitration decisions by the Beth Din are legally binding and can be enforced by the secular courts if both parties agree that the Beth Din can settle the issue. The parties use this arbitration procedure not only for religious and other reasons but also because it is quicker and cheaper than litigation. Decisions by Beth Din do not pose a challenge to the national law.

Can Islamic Sharia courts and tribunals be legitimately equated with Jewish rabbinical courts (Beth Din, or House of Judgment)? The two are similar in that both depend on religious faith and apply religious law, the Sharia is based on Islam, and the Beth Din on Jewish law supplemented by the Torah and the Talmud. But the differences are vastly more important than this similarity, and a number of them are apparent. Jewish law does not dictate the political life of Jews, nor does it seek to be incorporated into the national secular law. Indeed, interpretation of *halakhah,* decided by argument and vote, differs in Beth Dins.

Generalization about the work of the Beth Din is perilous. As already described, no one Jewish individual or institutional body determines conclusive interpretation of *halakhah*. Its regulations on issues of relationships between people and between people and power change constantly as the law is applied to real problems encountered in life, as well as on issues of religious practice.

The Beth Din is concerned only with civil cases. Above all, there is for the most part, if not complete, gender equality in its proceedings, which is contrary to the patriarchal nature of Sharia courts and Sharia law, which discriminates against women and places them in an inferior position.

A fundamental principle in democracies is that equality before the law must refer to all citizens. The rabbinical courts do not seek to be in disharmony with national law. By contrast, Sharia law has been used on the basis of religious principle to justify breaches or defiance of national, secular law—the question of polygamy being a notorious example.

Feminist writers such as Susan Okin have pointed out, without specifically alluding to Islam, that the values of some cultures or religions clash with the norms of gender equality endorsed in liberal democracies, even if democratic countries sometimes violate them in practice. Sharia law, but not *halakhah,* illustrates a major problem of multiculturalism in democracies in which there is a certain tension between commitment to equal rights and dignity for women, and the commitment to allow groups such as Muslims to claim the right to govern themselves according to their own culture.

The functioning of rabbinical courts also differs in different countries. In Israel they are part of the Israeli judiciary. In Britain they operate as alternatives to secular court action within the context of the Arbitration Act (1996). As an arbitration tribunal, the Beth Din is limited in Britain by law to civil proceedings and is not recognized as a substitute legal court. Its process of arbitration functions within the secular law.

In other countries as well as in Britain, the Beth Din does not deal with criminal law, but primarily with personal law: marriage, divorce, custody of children, and family property. In complex issues the Beth Din panel consists of *dayanin* (arbitration judges) who are authorities in Jewish law. Unlike the Sharia courts, women have sometimes been included in these panels.

The most familiar major function of the Beth Din is jurisdiction in divorce proceedings. Some Jews feel they must acquire a Jewish religious divorce, a *Get,* as well as a civil divorce to end marriage. It is true that the *Get,* when awarded, and written by a scribe, is presented by a husband to a wife, but usually, both parties must agree if the divorce is to go ahead. The final decision on jurisdiction is made by the participating couple, not by the Beth Din court. And the parties must still obtain a civil divorce to change their secular legal status. Aspects of the *Get* are somewhat complicated and controversial. Women have been denied a *Get* by the Beth Din if husbands refuse to divorce, whereas the reverse is not true. Reform Judaism, at least in Britain, has tried to alleviate this problem by granting religious divorces to women without the husband's consent on the grounds that an unethical law cannot be a Jewish law.

The nature of the interaction between the Beth Din and the secular court has changed from time to time. The secular courts may be asked to approve or disapprove decisions based on *halakah,* thus giving the secular courts a limited appellate function over the rabbinical courts But, contrary to Sharia courts, the Beth Din has never suggested that its decisions be incorporated into secular law. The Beth Din remains a significant institution for those Jews who choose to use its role to arbitrate on the basis of religious law. One can conclude that the legal decisions emanating from the rabbinical courts interact with those of the secular courts in various ways while the Beth Din takes care to maintain the wall of separation between church and state.

4. No Defamation of Islam

One of the important contributions of James Madison to American life was his impact on the framing of the Constitution of the Commonwealth of Virginia in 1776. One section of it states, "all men are equally entitled to the free exercise of religion according to the dictates of conscience." Another declared that "any citizen may freely speak, write, and publish is sentiments on all subjects, being responsible for the abuse of that right." The Bill of Rights of the US Constitution went even further, with the provision that Congress should make no law "prohibiting the free exercise" of religion or abridge the freedom of speech or of the press.

As a result of Islamic activity in recent years, the question has arisen whether restrictions should be imposed on the exercise of the right of free speech critical of religions or religious beliefs. Should those beliefs and belief systems be protected from adverse comment, or should there be tolerance by those who may be offended by the legitimate exercise of free expression in democratic societies?

Between December 12–14, 2011, the Organization of Islamic Cooperation (OIC)—formerly the Organization of Islamic Conference, a group of fifty-seven Muslim countries, with a headquarters in Saudi Arabia—met in Washington, DC with the Obama Administration to discuss the Istanbul Process, the issue of implementing the UN Human Rights Council Resolution 16/18 adopted without a vote on March 24, 2011. This Resolution reaffirmed the obligation of states to prohibit discrimination on the basis of religion or belief. It condemned any advocacy of religious hatred that constitutes incitement to discrimination, hostility, or violence, and expressed deep concern about "derogatory stereotyping, negative profiling and stigmatization of persons based on their religion or belief." It was noticeable that this Resolution did not use the term "defamation" of religions but used a softer term, "persons based on their religion or belief." The Resolution urged states "to take effective measures" to prevent discrimination against such persons. This Resolution was approved, a week after the DC meeting, unanimously by the UN General Assembly, on December 19, 2011.

The first such meeting launched by the secretary-general of the OIC to implement 16/18 was held in Istanbul in July 2011, and the third was to be hosted by the European Union. The irony in the DC meeting and in the Resolution is that the OIC has been active in trying to limit freedom of expression about its religion rather than protecting freedom of religion as a whole. This has been evident since the Cairo Declaration by the OIC in 1990, which declared that free speech must be consistent with Sharia law. The OIC intent is to limit rather than to protect speech. It has succeeded, under the pretext of fighting intolerance against religions, in persuading people to prevent criticism of Islam.

Many attacks have been made in recent years by Islamic groups in the Western world to prevent free speech. In April 2011 an episode of the TV program *South Park* was censured because of uncomplimentary remarks about the Prophet Muhammad. Earlier incidents of the same nature are well-known. The writer Salman Rushdie was victimized by a fatwa by the Ayatollah Khomeini against him for writing *The Satanic Verses*, which the Iranian leader held to be blasphemous. Theo van Gogh, the Dutch filmmaker of *Submission*, a film that connected the mistreatment of Muslim women to the Koran, was murdered by a Dutch-Moroccan Muslim in 2004. The editor of a Danish newspaper, Jyllands-Posten, was threatened for publishing twelve cartoons of the prophet on September 30, 2005, and the Danish artist who drew the cartoons was forced to live under police protection. The immediate consequences of the publication were riots by Muslims who killed over one hundred people and attacked Danish embassies. More surprising was the mounting of an art exhibition in Copenhagen that was critical of the editor and cartoonist for their free expression, which it found insulting.

The Dutch politician Geert Wilders was indicted for his comments on Islam and Muslims and threatened for his film *Fitna*, with its critical passages about the Koran, which he connected with Islamist jihad. It took several years of proceedings and legal battles before he was acquitted. The unorthodox French author Michel Houellebecq was indicted, though acquitted, for calling Islam "stupid" and "dangerous." The aging sex goddess Brigitte Bardot was convicted and fined on a number of occasions for critical remarks that were held to be racial hatred about Muslims The office of Charlie Hebdo, the French satirical weekly, was firebombed in 2011 after it had published a story that the prophet was to be a guest editor for a special edition of the journal, which would be renamed Sharia Hebdo in order to celebrate Islamic victory in Tunisia. Arrest warrants were issued first in Switzerland in 2002 and then in Italy in 2005 against the writer Oriana Fallaci for alleged remarks offensive to Islam in her book *The Force of Reason*. The remarks of Pope Benedict XVI, critical of the practice of forced religious conversion, at a speech at Regensburg University on September 20, 2006, were held to be "unfortunate and unwarranted."

There are two general problems concerned with these attacks on free speech: Islamic attempts to ban criticism of their religion by sponsoring international resolutions promoting the idea of "defamation of religions, an attempt to prevent criticism of Islam and its Prophet," and hate speech laws.

In April 1999 the United Nations Commission on Human Rights (now the UN Human Rights Council, UNHRC) for the first time adopted a resolution called "Defamation of Religions," introduced by Pakistan on behalf of the Organization of the Islamic Conference. The resolution purported to be concerned with "negative stereotyping of religions" but was really primarily interested in countering what it called the view that "Islam is frequently and wrongly associated with human rights violations and with terrorism." Since then this latter phrase has been incessantly repeated by international organizations, the UN General Assembly, from 2005, and the UN Human Rights Council, from 1999 to the present, which have passed resolutions aimed at "combatting the defamation of Islam."

One example was the resolution of the UN General Assembly 62/154 of December 18, 2007, which noted with concern that "defamation of religions could lead to social disharmony and violations of human rights of their adherents." The fundamental problem is that in this and all similar resolutions the only specific reference to religions was Islam, and "the negative projection of Islam in the media and the introduction and enforcement of laws that specifically discriminate against and target Muslims." The call was always to effectively combat defamation of all religions and incitements to religious hatred, against Islam and Muslims in particular.

The major player in this is the OIC which called for legislation by states to prohibit the defamation of religions thus seeking to criminalize incitement to hatred and violence on religious grounds. Two issues are relevant. The first is the reality that underlying the resolutions is that Islam is the only religion mentioned by name. The other is that international human rights laws exist to protect individuals in the exercise of their freedom of religion or belief, not religions as such. The OIC's defense is contrary to the principles of the Universal Declaration of Human Rights, adopted by the UN on December 10, 1948, which stated in Article 19 that "Everyone has the right to freedom of opinion and expression." The OIC"s position is to limit freedom of expression and freedom of religion.

Only in July 2011 was there a change with a statement by the Human Rights Committee, (HRC), a body of eighteen independent experts, "of high moral character and recognized competence in the field of human rights," set up to examine compliance with the 1966 International Covenant on Civil and Political Rights, which entered into force in 1976 and provided for freedom of expression. Blasphemy laws in countries like Egypt and Pakistan are in essence restrictions on free speech. The penal code of Pakistan proscribes imprisonment and even death for insults to religion and to the prophet Muhammad. Blasphemy laws tend to be broad in scope and weapons of political strategy to stifle dissent. At worst, they make it a criminal offence and punish with death those regarded as offending Islam.

The statement of HRC, General Comment No. 34, a comment on Article 19 of the 1966 International Covenant, said that blasphemy laws and prohibitions of displays of lack of respect for a religion or other belief systems were incompatible with universal human rights standards. Though recognizing the difficulty in implementing the goal, the Committee reaffirmed the central importance of freedom of expression that is crucial for the transparency and accountability that in turn are essential for human rights.

This conclusion is eminently justified, because the activity of the OIC is clearly a violation of the universality of human rights, though the OIC claims that the 1990 Cairo Declaration is not an alternative competing worldview on human rights. That Cairo Document, approved on August 5, 1990, by the then forty-five members of the OIC, declared in Art 22 (a) that "Everyone shall have the right to express his opinion freely in such a manner as would not be contrary to the principles of the Sharia"; in Art 22 (c) that "Information . . . may not be exploited or misused in such a way as may violate sanctities and the dignity of Prophets"; and in Art 24 that "All the rights and freedoms stipulated in this Declaration are subject to the Islamic Sharia."

Hate speech laws in a number of European countries have, since the defeat of Nazi Germany, tried to prevent or punish incitement to religious and racial hatred. Though the primary original intention was to reduce the extent of antisemitism, laws of this kind, on which there is no universal definitional agreement, for some time have been used to punish speech regarded as insulting to a race, nationality, ethnicity, or religion, and expressions of hatred founded on intolerance, including religious intolerance. In particular, Islamic groups to prevent criticism have tried to use them or to misinterpret the European and International Covenants on Human Rights and the Elimination of Religious Discrimination on which the laws are based.

The misuse of hate laws continues. Lars Hedegaard, the Danish journalist and historian, was prosecuted in 2012 for writing about a Norwegian book that dealt with the frequency of sexual abuse in Muslim families. The charge was that he had violated the hate laws of Holland. He was fortunate in being acquitted by the Dutch Supreme Court. Earlier, another well-known journalist, the Canadian Mark Steyn, had a complaint filed against him by an Islamic group arguing that his article touching on the growing influence of Islam in Europe constituted "hate speech." The complaint was not pursued by Canadian authorities. A case in 2002 involving two Australian pastors who had criticized Islam ended less happily when, after being prosecuted for hate speech, they were forced to make a public apology.

It seems to be clear that case law decided by the European Court of Human Rights has established that expressions constituting hate speech that are insulting to particular individuals or groups can be restricted by governments in their national law. Yet some ambiguity remains. The Venice Commission of the Council of Europe (The European Commission for Democracy in Law), a group of independent experts and distinguished academics, was established in 1990 as the Council of Europe's advisory body on constitutional issues. The Commission on October 17–18, 2008, concluded that the offence of blasphemy should be abolished, and that in democratic countries it was neither necessary nor desirable to create an offence of religious insult (insult to religious feelings) without the element of incitement to hatred as an essential component.

5. Racism in Arab Lands

Robert Fisk, whose anti-Israeli credentials endear him to critics of the Jewish State, wrote in an article in *The Independent* on May 7, 2012, of the pious silence by the politicians, prelates, and businessmen of Arab countries about the treatment of Asian domestic servants and discrimination against migrant labor, male and female.

The dirty little secret is finally out. Discrimination, intolerance, and racism in the Arab world persist in many forms: they affect women, all non-Muslims, dark-skinned people, blacks, would-be refugees, and migrants. Among those groups and peoples that have been denied complete or some political and civil rights are Kurds, the non-Arab people whose language belongs to the Iranian group; Berbers, the pre-Arab native people of North Africa; Turkmen, who speak their own language; the Christian Copts in Egypt; the Assyrians or Assyro-Chaldeans in Iraq, subject to both ethnic and religious persecution; and Jews. Christians and Jews are still regarded as *dhimmis* (protected people), defined in different ways but usually as second-class citizens. Extreme Islamists, regarding them as infidels, have used violence against many, including the Copts and the Bahais, as well as against Jews.

Recent years have seen even stronger examples of discrimination than is customary: the slaughter in Darfur; the massacre of Kurds by Saddam Hussein and their persecution by Syria and Turkey; the Algerian government repression of the Kaybles; the maintenance of apartheid of the Zaghawa people in the Sudan, especially in Darfur; the killing in July 2012 of the entire community of Bodo inhabitants of Takimari, in northeast India, by Muslims who killed the inhabitants, looted, and set fire to their homes. A reasonable calculation is that over the last twenty years more than 1.5 million black Christians have been killed or expelled from Southern Sudan, or are enslaved by the Islamist regime in Khartoum.

In his unjustly neglected book, *Race and Slavery in the Middle East*, Bernard Lewis recounted that many of the stories in the Arabian Nights portray blacks as slaves and as second-class citizens, while Arabs are "white." The Egyptian story is not a pleasant one for a variety of reasons. Egyptian Christian Copts, who have been present in the country for more than sixteen hundred years, now number about eight million. They are treated as second-class citizens and denied senior jobs. Their situation is likely to worsen now the Muslim Brotherhood and the Salafis have won the election with 70 percent of the seats in new parliament. Individual Copts and their churches have already been attacked. The Virgin Church in Assiut in Upper Egypt was burned. Copts have been sentenced to prison for allegedly insulting the Prophet. About two hundred thousand Egyptian Christians have tried to get visas to come to US.

Before he became Egyptian president, Anwar Sadat, who was dark skinned, was insulted as Nasser's "black poodle." Blacks suffer from discrimination in many countries, but Egypt has a long history of it. In recent years Egyptians have attacked black Africans. Riot police in 2005 cleared a camp of 2,500 Sudanese refugees, mostly from Darfur, at the Egyptian border with Israel. The Egyptians have killed numbers of African refugees trying to reach Israel. Black Africans report verbal harassment and negative language, such as being called "oonga boonga" or *samara* (black), as well as physical attacks in the streets by the public and by law enforcement officials in Egypt. Blacks have been stopped for arbitrary identity checks on the basis of skin color, or have faced arbitrary roundups.

In Basra, Iraq, blacks are treated contemptuously, as people in street talk call them *abd* (slaves). In Yemen, darker skinned individuals are known as *al-akhdam* (the servants). Kuwait has shown similar hostility to blacks. Two million black African migrants were treated as virtual slaves in Libya. Though slavery was officially abolished in Mauritania in 1981, it is probable that some 15 percent of its population is still enslaved.

Discrimination is rampant in the economic area. In the United Arab Emirates, the federation of seven emirates, the most well-known of which is Dubai, attractive to tourists with its high-rise buildings and luxury resorts. Tourists are unaware that the 2.5 million migrant workers in the country compose 80 percent of the population and 95 percent of the workforce. As the major group in the construction business they are treated terribly, a form of bonded labor or in essence slavery, in spite of the alleged UAE adherence to the 1965 International Convention on the Elimination of all Forms of Racial Discrimination. The migrant workers are abused by very low wages, years of debts to recruitment agencies, hazardous working conditions that result in a high rate of death and injuries.

Above all, there is outright slavery. Mauritania officially abolished slavery for a third time in 2007, but the legislation has not been enforced. We know Mauritania as an unpredictable country, one of the few countries and organizations that, like Yasser Arafat and the PLO, supported Saddam Hussein in the Gulf War in 1991. Today, some half a million are still believed to be enslaved in the country; the Haratin is the hereditary slave caste that speaks Arabic, the language of their masters. Similarly, slavery still exists in Yemen, in the provinces of Hudaydah and Hajja in the North, though it was officially abolished in 1962.

In contrast, the current Israeli story is more heartening. More than 120,000 of the Ethiopian Beta Israel community now live in Israel with full civil and political rights. Some are in mobile-home camps, but the majority are in towns and cities, helped by generous government loans or low-interest mortgages. Undoubtedly, problems such as a high unemployment rate exist in the attempt of Ethiopians, coming from a less developed society to become integrated into Israeli society. They have language problems and arrive with a low level of education. It is encouraging that they are beginning to participate in Israeli political and social life, to enter higher educational institutions, and to take positions in public bodies, including the diplomatic service. One Ethiopian woman was appointed as ambassador to her country of origin. A twenty-one-year-old Ethiopian born woman was crowned Miss Israel in 2013, and she named Martin Luther King, Jr. as one of her role models. Even the most prejudiced critics of Israel will hesitate to call these remarkable stories an illustration of racism.

6. Europe and the Coming Universal Caliphate

By her stream of books and articles over the last thirty years Bat Ye'or, an independent scholar not connected with any ideological or political group nor identified with any partisan organization, has made a singular and challenging contribution to the discussion of the historic and present role of Islam in politics and society, primarily in Europe but also elsewhere. Throughout that long literary career she has written on various subjects, but most important have been the works on the treatment of non-Muslims, or *dhimmis,* in countries under Islamic rule, and on the nature and impact of that Islamic rule.

Her writings are not only commentaries of a scholarly character and strong observations of an original kind, but they are also very much interrelated with and emanate from her personal history. This is the poignant story of a young Jewish woman forced to leave her native Egypt as the Jewish community that had existed in that country for over 2,600 years came to an end. Bat Ye'or chronicled that community in an early book in 1971, *The Jews of Egypt.*

If Bat Ye'or has been a formidable and courageous figure in discussion of Islamic activities, she has also been a controversial and politically incorrect one, whose work has sometimes been found by more conventional critics to be strident. It is understood that not everyone will agree with her assertions and her resolute conclusions and policy recommendations. It is equally clear that her arguments and analysis are presented strongly and clearly, sometimes emphatically, and with exact references, accumulation of accurate data, and a scholarly apparatus. In the present age of political correctness, when criticism of Islamic activities or even commentary on them in Western countries has been subjected to various forms of censorship or denial, and even violent personal assault, it is refreshing to read Bat Ye'or's well presented, stimulating, and insistent thoughts, and frequently her unfashionable views. Even if one is not always in agreement with them, it is salutary to read, consider, and take them into account.

Bat Ye'or began her original approach with the first of her major works, *The Dhimmi,* published in 1980, in which she provided a historical depiction of the texts of Islamic theologians and jurists and an account of the testimonies of eyewitnesses in various Islamic countries on the treatment of their non-Muslim populations, Christians and Jews. She extended her thoughts on this issue in further writings using pertinent Islamic documents.

In these works she challenged the mainstream position on the question held by many scholars. One of them, Mark Cohen, expresses this position in a number of writings, especially in his book *Under Crescent and Cross: the Jews in the Middle Ages.* The general argument by Cohen and others is that non-Muslims under Muslim rule were tolerated, though not treated in benign fashion, and were considered "protected people" who were guaranteed security of life and property, communal autonomy with their own leaders and judges and able to abide by their own laws in personal and family matters, and relatively free practice of religion. Though *dhimmis* were treated unequally in relations between them and Muslims, it is often argued that Jewish individuals were treated with more tolerance in Islamic countries than in countries under Christian rule. The orthodox view is that both Jews and Christians, in return for being "protected people" by Muslims, accepted their subordinate status as second-class subjects and the restrictions: taxes at higher rates than those for Muslims, tolls and customs duties.

Bat Ye'or, on the contrary, though agreeing that the condition of Jews in Islamic countries has varied, takes a more negative view of that condition and argues that the mainstream view is largely a myth. She argues that the myth started in the nineteenth century, when the Ottoman Empire, self-described as a tolerant Islamic regime, proclaimed it was the most suitable regime to rule Christians of the Balkans. Providing source data and analysis of that data, she holds that the condition of Jews was in general one of insecurity, humiliation, and subjection to a repressive system of rule over them. In rejecting the usually accepted view of the tolerant treatment of Jews under Islamic rule, she put forward and made familiar the term *dhimmitude*, the institutional subjection throughout history of non-Muslims to Islamic power and discrimination against them, in her path-breaking book *Islam and Dhimmitude*, published in 2002.

That subjection she argued involves fear and insecurity on the part of non-Muslims who were obliged to accept their condition of humiliation. She sees that condition as the outcome of Islamic belief and law that stems from the eighth century on. At its basis is the doctrine and jurisdiction of *jihad*, defined differently as struggle, striving, or holy war. This flows from three sources: the Koran, the *Hadiths* (the words and deeds attributed to the Prophet Muhammad), and the biographies of the Prophet.

For Bat Ye'or, *jihad* is central to the development of Islamic countries and to the requirement to spread Islam through the world by peaceful means or by war. She emphasizes this requirement for Muslims that the *Dar al-Islam* (the House of Islam) in which Islamic law prevails must according to doctrine overcome the countries containing infidels, the *Dar al-Harb* (the House of War).

Perhaps more important and pertinent for readers today than the historical argument in Bat Ye'or's writings is her assertion that the condition of non-Muslims remains the same and is still apparent in present-day practices in Muslim countries that apply or are inspired by Sharia (Islamic) law. Those practices are qualitatively different from Western conceptions of human rights and equality. Her challenging conclusion is that the Islamic emphasis on *Sharia* law and on *jihad* implies and even demands perpetual war against those who will not submit to Islam.

Bat Ye'or applies this line of thought to current affairs, concentrating on Europe. In her previous book *Eurabia, the Euro-Arab Axis,* published in 2005, she began an intensive study of the complicated and intense relationship between the countries of the European Union and Arab states, using the term Eurabia as a shorthand description of that relationship to indicate the increasing influence of Islam on European political and social life. Others may have been aware of this influence, but Bat Ye'or was the first scholar to dwell on and point out the exact details of that relationship. This began as a political reality in 1973, with informal alliances between the then nine countries of the European Community (soon to be renamed the European Union) and the Mediterranean Arab states. The relationship became more formal with the creation of the European-Arab Dialogue (EAD) in Paris in 1974, and the establishment of the Parliamentary Association for European-Arab Cooperation, with over six hundred members from European political parties who would consult with Arab representatives to provide an agenda for policy proposals by both sides.

The proposals led to cooperation and collaboration by Europeans and Arabs, through specially created organizations—diplomatic, parliamentary, and economic—on a wide range of issues; trade, media, culture, school textbooks, youth associations, tourism, immigration, and foreign policy. This interaction has resulted from a mixture of economic, political, and ideological factors: mutual concerns about oil supplies; Arab markets; European interest in Arab industrial development; political support in general for the Palestinians in the conflict with Israel, which they have criticized disproportionately; and a frequent anti-American viewpoint.

At the heart of Bat Ye'or's line of reasoning is her criticism of the Islamic voice and presence in Europe and her warning of its pernicious influence and of the resulting subservience of a considerable number of European politicians and media outlets. She envisages, not the hoped-for moderation of Islamic extremism or the Europeanization of Islam that some anticipate, but rather the Islamization of Europe, reflected in current European behavior and way of thinking. She does not sanitize the character of Islamic political culture. Nor does she minimize the extent of the appeasement currently displayed by European personalities in deference to Islamic interests.

At its harshest, this point of view would suggest that Europe, if its present activities continue in this same direction, will be lost to Islam. Europe, for her, is being transformed into Eurabia, a term first used in the mid-1970s by a French publication pressing for common European-Arab policies and advocating European support for Arab anti-Israeli policies. Eurabia is thus the enemy of Europe, though she holds that it is not agreeable to the majority of Europeans. It is, however, an ideology and a strategy for promoting an alliance between the European Union (EU) and the Arab world, which affects EU foreign and security policies and encourages automatic criticism of Israel. The danger today is that Islam is having an increasing impact on European life, not only in policy matters but also in the establishment of Islamic cultural and political centers in European cities, and in promoting the maintenance of the ties of Muslim immigrants with their homelands. European fashionable concepts of multiculturalism have aided this by suggesting that Muslims not become integrated into EU societies but rather remain participants in coexisting parallel communities.

Her new work, *Europe, Globalization, and the Coming Universal Caliphate,* continues, brings up to date, and expands the essential argument and analysis of the previous book, *Eurabia,* that Europe is not only being subdued and is on the way to succumbing to Islamic authorities and concerns, but is also acquiescing in its own subordination. She now argues that Europe has lost its moral compass in its apathy and reluctance to defend liberal democracy or unwillingness to recognize the true nature of Islamic terrorism and to act against it. Europe is renouncing or caring little for its Judeo-Christian identity. Though this work is relatively short, it contains a detailed presentation and a wealth of precise information not readily available elsewhere of the statements, activities, the political and diplomatic pressures by Islamic organizations and activists, the ambitious and unceasing proposals and intentions, and the supine response, with rare exceptions, of European leaders, groups, and media.

Bat Ye'or points out the various methods employed by Islamic bodies to achieve their objective: implanting Islamic values and traditions on Europe and the West in general; fostering the increasingly large Muslim immigration into the EU; and working to achieve ultimately the conversion of Europe into the Islamic orbit. She also makes clear the way in which globalization and concepts such as multiculturalism and relativism have helped the growing Islamization. She has challenging passages on the Islamic denigration of both Christianity and Judaism and on the Islamic threat to the State of Israel. It is also welcoming to find that she indicates the deliberate use made by Muslims to ascribe an attitude of Islamophobia to those who are critical of Islamic activities.

Even more welcome is Bat Ye'or's portrait of contemporary affairs. The EU has allowed large and increasing Muslim immigration into its countries, paid large sums of money to the Mediterranean Union and to the Palestinian Authority (PA), which it generally supports. She indicates the significance of the creation in December 2003 of the "Dialogue between peoples and cultures in the Euro-Mediterranean Area," a dialogue which is being implemented by a foundation purportedly reinforcing mutuality and solidarity. The EU has not taken heed of the prominent role of the Organization of the Islamic Conference (OIC), a religious and political organization representing fifty-six countries and the PA that nominally has a community of 1.3 billion throughout the world. Bat Ye'or sees the OIC as attempting to restore the Caliphate, which, deriving from the feud over the succession to the Prophet after he died in 632, became in medieval times the supreme sovereign of the Islamic empire, the head of both the religion and the state. She regards the intended Universal Caliphate, unifying Islamic countries into a single Islamic state, as the supreme controlling authority, one inspired by the Sharia and Islamic culture and values and aiming at the Islamization of the world. The OIC is concerned with Muslim immigrants in the EU and it interacts with European authorities through a variety of mechanisms including the Alliance of Civilizations.

In assessing the value of Bat Ye'or's work it is useful to put it in the context of contemporary life. As discussed in previous essays, European countries, as well as the United States and other countries, have witnessed and been subject to many examples of Islamic assaults against critics, including attempts to limit free speech and death threats, sometimes carried out. Some of the more egregious ones may be mentioned again: The assassination of the Dutch politician Pim Fortuyn in 2002 by an individual claiming he was denigrating Muslims. The death sentence imposed on the novelist Salman Rushdie in 1989 for being "disrespectful" of the Prophet. The prosecution of another politician, Geert Wilders, for critical remarks about Islam and the Koran. The murder of Dutch filmmaker Theo van Gogh in Amsterdam in 2004 by a Muslim. The cancellation of the production in Berlin of Mozart's opera *Idomeneo* because it included a scene indicating the severed head of Muhammad. The attacks on the Danish newspaper that had published cartoons of Muhammad. The self-censorship by Reuters and the Associated Press in refusing to refer to the perpetrators of 9/11 as terrorists. The introductions in the United Nations and other international bodies of resolutions banning "defamation of religion" in the attempt to prevent criticism of Islam.

Bat Ye'or's work therefore has noteworthy contemporary significance as the Western world confronts the danger of *jihad* and the fear of *dhmittude*. Her work is a virtual call to arms as she sees Western civilization in danger, a danger that many Westerners do not fully comprehend. She warns that if the process of Islamization continues in Europe, the United States will be challenged by an emerging Euro-Arab continent linked to the Muslim world and with considerable political and economic power in international affairs. If she occasionally overstates her case, there is no gainsaying her honesty, intellectual courage, and scrupulously accurate scholarship in confronting what she perceives as the myths of conventional wisdom and indicating the mindset of reluctance and apathy of those who ought to be more aware of present danger. It is well to ponder her argument that people hold on to destructive myths as if they were the only guarantee for their survival when, in fact, they are the path to destruction.

7. The Sad Plight of Christians in the Middle East

At this time of uncertainty and political vacuum in the Arab and Muslim countries in the Middle East, when more light should be shined on the disturbing and deteriorating situation of Christians in those countries, it is surprising and a commentary on the political climate in Washington that the US Commission on International Religious Freedom, created in 1998 to advise the president and Congress on the plight of persecuted religious groups, is being closed. The president is now therefore unable to be given such advice and to take specific action—such as economic or other sanctions, travel bans on government officials, and limits put on foreign aid—regarding countries designated by the Commission as of "particular concern" because of religious persecution in their territory.

Christians, of course, have been present in these countries for two millennia; they are not an exogenous entity intruding into a homogeneous Arab Muslim world. Christian communities and individuals have played a vital role in the Middle East, the cradle of Christianity as of other religions. Pope Benedict XVI, speaking in Castelgandolfo on September 2, 2007, is not alone in warning that "Churches in the Middle East are threatened in their very existence."

The Arab countries have not abided by the UN Declaration of Human Rights (Article 18) that "Everyone has the right to freedom of thought, conscience, and religion." Discrimination against non-Muslims has always been present in the Arab Muslim world. In the Ottoman Empire, as elsewhere, Christians were second-class subjects, except for a short period after 1856 when the Sultan conceded the principle of equality of the law to all subjects. The current reality is that Christians in the Middle East, probably numbering about fourteen million, are now facing aggravating hostility and persecution of various kinds. The Christians and their institutions—in a context of internecine wars in the area, a falling birthrate in the midst of an increase in the number of Muslims, and the political rise of Islamist groups—face physical brutality, destruction of their churches, discrimination in basic rights as well as in employment opportunities, boycotts of their businesses, and malignity in many forms of popular culture, television programs, and school textbooks. They are unable to practice or have difficulty in practicing their faith and fear prosecution by law for offences of apostasy—for which the penalty according to some interpretations of Sharia law is death, and blasphemy—devices intended to intimidate or prevent critical speech.

Even those regimes and ideas, such as Nasserism and Arab national-ism, that in the past exemplified to some extent moderation in religious matters regarding Christians now play a lesser role. Increasing violence and brutality against Christians is now evident in almost all the Arab countries except Jordan, under the relatively benign King Abdullah. Even there, those Muslims who converted to Christianity face severe discrimination.

The Christian plight is shown by the continuing decline in their numbers in the Middle East. In all, the Christians, Copts, Maronites, Assyrians, Greek Orthodox, and Armenians number less than twelve million, or 6 percent of the total population.

In Egypt the Christian Copts, members of a church dating from AD 451 and doctrinally similar to the Eastern Orthodox Church, are about 10 percent of the eighty-four million population. They suffer from attacks on them individually—in recent years over two hundred have been killed—and by assaults on their churches. The most egregious were the murder of Copts in January 2011; the attack on New Year's Day on the church in Alexandria, the worst attack in a decade, which resulted in twenty-one dead and seventy-nine injured; and the brutal police action against Christians protesting in central Cairo, in which twenty-seven were killed and over three hundred injured. Other churches have been burned, as in the Aswan area, or have been cordoned off. In a country that is now witnessing the rising influence of the Muslim Brotherhood (Freedom and Justice party) and the more extreme Salafi (al-Nour party), the Copts fear they are an endangered species.

In Iraq, violence against Christians, who have been present there since the second century, continues with killings and kidnappings. In the last five years eighteen priests and two bishops have been kidnapped. The Archbishop of Mosul was kidnapped and killed in 2008. Since 2004, over seventy churches, forty-two of them in Baghdad, have been subjected to some form of attack. A recent notorious instance was the slaughter of fifty-eight Christians during evening mass at the Syrian Catholic Cathedral in Baghdad in October 2010. Churches have been bombed in Baghdad and Mosul, seven on one day in July 2009 in Baghdad. Iraqi Christians once numbered about 1.5 million; they are now fewer than 250,000.

The intolerant theocracy in Iran, the constitution of which states that all laws must be based on the Islamic Sharia, has in the past year arrested over three hundred Christians, some of whom remain in prison. Christians, about one hundred thousand in 1979, are now almost nonexistent in the country's population of seventy-five million.

Saudi Arabia is the fount of Wahhabism, the thirteenth-century militant branch of Islam, revived in the eighteenth century by Sheikh Wahhab, which is critical of Muslims who are said to have abandoned the true faith. This extreme Islamic group argues that Islam must be restored to what it was at the time of the Prophet, and this should be achieved by action. As a result, Saudi Arabia is probably the most repressive Arab country because of the total ban on religious practice by non-Muslims and even the prohibition on bringing a Bible into the country. Christian prayer, even in private, is forbidden. School textbooks promote religious intolerance in general, as well as antisemitism. This bigotry is made even more unacceptable when witnessing the large sums spent by Saudi Arabia in building and sponsoring mosques and madrassahs abroad.

In November 2012, Saudi Arabia officially inaugurated an International Center for Inter-Religious and International-Cultural Dialogue in Vienna. Whether this is a genuine effort to foster dialogue or a propaganda device of cynical realpolitik to spread Wahhabism, using as a base a city that prevented in 1529 and 1683 the Muslim Ottoman Empire from conquering it, remains an open question. It is, however, an enticing notion that a country that does not permit any church, synagogue, or place of worship of any religion within its borders should suggest fostering a dialogue.

Not surprisingly, it is only in Israel that Christians of all denominations are able to practice their religion as they wish. They not only have full legal rights and religious freedom, they also play a role in political and social affairs; that role includes a justice of the Israeli Supreme Court, members of Parliament, and diplomatic representatives. Moreover, contrary to the experience in the Arab countries, the Christian population in Israel has increased fourfold in the last fifty years.

To escape persecution in the Arab countries, some Christians have converted to Islam; reports are that a considerable number of university graduates in Egypt have done so. Many have supported secular political groups in the hope of being protected. But above all, Christians have emigrated from those countries—some voluntarily but most because of the violence, threats, inability to practice their religion, and intimidation. The Arab countries are almost *judenrein*; now they are becoming devoid of Christians. The fate of those Christians will be an important litmus test of the consequences, agreeable or not, of the events that began in the Arab spring. Will the winds of change in the fluid politics of the Middle East allow the existence of a cultural and religious mosaic there, and a religious and political pluralism in which Arab Muslims can recognize the authentic status of citizenship and equal rights for non-Muslims? The West, especially the United States, should not be complacent about this.

8. Eyeless in Gaza

The proclamation issued by the Third International Christian Zionist Congress meeting in Jerusalem in February 1996 expressed its deep concern about the increasing threat posed by radical Islam to Israel, to Christian minorities in the Middle East, and to the world. By contrast, the communiqué issued by the eight Catholic bishops and one auxiliary bishop visiting the Holy Land as part of the Holy Land Coordination in January 2012 expressed no such concern.

The Catholic bishops, who included those from Evry (France), Liverpool (England), and Tucson (US), did appeal for tolerance and courageous leadership and the need for resumption of dialogue between the Palestinian Authority and Israel. But they also pointed out they had seen for themselves "occupation, fear and frustration dominate the life of people across the land." They made no critical comment about the validity of the information given them by Archbishop Fouad Twai, Latin Patriarch of Jerusalem, that the separation barrier, presumably meaning the fence built by Israel for security purposes, had caused people to emigrate, caused them to sell homes in the West Bank, and led to an increase in demand for housing in Jerusalem.

The most disconcerting remarks made by the bishops were those by Michel Dubost, who asked prisoners in his hometown of Evry to pray for people in Gaza, which he said was a large prison, and by William Kenney, auxiliary bishop in Birmingham, England, who asserted that two of the largest "open prisons" in the world were Bethlehem and the Gaza Strip.

It is saddening that leaders of the mainstream Churches, Catholic and Protestant, unlike Evangelicals, have expressed such little concern about the fate of Christians in the Middle East, let alone registered any support for Israel in its efforts to deal with the incessant attacks on it.

This lack of support, and animosity at its worst, can be illustrated by recent and forthcoming activities by the Christ at the Checkpoint conferences organized by the Bethlehem Bible College in partnership with the Holy Land Trust and by the World Council of Churches. The first Christ at the Checkpoint conference took place in 2010, and the third is to be held in March 2012.

The thrust of these conferences became clear from the outset. In 2010 a number of pronouncements were made. At that time Rev. Stephen Sizer, vicar of Christ Church, Virginia Water, Surrey, England, who was the main organizer of the 2012 conference, in his denunciation of Israel supported the call of the journalist Helen Thomas for Jews to "get the hell out of Palestine." The Lutheran priest, Mitri Raheb, acknowledged that a DNA test would show the similarity in origin of King David and Jesus, both of whom were present in Bethlehem, but no such similarity existed with Benjamin Netanyahu, who he said came from Eastern Europe, not Palestine. The British Anglican Rev. Colin Chapman recognized that Muhammad had bad experiences with the Jews of Medina, and therefore it must seem to Palestinian Muslims as if the Jews of the modern period were simply repeating the hostile behavior of Jews many centuries earlier toward the Prophet.

At the 2011 conference, Naim Ateek, former Palestinian head of the Sabeel Ecumenical Liberation Theology Center in Jerusalem, compared the fate of Jesus on the cross to that of present Palestinians. He saw Palestine as one huge Golgotha in which the Israeli government cruci-fixion system was operating daily. Elsewhere, he argues, with curious theology, "The original sin is the work of the violence of the Israeli occupation of the Gaza Strip and the West Bank." In his book *Justice, and Only Justice*, Ateek, calling for a liberation theology, contended that the Bible is a problem for Palestinian Christians because of its use in justifying Zionism.

The March 2012 conference attracted a considerable number of US theologians, especially Samuel Rodriguez, head of the US National Hispanic Christian Leadership Conference, and Tony Campolo, who was for a time a spiritual adviser to Bill Clinton, as well as others such as David Kim, head of the World Evangelical Alliance .

In connection with this conference, a Bethlehem Call manifesto had been published. The manifesto speaks of the Israeli occupation that has "reached a level of almost unimaginable and sophisticated criminality. This includes the slow yet deliberate and systematic ethnic cleansing and the genocide of Palestinians and Palestine as well as the strangling of the Palestinian economy." Taking it for granted that Israel is an apartheid state, it deplores the failure to resist the Israeli government; such silence "makes us accomplices in crimes against humanity."

This excessive rhetoric in an anti-Israeli document is familiar in recent publications of these mainstream Churches. The Bethlehem Call was preceded by the Amman Call of June 2007, which called for the end of Israeli occupation of Palestine. Following it was the Bern Perspective of 2008, issued after a conference co-hosted by the World Council of Churches, which wrote of the "decades of dispossession, discrimination, illegal occupation, violence and bloodshed in Palestine-Israel." The document recognized the distinction between the Israel of the Bible and the modern State of Israel: references to Israel in the Bible should be seen as metaphorical.

The Kairos Palestinian document of December 2009 spoke, on behalf of "us Christian Palestinians," of the tragedy of the Palestinian people. The Amman Call was introduced in September 2007 to participants in the meeting of the World Council of Churches in the UN Advocacy Week in Geneva. All the churches and Christians in the world were urged by the Council—which claims a membership of 580,000 adherents in 349 Protestant and Orthodox churches—to stand against injustice and modern-day apartheid in the "occupied" Palestinian territories.

Inherent in the activity of the mainstream churches is this strong animus against Israel on political grounds. This is familiar, with all those in the international community who criticize or condemn Israel and call for its elimination. What is different and disturbing in the arguments used by some in those churches of supersessionism or replacement theology, that Jews no longer had the promises God had given them, that the church had replaced the people of Israel in God's plan, and that biblical references to Israel really refer to Christians. Most troubling is the argument that Jewish Israelis are crucifying Palestinians as Jews of old had crucified Jesus. Images of the establishment of the State of Israel are equated with the killing of Jesus. Those Christian adherents who argue this way are not only eyeless about the real treatment of Christians in Gaza, but also have lost focus in their vision of Middle East politics.

9. The Disquieting Treatment of Christians by the Palestinians

In the voluminous commentaries on the Middle East today, very little attention has been given to the sad fate of Christians in the Arab and Muslim countries. Even less attention has been paid to the contrast between the treatment of Christians in Israel and their treatment in Arab countries. In Israel Christians have religious freedom and their numbers have increased. In Arab countries the religious freedom of Christians is restricted and their number has been reduced because of harassment, fear, and persecution. It is well to remember the words of Martin Luther King: "In the end we will remember not the words of our enemies but the silence of our friends."

Christians have been a presence in the Middle East for two millennia. Hundreds of churches and monasteries were built after Constantine legalized Christianity in 313. Yet after the Islamic conquest in 638, Christians have been subjected to Arab and Muslim rule for centuries. Their status in the Ottoman Empire was that of *dhimmis,* non-Muslims who were protected but who were second-class citizens. In this millet system based on religious affiliation, Christians were tolerated but they were also in a state of perpetual humiliation, even of subjugation.

Population statistics today are questionable, census is difficult in the various countries of the Middle East, and demographic trends and accuracy of religious affiliation are political issues and must be treated with caution. However, it is evident that under Muslim rule Christians became a minority in the area of Palestine. In recent years the Christian population has declined not only numerically but also as a proportion of the overall population. This decline has been due to a number of factors: Christian emigration, a higher Muslim birthrate; poor economic conditions; the rise of Islamist groups, especially Hamas and Islamic Jihad; growing insecurity; the use made of Christian towns such as Beit

Jala as a base by Palestinian fighters for sniping against Israeli areas in Jerusalem; and Christian concern about their fate in the political future.

Critics of Israel have argued that the departure of Christians from the area of Palestine is due to the "Israeli occupation." No doubt measures taken by Israel for security reason have caused some economic difficulties and led to some departure. But the general accusation ignores the reality that two-thirds of Christian Arabs left the areas between 1949 and 1967, the period when Jordan occupied and annexed the West Bank, and Egypt controlled Gaza, years before Israel controlled those areas.

The discriminatory treatment of Christians by the Muslim majority and the consequences of continuing Arab hostility toward the State of Israel has led to increasing migration from the West Bank and Gaza, the areas controlled by Muslims. Christians in those two areas now account for only about forty thousand people, 1.5 percent of the total. The towns of Ramallah and Bethlehem, which depended on the Christian tourist and pilgrim trade, both lost their Christian majorities. In 1995, the number of Christians in Bethlehem was two-thirds of the population; today it is now less than 20 percent. According to the1947 census held by the British, there were twenty-eight thousand Christians in Jerusalem; in 1967, after nineteen years of Jordanian rule, there were eleven thousand. Today there are less than ten thousand. By contrast, the number of Christians in Israel has increased from 34,000 in 1949 and 120,000 in 1995 to over 180,000, now numbering about 9 percent of the Israeli Arab population, and 2 percent of the total population in all of Israel.

The Christian community in the West Bank and Gaza has a medium age of thirty-two compared with the Muslim median age of sixteen. By comparison with the Muslims, its members are older when they marry, have a lower fertility rate, are better educated, are twice as likely to have a university degree, have a higher income, and are more likely to be in white-collar and business professions.

Discrimination against, hostility toward, and intimidation of Christians by Palestinians has taken a number of forms. From 1949 to 1967, Jordan occupied the West Bank; its laws forbad Christians from buying land and houses in the Old City of Jerusalem; all schools were closed on Muslim holidays; mosques were deliberately built near churches. The Palestinian Authority formulated a Constitution in 2003 that declared that Islam was "the official religion." The Constitution also declares that in a Palestinian state the principles of Islamic Sharia law are to be the main source of legislation. The statement that "respect and sanctity of all other heavenly religions shall be maintained" is contradicted in practice by the attacks and condemnation of Christians in mosques, sermons, and publications of Islamic groups. Furthermore, the Palestinian legal and judicial system does not provide protection for Christian land owners and enforces discrimination in educational, cultural, and taxation policies.

More drastically, Christians have suffered direct harassment. They have been intimidated and maltreated; money has been extorted, land and property confiscated, and Christian women have been abused, raped, abducted and been subjected to forced marriages. Attempts have been made to impose the Islamic women's dress code on them. The Palestinian Authority has denied Christian, as well as Jewish, ties to Jerusalem. Christian holy sites have been disparaged or insulted. The Palestine Liberation Organization in July 1997 evicted monks and nuns from the Holy Trinity Monastery in Hebron. Palestinian gunmen positioned themselves in or near Christian homes, hotels, and churches during fighting against Israel. The most notorious example of Palestinian insult was the takeover on April 2, 2002, of the Church of the Nativity in Bethlehem by over 150 gunmen who used the Church to fire against Israeli soldiers, who out of respect for the Church did not return fire. Priests, monks, and nuns were essentially hostages of the Palestinians, who apparently stole gold and other property including prayer books.

Theft of Christian land and property as well as desecration of Christian institutions and disparagement of the religion has occurred. There are allegations of Christians being forced off their land by gangs upheld by a corrupt judiciary. Businesses have had to pay protection money to maintain their existence. Individuals who have converted to Christianity have been threatened. Armed Muslims in September 2005 crying "Allahu Akbar" attacked the Christian city of Taibe, setting fire to homes and businesses and destroying a statue of the Virgin Mary, after a Christian man dated a Muslim woman from a neighboring village. The woman was already dead, having been poisoned by her own family in an honor killing.

Christian graves in the Gaza Strip have been dug up. Anti-Christian graffiti has appeared, and Christian cemeteries and statues have been defaced. A Muslim mob in February 2002 attacked churches and Christian shops in Ramallah. The First Baptist Church of Bethlehem was firebombed on at least fourteen occasions, and the pastor, Naem

Khoury, was shot. In Gaza in June 2007 a leader of the Baptist Church, one of the oldest in the area, which contains Gaza's only Christian library, was kidnapped and murdered. The Sagrada Familia school in Gaza was fired, and the nun's building in the Convent of the Sisters of the Rosary in June 2007 was looted, and holy images and sacred books were burned.

In a speech in Paris, reported in *L'Osservatore Romano* on September 17, 2008, Pope Benedict XVI, concerned about developments in Muslim Middle East countries, suggested that they might consider the concept of "positive laicity," a term he borrowed from then French President Nicolas Sarkozy. The term refers to societies in which various religions should be allowed to exist, all of them separate from the state, and all treated in a positive fashion. The pope was conscious of the danger facing Christianity if Islamic fundamentalism is successful and theocratic Arab regimes are created. Unlike the Palestinian Muslim treatment of its Christian minority, Israeli policy is built on a separation of religion and state in a society that is pluralistic and upholds freedom of religions and human rights. In view of the comparative records of Palestinian Muslim and Israeli actions toward their Christian minorities, Israel comes closer to the positive laicity suggested by the pope and President Sarkozy than Muslim Palestinians.

10. Evangelicals: Righteous Gentiles for Israel

Jews in democratic countries are disproportionately more disposed than other groups to prefer the left spectrum of political and cultural affairs. That spectrum is in general unfriendly to the evangelical Christian movement. Therefore, it is not surprising that only 20 percent of Jewish Americans hold a favorable opinion of the Christian right, the members of which tend to be favorable to the Republican Party. Yet it is strange when one considers that fact that evangelical Christians have been strong supporters of Israel. A reasonable conclusion might be that for many American Jews, social and cultural values are more significant than support for Israel. Clearly, differences between many Jews and Christian—especially evangelical—churches exist on social questions such as abortion, women's rights, gay and lesbian rights, and political ones such as separation of church and state. Equally, such differences do not and should not prevent a cordial and supportive relationship between those churches and the State of Israel. Jews, inside and outside Israel, should willingly acknowledge the helpful role of evangelical Christians.

It is evident that many Christian evangelicals have supported Israel politically and financially since its creation. Indeed, evangelicals may claim to be the strongest single group supporting Israel. Theologically, a considerable number of evangelicals believe that Jews must possess their historic right before Jesus can return. With the return of Jews, God's Chosen People, to Israel and the Holy Land, evangelicals await the coming of the apocalypse, the return of Christ, and the conversion of Jews.

This view results from dispensationalism, a distinctive way of understanding the prophecies in the Bible: an interpretation of history as a number of dispensations or epochs, each of which reflects a particular way in which God deals with people. Specifically, Israel is seen as playing a key role in events that will lead to the Second Coming of Jesus Christ. Accordingly, the holders of this view support the existence of the State of Israel and believe it will play a role in world affairs. Among the groups holding this position are the National Unity Coalition for Israel, Eagle Wings, Christian Friends of Israel, the National Leadership Conference for Israel, Christians United for Israel, which claims a membership of over one million, and Bridges for Peace.

Evangelical supporters sometimes refer to the Biblical passage in Ezekiel (36: 24). Ezekiel, writing at the time of the Babylonian captivity, declared that God was speaking to the house of Israel: "I will gather you out of all countries, and will bring you into your own land." Evangelical support also results from Christian appreciation of contemporary Israel as a democratic nation, exemplifying individual freedom, the rule of law, and the embrace of modernity in a geographical area devoid of these attributes. Endorsement also results from the realistic understanding that Israel has been subject to constant attack by modern Pharaohs in the Middle East and elsewhere who call, directly and indirectly, not only for boycott and divestment of the State but also for the elimination of the State of Israel.

For evangelicals, religious and political beliefs merge. God maintains the Biblical covenant with the Jewish people, though they were and are not perfect, and the religious belief in Jewish sovereignty over the Holy Land is deeper than the geopolitical argument. However, some parts of that covenant regarding the exact territory of the Promised Land are more controversial than others in concrete interpretation for evangelicals. In particular, Genesis (15:18)—"Unto thy seed have I given this land, from the river of Egypt unto the great river, the river Euphrates"—is a statement open for discussion. Public opinion surveys

183

show that evangelicals are likely to say that religious belief was the single biggest influence leading them to sympathize with Israel, to believe that God gave the land of Israel to the Jews, that Israel fulfills the biblical prophecy about the second coming of Jesus, and to declare that they are more sympathetic to Israel than to the Palestinians.

Surveys also show that in the first decade of the twenty-first century the greatest increase in support of Israel of any religious group came from evangelicals. That support may partly result from the attempt to force the Second Coming. It is more likely to stem from a variety of factors: God's promise to bless those who bless the Jews; appreciation that Jews provided the basis of Christianity; remorse over the Holocaust and over the past animosity of Christian churches toward Jews; the belief that God will judge people on how they treat Jews; the appreciation of the democratic and religious free society that exists in Israel.

Christian Churches, as a result of international pressure organized by Palestinians and their allies, now have to consider resolutions calling for boycott, divestment, and sanctions against Israel. Unlike the Evangelicals, mainstream Protestant churches have been sympathetic to Palestinian Christians and the Palestinian narrative for some time and have sought to raise awareness of what they call persecution or oppression of the Palestinians. Increasingly, they recommend economic action against Israel and those who do business with it.

The Evangelical Lutheran Church in America represented the evangelical position when it rejected divestment proposals regarding Israel in 2007 and 2011. By contrast, mainstream religious adherents have differed on this question. To its credit, the United Methodist Church, in spite of considerable pressure, on May 2, 2012, at its meeting in Tampa rejected a resolution calling for the Church to join the Palestinian-inspired boycott, divestment, and sanctions campaign against three companies trading with Israel. The UMC had rejected similar resolutions at its previous General Conference in 2008. The UMC in 2012 by a vote of two to one opposed action against Caterpillar, which supplies bulldozers to Israel; Hewlett-Packard, which provides advanced biometric technology; and Motorola Solutions, which supplies surveillance equipment. Those in favor of boycott might remember that the Palestinian Authority also buys Caterpillar products.

However, the UMC spoke with an uncertain voice. By a sixty to forty vote, it did adopt a resolution recommending nations should prohibit the import of products manufactured in "Israeli settlements on Palestinian land." It is perhaps a warning sign that members of the UMC in some geographical areas did support both boycott and divestment resolutions against Israel. Palestinian pressure attempted to influence the vote at the general assembly of the Presbyterian Church USA in June 2012 on a divestment resolution. Though the assembly did not do so, the leaders of the Presbyterians, together with other Christian leaders, in October 2012 called on Congress to reconsider giving aid to Israel because of alleged human rights violations.

Mainstream American churches and missionaries in the past, fostering Arab nationalism for religious reasons, promoted anti-Zionism, if not always antisemitism. The Protestant churches have passed resolutions to divest their funds from companies selling military and security equipment to Israel. The existence of Israel as a legitimate state is now being challenged in a number of ways and a variety of media: by a Palestinian-inspired offensive to portray Palestinians as suffering from human rights abuses and colonial crimes committed by Israel; by the Electronic Intifada, a Chicago-based news website; by the United Methodist Kairos Response; by individuals and groups, such as writers and academics like Grace Halsell, Timothy Weber, Tony Campolo, and Gary Burge (Wheaton College), as well as attendees, especially Stephen Sizer, the anti-Zionist Church of England priest, at the Christ at the Checkpoint Conferences organized by the Bethlehem Bible College.

The argument of individuals and groups of this kind is based on a number of political factors stemming from acceptance of the fallacious Palestinian narrative of victimhood and unending Israeli oppression of Palestinians, rather than on theological issues. Like the Palestinians, they identify Jesus as a Palestinian rather than a Jew, and one who was oppressed and persecuted as a Palestinian rather than as a Jew. They see Israel, on the other hand, as responsible for the unending violence in the Middle East and refusal to agree to Palestinian rights. They minimize the existence of antisemitism and ignore Islamist attacks on Israel. They refuse to accept Israel, now in existence for sixty-four years, as an independent, self-governing entity. Instead, they advocate the creation of a Palestinian state, sometimes alongside the State of Israel, but often in place of it.

It is therefore heartening to learn of those evangelicals such as the members of the Pentecostal-Charismatic Faith Church in Hungary, the largest evangelical church in Europe, who are opposing this attempt to disparage and to delegitimize the State of Israel.

An interesting individual who has issued an important rejoinder to the disparagers of Israel is Dr. Kenneth Meshoe, member of the South

African Parliament, president of the African Christian Democratic Party, and pastor of a South African Church. What is particularly significant about pastor Meshoe is that he, as a black South African, on a number of occasions has nullified the lie spread by the Palestinian narrative that Israel is an apartheid state. At the international conference of legislators held in Budapest on October 31, 2011, he replied to the kind of fulminations published by the Electronic Intifada that Israeli actions are "the epitome of apartheid" and aim at the systematic destruction of Palestinian society. He describes those who promulgate the lie of Israel as apartheid as ignorant of the true nature of the impact of apartheid on black South Africans, an experience quite different from that of Palestinians in nature and intensity. South African blacks were treated as second-class citizens and were denied basic human rights. By contrast, he points out that in Israel there are no laws discriminating against people on the basis of their color or on the basis of their religion. Palestinians have not suffered the pain of apartheid experienced by black South Africans.

Pastor Meshoe amplifies his general remarks by specific examples. He calls attention to the fact that in South Africa there were separate modes of transport for blacks and whites; there were coaches in trains only for black people, and others only for whites. Segregation was present in schools, hospitals, public places, city parks, benches, chairs, beaches. No such segregation exists in Israel.

In view of this empirical evidence, why do members of some churches and their leaders argue that Israel is an apartheid state? Whatever the motive of these people, Palestinians have used this falsehood to persuade them to gain sympathy for their cause. By doing so, they and their allies in the churches as elsewhere—purportedly concerned with Palestinian suffering—are their own worst enemies. By maintaining the animosity against Israel, they are preventing a peaceful process of negotiation to resolve the conflict.

11. The Arab Spring and Reality

In a speech in Istanbul on March 18, 2012, Khaled Meshal, leader of Hamas, heralded the Arab spring as a milestone in the history of Muslims. He saw it as a fight against corruption, as aimed at honor, in favor of freedom, reform, and democracy, which would lead to economic growth and to political and economic development. Above all, it would also strengthen the unity of the Arabs against Israel, and therefore the Arab nations will strongly support the Palestinian cause against Zionist policies. For Meshal, Israel remains an invader state, a state of crime and terrorism, and the fight against it must be continued in political, diplomatic, press, and propaganda fields.

Meshal, following the current nonmilitary international campaign against Israel, shrewdly avoided any mention of violence and was in line with the ongoing activity of the international community to engage in the struggle against Israel by the use or misuse of the law and by a fallacious narrative of the inadequacies or deficiencies of Israel. However, he has not appreciated that the Arab spring will be a little late this year, a little late arriving. Expectations that the cries of freedom and democracy by demonstrators against the Arab regimes in Tunisia, Libya, Syria, and Yemen would lead to real political change and to the creation of democratic institutions have been dispelled by the realities of Arab societies and politics.

Among those realities are the downfall of four Arab rulers, in Tunisia, Egypt, Yemen, and Libya. The fight of Bashar al-Assad and his regime to retain power in Syria using the slogan "There is no God but Bashar" has been transformed into a brutal civil war, largely if not wholly between the minority Alawite regime and the Sunni majority population, in which other countries have become involved. By serendipity, another of these realities, occurring in the same week as Meshal's speech, was the decision emerging from the meeting of major tribal leaders, military commanders, and political figures in Benghazi, Libya. This group called for Cyrenaica, the eastern part of the country, to be a semi-autonomous state, called Barqa, from central Libya to the Egyptian border in the east and to Chad and Sudan in the south. It would have its own legislature, police, and courts, and Benghazi as its capital; the central government in Tripoli would control foreign policy, the army, and oil supplies.

This is a reminder that Libya was an artificial country created by Italy in December 1951 by combining three provinces: Tripolitania in the west, Cyrenaica in the east, and Fezzan in the southwest. Even more, it was a reminder that Libya, like many of the Arab states, was essentially a tribal society in which people were more loyal to their tribe than to the state. In Libya over 140 tribes and clans, interrelated through alliances, and of whom about 30 have influence on affairs, exist in a society with tribal feuds and divided by uneven distribution of oil wealth and polarization between rich and poor, by geographical tensions, and different rebel militias. To retain power, Gaddafi, who himself came from the Gadhadfa clan—which was allied with ten others by marriage, to which he gave special privileges—had coopted

187

tribes, persuading them with cash, various perks, and jobs, especially in the security services and military. He also controlled the military, well armed with four thousand tanks and other armored vehicles, four hundred combat aircraft, and twenty thousand portable surface-to-air missiles. He fell when part of the army split from him and joined the rebels or mercenaries in the country. The question now is how tribal loyalties will be expressed in any fair election.

The Libyan situation illustrates the issue of the major forces and the balance of power in Arab countries, between tribal leaders linked by family and blood; the army, previously the most stable institution based on honor and virility; and the Islamic mosque, a meeting place not only for religion but also for fraternity and the transmission of ideas and allegiances. Tribal alliances abound in Libya, Yemen, and Jordan. In Syria, suffering from the brutalities of the Alawi-dominated Bashar Assad regime in killing thousands of its own citizens, parts of the country are really tribal areas, hostile to the regime and getting aid and weapons from Sunni Muslim insurgents. On the other hand, Egypt from 1952 on has been dominated by the military: General Mohamed Neguib (1953–54); Colonel Gamal Abdel Nasser (1954–70); Colonel Anwar Sadat (1970–81); and General Hosni Mubarak (1981–2011). Even today it is not clear whether there will be in Egypt an alliance or relationship between the military, which refused to fire on the protesting crowds in the streets, and the Islamists.

The Arab spring, the term inappropriately borrowed by commentators from the Prague spring of 1968—the liberalization movement to free Czechoslovakia from the domination of the Soviet Union—started not with any similar political ideology of liberalization but from the self-immolation of a twenty-six-year-old street vender in Tunisia, and then rioting in Egypt. The consequent winds of change have varied in the different Arab countries and had unintended consequences. Two factors in the wind were surprising. One was the absence or lack of support for any anti-Israeli slogans. The other surprising factor about the outpouring of people in the street and the ending of entrenched regimes is that the activity, hardly a movement, had no leaders, no individual theorist inspiring it, and no real agenda or objectives other than the overthrow of the existing regimes, and a general aspiration for economic and political improvement. Mobilization and communication took place in diverse ways through the Internet, social networks, and cell phones, and an Arab version of Facebook, not through political manifestos.

Changes have occurred. Saudi Arabia, in spite of its intolerant Wahhabist adherents, has agreed to allow women to vote and run for municipal office, though they are still not allowed to drive. Elections have been held in Tunisia and Egypt and in the Gulf Cooperation Council countries. About a quarter of the new Tunisian legislature are women. But secularism is in crisis, and few could have envisaged that Islamic groups would have benefited from something they did not start and would emerge politically to the degree that they have. The Arab spring has become an Islamic spring.

In Tunis, the Islamist Ennahda (Renaissance) party gained 41 percent of the vote and 87 of the 217 seats. In Morocco the PJD (Justice and Development party) won 30 percent of the vote and has been the ruling party since November 2011. In Egypt for over half a century the military rulers—Nasser, Sadat and Mubarak—had limited the place of religious groups in public life. Now the Islamic parties there got 70 percent of the vote; the relatively moderate and politically astute Muslim Brotherhood (FJP) is the leading party, but the real surprise has been that the more extreme Islamic group, the Salafist Al-Nour party, which has only been in existence for nine months, and which is opposed to alcohol, pop music, and Western culture, got 29 percent. Islamic groups in other countries—Hama in Gaza, Islamic Action Front in Jordan, the FIS in Algeria, the AKP (Justice and Development party) in Turkey—have all been influenced by the Muslim Brotherhood, created in 1928 by Hasan al-Banna, who called for a political system based on Islam. All the groups assert they will end corruption, promote justice and dignity, and continue the welfare system for the poor they have begun.

The present reality is mixed and diverse in the different countries. Egypt has closed civil society groups including some financed by the United States, which continues to provide the country with $1.3 billion a year in military aid. It has also reduced female representation in parliament and other groups. Turkey has harassed the media, the military, judges, and the middle class. Though the Arab League in November 2011 called for sanctions on Syria, including a travel ban on senior officials, freeze on government assets, and ban on commercial exchanges, some Arab countries were unwilling to abide by this. Russia remains interested in selling arms to Syria and since 1971 has had a naval base at the Mediterranean coast port of Tartus, Syria's second-largest port. In early 2012 Russia sent a naval flotilla led by an aircraft carrier to the port to show support for Syria as well as attempting to block sanctions imposed on the country.

The crucial question for the world, and especially for Israel, is whether these groups, now influential and stronger than ever before, can adapt to a more moderate position. Does the Egyptian Muslim Brotherhood genuinely believe in a free market and equality of faith and gender, especially the rights of women and religious minorities, as it claims? More specifically, will the Arab community, presently engaged in national fashion in problems of their own countries, become more concerned with Israel? It is an ominous signal that the Egyptian Islamists have threatened to revoke the 1979 peace treaty with Israel. Spring may become a cold winter.

12. God Save the Queen

By long tradition, the British monarch refrains from making political statements of any kind. The monarch may give advice but must not be drawn into the political arena except very occasionally, such as the appointment of a prime minister if the choice is not automatically clear to all and there are alternative candidates available. Her official utterances are expected to be noncommittal, bland, and even banal.

It was therefore surprising that in September 2012 the political views of Queen Elizabeth II were made public when the British Broadcasting Corporation (BBC) apologized to her for its breach of etiquette after one of its correspondents had revealed the nature of a conversation, which should have remained private, he had with the Queen some years earlier. At that time the Queen had said she was "pretty upset" it was not possible to arrest Abu Hamza, the extremist Islamist preaching in the Finsbury Park mosque in north London, and had raised the issue with the then home secretary, the government minister responsible for internal affairs and security. The Queen was troubled that "this man surely must have broken some laws." She was also annoyed he had called Britain "a toilet."

Hamza, fifty-four years old, son of an Egyptian army officer, naturalized British citizen by marriage to an English woman in 1984, had been born in Alexandria, Egypt in 1958, studied civil engineering, and came on a student's visa to Britain in 1958. He fathered eight children with two different wives, one of whom, a Moroccan-born wife, lives in a five-bedroom home financed by British taxpayers at a cost of £1 million. Hamza had been a heavy drinker and at one point was employed as a bouncer at a strip nightclub in Soho, London. He became a Muslim holy man in the 1990s and as a Muslim extremist went to Afghanistan, where he claimed he lost both his hands and one eye fighting against the Soviet Union.

Returning to London, he appeared at his mosque in Finsbury Park, using it from 1996 on to denounce Western democracies with his violent, fiery, inflammatory rhetoric; to recruit Islamic radicals, preaching jihad; and allegedly to plot terrorist attacks. He called for aid for the Taliban and for jihad in Afghanistan in 2001. He publicly praised Osama bin Laden as a "hero." He conspired to set up a jihadist training campaign in Bly, Oregon, 2000–2001. Among others he influenced by his sermons to his congregation in his mosque were Richard Reid, the failed shoe-bomber, now serving a life sentence in the Supermax prison in Colorado, and one member of the September 11, 2001, bombers. Hamza was said to be the leader of a terrorist cell called Supporters of Sharia.

Hamza was arrested in Britain in 2004, charged with terrorist offences, which included six charges of soliciting to murder, four charges of stirring up racial hatred, and one charge of owning a terrorist encyclopedia. When arrested, police found thousands of videos and audiotapes in his home calling for holy war against nonbelievers. He was found guilty and sentenced to seven years in jail. The legal proceedings had cost considerable amounts of public money. From his maximum-security prison in London he fought extradition to the US for eight years, arguing he would suffer torture or inhuman treatment in an American prison.

Hamza had also been charged in the United States on eleven counts, including his participation in the kidnapping of sixteen hostages in Yemen in 1998, of whom four—three Britons and an Australian—were killed. The US therefore for years has been calling for his extradition from Britain to face charges of terrorism, and Hamza and his lawyers used every legal device to prevent that, including the allegation that prison in the US would be cruel and unusual punishment.

The British High Court in 2008 ruled that the US request for extradition of Hamza was lawful and that Britain should comply. However, because of the opposition of human rights advocates and an appeal by Hamza, the government was forced to delay extradition. The European Court of Human Rights in Strasbourg in August 2008 ruled that he should not be extradited until judges examined his case again.

In April 2012 the European Court changed its mind and ruled that the extradition of Hamza and four other alleged terrorists would be lawful and would not violate their human rights since they would not be subject to "ill-treatment" in America. This decision was upheld by a British High Court panel of judges, which rejected an appeal by

Hamza's lawyers. Apparently, both European and British judges had now agreed that if Hamza were tried in an American court and put in an American jail with TV, newspapers, books, and telephone rights, he would have acceptable housing.

Under the terms of the extradition agreement, Hamza and the four other terrorist suspects extradited to the United States cannot face the death penalty if found guilty or be sent to Guantanamo. They must be tried in federal civilian courts and may be defended by court-appointed lawyers.

Queen Elizabeth must not be the only Briton to be delighted that this undesirable man was flown out of the country from an RAF base in Suffolk to New York and was brought to a courtroom in Manhattan on October 6, 2012, to face charges of terrorism. Ironically, the courtroom was just a few blocks from the scene of the 9/11 attacks. The Queen inadvertently did the judicial system a great service by bringing to light the need to bring terrorists to justice.

It is now up to the American judicial system to ensure that, in spite of the difficulty and legal costs involved, it is conscious of this need and will act accordingly. The system might heed the statement of the British Lord Chief Justice that it was unacceptable that a case such as that of Hamza's should take eight years to go through the courts.

13. Gender in the Middle East

An examination of the role and status of women in Israel and the Arab and Muslim countries is enlightening. A number of factors are relevant in such examination. First. Israel is an essentially democratic country in which the data about women is collected accurately and is well-known. By contrast, accurate information about the Arab societies is difficult to obtain since these countries lack the mechanisms of a democratic society: valid statistical analysis resulting from a free press, free association, and an independent judiciary.

Secondly, whereas Israel is a single country, the Arab and Muslim world in the Middle East, including the twenty-two members of the Arab League, is now at different levels of development, and thus generalization is difficult. The Gulf countries, particularly Bahrain and Qatar, are at one end of the scale, and Yemen is at the other. Moreover, changes in the Arab countries, starting with the Arab Spring, have led to differing results depending on the relative strength in them of traditional culture, Sharia law, Islamic forces, or the move to modernity.

Nevertheless, enough information is available to make comparisons. The contrast between the state of women in Israel and in Arab states is striking and has been illustrated in the World Economic Forum's 2012 Global Gender Report, which analyzed the magnitude and scope of gender-based disparities in 135 countries, based on economic participation and opportunity, educational attainment, health and survival, and political empowerment–based criteria. The Report ranked the four Nordic counties at the top of the list; the United States was number seventeen and Israel was fifty-five. The Arab countries were at the bottom of the list, with none being in the top one hundred. Yemen was the last at 135; Jordan was 117, Egypt was 123, Oman was 127, and Saudi Arabia was 131. The Arab countries lag behind other regions in the world regarding economic participation and opportunity and political empowerment of women.

Though some discrimination and inequalities still exist regarding women in Israel, the place and status of women there is considerably higher than in any of the Arab countries. The Israeli Declaration of Independence of 1948 clearly states that the State of Israel "will ensure complete equality of social and political rights to all its inhabitants irrespective of religion, race, or sex." Israel has passed the Equal Employment Opportunities Law concerned, among other things, with equal rights of women and protection against sexual harassment and violence. Discrimination based on gender as such is therefore legally prohibited, though disparities remain. The Israeli parliament, the Knesset, has a committee on the status of women that is concerned about issues of discrimination and inequality.

Women, who now account for half of the Israeli population, participate in Israel life in every way: in national and local politics, in administrative positions, in the judiciary, in the workplace, in the military, and in education.

Women have equal rights in voting and in ability to participate in politics. In the current Knesset, women, mostly from center or left of center parties, now number twenty-four and comprise 20 percent of the membership (MKs). Women have chaired committees, usually those dealing with domestic or social issues. One has been speaker (Dalia Itzik, 2006–2009) and others have been deputy speakers. They have been most active in issues of equal pay legislation, affirmative action, and violence against women.

Israeli political parties differ in their treatment of women. The three major parties, Kadima, Likud, and Labor, as well as some of the smaller parties, have guidelines for increasing the number of women in leadership positions. They vary between 20 and 40 percent. The leader of Labor in 2012 is a woman, Shelly Yachimovich. However, the religious parties, Shas and United Torah Judaism, have no women members.

The most prominent woman to have been not only an MK but also a political leader is Golda Meir, one of the signers of the Declaration of Independence, who became a cabinet minister, ambassador, and prime minister (1969–1974). Tzipi Livni was the leader of Kadima, the largest party in the Knesset, and vice prime minister. In all, ten women have been cabinet ministers.

Women are playing an important role in the courts. For many years at least one member of the Israeli Supreme Court has been a woman. Recently, five women have served as judges on the fifteen-person Supreme Court. Dorit Beinisch, in 2006, after ten years on the court was the first woman to be appointed as its president. She had already been the first woman state attorney of Israel. Women now account over half of all magistrate and district court judges, and over 40 percent of all lawyers in Israel are women.

Women have also been appointed or elected to positions of all kinds: government ministers, heads of political parties, mayors, local council members, state attorneys, members of religious councils. It is mandatory for women, as for men, to serve in the military (IDF), on land, sea, and in the air, except that they serve for two years compared to the three years of men. They account for over a third of all the IDF and for about a quarter of its officers. In June 2011 a woman was appointed for the first time to be a major-general in the IDF.

Women now constitute about half of the total workforce; working women are more than half of the total number of women in the country. They are less likely than men to be self-employed. Though disparities have been declining, on average women earn about two-thirds of what men earn and are less likely to be in higher-paying professions. There are two reasons for this. Men work about ten hours longer a week, and women enter more than do men lower-paying professions, such as teachers, secretaries, and saleswomen. Almost 60 percent of employees in the civil service and the public sector are women, who fill most of the low-level positions. Over 40 percent of women are employed in these sectors.

A survey in 2012 by the International Institute for Management Development places Israel in eleventh place out of fifty-nine developed countries regarding the participation of women in the workplace, and twenty-fourth regarding the proportion of women serving in executive positions. An interesting comparison is that in Germany today the percentage of women in managerial positions in private industry is comparable, about 27 percent. The number of women in executive positions in Israel amounted to 72,600, about 5 percent of all employed women, in 2011. Interestingly, men in executive positions amounted to 8.7 percent of total employed men, little more than women.

Women are at every level in the Histadrut, the federation of labor unions. It has been a rule that 30 percent of its leadership must be women, but none have risen as high within the Histadrut as Golda Meir, who headed its Political Department before becoming a politician.

Social expectations and customs limit women's advancement. Daily responsibility for children still resides with mothers rather than fathers. The typical school day ends around 1 p.m., but the workday ends several hours later, thus handicapping women's involvement in the workplace.

Israeli women are the best educated women in the Middle East. Over half have gone to institutions of higher learning, making Israel about seventh in the world regarding the percentage of women studying in higher educational institutions. About 60 percent of university students and graduates are women. The Women in Science program provides a stipend after PhD. In the life sciences, particularly the biomed industry, women are more prominent than men, but the reverse is true in the field of engineering. Women constitute about a quarter of university faculty. In 2009 the Nobel Prize for Chemistry was awarded to Ada Yonath.

The major hindrances limiting parity for Israeli women arise over personal status, especially marriage and divorce. Marital affairs are handled by the rabbinical courts as a result of the arrangement reached in 1947 between David Ben Gurion and the religious parties. The religious authorities operate on the basis of Torah law, according to which a Jewish woman can initiate divorce proceedings but her husband must give his consent to make the divorce final. The result is that many women are unable to remarry or to have legitimate children if their husbands refuse to grant divorces. One aspect of religious discrimination against women has been remedied. Until 2011 the sexes were separated, with women having to sit at the back, on the Mehadrin bus lines that served the ultra-Orthodox Jewish areas of Jerusalem. The Israeli High Court in January 2011 abolished them, stating that segregation was illegal.

Religious restrictions remain problematic over two issues: the orthodox refusal to allow women to pray and read Torah at the site of the

Western Wall in Jerusalem and the restraining code placed on women's dress by the ultraorthodox citizens.

Arab Israeli women have the same rights and privileges as Jewish women. They have the right to vote and to be elected to public office. Practices in Arab countries such as polygamy, child marriage, and female sexual mutilation are forbidden in Israel. A number of Arab women have been members of the Knesset.

The Arab Countries

The United Nations Arab Human Development Report of 2002, written by a number of Arab intellectuals, painted a picture of Arab society that is critical of the inferior status of women regarding freedom, empowerment, and education. The Report indicated that "The utilization of Arab women's capabilities through political and economic participation remains the lowest in the world in quantitative terms, as evidenced by the very low share of women in parliaments, cabinets, and the work force. . . . In some countries . . . women are still denied the right to vote or hold office. And one in every two Arab women can neither read nor write." The Report explained that society as a whole suffered when a huge proportion of its productive potential was stifled.

The Arab world is not a monolithic bloc as far as the political and civil rights and the role of women are concerned. There are considerable differences among the women themselves, rich or poor, educated or uneducated, urban or rural; caution is required in making generalizations. Furthermore, since the publication of the Report the situation for women has changed to differing degrees in some of the countries. At the same time it is apparent that the struggle for women's rights is not synonymous with moves to democratize the whole system and to limit executive power.

One generalization is appropriate. In the Arab countries, women—because of the Islamic religion but also for political, economic, and educational reasons—still occupy a subordinate place in society. In many ways they face discrimination and are denied free choice in personal behavior and in the rights that men enjoy.

In personal relations they suffer discrimination within the family and in marriage relations, being obliged to marry as a minor. Tunis has been an exception by outlawing polygamy and forbidding a woman under eighteen to marry.

In the Arab world differences exist about veiling. Is it a manifestation of male control? Is it a symbolic act? Is it a protest by lower-middle-class women? Is it a political act, as it was in Algeria? Dress code varies in different Arab countries. It varies from loose scarves to veils and full-length coverings such as the *burqua*. Saudi Arabia is the most traditional, and many women wear not only the hijab (head covering) but also the *abaya*, a black garment covering the whole body. However, in a number of other countries the veil is not mandatory.

Discrimination and restrictions on women stem from both tradition and the Muslim religion. To some extent the extent of those restrictions regarding educational and economic opportunities depends on the wealth and social class of women. The Sharia, Islamic law, and tribal custom define the rules of social behavior for women, as for men, in most Arab countries. Those rules have traditionally meant limitations on political and social freedoms, on the right to education, and on access to most occupations, and legal discrimination.

Women are not totally free to travel. They have difficulty in obtaining a passport. In some countries they are not allowed to travel alone or have to get permission from their guardian. In Saudi Arabia, where women are not allowed to drive a car, all women must have a male guardian who has rights over and duties to them. His permission is necessary for women to travel outside their home.

Women are in practice not involved in deciding on their own marriage. Moreover, polygyny is legal while polyandry is forbidden. Women are forbidden to marry non-Muslim men. There is no minimum age for marriage in Saudi Arabia. By tradition, rules have meant that Arab women marry at a young age to a man chosen for them. A husband can get a divorce even without agreement of his wife. The reverse is not the case. It is difficult for women to get a divorce. Women are handicapped in other ways. Polygamy is legal, though now infrequently practiced. Ritual sexual mutilation of women prevails in some rural areas. Honor killings of women for adultery still occur.

Social norms make it difficult for Arab women to have full legal rights. Women have been treated unequally in court and have been deprived of an equal share of inheritance. In no Arab country do women have equal rights or have equal opportunities with men.

In the Arab Muslim Middle East no woman has been a political leader or head of state. Throughout history, until fairly recently, they have devoid of political rights. There are few feminist movements in the Arab countries.

However, since 1949, when women were granted the vote in Syria, and 1952 in Lebanon, they now can vote in national elections in most

Arab countries, the most important exception being Saudi Arabia. They have played a small role in most of the parliaments in Arab countries. Nasser gave women the vote in 1956, though he closed all independent feminist orgs. The first female elected as a member of parliament in the Arab countries was a woman in Egypt in 1957.

To this point the most prominent political and economic role played by women has been in Tunisia, where they constitute about a quarter of the workforce and also won 49 of the 217 seats on the Constituent Assembly elected in 2011, and constitute about a quarter of municipal councilors. It was noticeable that women played an active part in the protest movement in Tunis in January 2011 and played some role in Egypt, Libya, and Yemen. In Libya they hold thirty-three of the two hundred seats in Parliament. Women have not been successful in either Egypt or Syria.

Women have complained that conservative and extreme Islamists have opposed female participation in political life and discouraged women from voting. In a surprising move, Saudi Arabia announced in September 2011 that women will be allowed to vote, to nominate candidates, and to run for office in future municipal elections, though not yet national elections. In addition, women will be allowed to participate in the Shura Council, the Consultative Council appointed by the king. Up to now women have not been members of political organizations. They have been able to hold positions on commercial boards.

Women in the Arab countries have to balance, in a way even greater than those in the Western world, the ties to family and community with the desire for personal satisfaction and accomplishment. Like many Western women, the problem is to live a balanced life. They play their role in male-dominated societies, even as some now seek women's empowerment. The ability of women to work varies in the different countries. In some of the wealthier countries with rapidly growing economies, such as the Gulf Countries—Bahrain, Kuwait, Oman, Qatar, and the United Arab Emirates—the number of women as business owners, especially as members of family businesses, as teachers, and as scholars, is growing. In what is a significant change in the region, women are being trained to work in these professions, particularly to work outside the home. Many work as teachers and nurses.

Attendance of Arab girls in schools varies widely. One classification suggests that more than 40 percent of Arab women are illiterate; in Yemen the figure is about 55 percent. In other countries literacy has been rapidly increasing. Instead of being discouraged, as has historically been the case, young women have increasingly gone on to secondary education. In a number of Arab countries the enrollment rate for women in college is larger than that for men; in Saudi Arabia it is almost 60 percent of all university students. Most of the women students have degrees in education or the social sciences.

Saudi Arabia can illustrate the present problem for Arab women. Tradition prevails in that gender inequality is official. Women have an inferior personal status. Men are allowed four wives, can divorce at will, have dominant position in custody of children and in inheritance issues. Women, always expected to be obedient to their husbands, suffer considerable domestic violence.

Women are restricted in work opportunities, partly because of difficulty in transport facilities. A recent United Nations report shows that the economic participation rate of women in Saudi Arabia is only 22 percent. They mostly work in the public sector especially in education and medicine. They can own and manage property and other assets. It is calculated they own 40 percent of real estate and 20 percent of stocks. They are not allowed to drive; they cannot travel abroad without permission, and there are restraints even on movement within the country. As a result women rarely walk the streets alone.

Women are considered legal minors under the control of their nearest relative. The religious police are concerned with public moral behavior, including dress. They have been notorious in this control of behavior. Women have never been leaders in religious institutions.

If women go to court they must rely on a male relative or lawyer to represent them. Since the face of a woman is covered, her guardian must identify her in court. In spite of this restriction, since 2007 women have been allowed to study law. The general educational system, which is free for all from six to fifteen, has improved for women; forty-four thousand have graduated from universities, and 80 percent of all PhD degrees have been awarded to women.

There have also been some positive changes in the mixed bag of Saudi rules. Women are segregated in dining places, hospitals, parks, banks, government buildings, and in taxis, but since 2007 can check into hotels and can rent apartments on their own. Slavery was outlawed in 1962, but there is still involuntary servitude; about 1.5 million domestic workers get no protection.

The crucial question is whether any winds of change in the future will improve the condition and status of women in the Arab countries. Presently, the difference between that status and the status of women in Israel is vast.

The question must be asked whether Western feminist organizations, especially the newly created UN Women (The United Nations Entity for Gender Equality and the Empowerment of Women), set up in 2010, will act on behalf of women in Arab and Muslim countries in the Middle East to help them become full citizens with equal rights in their countries. They should heed the Report of 2002, mentioned at the beginning of this article, which suggests the changes for improvement that will affect not only the well-being of Arab and Muslim women but also that of Arab societies as a whole.

14. Is Islamic Ideology Totalitarian?

Several essays in the book address the issue that Islamic thought and activities pose a serious threat to democratic societies. They range from those examining the historical record of relations between Islamic and Western countries to that of the historian Bat Ye'or, who strongly contends that the Islamic threat to Western civilization is an imminent and possibly unavoidable danger.

Indeed, Islamic practices are qualitatively different from Western concepts of human rights and equality. The distinction between the system of state sovereignty devised over 450 years ago and the Islamic concept of rule is critical. The Peace of Westphalia, the series of peace treaties signed in 1648, ended the Thirty Years' War among the countries in the Holy Roman Empire and the other destructive wars plaguing Europe, although it did not lead to peace throughout Europe. However, it was significant for leading to European, and later international, agreement on and acceptance of the idea of the sovereignty of nation-states. Sovereignty, the supreme power in a given area, was to be embodied in a state that could exercise authority within its borders and prevail over challenge from religious dignitaries and other forms of influence.

This configuration of sovereign states in international relations entailed a number of factors: territorial integrity of the state, ultimate power of decision-making by the state authorities, and no interference by outsiders in the domestic activities of the state. Thus, individual states, not any supranational authority or religion, became the actors in international relations. States became the legal expression of nations, people bound by ties of different kinds but primarily by language, culture, common history, and common values.

Since 1648 the principle of national sovereignty has often been disregarded in practice. Equality between states has existed more in theory than in practice. The principle of nonintervention in the affairs of other states has not been observed. State sovereignty has been challenged by international agreements, by attempts to formulate binding international law, and recently by the International Criminal Court. The processes of globalization, with increasing interdependence of markets and businesses in the world, and modernity with its influence on culture and economic life and the movement of people and goods beyond a local area, have qualified state sovereignty. Nevertheless, the political system of sovereign states stemming from Westphalia remains in existence, as shown by the 193 states that now, at least legally, exercise sovereignty in their own territory and are members of the United Nations.

However, ideologies in the twentieth century, primarily Marxism and Nazism, laid claim to control or influence nations on a worldwide basis. Hitler wrote of the personality and conception of "the *Volkish* state" that would be spread throughout Europe. Soviet Marxism called on "workers and oppressed people in the world" to unite. Today, with the rise of Islamists to power or influence in Egypt, Tunisia, Yemen, and Iran, the world is faced with another ideology, Islamism, a comparatively modern term. That ideology competes with, and in some Arab countries has supplanted, Arab nationalism as a uniting factor for political activity.

There are two ultimate aims of that extreme ideology. One is to restore wherever possible the Muslim Caliphate, the first system of government set up in Islam in the seventh century, by uniting Muslim nations through political action or by force. The Muslim ruler applies and enforces the holy law of Islam. The second related aim is to have people convert to Islam or to have them—in the case of the protected religions of Christianity and Judaism—submit to Islamic rule.

It is not always easy to distinguish between Islamism, supposedly the ideology of an active minority, and the religion of Islam. This is because Islam, in Bernard Lewis's words, "is not only a religion in the narrow Western sense but a whole civilization which grew up under the aegis of that religion." In contrast to the Westphalian system of a secular state sovereignty, Islam has a political identity and allegiance transcending all others. Sovereignty or supreme power belongs to Allah. In practice that power rests in the ruler who acts on the basis of Sharia, or Islamic law. It is an open, though important, question whether the essence of and interpretation of the political identity of Islam is the call for jihad, or struggle, a key element of the Muslim faith.

Even agreeing that Islamism is not synonymous with the religion of Islam it is not easily differentiated from it, because the religion is founded on a community of believers (the *umma*) and legal, social, and moral prescriptions to which they adhere. The two, Islamism and the religion of Islam, share values to a considerable degree. If they differ it is not because of incompatible views but on tactical questions of the manner of implementing those views. The objective for both is to promulgate Islamic rule throughout the world. However, that rule is not imposed on the non-Muslims, members of the two permitted religions, individuals who can practice their religion but who accept their status of inferiority.

Can Islamism be compared with the two former totalitarian ideologies, Communism and Nazism, with their outreach to the world? Certainly Margaret Thatcher thought this was the case. In an article in *The Guardian* on February 12, 2002, she wrote of Islamic extremism that "like Bolshevism in the past it is an armed doctrine. It is an aggressive ideology promoted by fanatical, well-armed devotees." Even without strong rhetoric of this kind, the analogy is plausible because of the similar ambition of the "secular political religions" of Communism and Nazism, and Islamism, an extreme religious political ideology to convert people throughout the world. Islamism is based on a religion claiming universal truth.

In his book *The Curse of Ideas*, Robert Conquest wrote that for Lenin, "Marxism provided a whole theory of history. . . . It divided humanity into irreconcilable sections engaged in a struggle to the death." Islamic extremists hold that their doctrine is superior to that of Western systems, which they view as corrupt. In areas controlled by Islamic forces, that control leads to the removal of non-Muslim influences and power. The Islamist ambition is the exercise of power and control, and the imposition of Sharia law that is not limited by boundaries of individual national states. In the past, relatively benign Muslim rulers granted a degree of religious toleration to non-Muslim minorities in return for tribute paid to them. Islamic extremists, with their insistence on Sharia law and aggressiveness in action, are unlikely to act in similar benign fashion.

Islamism is a term that is controversial and has been defined in different ways, both intellectually and in practice. It has also taken somewhat diverse and varied forms in individual countries. The diverse forms of Islamic activism and ideological differences in the Sunni Muslim countries thus make generalization about Islamism difficult. The countries differ in their interpretation of Sharia law and the degree of austerity or flexibility in their Islamic jurisprudence. It may also means differing relationships in levels of hostility between individual Islamic countries and the democratic countries of the West. In this relationship perhaps the most troubling is the anti-American rhetoric and the anti-Israeli animosity of many Islamists.

The different forms of Islamism have also been expounded on by a number of Muslim intellectuals, the most well-known of whom are Sayyid Qutb, Abul Ala Maududi, and Hasan al Banna. For insight into contemporary affairs it is worth recalling that one of the students of Qutb was Ayman Zawahari, who was the ideological teacher of Osama bin Laden. The most notable modern Shi'a counterparts of this Sunni group are the late Ayatollah Ruhollah Khomeini and the Islamic Republic of Iran that he founded, Moktada al-Sadr in Iraq, and the Hezbollah in Lebanon.

Some Islamists, such as the Muslim Brotherhood in Egypt, claim to advocate peaceful change and present themselves as sensible pragmatists. Others, such as the Taliban, Algerian Islamic Salvation Front, and the Egyptian Jamaa Islamiya, call for violent jihad directed against non-Muslims and apostates. The essence of Islamism, or Muslim radicalism, is the assertion that a strict interpretation of Islamic theology, the Koran, Hadith, and commands of the Prophet, should guide the life of all Muslims in personal, political, and social areas. It is a plan for global action, responding to contemporary modernity. It also rests on the historical reality that the Prophet was a sovereign ruler, a leader who by force established the Islamic state in Medina and whose followers conquered parts of Asia, Europe, and North Africa.

Maudidi argued that Islamic states must be established based on pure Islam. He held that Islam is a militant ideology and has a program that seeks to alter the social order of the whole world and rebuild it in conformity with its own tenets and ideals. Islamic Jihad would destroy non-Islamic systems and would bring about a universal revolution.

Hasan al-Banna, founder of the Muslim Brotherhood in 1928, called not only for political systems to be founded on Islamic rule, but also for jihad to be the way in which the mission of spreading Islam would be fulfilled. The Brotherhood would work for pan-Islamic unity, religious solidarity, and a united Islam against Western domination.

More extreme concepts were expounded by the Egyptian Sayyid Qutb, the major intellectual influence on the Brotherhood after Banna's death in 1949. Qutb called for a more aggressive attempt not simply to defend the home land of Islam, but to carry the movement of Islam throughout the world to the whole of mankind. In addition, Qutb used the Islamic concept of *takfir* (declaration that someone is an apostate) to threaten and justify attacks on Muslim rulers who did not rule on the basis of pure Islam and thus could be declared an infidel who should be removed from power. Non-Muslims can be tolerated but apostates cannot, and the penalty is death. For this reason, and not because he had made peace with Israel, President Anwar Sadat was assassinated in October 1981 by Egyptian Islamic army officers who considered him to be unfaithful to true Islamic principles.

Assassination of unwelcome individuals has been a familiar experience in the Muslim world since soon after the death of the Prophet. The Shiite group known as the Assassins founded in the eleventh century lasted two centuries. In recent years the presidents of Egypt, Syria, and South Yemen, the would-be president of Lebanon, and the prime minister of Iran have all suffered this fate.

Differences have naturally been expressed within the forces of Islamism. The Muslim Brotherhood in Egypt and similar groups elsewhere purport to be moderate in their political tactical policies, claiming to be reformist not revolutionary and to conceive of change through political action. In contrast, the more extreme Salafi movement emphasizes the spread of the Sharia, the Islamic faith, and its moral order that will overcome countries of unbelief, an emphasis to be implanted by jihad or armed struggle against non-Muslim power.

However, both are expressions of political Islam in the Muslim world. Future events will decide if Muslim states will become or remain tyrannical or whether political systems based on some limited form of government will prevail. The key problem for the world is whether Islamic control in Arab countries will continue to be an obstacle to reform and will prevent the emergence of secular democratic changes. The West must still be cautious that the forces of political Islamism and jihadist activism do not advance a worldwide ideology, posing a threat to the rest of the world, as did Marxist Communism and Nazism.

4

The Palestinian Narrative

1. The Palestinian Narrative of Victimhood

One controversial aspect of modern thought, based on the thesis that the full truth is unknowable, is interpretation of historical events and present behavior by designing a narrative. Nowhere is this more apparent than in the effort of those critical of Israel to design or accept a Palestinian narrative to serve as the basis of an ideological campaign to condemn the State of Israel and to undermine its moral fabric.

This narrative focuses on a number of issues: the original sin of the creation of Israel; the Nakba (catastrophe) of 1948; the Israeli responsibility for violence and the various wars in the Middle East; the dispossession of a native people by intruders; the seven-thousand-year historic association of Palestinians with the land of Canaan; the deliberate creation by Israel of large numbers of Palestinian refugees who are unable to return to their homeland; and the supposed indignities and injustices done to innocent and blameless Palestinians who have become victims of the powerful Israeli aggression and colonialism—even of genocide and apartheid. Parenthetically, one of the oddities in all this is the use by Muslims of the Christian concept of original sin to refer to Jews.

Much of this narrative is deliberate fabrication and attempts to denigrate the Jewish relation with the land of Israel, or is nonsensical. Yasser Arafat at the Camp David Summit said that the Temple had been in Nablus, not Jerusalem. Others have argued that the Biblical Hebrew tribes were Bedouins and that Israeli Jews stem from Khazars who converted to Judaism. Some suggest that Jesus should be defined as a Palestinian, apparently ignorant of the fact that Palestine does not appear in the Bible.

Unmentioned in this curious narrative is the reality that most people now defined as Palestinians came into the area as migrants from Arab

countries, or were wandering Bedouins, or were imported for commercial reasons by Ottoman authorities or the British mandate authorities,
or were attracted by the success of the Zionist settlement. Palestinians
have no language or dialect distinct from Arab neighbors.

The Nakba myth is the one most often invoked with its emotional
appeal. What is unsaid in the Arab Palestinian lexicon of catastrophe is
that the Jewish community did not seek the war of 1948–49. Moreover,
the real start of the war between the two sides was November 30, 1947,
the day after the UN General Assembly Partition Resolution, when
Arab gunmen ambushed two buses full of Jews, killing a number of
them, and other Arabs fired on civilians in the streets of Tel Aviv. The
Arab Higher Committee called for a general strike against Jews, during
which an Arab mob looted part of Jerusalem. Hostilities then began
between the Jewish Haganah and Palestinian Arab village militias and
four thousand troops of the Arab Liberation Army sent into the area
from Syria after being trained there by the Arab League. On May 15,
1948, the day after Israel was created, the Arab states, except Lebanon,
and Iran invaded Israel and attacked its territory, with the objective of
eliminating the State of Israel.

All of these spurious charges in the Palestinian narrative have
become part of the campaign to challenge the legitimacy of the State
of Israel, and even to call for its elimination. But it is the last—the
concept of Palestinian victimhood, people embracing the mantle of
victims—that has given most resonance to international support for
the Palestinian cause. It accounts for the obsessive concentration on
the Israeli-Palestinian conflict that, disregarding the millions killed or
oppressed in other countries today, is viewed by so many in the international community as well as by the Palestinians as the world's most
important and dangerous conflict.

The narrative of victimhood uses myths and symbols as well as
controversial interpretation of events and actions. It is also sometimes
formulated in extreme fashion. Palestinians become the new Jews suffering a new Holocaust. Jews become the new Nazis. The narrative
denies Jewish historic national identity; to this end Palestinians have
destroyed archeological evidence of the ancient kingdom of Judea.
The Western Wall in Jerusalem is not accepted as a Jewish historic
site. Excessive rhetoric and idiosyncratic judgments of this kind are
rarely, if ever, applied to the truly despotic and authoritarian regimes
in the world that commit crimes against humanity and violations of
human rights that are not censured.

The formulation of the Palestinian narrative of victimhood is pernicious in a double sense. It poisons the international attitude to Israel and prevents any kind of accommodation or possible negotiation between Israel and the Palestinians to reach a peaceful settlement of the long conflict. It is a Freudian projection of blaming others for self-failure; for the Palestinian civil wars that killed rival leaders; for the failure to develop, or to create institutions and an infrastructure for their own society or a sovereign state of their own, or to establish a unified military and political apparatus in 1947. The narrative omits not only the Palestinian refusal to accept any proposal for partition but also the reluctance or unwillingness to take positive action to help resolve their problems, even after the 1948–49 war when Egypt and Jordan occupied what Palestinians now regard as their territory. It also ignores the present friction between Fatah and Hamas that prevents the emergence of a central political and military system, and which cannot be blamed on Israel or any outside party.

Equally important is the fact that Israel is the political canary warning of the presence of poisonous political traits that intimate impending danger to the world, particularly to the United States and Western democracies. Concurring in the validity of the Palestinian narrative leads on the part of Western critics to a standpoint of moral relativism and a stance of appeasement, a mindset that has as its outcome an inability or refusal to defend the West against contemporary threats and the clear and present danger to its culture and way of life. At its worst this leads to the view that the "war on terror" is unwinnable or should not be fought, or that the West is to be eternally found guilty for its past colonial empires and activity.

The world has been through this before. The willingness of people to respond to the call for support of distasteful totalitarian regimes, Nazism and Stalinism—a support intensified by propaganda, the media, and some academics, and justified by some well-meaning people, the kind that Lenin once called "political idiots"—is akin to those who blindly accept the Palestinian narrative both of their general victimhood or of individuals seen as heroic figures. Progressive-minded individuals, as Albert Camus wrote in his *Notebooks*, "reknit the sleeve of reasoning torn apart by the facts."

One such figure is Rachel Corrie, the twenty-three-year-old American student who had worked with the radical International Solidarity Movement, which describes itself as "a Palestinian-led movement committed to resisting the Israeli occupation of Palestinian land," but which organized the Mavi Marmara flotilla to go to Gaza, and whose co-founder Huwaida Arraf is said to work with Hamas. Corrie was accidently killed in Gaza in 2003 after kneeling in front of an Israeli bulldozer that she was deliberately trying to block, and she has become a martyr and symbol of heroic defiance of Israel and of Palestinian resistance. The symbolism extended to her name being used as one of the boats in the 2010 Gaza flotilla.

The narrative of her activity does not dwell on her reckless behavior in a war zone where the bulldozer was clearing brush to prevent illegal weapons being smuggled by terrorists into Gaza. It also ignores the activity of the International Solidarity Movement, which has engaged in illegal and violent actions against Israeli soldiers, and which helped the terrorists who in 2002 occupied the Church of the Nativity. Rather, the incorrect version of Corrie's negligent behavior has penetrated the theater as well as public life.

One example is the eight-minute play *Seven Jewish Children* by Caryl Churchill, produced in London in 2009, a display not only of radical chic, but a presentation that, consciously or otherwise, has overtones of the historic blood libel charge against Jews, as well as of alleged bad treatment of Palestinian babies. Another was the play *My Name is Rachel Corrie*, based on her writings. However, in August 2012 the Haifa District Court in Israel held that her death in the Gaza Strip by the bulldozer was a regrettable accident, that the driver of the bulldozer did not see her, and that she was not killed intentionally or unlawfully by the State of Israel.

The Palestinian narrative has been accepted by those supporters of the Palestinian cause reveling in a fanciful, romanticized violence and revolutionary myth, and presentation of the superior virtue of Palestinians, regardless of their actual behavior. For some, the Palestinians are seen as the embodiment of "the wretched of the earth," the phrase used by Franz Fanon to justify the Algerian struggle against France. This ignores the benefits and the assistance, political, economic, and military, and the diplomatic and propaganda support that the Palestinians have got from the radical left and the Third World by using their narrative of victimhood and proclaiming their lack of human rights.

It is the misfortune of Israel that the Palestinians have been elected to be the main symbol of the oppressed of the world. Traditional antisemitism has often used Jews as scapegoats, supposedly responsible for most of the problems of the world. George Orwell remarked in 1944, "However true the scapegoat theory may be in general terms, it does not explain why the Jews rather than some other minority group are picked on, nor does it make clear what they are the scapegoat for."

By tortuous logic and pathological intensity Israel has now become the contemporary scapegoat for racism, oppression, and colonialism in the world. Jewish nationalism is identified as imperialist and racist, while Palestinian nationalism is the nationalism of the oppressed. While recognizing the real problems that the Palestinians encounter, it is time to state forthrightly that the Palestinian narrative, with its false presentations, is not to be equated in moral abhorrence to Auschwitz. Antisemitism and anti-Zionism is not a formula for equity for the Palestinians. Only a peace between Israel and the Palestinians who are willing to accept the existence and legitimacy of a Jewish state can lead to that end.

2. The Palestinians Are an Invented People

The statement by Newt Gingrich during his candidacy in the 2012 American electoral campaign that the Palestinians are an "invented people" was criticized by political opponents as indicating a lack of sobriety and stability on his part. Yet, whatever one's views of the sagacity or judgment of Mr. Gingrich on other issues, or one's opinions on the more general issue of the desirability and character of a Palestinian state existing alongside the State of Israel, the accuracy of his statement cannot be denied.

The conclusion stems from two factors. One is that Arabs living in the area now known as Palestine were regarded, both historically and in contemporary times, not as a separate entity but as part of the general Arab people. This fact has been acknowledged by statements of some Arab leaders, by analysis of independent scholars, and in objective official reports. The second is that no independent Palestinian state has ever existed, let alone one that manifested a Palestinian identity.

A few examples can illustrate this. The first Congress of Muslim-Christian Associations in the area met in February 1919, to consider the future of the territory formerly ruled by the Ottoman Empire, which entered World War I on the German side and which came to an end after the defeat of that side in the war. The Congress declared, "We consider Palestine as part of Arab Syria as it has never been separated from it at any time. We are connected with it by national, religious, linguistic, moral, economic, and geographical bonds." The celebrated scholar Philip Hitti, testifying before the Anglo-American Committee in 1946, stated there was no such thing as Palestine in history, "absolutely not."

The important United Nations Special Committee on Palestine (UNSCOP) in its report of September 3, 1947, remarked that Palestinian nationalism, as distinct from Arab nationalism, was a relatively new phenomenon. It concluded that Palestinian identity was only part of a rich tapestry of identities, mostly predicated on Arab and Islamic solidarity.

The Palestinians themselves reached the same conclusion. Ahmad Shuqairy, then Palestinian spokesperson, told the UN Security Council in 1956 that Palestine was nothing more than southern Syria. The head of the Military Operations Department of the Palestine Liberation Organization (PLO), Zuhair Muhsin, declared on March 31, 1977, that "Only for political reasons do we carefully underline our Palestinian identity . . . the existence of a separate Palestinian identity is there for tactical reasons." The PLO in its own Charter or amended Basic Law (Article 1) says that Palestine is part of the Arab nation. Azmi Bishara, former Arab member of the Israeli Knesset, said, "There was no Palestinian nation. I think it is a colonialist invention . . . until the end of the nineteenth century, Palestine was the south of Syria."

That Arab nation never included a state known as Palestine. Indeed, the inhabitants of the general Palestinian area were subjects, not of an Arab nation, but of the Ottoman Empire, which ruled the area and lasted from 1516 until the end of World War 1. This was the last generally recognized sovereign power in the area. The area of Palestine was a district of the Empire, officially a *vilayet* (province), not a political entity. No independent Palestinian state has ever been established, nor was there a single administrative or cultural unit of Palestinians. Arabs in the area were not different in any way from other Arabs in the Middle East area. Nor was Israel established on the ashes of any state other than that of the Ottoman Empire.

The first official naming of Palestine as a distinct, defined territorial area came with the decision of the League of Nations, dealing with areas of the former Ottoman Empire, to create a Mandate for Palestine. This was accorded to Great Britain, which ruled the area from the Mediterranean Sea to west of the Jordan River, from 1922 until May 1948. In 1922 Winston Churchill, then British colonial secretary, excluded the area east of the Jordan River from the Mandate. This became the emirate of Transjordan, later the kingdom of Jordan, ruled by Abdullah, son of Sharif Hussein of Mecca.

All people living in that area were regarded as Palestinians, without any ethnic connotations. Ironically, the name was used not by Arabs but only by Jews in the area, as in *The Palestinian* (now the *Jerusalem) Post*, and the Palestine Symphony (now Israel Philharmonic) Orchestra. Only after the State of Israel was established in May 1948 did the term Palestinian become exclusively used in referring to Arabs in the area.

It is now clear that a concept of Palestinian identity and nationalism has emerged and become a political factor. Whether it first emerged from literary societies and missionary groups a century ago, from the impact of the Arab Revolt of 1916–1918 in the Hijazi desert in Arabia, or as imitation of the actions of the Young Turks who in 1908 seized power in the Ottoman Empire is irrelevant. The new concept became important as a claim to self-determination by Arabs in the period after World War I in reaction against the increasing importance of Zionism and the assertion of self-determination by the Jewish people. One might say it was even an imitation of the Zionist movement.

The essential problem is not simply a terminological one, a refusal to acknowledge that the category of Palestinian identity is a recent invention. Rather, the insistence on a presumed time-honored right of a Palestinian people to the disputed land is being used as a weapon against the right of Israel to exist. Such an insistence is a handicap to a peaceful negotiated agreement between Palestinians and Israel.

3. The Palestinian Refugee Issue

Whether or not a Palestinian state is unilaterally declared in the future, crucial differences between Israel and any Palestinian authority remain, the most controversial of which is the refugee question, an issue that has political and legal as well as humanitarian dimensions and touches on collective guilt feelings. The controversy over Palestinian refugees is the longest, most deliberately protracted, and most discussed of refugee problems in the world. After sixty years it remains unresolved, while most other refugee problems have been resolved.

World War II ended with some forty million refugees in Europe. Central Europe was a site of displaced persons (DPs), those forced to flee their homeland, prisoners of war, individuals who had been deported or had been in forced labor camps, and Jews who had survived the Holocaust. In 1947 about nine hundred camps of DPs existed. They were administered by various bodies: by the Allied occupation forces, by the United Nations Relief and Rehabilitation Administration (UNRRA), and then by the new international organization for refugees,

(UNHCR). This body was originally set up in December 1950 for three years, to protect and assist refugees. The UNHCR, which deals only with actual refugees, has provided humanitarian assistance for over twenty-five million people throughout the world, and has tried to find permanent solutions to refugee issues.

These refugees were settled in various countries. Germany and Poland exchanged millions. Similar relocations, involving fourteen million, took place between the countries of India and Pakistan in 1947; less than 2 percent of these returned to their original home or recovered their property. Solutions were found for others who were dislocated: Hungarians in 1956; Czechs in 1968; Cubans from the 1960s; Algerians and French *pieds-noirs* after the French-Algerian war; the million and a half boat people persecuted by Vietnamese communists; those fleeing the Balkan war, 1991–95; the three million fleeing the Rwanda genocide in 1994; the Afghans escaping from the Soviet invasion of their country in 1979.

However, as a result of the Cold War and recent wars, over fifteen million are now refugees and another twenty-seven million are internally displaced all over the world. Over half are in Asia, and about a quarter are in Africa. But the international community still focuses more on Palestinians than it has on others who were displaced. This is clear from the discrepancy between the UNHCR with its staff of 7,600 in 126 countries in the world and the United Nations Relief and Works Agency (UNRWA) with its 23,000 dealing only with the Palestinians.

Wherefore are Palestinian refugees different from all other refugees, and why have they drawn so much attention and comment compared with others? First is the problem of definition; Palestinian refugees are classified by a set of criteria different from others. In the Geneva Convention Relating to the Status of Refugees of July 1951 (Article 1A(2), which led to the creation of the UNHRC, a refugee is one who, for various reasons, "is outside the country of his nationality and is unable to avail himself of the protection of that country . . . or is unwilling to return to it." In 2011, 147 states are parties to the Convention. But this definition does not apply to Palestinian refugees. Article I (D) states that the Convention "shall not apply to persons who are at present receiving from organs or agencies of the United Nations other than the United Nations High Commissioner for Refugees protection or assistance."

The United Nations had set up the UNHCR to deal with refugees throughout the world, but it also established a special unit, UNRWA, on December 8, 1949, whose mandate was to provide relief and works programs only to Palestinian Arab refugees who had gone to the West Bank, the Gaza Strip, Jordan, Lebanon, and Syria. Its mandate did not define a refugee, but in practice UNRWA uses a broad definition: those whose normal place of residence was Palestine during the period between June 1, 1946 and May 15, 1948, and who had lost both home and means of livelihood as a result of the because of the 1948 conflict, and the descendants of such persons.

Over 70 percent of those regarded by UNRWA as Palestinian refugees reside in the areas in which UNRWA operates. With a local staff of over twenty-three thousand, most of whom are Palestinians, working in its fifty-nine camps, UNWRA is clearly political in its support for the Arab cause. The essential question is why those camps still exist. The Arab states have not contributed any significant amount to the operation of UNRWA (most of the funding comes from the United States and the member states of the European Union.). They have done little to solve the refugee problem.

As early as 1952 General Sir Alexander Galloway, then UNRWA director in Jordan, said, "The Arab states do not want to solve the refugee problem. They want to keep it as an open sore, as an affront to the United Nations, and as a weapon against Israel. Arab leaders don't give a damn whether the refugees live or die." Not surprisingly, he was fired.

Even more important, UNRWA itself has not resolved the refugee issue. Indeed, with its maintenance of camps for sixty years UNRWA has perpetuated the refugee status of Palestinians, generation after generation, by providing them with the benefits of a welfare state, including housing, medical care, social services, and education, and not encouraging them to reside in and develop by productive activity the areas of the West Bank and Gaza, or to find a home in an Arab country. It has allowed the great grandchildren of the original refugees to cling to the idea that they will, under the claim of a right of return, someday live in the area that is now Israel. This attitude was made clear by James G. Lindsay, general counsel of UNRWA between 2002 and 2007, who wrote, "UNRWA encouraged Palestinians who favor re-fighting long-lost wars, discouraged those who favor moving toward peace, and contribute to the scourge of conflicts that have been visited on Palestinian refugees for decades."

Who should be considered a refugee? Logically, only first-generation refugees, those resulting from the 1948 and 1967 wars, should be so considered. Palestinians insist on a more extensive definition, including spouses, children, and grandchildren of refugees, even though Israel is not the state of origin of the vast majority of these refugees.

Differences arise over the numbers of those displaced in 1948 (either several hundred thousand, as Israel suggests, or a million in the Palestinian formula), and in 1967, either one hundred thousand (Israeli view) or three hundred thousand (Palestinian). There is thus legitimate skepticism over the meaningfulness of the figures of 4.25 million Palestinian refugees given by UNRWA. These include 1.7 million in Jordan; 1 million in Gaza; 0.6 million in the West Bank; 0.4 million, most in nine camps, in Syria; and 0.4 million in Lebanon. They have not been treated in brotherly fashion. In Syria, though refugees may have been born and raised in the country, they are not allowed to vote or hold political office, cannot buy farmland, and cannot hold passports.

The crucial issue centers on the Palestinian demand for the right of return for those who claim they would be returning to their homes that they left sixty years ago. The demographic figures consequent on any large-scale entry of Palestinians into Israel show clearly that such an event would be a threat to the nature of the Jewish state.

The right of return is argued on the basis of UN General Assembly Resolution 194 (III) of December 11, 1948, but this Resolution does not state there is an unconditional right for Palestinians to enter Israel. The exact text of Article 11 of the Resolution is open to various interpretation or emphasis. It reads, "the refugees wishing to return to their homes and live at peace with their neighbors should be permitted to do so at the earliest practicable date, and that compensation should be paid for the property of those choosing not to return." It continues in instructing the Conciliation Commission (CCP) "to facilitate the repatriation, resettlement and economic and social rehabilitation of the refugees and the payment of compensation." At first, the policy of resettlement was tried, in Jordan, Gaza, and the West Bank, but it soon ended for political and financial reasons.

At the Lausanne Conference convened by the CCP from April to September 1949, which tried to resolve disputes stemming from the war, Israel offered to accept one hundred thousand Palestinian refugees, contingent on Arab parties agreeing to a peace settlement. However, those parties, who refused to talk directly with the Israeli representatives, refused the offer.

Ironically in this discussion of the issue, it was the Arab states— Egypt, Iraq, Lebanon, Saudi Arabia, Syria, Yemen—that voted against

Resolution 194. Moreover, any such claim for return does not rest on any accepted principle of international law.

The Palestinian demand for the right of return is a political maneuver, rather than a genuine humanitarian concern. This interpretation is substantiated by the reluctance of Arab states to aid their fellow Arabs in any meaningful way. Most significant has been their general refusal to grant citizenship to refugees except in two instances. Lebanon did grant citizenship to some Christian Palestinians, and Jordan granted citizenship to Palestinians living in the area of the West Bank after it unilaterally annexed the area in 1950.

At best, the Arab states have paid scant attention to the League of Arab States Casablanca Protocol of September 1965 that agreed on the right of Palestinian refugees to work, to have freedom of movement, and to have full residency rights. These rights have often not been observed, and indeed to some extent have been revoked. The conclusion is justified that the Arab states have wanted to maintain the separate status of Palestinians to use as a weapon, a political football, against Israel.

An issue that will never be conclusively resolved to satisfaction of all parties is responsibility for the existence of the Palestinian refugee problem in the first place. Yet the answer is at the heart of the moral issue concerning the refugees. Their displacement largely stems from the consequences of the war started by Arab leaders who refused to accept the UN General Assembly Resolution 181 (II) of November 29, 1947, which called for the creation of two states, one Jewish, the other Arab. Instead they attacked the newly created State of Israel, in the hope of destroying it, and lost the war.

The historical evidence is that, while Israeli forces committed some blunders in the heat of war, Palestinians, about seven hundred thousand, fled from their homes in 1948–9, mostly on orders from their own Arab military and civilian leaders, and as a result of fear and panic, hoping to return when the Arabs had won the war. The Palestinian narrative, viewing the establishment of Israel and the 1948–49 war as the *Nakba*, or catastrophe, lacks veracity in arguing that Israeli military or officials deliberately planned to expel the Palestinian population. The instructions by the Arab Higher Committee and Arab community leaders in ordering Palestinians to leave Haifa, Tiberias, Jaffa, and Jerusalem and other places are thoroughly recorded. So is the record of Israelis, such as Shabtai Levy, mayor of Haifa, asking the Arabs not to leave their homes. However, many did, and most of the Palestinians were displaced from one part of Palestine to another.

What is to be done? According to the Oslo Accords, the refugee issue would be resolved through the final status negotiations. Palestinians have options: resettlement in a country other than Israel, the West Bank, or Gaza; integration into the country in which they are living; or voluntary repatriation. A logical conclusion is for the Arab states to absorb and grant citizenship to a considerable number of the refugees in their midst, but in view of the past and present discord in the Arab world this solution is hardly likely. Palestinians were expelled from Kuwait in 1991 and from Libya in 1995.

Israel might take a small number of those prepared to live in peace. Mahmoud Abbas himself in 2009 said it was not logical "to ask Israel to take five million, or indeed one million." Hamas, however, has rejected any concessions on the refugee issue. The most likely outcome would be for Israel to make some payment of reparations for lost property and damages. Yet, fairness suggests that such a solution should be paralleled by similar payments for those Jews forced to leave the Arab countries after 1948, an episode that has received less attention than the fate of the Palestinians.

4. Is a Palestinian State Viable Today?

Beyond the issue of bad faith and irresponsibility of Palestinian authorities in calling for a unilateral declaration of a Palestinian state is the question of whether such a state is politically and economically viable. Politically, would it meet the four qualifications for statehood mentioned in the Montevideo Convention on the Rights and Duties of States signed on December 26, 1933: a permanent population; a defined territory; a government; and a capacity to enter into relations with other states?

Were a Palestinian state to be established today, few of those qualifications would be met, and it is probable that it would become a failed state. Consider the question of population. Over two million Palestinians live east of the 1947 armistice lines, another million in the Gaza Strip, and about a million in Israel, with Israeli citizenship. Over half of Jordan's population is Palestinian in origin. That hardly epitomizes a permanent population within a defined territory. Hundreds of thousands more are located in surrounding Arab countries.

Millions are registered as refugees in the camps run by UNRWA (the United Nations Relief and Works Organization). UNRWA defines a refugee as a person descended from those displaced in the 1948–49 war, irrespective of current citizenship or place of birth. There are two other problematic factors. It is unclear what part of the diffused Palestinian population would want to live in a Palestinian state; certainly Israeli Arabs have no such desire. Also, the politically explosive issue of Palestinian insistence on the right of return for refugees makes demographic counting futile.

Palestinian geography is no more identifiable. In spite of constant references by political actors to the 1967 lines as the defining borders, the territory of a Palestinian state still remains undefined. The geography and borders can only result from good-faith negotiations between Israel and appropriate Palestinian representatives.

The immediate problem is the nature of those representatives. Certainly, Hamas does not qualify, and negotiation is impossible if Hamas is included in any Palestinian governing entity. As recently as February 2012, Ismail Haniyeh, the leader of Hamas in Gaza, stated, "The resistance will continue until all the Palestinian land including al-Quds [Jerusalem] is liberated and all the refugees return." Its stated objective is the establishment of an Islamic state in the whole of Palestine, which includes what is now Israel. Hamas emphasizes armed struggle to a greater degree than does the PLO.

Since the Oslo Accords of 1993, the Palestinian Authority (PA) exists as a quasi-government, exercising authority in the West Bank and, for a time, in Gaza. However, no real infrastructure has been created, and full autonomy did not follow Oslo. Instead, Yasser Arafat, as president of the PA, created both a *mukabarat* (secret services), which absorbed 60 percent of the PA's budget, and a corrupt and unaccountable regime that largely remains today. The PA today does not have the monopoly of the legitimate use of physical force. It was defeated politically and militarily by Hamas, which controls Gaza with its own security forces, provides some services for the population, but above all engages in militant aggression against Israeli civilians. In essence there are two Palestinian governments in continuing conflict. Attempts at reconciliation between the PA and Hamas have failed up to this point.

At present the fourth requirement, that of living in peace with the Israeli neighbors, appears improbable. Although Yasser Arafat, as part of the Oslo Accords, appeared to recognize the State of Israel, the Palestinian Covenant, containing the statement that the "partition of Palestine in 1947, and the establishment of the State of Israel are entirely illegal" has never been formally amended. Even more starkly, the Hamas Covenant of August 18, 1988, advocates the destruction of Israel by jihad. Its very beginning is that "Israel will exist and will continue to exist until Islam will obliterate it, just as it obliterated others before it." Hamas has tried to implement this by its constant attacks against Israeli civilians.

Equally important as the political problems is the economic outlook. Both the World Bank and the International Monetary Fund have issued optimistic, if misguided, reports in recent years, noting that if the PA maintains its performance in nation-building and in delivery of public services, it is well positioned to establish a state in the near future. One can accept that the PA has strengthened some institutions and developed certain services in the territory it controls, and that the Palestinian economy has grown, a growth estimated at 9.3 percent in 2010.

But is the PA's economic performance record fundamentally sound? First, the growth stated is from a very low base established in the second intifada in 2000. It does not appear to be sustainable. It is still primarily confined to the nontradable sector, in which the fastest growing parts are agriculture, hotels, and restaurants, and the payroll of the PA. Manufacturing output, in contrast, has fallen. Finally, the growth is largely the result of funds given by donors who are more reluctant to supply funds because of the extremism of Hamas.

Unemployment in the West Bank and Gaza is among the highest in the world. It peaked in 2002 at about 30 percent; now it is 16.9 percent in the West Bank and 37.4 percent in Gaza. The situation is particularly serious for youth, whose unemployment reached 25 percent in the West Bank and 52 percent in Gaza. GDP per capita has fluctuated widely, but real wages have decreased in value. Paradoxically, Israel and its settlements are a major employer of Palestinian labor, now numbering about 130,000, who account for about one-quarter of Palestinian payroll. Equally, the main trading partner is Israel, which accounts for 89 percent of Palestinian exports and 81 percent of imports. About one-fifth of the Palestinian population lives in poverty.

Because growth is largely donor driven, a vibrant private economic sector is lacking. Between 1994 and 2011 the European Union gave EUR 5 billion in development aid to the Palestinians, including EUR 525 million in 2011, and individual European countries gave separate aid. It is unlikely that outside funding—from the United States, the European Union, and Arab states—would be maintained at present levels, let alone increased, while Hamas is part of any Palestinian governing authority. In recent years Arab states have become less generous: in 2009 they gave the Palestinians $462 million, in 2010 $287, and so far in 2011 $78 million. Of the $971 million pledged to the Palestinians, only $330 million has actually been given. Consequently, the PA is heavily in debt.

No doubt some improvement in the Palestinian economy would occur if Israel reduced restrictions on movement and access, imposed for security reasons. But such changes would do little to remedy the fundamental systemic problems of the Palestinians. Would a Palestinian entity automatically become a failed state akin to Somalia, Chad, or Zimbabwe, where anarchy, civil war, and ethnic and religious strife prevail? If the fundamental issues concerning Israel are resolved, and if Hamas is prepared to accept the State of Israel, both highly unlikely at the moment, a state of Palestine could be as viable as other struggling Arab states. But if the state is established under present conditions the outcome is likely to be less felicitous. To attempt to establish such a state now might well jeopardize the chances of its viability and success in the future.

The present reality is discussed in the following essay.

5. A Palestinian State Is Not Now Economically Viable

Over the last year Palestinian authorities have spent a great deal of time calling for a unilateral declaration of a Palestinian state while refusing to resume peace negotiations with Israel. They garnered political support for this in the UN General Assembly in September 2011. However, a new report from the World Bank, written in April 2012, and made public in July 2012, indicates that the efforts of the Palestinians and their supporters would have been more usefully employed in thinking about the economic viability of such a future state.

The essential conclusion of this sobering World Bank report, which contradicts the more optimistic and inaccurate picture of the Palestinian economy presented by the International Monetary Fund in 2011, is that although the Palestinian Authority (PA), the official representative group established in 1994, has made steady progress in many areas toward establishing the institutions required by a future state, the economy is currently not strong enough to support such a state. The report is implicitly a stinging commentary on the poor state of the Palestinian economy, especially by comparison not only with the economy of Israel but also with that of Jordan, and on its decline due to the Palestinian violence which erupted in the second Intifada in September 2000.

The crucial problem according to the report is that the Palestinian economy has become increasingly dependent on foreign aid to drive its growth, and this is insufficient for economic sustainability. Foreign aid has given the Palestinians billions of dollars. By 2008 that aid was about 56 percent of GDP. This led to GDP growth of 7.7 percent between 2007 and 2011; in some years it reached 9 percent a year.

But the growth is artificial and is not sustainable for three reasons. It has funded government expenditures and been largely in government services, real estate, and other nontradable sectors. The productive sectors have declined in importance: there has been a decrease in manufacturing from 13 to 10 percent and in agriculture from 9 to 6 percent. The inflow of foreign aid in 2007 led to some improvement in GDP in the West Bank.

Gaza, now with a population of about 1.6 million, over half of whom are under the age of sixteen, experienced growth because of the foreign aid and the expansion of trade through tunnels from Egypt. Reliable reports claims there are more than six hundred millionaires living in the Gaza Strip, most of whom have made their wealth from the proceeds of the goods—fuel, cement, vehicles, drugs, electronics, medicine, cigarettes—coming out of these tunnels. The tunnel trade between Egypt and Gaza is estimated to be more than $700 million a year. The Hamas government, by taxes, customs duties, and daily fees on these goods, gets about a quarter of its budget from them. In addition to the tunnels, Gaza is able to import goods, particularly building materials, and to get electricity and fuel from Israel.

Gaza has benefitted by funds, about $240 million, from the Islamic Development Bank, led by Saudi Arabia, by the UN reconstruction program bringing Gaza about $200 million, and grants from Turkey, including one for a teaching hospital in the Islamic University of Hamas.

However, the Palestinians now face a crisis, because important donor countries have so far not sent aid or have sent less aid in 2012. The PA now has a debt of $1.5 billion, in its budget of about $4 billion, and a cash shortfall of $500 million. It has been promised $100 million from Saudi Arabia, an amount insufficient to end the crisis.

Those who admired the second Intifada, heralded by Yasser Arafat in 2000 but which in fact resulted in violence for over two years and halted progress to peace negotiations, will now realize that it was a disaster, a severe blow to the Palestinian economy. The violence resulted in the West Bank and Gaza suffering a severe economic contraction. Between 1999 and 2002, real GDP fell by 27 percent. In 2007 real per capita GDP was 23 percent below the 1999 level. Industry, agriculture, tourism, and some other services declined. Public administration, defense, and public services such as health and education grew from 20 percent of GDP to more than 27 percent.

The report argues that the PA must increase private sector growth, must improve its trade infrastructure to lower costs and increase efficiency, must improve the investment climate, and must improve the quality of the workforce. Sustained economic growth entails a strong dynamic private sector that can generate jobs both to employ a rapidly growing population and to provide resources for government to provide services.

That necessary dynamism is lacking. The Palestinian private sector is overwhelmingly dominated by small family-owned businesses. The high cost of doing business lowers competiveness. The Palestinian businesses mostly focus on the local market. In addition, relatively high wages, compared with other countries such as Turkey and India, high transportation costs, and low level of innovation also reduce competitiveness.

Yet, even with significant growth, it is unlikely that the PA can support an administration of the current size. It must reduce costs, raise revenues, and move to fiscal sustainability. Politically, the report recognizes that investment would be increased if a peace agreement is reached between the Palestinians and Israel.

The Palestinian economy over the last decade has been characterized by high levels of unemployment and underemployment, some of the highest rates in the world. It has varied between 20 and 30 percent. These rates are accompanied by low levels of labor force participation, which have been about 41 percent. Even more troubling has been the decline in youth employment and economic participation, and the very low level of female labor participation. In 2010 youth unemployment was in general about 34 percent, and was 53 percent in Gaza. One interesting form of activity was the building by Hamas in Gaza of hundreds of tunnels under its border with Egypt. That activity benefitted Bedouin tribes, Hamas Islamist radicals, and corrupt Egyptian officials.

During the last decade, the rate for women participating in the labor force was below 16 percent. The result of this high unemployment and the decline in private sector wages relative to government wages has led to high levels of poverty; in 2009 it was 22 percent in the West Bank and 33 percent in Gaza. About 80 percent of Gaza households get some form of assistance.

The report makes the obligatory criticisms that Israeli restrictions significantly impact Palestinian's ability to trade and remain the biggest impediment to investing because they create high uncertainty and risk, and that Palestinian goods have difficulty entering the Israeli market. It ignores the fact that those restrictions that remain are due to security needs. Moreover, it says nothing about the aspects of Israeli culture, its climate of innovation, and the overcoming of adversity, that help explain the large disparity between the GDP per capita of Israelis and Palestinians.

How can the viability of the Palestinians be increased? Clearly, there are problems to be resolved besides the acute one of differences between Fatah in the West Bank and Hamas ruling Gaza since 2007. If the Palestinian narrative has gained some resonance in the political realm, the PA has lacked competence in economic matters and not been devoid of corruption. It could try to build a better business environment. To help business and investment it could reform the legal system, especially relating to land, now composed of a disparate group of layers of Ottoman, British Mandate, Jordanian, Egyptian, and Palestinian laws that differ between Gaza and the West Bank, and Israeli Military Orders. Although the report speaks of the well-educated, entrepreneurial population in the West Bank, it is apparent that the skill level of Palestinian workers needs to be improved by more emphasis on cognitive and behavioral skills, such as discipline and work effort.

Most importantly, and not sufficiently stressed by the World Bank report, are the benefits that would accrue to the Palestinians with a peace settlement. Economically, they would include a well-balanced customs union between a future Palestinian state and Israel, and a nondiscriminatory policy of free trade agreements. Ending the violence is the fundamental requisite for economic and political progress.

6. The Controversial Life and Death of Yasser Arafat

Yasser Arafat is virtually unique in having both the facts about his birth, family background—in a shopkeeper or textile family—and early life grounded in obscurity or given conflicting versions and also leaving the nature and cause of his death a subject of controversy.

Who or what caused the death of Yasser Arafat in Paris in November 2004? Lawyers on behalf of his family—his widow, Suha, and daughter— called for an independent judge to be appointed to inquire into the matter. French independent judges, without connection to political authorities, have the power to call witnesses and to take testimony. The investigator can even order that Arafat's body be exhumed from his grave in Ramallah, and have it tested. He or she can then present any evidence to a court presided over by another independent judge.

Some of the essential facts concerning his death are clear. Arafat, who had been ill with flu for weeks in Ramallah, was flown to France and in frail condition was taken to the Army Teaching Hospital in Clamart, outside Paris, on October 29, 2004. He was diagnosed as suffering from a blood disorder that leads to the formation of small blood clots throughout the body. He fell into a coma and died on November 11. At the hospital he underwent a considerable number of medical tests and was examined by over thirty medical personnel, some of whom were knowledgeable about radiological toxins. The French doctors could not establish the exact cause of death and refused to give details of his illness.

The assumption that became popular was that he died from a stroke caused by a bleeding disorder that resulted from an unidentified infection or liver disease. Another view was that he died of a brain hemorrhage. Allegations were also made that Arafat was poisoned, even though he did not suffer the extensive kidney or liver damage expected from one who had been poisoned. Nor did he lose his hair or have his bone marrow damaged. Other rumors, however, surfaced that he died from cancer, or cirrhosis of the liver, or from AIDS, the result of a liaison with one of his bodyguards. He did not get a routine test for AIDS. Standard toxicology tests did not detect anything out of order. For some reason his widow, Suha, refused at the time to have an autopsy performed on Arafat's body. His urine samples and vials were destroyed in 2008.

For an equally strange and seemingly bizarre reason Suha kept his toothbrush, stained underwear, his kaffiyeh headscarf, and other objects stained with saliva and sweat, in her possession. Now, eight years after his death, believing that a crime was committed, she sent these personal effects of Arafat to be analyzed by the Institut de Radiophysique in Lausanne, Switzerland. The doctors there did not find any traces of common heavy metals or conventional poisons in these effects. According to Al Jazeera television, the Swiss scientists did, however, find on the items supplied by Suha what is reported to be abnormal levels of an obscure poison, polonium-210, a highly radioactive element, an element that decays rapidly. That poison while unfamiliar is not unknown. Marie Curie who discovered the element in 1898 died of an accidental exposure to it. The Swiss findings at this point appear to be inconclusive. Thus only an autopsy can help clarify the issue.

The question, still to be resolved, is how the polonium at this point may have got onto Arafat's old effects. The most familiar case of a victim who died from the poison is Alexander Litvinenko, the former agent of the KGB and of the FSB (Russia's Federal Security Service) who fled to Britain from Russia for fear of prosecution, and who died as a result of Russian action after drinking a cup of tea in a London hotel in 2006. For some time there has been speculation that Napoleon was murdered because of the arsenic in his hair while he was isolated on the island St. Helena. Some Palestinians now speculate on the possible poisoning of Arafat while he was isolated in the suburbs of Paris, though the French hospital had apparently, according to Roland Masse, a prominent doctor, tested Arafat for radiation poisoning and reported negatively.

The mystery of his death remains. His wife, Suha, born a Christian and now forty-eight years old, has been living a lavish life style at a reputed cost of $500,000 a month in Paris and Malta. She is probably knowledgeable about the large amounts of money, which have never been located, that Arafat accumulated from PLO sources. Suha was a major shareholder in the company al-Bahr (the Sea) run by the PLO treasurer. Though in 2004 she had refused to allow an autopsy, she did in 2012 ask the Palestinian Authority for the body to be exhumed from its limestone mausoleum in Ramallah, and this was done. Experts took samples from the corpse on November 22, 2012, to test for radioactive indications. It was delightful irony that one of the three experts was a Russian, whose fellow citizens were responsible for the murder of Litvinenko. A report is expected in spring 2013.

Arafat's PLO associates and inner circle were unhappy at the amount of money he siphoned off from Palestinian funds. An audit in September 2003 by the IMF of the Palestinian Authority revealed that between 1995 and 2000 Arafat had diverted $900 million from public funds—including money from gas, tobacco, and alcohol taxes—to a private bank account he controlled. His private wealth, hidden in more than two hundred bank accounts around the world, has been calculated to have been more than $1 billion. Perhaps there is no mystery about whether he came to an untimely end. After all, a man aged seventy-five, not in good health, might have died a natural death of old age.

7. The Palestinians Reveal the Ties of Jews to Palestine

The Palestinians have inadvertently contributed to the truth of the historic relationship of Jews with the land of Israel by asking the World Heritage Committee (WHC) of UNESCO to recognize, on an emergency basis, Battir, a village about five miles west of Bethlehem, as a World Heritage Site and add it to the 936 sites already maintained by UNESCO. Unwittingly, the Palestinians have given the world the opportunity to learn about that historic relationship.

Though not a state, the Palestinians in October 2011 were granted full membership in UNESCO, which they hoped would lead to international recognition of a state of Palestine. As a consequence of this membership, they are a party to the proceedings of the WHC, which has twenty-one changing members, presently including Russia, Qatar, Algeria, and the United Arab Emirates, but not including the United States or Britain.

The request regarding the recognition of Battir is connected with two issues: a protest against Israeli plans to extend its security fence near the village, and the Palestinian's more ambitious claim to be accorded by UNESCO the heritage over the basilica of the Church of the Nativity, a World Historic Site regarded as the site of the birthplace of Jesus, and the Pilgrimage Route, Bethlehem. Already, UNESCO has designated two Jewish sacred sites—Rachel's Tomb, the burial place of the matriarch Rachel, the wife of Jacob, and the Cave of the Patriarchs where Abraham and Sarah were buried in Hebron—not as Jewish holy sites but as mosques. Only the United States voted against this proposal, which was approved by forty-four of the fifty-eight members of the board of UNESCO.

The claim made by the Palestinians for Battir to be recognized as a heritage site is ostensibly based on its unusual topography of historic terraces supported by dry stone walls and its Roman irrigation system. Indeed, the village was awarded the UNESCO Melina Mercouri Prize for its ancient Roman irrigation system. The Palestinian Authority (PA) asserts that the village is a "historically sensitive area . . . where a millenary irrigation system is still in use to water the vegetable gardens of Battir." The village, which has grown in recent years to a population of four thousand, does have seven natural springs, an old Roman bath, and an irrigation system that waters fruit and vegetables.

However, the reason for the Palestinian request is more political than aesthetic. The PA argues that Israel is planning to build part of its security fence through the valley and that it will damage the site that it claims, in accordance with the UNESCO operational guidelines concerning the acceptance of World Heritage Sites, is "representative of a culture."

The Palestinian complaint is that the Israeli fence will deny the ability of the residents to enjoy their natural heritage and sustain the land. The village, they argue, should be maintained as a Palestinian and humanitarian heritage. The complaint has gone to the Israeli Supreme Court, which will adjudicate the question of the exact route of the fence, including whether it should be rerouted, and consider whether the route is in accordance with Israeli security considerations.

All will admit the pleasant nature of the village and its picturesque character. Yet the ambitious Palestinian claim is deficient in a number of ways. Though the Roman irrigation system is historically interesting, in fact the village gets most of its water from the West Bank Water Department, the public water network established in 1980. The village has grown substantially since then, and the natural heritage is more threatened by the increased housing development than by any Israeli action. Moreover, pretty though the area might be, it does not meet the objective requirements of UNESCO that a heritage site be a place of beauty, of importance, and of outstanding universal value.

But most important, the Palestinians have unwittingly drawn attention to the historic Jewish relationship and claim to the land of Palestine. The original name of Battir was Betar, the last fortress of Simon Bar Kochba (son of a star) in his revolt against the Romans in 132–135. The revolt led to the creation of an independent State of Israel over parts of Judea for over two years before being crushed by the Roman army of six legions. The result was the killing of thousands of Jews, perhaps half a million, and the loss of Israeli independence and of Jewish religious and political authority. The Romans did not allow the Jews to bury their dead in Betar.

A Jewish entity was not again the center of religious, cultural, and political life until the twentieth century, but Betar remained an important symbolic reminder of the Jewish past. The Revisionist Zionist youth movement, formed in 1923 by Vladimir Jabotinsky, took its name from the fortress. It played a role in fighting against Nazi Germany in World War II. Interestingly, Jabotinsky's main political opponent, David Ben Gurion, is said by some to have taken his Hebrew name from one of the generals who fought in Betar.

Betar is a reminder of courage, of fighting against overwhelming odds, of struggle against those who would eliminate Jews, and of self-assertion in pursuit of independence. By their action the Palestinians have allowed the international community to become aware of the Jewish history of Betar. Israelis, confronting the immediate menace of Iran, the existential threat and the relentless assault against their country, can once again evoke the historic lesson of Betar in their response to the danger they face. That response will now, as in the past, embody the words of Pericles's great funeral speech: "happiness requires freedom and freedom requires courage."

5

The Arab-Israeli Conflict

1. Negotiations, Not Unilateral Declarations

The conflict between Israel and the Palestinians can be resolved only by negotiations between the parties, not through unilateral declarations by one side. A unilateral declaration of a state would mean renouncing the many attempts made in many forums over the last sixty years to resolve the Israeli-Palestinian conflict by a negotiating process in which the Palestinians have taken part on many occasions. It would constitute a breach by the Palestinians of their past agreements and legal obligations. It would be an act of bad faith.

The initial obligation is that the cease-fire lines, established through the armistices following the 1948–49 war between Israel and the Arab states, were to remain in force until "a peaceful settlement between the Parties is achieved." Following the wars of 1948, 1967, and 1973, the basis for resolution of the conflict became United Nations Security Council Resolution 242 of November 22, 1967, and UNSC Resolution 338 of October 22, 1973.

Resolution 242 called for efforts to achieve a settlement based on a "just and lasting peace" and on the right of states in the Middle East to live in peace, within secure and recognized boundaries. Boundaries would be determined by negotiation, not by force or by unilateral action of any of the parties, nor were they to be imposed. Resolution 338 repeated the call for negotiations between the parties.

Negotiation achieved two peace treaties. The Israeli-Egyptian treaty on March 26, 1979, encouraged negotiation by inviting "the other Arab parties to the [Arab-Israeli] dispute to join the peace process with Israel." The Israeli-Jordan treaty of October 26, 1994, stated that disputes arising out of the application or interpretation of the treaty should be resolved only through negotiation.

The preamble of the Camp David Accords on September 17, 1978, provided a framework for negotiations to establish an autonomous self-governing authority in the West Bank and Gaza. Palestinians were urged to join in discussion of the autonomy and the election of such an authority but did not do so.

At the Madrid Conference on October 30, 1991, the objective was to foster negotiations on two tracks, bilateral and multilateral; one was for an interim self-government arrangement, and the other for permanent status agreement. The Madrid Conference led to the Oslo I Accords of September 13, 1993. These Accords were the first public face-to-face bilateral negotiations between Israel and the Palestine Liberation Organization (PLO). The hope was that they would lead to further negotiations in which "final status issues" would be resolved.

The Accords, signed by Prime Minister Yitzhak Rabin and Yasser Arafat, chairman of the PLO, and by President Bill Clinton, provided for the creation of a Palestinian Authority (PA) that would have responsibility for the administration of territory under its control. By exchange of letters between Rabin and Arafat, the former recognized the PLO as the legitimate representative of the Palestinian people, while Arafat acknowledged the right of Israel to exist and renounced the use of terrorism and other violence.

Oslo I laid out a five-year timetable, an interim period during which permanent status negotiations would take place in stages. During this period a Palestinian Interim Self-Government Authority and an elected Council would be established in the West Bank and the Gaza Strip. Israeli would withdraw from the Gaza Strip and the Jericho area. The Palestinian Authority would have power over education, health, culture, social welfare, direct taxation, and tourism. Other subjects, Jerusalem, settlements, refugees, security, and borders were to be negotiated later.

Oslo I was to be followed by confidence-building measures. These have taken a number of forms, the more important ones being the Gaza-Jericho Agreement, August 29, 1994; Oslo II, September 28, 1995; the Hebron Protocol, January 17, 1997; the Wye River Memorandum, October 23, 1998; the Sharm el-Sheikh Memorandum, September 4, 1999; the Camp David Summit, July 2000; and the Annapolis Conference, November 2007. They were supposed to lead to the implementation of Security Council Resolutions 242 and 338, as well as prohibit all forms of incitement to violence or terror.

The Gaza-Jericho Agreement dealt with the transfer of powers and responsibilities. Israel would be responsible for Israelis and the settlements in the areas; the PA would be responsible for public order in general and for many civil matters. Israel was to withdraw from Gaza and Jericho while retaining control and supervision over air space.

On September 28, 1995, the Interim Agreement, known more familiarly as Oslo II, provided for redeployment in the West Bank, including Palestinian self-rule in a number of cities. The West Bank was divided into three areas, A, B, and C. Area A was to be under full control of the PA; area B under joint Israeli and Palestinian control; and area C under Israeli control. The Hebron Protocol, signed by Arafat and Prime Minister Netanyahu, provided for withdrawal of Israeli forces from most of Hebron within ten days, and then further withdrawal from the West Bank, apart from settlements and military locations, before mid–1998.

The Wye River Memorandum, signed by Netanyahu and Arafat on October 23, 1998, focused on implementing Oslo II. The two sides agreed to resume permanent status talks. The Memorandum stated, "neither side shall initiate or take any step that will change the status of the West Bank and the Gaza Strip in accordance with the Interim Agreement." On September 4, 1999, Prime Minister Ehud Barak and Arafat at Sharm el-Sheikh signed another Memorandum to implement Oslo II and other agreements. Again it was agreed that neither side would initiate or take any step that would change the status of the West Bank or Gaza.

An attempt to negotiate a "final status settlement" at the Camp David Summit in July 2000 in talks between Barak, Arafat, and Clinton failed, but the two sides reaffirmed the decision that their differences could be resolved only by good-faith negotiations. A further attempt at a settlement was made in late January 2001 at Taba. This Summit focused on four main themes: refugees, security, Jerusalem, and secure and recognized borders. However, the talks were discontinued on January 27, 2001, partly because of the reluctance to compromise on the part of the Palestinian delegation, and partly because of the preparations for the special Israeli election.

At a summit meeting at Sharm el-Sheikh in February 2005, Abbas continued to adhere to the principle of negotiation. In his speech of February 8, 2005, he reiterated "our adherence to the peace process points of reference, the resolutions of international legitimacy, the agreements signed between the PLO and the government of Israel, and the roadmap (of the International Quartet)." At the conference in Annapolis, Maryland in November 2007, Prime Minister Ehud Olmert and Abbas attempted to negotiate a peace settlement along the lines of President Bush's roadmap for peace.

For Palestinian authorities, to introduce a unilateral declaration of independence would be a breach of their obligations, especially those of Oslo II. It should be recognition of necessity, as well as adherence to moral obligations, for Palestinians to accept that direct negotiations with Israel are the only way to achieve a just and lasting peace.

Nevertheless, on September 23, 2011, Mahmoud Abbas, self-styled president of Palestine, in a letter to the UN secretary-general applied "on behalf of the state of Palestine" for admission to the United Nations. By November 2011 the Palestinians had been unable to gain the nine votes necessary for approval by the Security Council, and the application failed.

Though the Palestinian attempt to gain full United Nations membership did not succeed, the Palestinian Authority did gain membership in UNESCO, where the United States does not have veto power. Moreover, on November 29, 2012, a date chosen as symbolically reminiscent on the sixty-fifth anniversary of the historic November 1947 UNGA Resolution that called for two states to be established, a Resolution in the UNGA to upgrade the PA to "nonmember observer status" was passed by 138-9 with 41 abstentions. Canada joined the US in voting against the Resolution, while France, Spain, Italy, and Switzerland were among the countries voting for it. The members of the European Union who voted for the Resolution should have remembered the past history of the policy in the 1930s of trying to appease Nazi Germany. Neville Chamberlain and likeminded others were a dismal and tragic failure. Europeans ought to be wary of similar appeasement today.

The Resolution was passed, though none of the qualifications for statehood mentioned in the Montevideo Convention of December 1933 (permanent population, defined territory, government in control of that territory, ability to engage diplomatically) are valid regarding the Palestinians. It was noticeable on the occasion of the vote that Mahmoud Abbas, president of the PA, instead of unequivocally declaring his recognition of the legitimacy of the State of Israel as called for in the 1947 Resolution, took the opportunity to denounce Israel in strong language. His rhetoric about Israel included charges of racism, ethnic cleansing, and dispossession, and being synonymous with "an apartheid system of colonial occupation." He also did not acknowledge that a unilateral action of this kind was another breach by the Palestinians of past agreements and legal obligations.

The PA in its status as a nonmember observer state does not have voting rights at the UN. Only the UN Security Council can approve any country to become a member state. But the PA can now pursue membership in international treaties and in other United Nations and international specialized agencies, such as the International Civil Aviation Organization, the International Atomic Energy Agency, and others, perhaps even the International Criminal Court. Since only genuine states or the UN Security Council can refer complaints to the ICC, it is questionable whether the Palestinians could bring charges in the Court against Israel or to press for an investigation of practices in the disputed territories. Another issue is the possibility of charges being brought against the Palestinians, especially Hamas, for war crimes against Israeli civilians if the Palestinians are given and accept the jurisdiction of the ICC.

2. The Palestinians Must Eliminate the Negative

Forty-five years after the events, declassified transcripts were released in June 2012 of the Israeli cabinet and government committee meetings in the days after the Six-Day War, which ended on June 10, 1967. The documents provide a valuable insight into the diverse efforts of those Israeli leaders to reach a desirable peace settlement with the countries and groups who had been at war with Israel. The evidence of the varied opinions of Israeli ministers, all eager to reach a peace treaty and an understanding with the Arab states and the Palestinians, reveals an extraordinary and revealing contrast with the long-term totally negative view of the Arab parties, a consensus that was exposed at the summit meeting of the Arab League on September 1, 1967, in Khartoum.

This unconditionally negative position taken by Arab leaders still persists on the part of the Palestinians. The ostensible reasons for their continuing refusal to enter into negotiations with Israel are that Israel must first accept the "pre-1967" borders (borders that have never been established); it must agree to Jerusalem, or part of it, as the capital of a Palestinian state; and it must end all construction in areas acquired by Israel as a result of the 1967 War.

The Palestinian intransigence, the refusal to accept compromise arrangements, is an all-too-familiar phenomenon. The Arab leaders at the London Conference in 1921 refused to establish an Arab Agency in Palestine parallel to that of the Jewish Agency, which then organized an infrastructure of political and social institutions that became the basis of the State of Israel. Those Arab leaders refused to participate with the

Jews in any plan or in a joint legislature, in which they would have been the majority. In 1922 the Arabs rejected the proposal for a Palestinian Constitution with a Legislative Council in which again they would have formed the majority, and boycotted the election for the Council.

The Arab Higher Committee in 1937 rejected the idea of two states first officially proposed by the British Peel Commission Report. The report had recommended a Jewish state in about 20 percent of Palestine, about five thousand square kilometers, while most of the rest was to be under Arab sovereignty. The Jewish state would have been small. An Arab state would have included what is now the area of the West Bank, Gaza, the Negev, Beersheba district, and part of Jerusalem. The Report also suggested a transfer of land and an exchange of population between the two states. The Peel Commission Report was accepted, in principle, by the Jewish Agency, though it meant that the Jewish state would be a small one, but it was totally rejected by the Arab Higher Committee, which called for a single state in all of Palestine.

At the last attempt before World War II—the Round Table Conference organized by the British Colonial Secretary in London in February 1939—to reach some agreement, failure was inevitable as the representatives of the five Arab states and the Arabs in Mandatory Palestine who were present refused any direct contact or discussion with the Jewish representatives, or even to sit in the same room with them.

The most crucial negative Arab decision was its refusal to accept United Nations General Assembly Resolution 181(II) of November 29, 1947. This Resolution adopted the recommendation of the UN Special Committee on Palestine (UNSCOP) that Western Palestine, that is the area outside of Jordan, be partitioned into two states—one Jewish, one Arab—and an internationalized Jerusalem (a *corpus separatum*). The Jewish state would have about 55 percent of the area, but not have the historic areas of Judea and Samaria. The Arabs would have most of the Galilee District. The Resolution was accepted by the Jewish leaders but rejected by the Palestinian Arabs and by six of the seven member states (Jordan was the exception) of the Arab League.

The League was founded in Cairo, where its headquarters remains, in March 1945, purportedly to promote political and economic cooperation between the Arab states, but its real purpose was to oppose the Jewish settlement in Palestine and then the State of Israel after it was established. In essence it and its successor the Arab League was at first largely a tool of Egyptian foreign policy, but its summit conferences did lead to the creation in 1964 of the Palestine Liberation Organization

(PLO), and then to the suspension of Egypt after its peace treaty with Israel.

In the Six-Day War in June 1967, Israel achieved a surprisingly rapid victory over its Arab opponents, leaving it in control of the Sinai Peninsula, the Golan Heights, Gaza (which had been ruled by Egypt), the Jordan River and the Suez Canal, and the West Bank—so named by Jordan, which had annexed the area with almost unanimous international disapproval. Israel had defeated three Arab armies and had captured territory four times the size of Israel.

The Israeli documents now released show a startlingly different attitude among Israeli leaders from that of the total negativism of Arabs and Palestinians. They show clearly, while there were acute differences among them about the fate of the territories captured in 1967, almost all Israelis were eager to trade land for peace.

The discussions and proposals were not initially intended to be policy proposals but were to be directives to Abba Eban, Israeli foreign minister who was participating in the Special Session of the UN General Assembly, the diplomatic maneuvers at the United Nations on the Israeli-Arab conflict. The ministerial discussions have to be put in the context of Israeli concern about any UN action after the memory of at least two issues: Israel was forced to withdraw from the Sinai after the 1956 war and to rely on United States guarantees and the UN observer force there which proved ineffective; and the speedy compliance in May 1967 of U. Thant, secretary–general of the UN, without the required approval of the UN General Assembly, to accede to President Nasser's demand that the United Nations Emergency Force in the Sinai be withdrawn. The Israeli ministers feared that pressure would again be exerted on the state as in 1956 and May 1967.

It is also relevant that the Israeli government was a unity one under Prime Minister Levi Eshkol, and included members of Gahal (Menachem Begin and Yosef Safir) and the Rafi party (Moshe Dayan, the minister of defense). Not surprisingly, there were strong differences of opinion on the issues of security, borders, refugees, and water, preventing complete agreement.

However, consensus was reached on some issues. First, Israel should withdraw from captured territories only if the Arab states agreed to make peace and end the boycott of Israel. Most important, Israel would return the Sinai Peninsula to Egypt and the Golan Heights to Syria in return for a peace treaty, or strong security guarantees. The cabinet also agreed both that east Jerusalem would not be returned to Jordan, which had ruled it, and that Egypt had no greater claim to Gaza and Jordan no greater claim to the West Bank than had Israel, as all three countries had captured the area through war.

Some ministers thought that the demand for peace treaties was unrealistic. Instead, they grappled with a variety of contradictory alternatives: control over the Gaza Strip, freedom of navigation in the straits of Tiran; demilitarization of the Sinai and of the Golan Heights; control of the sources of the Jordan River; rule over the West Bank; end of any Israeli rule in the West Bank; military rule during a transition period; self-rule for the Arab inhabitants of the West Bank while Israel controlled foreign affair and security.

The ministers all spoke of peace with security arrangements, though there were differences on the issues of the destiny of the West Bank, and on whether peace treaties should be based on international frontiers. The positive answer to the latter issue was finally approved by a majority of one, ten to nine. It was decided that a peace agreement should ensure freedom of navigation in the Straits of Tiran and Bay of Aqaba and the Suez Canal, freedom of flight over them, and demilitarization of the Sinai Peninsula.

The formula agreed to by unanimity on June 19, 1967, was that "Israel proposes the conclusion of peace treaties with Egypt and Syria on the basis of the international frontiers and Israel's security needs." This was presented to those two countries, but no positive response to this formula came from either Egypt or Syria. Instead, the Arab Summit leaders at Khartoum announced on September 1, 1967, the three "nos:" no peace with Israel, no recognition of Israel, no negotiations with Israel.

As a result of Khartoum, Prime Minister Eshkol wrote a month later that "I doubt whether the government would approve the decision of June 19 exactly as it stands." Indeed, the decision became invalid in view of the continuing Palestinian refusal to negotiate.

What these newly released Israeli documents show in dramatic fashion is the fervent eagerness of all the Israeli leaders, no matter how they differed on specific issues, to reach a peace agreement with their Arab neighbors. For any hope of peace the Palestinians must accentuate the positive.

3. Stumbling on the Road to Peace in the Middle East

In September 2011 the Palestinian Authority introduced in the UN General Assembly meeting in New York a resolution calling for support of its unilateral declaration of independence and for a Palestinian state. The resolution passed in the UNGA but was not approved by the UN Security Council.

It is an open question whether such an attempt was a genuine effort to incorporate the principle of self-determination into a viable state. Rather, it might be a device to garner support in the international community for the continuing Palestinian policy of refusing to acknowledge in any authoritative fashion the existence and legitimacy of Israel. Supporting a unilateral declaration presents problems not only for Israel but also for the United States and the Western democratic world.

The resolution called for a Palestinian state along the 1949 armistice lines. This is both a questionable proposition and an act of bad faith. The resolution was based on the UN General Assembly Resolution 181 (II), the Partition Resolution, of November 29, 1947, which called for the creation of independent Arab and Jewish states, and a special international regime for the city of Jerusalem. The boundaries of all those entities were laid down in the Resolution. On this basis the State of Israel was established. However, the Arabs rejected the Resolution, and thus did not create a Palestinian state. The Arab argument was that by accepting the Resolution it would recognize the right of the State of Israel to exist.

This refusal to accept the State of Israel alongside a Palestinian state was reinforced at the Arab League Summit Conference in Khartoum on September 1, 1967, which upheld the rights of the Palestinian to their land but stated that the basic Arab commitment entailed non-recognition of Israel, no conciliation or negotiation with it. A Palestinian unilateral declaration of independence would be based on this pronouncement. Would the United Nations be abrogating the right of the State of Israel to exist?

The General Assembly approved the Palestinian declaration by a large majority. It was then introduced into the Security Council for endorsement and action. It did not receive the necessary nine votes to pass, but in any case the United States should at that point have exercised its veto for four reasons.

By this action it would demonstrate its support for the existence of Israel. It would reveal the bad faith of the Palestinian Authority in not abiding by all UN agreements, since Security Council Resolution 242 of November 22, 1967, states that the conflict with Israel should be resolved by peaceful negotiations, not by unilateral declarations. The important Declaration of Principles of September 13, 1993, between the two parties required that all disputes should be resolved by negotiations.

The passage of the resolution by the Security Council would mean that all issues—borders, refugees, Jerusalem—remained unresolved. The United States would also be aware that, according to present arrangements, a Palestinian state would include Hamas in its governmental structure, which would not bode well for peaceful resolution of the conflict with Israel, or even for Palestinian institution building.

A further disturbing problem might then arise. After a US veto, the Palestinians could resort to UN General Assembly Resolution 377, the "Uniting for Peace" resolution, introduced by the United States and adopted by a vote of fifty-two to five on November 3, 1950. This resolution stated that where the Security Council, because of lack of unanimity of the five permanent members, failed to exercise its primary responsibility for the maintenance of international peace and security, the General Assembly could then consider the matter immediately and make recommendations to members for collective measures, including the use of armed force when necessary.

At best, this would lead to a dispute between the respective power of the UN Security Council and the General Assembly. It is improbable that the United States would call for reversing a resolution it had introduced sixty years earlier.

At worst, it might allow hostile countries to engage in military activities against Israel, as well as allow Palestinians to act on their own.

The wisest policy for the international community is to persuade the Palestinian authorities that a unilateral declaration is harmful both to the peace process and to themselves.

4. Unilateral Declaration of a Palestinian State

In 2011 Palestinian spokesmen did call for a unilateral declaration of a state of Palestine and for international recognition of it on pre-1967 lines, including East Jerusalem.

This is not the first time that such a demand has been made by Palestinian authorities. On November 15, 1988, Yasser Arafat at the Palestine National Council meeting in Algiers proclaimed in a Declaration of Independence the "establishment of a state of Palestine on our Palestinian territory with its capital, Jerusalem." Arafat, chairman of the Palestine Liberation Organization (PLO), assumed the title president of Palestine. This Declaration did not specify any territorial borders of the state, but it did refer to the United Nations General Assembly (UNGA) Resolution 181 of November 29, 1947, for its legitimacy.

This was a surprising basis for a Palestinian claim. UNGA Resolution 181, the Partition Resolution, called for the establishment of two states, one Jewish, one Arab. The Zionist organization accepted the Resolution and on its basis established the State of Israel in May 1948. But the Arab parties not only did not accept it, they also strove to overturn it by attacking Israel on the day of its creation. The Arab League on April 12, 1948, declared its intention to liberate Palestine, which would "be handed over to its owners to rule in the way they like."

The 1988 Unilateral Declaration described the entity to be established as the state of the Palestinians "wherever they may be." Following this the UNGA adopted, by a vote of 104-2-36, Resolution 43/177 on December 15, 1988, which acknowledged the proclamation of the state of Palestine and authorized the PLO delegation, an observer body, henceforth to be called Palestine, though it did not say it was a state. About ninety nations did, however, recognize it. The Palestinians twice proclaimed they would form a state: in 1999 and in 2008, when Kosovo had unilaterally seceded from Serbia.

About any present Palestinian declaration two factors are pertinent. The first is the reality of whether Palestinians are ready and whether the criteria understood in international law as necessary to create a state have been fulfilled. Several issues present problems. There is an absence of independent governmental control and sovereign authority with sole right of decision-making independent of foreign control. With the division of power between Fatah in the West Bank and Hamas in Gaza, stability is not assured, nor is the certainty of central control over a permanent population.

Constitutionally, there is an uncertain, perhaps improper, situation since the term of President Abbas expired in January 2009, and no one has been legitimately chosen to fill the position he still occupies. So far a state of Palestine has no defined borders nor have crucial issues—Jerusalem, refugees, settlements, boundaries—been agreed upon between the Palestinians and Israel. Relations between the more moderate Muslim Palestinians and the extreme Islamist forces in Hamas and in the Middle East remain tentative. The necessity of security guarantees for Israel has not yet been generally acknowledged by Palestinians.

The second factor is even more crucial. A unilateral action would be contrary to the legal understandings reached between Israel and the Palestinians. It is ironic that the Palestinian argument should be based on UN Resolution 181, which the Arabs rejected and which goes counter to their familiar argument for a one-state solution. More important, since 1949 all resolutions and agreements, from Resolutions 242 and 338 on, have rested on the assumption that resolution of the Israeli-Palestinian conflict by negotiation is the foundation of the peace process.

The Declaration of Principles on Interim Self-Government Arrangements, the Oslo Accords, signed between Israel and the PLO in Washington on September 13, 1993, agreed to the establishment of a Palestinian Authority for an interim period of not more than five years pending the outcome of permanent status negotiations based on Resolutions 242 and 338. The Interim Authority was to be given a limited number of powers previously exercised by the Israeli Military Government. It would have only the agreed-upon powers, responsibilities, spheres, and authorities that were transferred to it. Israel would withdraw from parts of the West Bank and Gaza. In a mutual exchange, the PLO was recognized as the legitimate representative of the Palestinian people, while the PLO recognized the right of Israel to exist.

The second Oslo Accord, the Israeli-Palestinian Agreement of 1995, set up the Palestinian Authority, which was given certain powers while all others were reserved for Israel, which withdrew from many of the West Bank towns. The Accord defined the powers and responsibilities of both sides. The 1995 Agreement specifically stated (Article 9) that the PA "will not have powers and responsibilities in the sphere of foreign relations." What is particularly important is that the Agreement also said (Article 31) that neither side shall initiate or take any step that will change the status of the West Bank and the Gaza Strip pending the outcome of the permanent status negotiations." A unilateral action by the Palestinians would therefore mean the unraveling of the agreements made, and negate the validity of the compromises reached so far. It would signify an act of bad faith.

5. Discrimination? The Reality of Nationality and Citizenship

Following its victory in the 1967 war, Israel has been accused of discrimination, racism, and colonialism. The charge of discrimination relates to a number of Israeli issues, particularly the complex one of defining an Israeli. By law, Jewish nationality is different from Israeli citizenship. The 1952 Citizenship Law affords Jews both nationality and citizenship, while Palestinians hold only citizenship. The July 1950 Law of Return is not discriminatory against anyone but is positive in that it entitles Jews from any country to enter *Eretz Israel* and be given nationality and legal and political rights. This refers to individuals with a Jewish mother or grandmother, those with a Jewish father or grandfather, and converts to Judaism. In essence, it is a unique example of a state being founded on a combination of nationality, ethnicity, and religion.[1]

Jewish nationality is extra-territorial and embraces Jewish citizens of other countries. Understandably, Jews who are considered to be involved in an activity directed against the Jewish people or are likely to endanger public health or the security of the State can be excluded from citizenship. In the amendment of the law in 1954, those persons "with a criminal past likely to endanger public welfare" can also be excluded. The crucial point, however, is that the law is not discriminatory against non-Jews. Individuals who are not Jewish can become citizens by birth, by naturalization, by residence, or by marrying an Israeli citizen; Israeli laws on these issues are consonant with those in other democratic countries.

It is noticeable that Israel was one of the few countries to give shelter and then citizenship to a number of Vietnamese boat people who sought political asylum in the late 1970s. It also gave refuge to thousands of Sudanese, especially from Darfur, to others from Liberia, and in 2012 to other Africans fleeing their country. Work permits, now numbering more than two hundred thousand, have been issued since the 1980s to foreign workers from Asian, African, Latin American, and Eastern European countries.

The concept of Jewish nationality stems from the belief in the existence and continuity of a Jewish people who have shared some commonalities for over three thousand years. This existence has sometimes been denied by those questioning what they call the myth of supposed links between different Jewish communities in the world. At an extreme, this argument rejects the idea of a Jewish people who went into exile and denies a bond between those Jews and the land of Israel. The argument that Ashkenazi Jews stem not from the Middle East but from the conversions in the eighth century in the Khazar Kingdom—now in south Russia in the Caucasus—is familiar from the book by Arthur Koestler.[2]

Even more extreme is the view that there never was a Jewish people, which is an invented entity. This implies there are only Jewish religious communities that have sprung from conversions throughout history. The exile from the Holy Land never happened, and thus there was no return to it. Several conclusions are presumed to follow from this argument. One is that the creation of a national Jewish identity told in the Bible is a myth. Some extreme post-Zionists hold that the Zionist movement starting in the late nineteenth century deliberately formulated the idea of a common Jewish ethnicity and a historical continuity that is unwarranted.

The argument that most Jews descend from nations that converted to Judaism at different times, and that therefore Palestine is not the homeland of the Jewish people, was formulated a generation ago by some Tel Aviv intellectuals popularly known as the Canaanites. They tried to separate the concept and existence of an Israeli nationality from that of a Jewish people linked by ties of the past and whose ancestry did not originate in Palestine. The political objective in these arguments is to assert the place and at least equal rights of Palestinian Arabs in contemporary Israel. Arguments of this kind denying the bond between the Jewish people and the land of Israel may well be correlated with the denial by their proponents of the right of the Jewish people to a state of its own.[3]

Yet it has long been understood that the Jewish people consists of individuals linked not only by a common religion of Judaism in its different forms but also as a common ethnic community with historic memories of a shared past and culture, a certain solidarity, and a bond felt by descendants of those dispersed from Judea and Samaria to their ancient homeland. Race is not the definition of Jewish identity. Genetic research suggests that Ashkenazi Jews, most of whom lived in Eastern Europe and Russia, and Sephardim, descendants of Jews who had lived in Spain and were exiled at the end of the fifteenth century, have common genes. This does not imply that the origins of Jews are ethnically and biologically pure.[4]

Some notable Jews, including Louis Brandeis, Martin Buber, Albert Einstein, and Isaiah Berlin, have addressed the subject of Jewish identity. In a speech on April 25, 1915, to the conference of the Eastern Council of Reform Rabbis—"The Jewish Problem: How to Solve It"— Brandeis, while admitting that the Jews were not an absolutely pure race, remarked that a "common race is only one of the elements which determine nationality. Conscious communities of sentiments, common experiences, common qualities are equally, perhaps more, important. Religion, traditions, and customs bound us together, though scattered throughout the world." Among those experiences was common suffering. Buber in similar fashion held that the Jewish people were like no other because from its earliest beginning it has been both a nation and a religious community. Einstein too saw Jewish nationality as a fact, and held that "the Jewish nation is a living fact in Palestine as well as in the Diaspora."[5]

Isaiah Berlin's answer on January 23, 1959, to Prime Minister David Ben-Gurion, who had asked his opinion about the relationship of religion and nationalism in the formulation of Jewish identity, showed the complexity of the issue. Berlin wrote, among other matters, that "historically, the Jewish religion, the Jewish race, and all the factors which combine into Jewish culture, have combined into a single, persistent entity, incapable of being neatly fitted into the political pattern of a modern state of a Western type."[6]

A further indication of the complex issue is illustrated by the decision of Beth Hatefutsoth in Tel Aviv to change its name from the Museum of the Jewish Diaspora to Museum of the Jewish People, thus indicating the bonds between the Jewish people and the State of Israel by linking Jews living in Israel with those anywhere else in the world. The view of post-Zionists that the State of Israel should be a state of all its citizens rather than a Jewish state may be intellectually arguable, but this ideological political position does not require doing violence to the true history of the Jewish people.

Have the minorities within Israel, the Arab population including Bedouins and Druze, who now make up about one-fifth of the population, experienced discrimination? Certainly inequalities in the social and economic system and restrictions have existed, and to some extent persist in the Israeli multicultural society, with its divisions along national, religious, ideological, and ethnic lines. Yet a fair and objective assessment would be that many of the past and present restrictions result from the requirements of security, as protection not only from wars instigated by Arab countries but also from relentless attacks by Palestinians and terrorists, especially by suicide bombers, on civilians. One example of restriction is the case within Israel when Israeli Arabs have found difficulty in gaining employment in industries connected with military affairs.

A noticeable recent change is a greater effort in Israel to minimize or close the differences regarding the Arab minority in a variety of areas. They include economic development; employment opportunities, especially in the civil service; public buses; funding of Arab municipalities; new housing on state-owned land; and employment guidance centers.

The convincing response to the charge of discrimination is that Israel has shown positive concern for minorities. The Israeli Court has made a number of decisions upholding the rights of Arabs. Israel has established seven Bedouin towns in the Negev to encourage settlement of the traditionally nomadic tribes. Land was made available at deliberately low prices for Bedouins, and non-Bedouins are now not allowed to lease any of that land. The Israeli Supreme Court (*Eliezer Avitan v. The Israel Land Administration et al.*, HCJ 528/88) decided that there was a public interest in assisting Bedouins to settle permanently in urban communities, thus justifying a policy of preferential treatment or affirmative action for a minority group.

Whatever differences may be held by commentators on this issue of the nature and degree of discrimination against minorities, there is virtual unanimity on the existence of full political and legal rights for Israeli Arabs. They have legal protection for their property rights and have free access to the courts and to due process procedures. Arabs participate in political activity, not only in voting but as members and advocates of various political parties, including specifically Arab ones. Indeed, Israel Arabs have a free press in their own language and are free to express their views, including criticism of the existing government and what they perceive of as mistakes or injustice, in uncensored fashion in parliament and on television.

The fundamental reality is that Arabs in Israel are freer, including freedom to leave the territory of the State, than are Arabs in any Arab country. That was shown in laudatory fashion when the Israeli Supreme Court, which meets as the High Court of Justice when reviewing the activities of public authorities, overturned the disqualification by the Central Elections Committee of two Arab parties running candidates for parliament that were accused of supporting terrorist activity against the State of Israel and refusing to recognize it.

According to a survey done at Haifa University of Arab-Jewish relations in 2011, the Arab perceptions are mixed. Though 73 percent of Arab respondents believed that the government treated Arabs as second-class citizens, and 19 percent denied Israel's right to exist, 63 percent said they preferred to live in Israel than in any other country, and 71 percent felt that Israel was a good place to live.

Though no independent Arab party has of yet been part of any Israeli coalition government, Arabs have been members of parliament (the Knesset), members of governments, parliamentary officials, diplomatic representatives, and a judge on the Supreme Court. Arabs are exempt from military service. They participate in almost every sector of Israeli life, including the Israel soccer team in international games. The Arab writer Emile Habibi was honored with the major Israeli literary prize in 1986.

Interestingly, members of the one hundred thousand Arabic-speaking Druze minority, about 1.5 percent of the total population, do serve in the military; after the establishment of the State of Israel they declared that as Israeli citizens with full rights they would also accept full duties of citizenship. The Druze, after changing sides during the war in 1948, volunteered for the Israeli army, along with Circassians and Bedouins. The Druze are subject to conscription, but the Bedouins who enter the military are volunteers. The Druze have their own religious courts dealing with marriage and divorce; they also have members in the Knesset and hold some executive positions.

Arabic is an official language in Israel, and most official signs have Arabic translations of the Hebrew language. Arab students may be taught in Arabic-language schools and may attend universities in Israel in increasing numbers: in Haifa in 2009 the proportion is about 40 percent of the total number of students. Palestinians in the West Bank as well as Israeli Arabs can petition the Supreme Court about Israeli actions in the areas in which they reside.

Arabs, not only those who are Israeli citizens but also those in the West Bank and Gaza, have access to Israeli medical and social services. About 40 percent of the patients in the pediatric oncology department of Tel Hashomer hospital in Tel Aviv come from the West Bank and Gaza. Arabs get professional advice to assist with housing permits.

In this recounting of the place of Arabs in Israel it is clear that Arabs living in the West Bank, in Gaza, and in East Jerusalem, who before 1967 had Jordanian passports, are not Israeli citizens, but carry Palestinian identity cards issued by the Palestinian Authority which was established by the Oslo Accords, the agreements between representatives of Israel and of the Palestinians, in September 1993.

6. Occupied or Disputed Territories?

The international community has on many occasions been hostile to Israeli control of captured territory resulting from war. The pattern is familiar: a majority in the UN Security Council opposing this Israeli control and approving resolutions that the areas captured by Israel are occupied territories. Other bodies such as the International Committee of the Red Cross and the International Court of Justice have made similar pronouncements, holding that Israeli settlements or occupation of territory have no legal validity and constitute a serious obstruction to achieving a peace agreement in the Middle East.

Though this point of view has now become familiar in political discussion of Israel's policies, it is open to challenge. First, in view of the history of the area it may be more appropriate to talk of the territories in the Palestine area as disputed rather than as occupied. To use the latter term is likely to prejudge the outcome of any negotiations over them. The territories have not been under the legitimate sovereignty of any state, certainly since 1948, and therefore no nation has any clear legal right to them.

At Arab insistence the Armistice Agreements of 1949 did not establish permanent borders; they were to be decided by negotiations. It is worth remembering that between 1949 and 1967 neither the United Nations nor other international organizations referred to the rule of Egypt over Gaza and of Jordan over the West Bank as rule over *occupied* territories. Palestinian Arabs in Gaza were not given citizenship by Egypt and were restricted in travel and work possibilities; unemployment was very high. It is also often forgotten that Syria conquered a few kilometers of Israeli land during the war, including Hamat Gader and access to the northeastern shore of Lake Kinneret, and still holds it.

Israel controls the disputed territories not because of any interest to occupy them, but because they resulted from victory in wars waged against it by Arab forces. It is sometimes forgotten that, when in 1967 Israel captured the West Bank, it was Prime Minister David Ben Gurion who suggested that all territory, except Jerusalem, be returned to Jordan. In any case, Israel unilaterally withdrew all forces from Sinai in 1979, from southern Lebanon in May 2000, and, by decision of Prime Minister Ariel Sharon, from Gaza in 2006. Surprisingly, Sharon, usually depicted as a hawk for most of his military and political career, at this point believed that Palestinians might be prepared to live in peace with Israel. Israeli withdrawal from Lebanon was greeted with over four thousand Katyusha rockets aimed from there against northern Israel.

A legal opinion on the territories was proffered in 1970 by Stephen Schwebel, former State Department legal advisor and then a judge and head of the International Court of Justice in The Hague (1981–2000). He wrote, "Where the prior holder of territory had seized that territory unlawfully, the state which subsequently takes that territory in the lawful exercise of self-defense has, against that prior holder, better title."[7] Schwebel distinguished between territories resulting from "aggressive conquest," such as that of Japan and Nazi Germany before and during World War II, and those resulting from a war of self-defense, as in the case of Israel. Israeli law does not apply in the territories that have not been annexed. Instead, international law applies to them (HCJ1661/05 *Gaza Coast Regional Council v. The Knesset et al.*)

Jerusalem is a separate problem. As a result of the 1948–9 war, Israel captured the west part of the city, while Jordan captured east Jerusalem and the Old City and annexed them in 1950. The state of Jordan had no historic connection with the areas. Only two countries, Pakistan and Britain, recognized that claim, and Britain only de facto, not by full legal recognition. During the period between 1949 and 1967, in Arab-controlled areas of Palestine Jewish sanctuaries and cemeteries were desecrated. In the 1967 war Israel captured east Jerusalem and subsequently applied its "laws, jurisdiction and administration" to it. By the Israeli Basic Law of July 30, 1980, "Jerusalem, complete and united is the capital of Israel." Thus east Jerusalem was annexed by official decree.

Not unexpectedly, the UN Security Council by Resolution 478 of August 20, 1980, censured Israel, declared the action "null and void" and called for it to be rescinded. It also called on countries with diplomatic representatives in Jerusalem to move them elsewhere; most countries complied. The result is that no country presently has an embassy in Jerusalem. The United States Congress on October 23, 1995, implicitly accepting that a country has the right to choose its capital, passed a law stating that Jerusalem was recognized as the capital of Israel, and that the US embassy should be moved from Tel Aviv to Jerusalem, no later than May 31, 1999. For political reasons this has not yet been fulfilled.

The Need for Security

Why does Israel control any Palestinian areas outside of the Green Line? And why is there a Palestinian refugee problem? Despite the perplexity of well-intentioned persons and groups, the answer to both is really simple. These circumstances are the consequence of the 1948–49 and 1967 wars between Israel and Arab—including Palestinian—forces, which had launched the wars or threatened Israel. The Arabs and Palestinians had tried to destroy the State of Israel and had caused their own fate. Similarly in regard to the refugees, in the absence of the Arab-instigated wars the Palestinians would not have left their villages and homes, nor would the State of Israel have had to deal with this issue. The Palestinian refugee problem, as Benny Morris pointed out in his 1988 book, *The Birth of the Palestinian Refugee Problem, 1947–49*, was "born of war, not by design, Jewish or Arab."

The ultimate objective of the Zionist movement was to establish a state for the Jewish people. To that end Zionists in the early twentieth century had been building in the Yishuv (the Jewish community in Palestine) political and social institutions, and a trained militia, the Haganah, (defense). The Haganah set up in 1920 as a paramilitary force to protect Jewish farms and kibbutzim developed into an underground army. Palestinian Arabs had not developed a similar infrastructure.

The crucial reality is that the Palestinian spokesmen and the wider Arab world, for the most part, had refused to accept division of the land and a two-state solution, a Jewish and an Arab state. The option of a Palestinian state was readily available. Partition was first officially proposed by the British Mandatory Administration and by most of the British Peel Commission in 1937, which went beyond its given task of examining and reporting on the causes of the 1936 Arab Revolt and then proposing methods for removing the causes of Arab and Jewish grievances. The Commission rejected the possibility of dividing the country into cantons and recommended a Jewish state in about 20 percent of Palestine, but without exact details, with most of the rest to be under Arab sovereignty as the best palliative for "the disease from which Palestine is suffering."

For its own political reasons the Soviet Union in October 1947 declared its support for partition of Palestine. Two months later, on December 11, Britain announced it was going to withdraw its administration and army from Palestine in 1948. Its mandate from the League of Nations was transferred to the new United Nations. The historic step toward partition into two states was taken in the November 29, 1947, United Nations General Assembly Partition Resolution 181. This Resolution was rejected by the Palestinian Arabs and by six of the seven member-states of the Arab League; only Jordan abstained. The constant Arab position from the 1930s was insistence on the whole of Mandatory Palestine as an Arab state, not on any two-state solution or even a bi-national state.

The latter solution was at one point supported by the left-wing Jewish party, Hashomer Hatzair, some of whose members were admirers of Stalin, by scholars like Martin Buber and Hebrew University President Judah Magnes, and even for short time in 1922 by Vladimir (Ze'ev) Jabotinsky, leader of the militant New Zionist Organization, and for a very short time in the early 1930s by David Ben Gurion, then chairman of the Jewish Agency Executive and leader of Mapai, the Social Democratic party.[8] Jewish proponents, such as Magnes, of a bi-national state lessened their advocacy after the murder by Arabs in April 1948 of the convoy of Jewish medical staff and faculty going to the Hadassah Hospital and Hebrew University on Mount Scopus.

The fighting in November–December 1947 and subsequently in May 1948 resulted from the Arab attempt to destroy Israel, to prevent implementation of a two-state solution, and to refuse any compromise on the partition of Palestine. On the future of the territory the Arab states were divided. Egypt was thought to have had designs on some of the land in the south. Syria was interested in the northern area and claimed some of the land near Lake Galilee, including the town of Al-Hamma which it saw as part of Syria.

The ambition of Abdullah, the emir of Transjordan who became king of the Hashemite Kingdom (later renamed Jordan) in 1946, was to annex Palestine or parts of it to create a Greater Syria.[9] Not simply the most virulent but the general Arab rhetoric at the time suggested that the Arab attacks were aimed at driving Jews into the sea. During the 1948 war Arab forces did expel Jews from the Gush Etzion area and from the Jewish Quarter in the Old City of Jerusalem, and from captured areas such as Neve Ya'akov and Atarot, north of Jerusalem.[10]

Indeed, no Jews were allowed to remain in or return to territory captured by the Arabs, who in areas they occupied desecrated and destroyed some cemeteries, notably the ancient one in Jerusalem, where Jews were buried. Interestingly, in symbolic memory of this, Kfar Etzion, close to the scene of the 1948 massacre, was the first Jewish settlement re-established in the areas captured by Israel in the 1967 War. Similarly, another settlement was established in 1968 in Hebron, a town with a long Jewish history, and where Jews had been massacred by Arabs in 1929.

The extreme Arab position was that Jews should be expelled from the area of Palestine. This idea of expulsion had been voiced as early as 1919 by Arab leaders when testifying to the King-Crane Commission, which was appointed by President Woodrow Wilson to inquire whether people in the Middle East lands wanted independence. It was to be reiterated by the Palestinian leader the mufti of Jerusalem (grand mufti of Palestine), Haj Amin al-Husseini. Together with other Palestinian Arab representatives he called in the 1930s for an all-Arab congress that would make the Palestinian question a wider Arab and Islamic political cause by alleging that Jews were seeking to control the Muslim Holy Places in Jerusalem.

The mufti further organized in 1931 a General Islamic Congress in Jerusalem, which set up a Permanent Secretariat that would seek to raise funds for Islamic shrines in Palestine. He also called for a band of jihad fighters who would use violence to deter Jewish immigrants from settling in Palestine.[11]

The mufti thus had made the Palestine issue one that would involve both the wider Arab and the Islamic world, and that involvement became more manifest with the Arab Revolt in Palestine that began in April 1936. As a consequence, Britain invited Arab leaders from six countries to the London Conference in 1939 to discuss a solution to the Palestine conflict. Not surprisingly, those leaders supported the Palestinian demands for an end to Jewish immigration and sale of lands to Jews, and for an Arab state in Palestine. The Arabs thought the British compromises, to limit Jewish immigration to seventy-five thousand over a five-year period, were insufficient and publicly condemned the May 23, 1939, British White Paper on Palestine, the MacDonald White Paper.[12]

The League of the Arab States formed in March 1945 was actively involved in the Palestinian conflict. In June 1946, in an effort to reconcile conflicting Palestinian groups, it set up the Arab Higher Committee, with the mufti al-Husseini as president. Since he was in refuge in Cairo, that city became the locus of the Arab League, which generally accepted the extreme proposals of the mufti as common policy. Included in that policy was the imposition of an economic boycott on so-called Zionist industry and trade in Palestine, a policy that had been urged by the Arab League in 1922. Though this was only partially successful, it did as a byproduct also lead to a boycott on all Jewish trade as well as increased antisemitism in Arab countries.

At the London Conference, September 1946–February 1947, the last attempt by Britain to reconcile the conflicting points of view, the Arab League strongly rejected any plan for partition of Palestine or for any Jewish state. The British government refused to recommend any particular solution.

In October 1947 the Arab League set up a Military Committee with representatives of five countries. Two months later this Committee was given weapons, money, and authority to dispatch a force of three thousand volunteers to Palestine, who then crossed into the area and began attacking Jewish settlements. The Arab countries did invade Palestine, but their leaders, limited by personal rivalries and conflicting ambitions, were divided among themselves on the character and tactics of that invasion.

In March 1948 the mufti, al-Husseini, stated that the Arabs would continue fighting until the Zionists were annihilated by a holy war and the whole of Palestine became a purely Arab state. At best, this might include Jews who had lived in Palestine before 1914 or 1917. The latter date refers indirectly to the Balfour Declaration of November 2, 1917, in which Lord Balfour, then British foreign secretary, stated in a letter to Lord Rothschild, a zoologist who was Britain's wealthiest Jew, that "His Majesty's Government view with favor the establishment in Palestine of a national home for the Jewish people, and will use their best endeavors to facilitate the achievement of this object." This declaration proclaimed not only the right of Jews to establish a national home in Palestine, but also that this right was given to the "Jewish people" as a whole.

The mufti, al-Husseini, discredited because of his association with and aid to Nazi Germany, had been an officer in the Ottoman army in World War I. He had led the Arab resistance and riots against Jews in 1929 and 1936 in his role as head of the Supreme Muslim Council. During World War II he lived from 1941–1945 in Germany, meeting occasionally with Adolf Hitler and more frequently with SS leader Heinrich Himmler and Adolf Eichmann to discuss solving the Jewish problem, recruiting Muslims for the Nazi war effort, and raising an SS unit of Muslims in the Balkans to fight with the Nazis.

One Nazi proposal was that the mufti would head a postwar government in Palestine, in which only those Jews who had lived there before 1914 would be allowed to stay.[13] After the Nazis defeat, the mufti of Jerusalem now called on Palestinian Arabs and all Muslims to slaughter the Jews in Palestine. In similar rhetoric the mufti of Egypt, Sheikh Muhammad Mahawif, proclaimed in April 1948 that a jihad, a holy war, was the duty of all Muslims in Palestine because the Jews intended to take over all the lands of Islam, a new version of the historic allegation of a Jewish conspiracy to rule the world.

The struggle for Arabs and Palestinians was now a complex mixture of religious, territorial, and national objectives. Benny Morris, paying perhaps too much attention to Muslim rhetoric of the time, has argued that the struggle in fact became a Muslim holy war against infidels.[14] On the very day—May 14, 1948—of the declaration of the establishment of the State of Israel, the secretary of the Arab League, Abd al Rahman Hassan Azzam, proclaimed that the war starting that day would be one of annihilation in which the Jews would be swept into the sea and the story of the slaughter would be told like the campaigns of the Mongols and the Crusaders. The Jews, on the other hand, at first simply fought for survival, as at Nirim and Degania in May 1948, and to defend their state, not for conquest. Later, as they gained victories, they held the newly captured land. Consequently, about two thousand square miles were added to the original six thousand square miles of Israel.

7. A Fence for Defense

The terrorist attack initiated by the Popular Assistances Committees of Hamas against southern Israel on August 18, 2011, particularly because of its complex military nature, is a pressing reminder of the unrelenting assaults by Palestinians on Israeli citizens. It reinforces the case for Israel to maintain appropriate defensive structures, such as the fence in the West Bank, to prevent similar attacks and suicide bombings in other parts of the country.

Considerable rhetoric has been directed against Israel for the fence. It is understandable, as Robert Frost wrote in his poem "Mending Wall," "Something there is that doesn't love a wall, that wants it down." Yet historical experience—such as Hadrian's Wall and the Great Wall of China, and more recently the fence between the Soviet Union and Finland and Norway, as well as manifold contemporary examples—show how effective they can be.

The first point is that barriers are very common. They exist throughout the world, in every continent, for a variety of reasons. Some, as in the Soviet Union and Communist countries and especially the Berlin Wall from 1961 to 1989, are created to prevent their citizens from leaving their territory. Many others exist to prevent people from entering a territory, either a country or a particular area within it. Some have been established to separate parties involved in a conflict or to prevent the conflict altogether, as in Belfast in 1969 and in Londonderry; Cyprus in 1974; Kuwait-Iraq in 1991; Kashmir in 2004; and the two Koreas in 1953. Some have been set up to prevent undesirable activity, as in India to stop drug smuggling and terrorism from Burma, or on the Kazakh-Uzbekistan border.

In Morocco, since 1995, Ceuta and Melilla, autonomous cities of Spain, have established metallic border fences to stop illegal emigration to Europe and smuggling. Morocco, between 1980 and 1987, built a 2,700-kilometer barrier of sand and stone, the so-called Berm wall, in western Sahara, to prevent attacks by the Front Polisario. Botswana in 2003 built an electrified barbed wire fence of 310 miles along its border with Zimbabwe. Brunei began building a short fence along its border with Limbang in Borneo. South Africa built a barrier against Zimbabwe and Lesotho to stop illegal immigration and plunder, and also against Mozambique. Saudi Arabia in 2004 tried to stop entrants from Yemen. Thailand by means of a fence attempts to prevent Muslim fighters from Malaysia from crossing its borders. Greece built a wall at the Evros River, its border with Turkey, to stop immigration by people from Muslim Asian and African countries. The European Union has the Schengen plan to control immigration by outsiders into member countries. China created a barrier against Hong Kong. India has built a number of barriers to prevent illegal immigration from Bangladesh, Nepal, and Burma. Even the United States is familiar with the issue, having built the eighty-one-mile barrier to prevent immigration and smuggling of contraband and illegal drugs from Mexico. While not all have been successful, many have achieved their goals.

Barriers against terrorism are also common. The more important ones are those built by Russia against Chechnya, Pakistan against Afghanistan, Malaysia against Thailand, India against Burma, and Egypt against Gaza in 1979. But clearly the most familiar and the one most criticized is the security fence established by Israel in the West Bank. The multi-layered fence, including barbed wire, high walls, electronic equipment, and vehicle-barrier trenches, was the response to prior suicide bombings and terrorist attacks on Israeli citizens. Between 2000 and July 2003, when the first part of the fence was built, seventy-three suicide bombings had killed nearly three hundred Israelis and wounded almost two thousand. Since 2003 the number of attacks and consequent casualties has been sharply reduced. In 2010 the number of Israeli fatalities was nine, and in 2012—none. Nevertheless, critics refer to the fence as a wall; they disregard its real purpose and accuse Israel of building it not for security but as a device to annex territory in the West Bank, to acquire water resources, and to predetermine future borders with any Palestinian entity. Among other things they condemn Israel for imposing collective punishment on the Palestinian population by use of the fence.

Much of this critical argument rests on the opinion that the fence has been built within occupied territory, not within the area of the 1949 cease-fire lines, the Green Line, and is therefore a violation of international law. This point of view was upheld by the advisory decision of the International Court of Justice in The Hague in 2004. The Court called for the fence, or barrier, to be removed, explaining that Israel could not consider the lawful inhabitants of the occupied territory as a threat, and had imposed restrictions of various kinds on Palestinians in the area. Israel could not "rely on a right of self-defense or on a state of necessity in order to preclude the wrongfulness of the construction of the wall."

As a responsible member of the international community, Israel has been conscious of the criticism and the problems. The Israeli government has reviewed and altered the route of the fence in response to stated concerns. It modified the number of checkpoints to reduce hardships. The Israeli Supreme Court ruled in June 2004 that a part of the fence did violate the rights of Palestinians, and some rerouting took place on a number of occasions after that.

No doubt the building of the fence has had an impact on the life of Palestinians, on closure of roads, some loss of land, on access to water resources, economic life, and access to Israeli educational and health facilities. Yet two salient points are relevant to consideration of these inconveniences. The first is the dramatic success of the fence. Terrorist attacks in West Bank areas where the fence has been constructed have virtually stopped; the attacks now come from Hamas terrorists in the Gaza area and near the Egyptian border, areas that do not have a similarly efficient fence. The other is the nature of the chorus of criticism by international bodies. Those bodies—such as the Red Cross, human rights organizations, the World Council of Churches—have condemned the Israeli fence but remain conspicuously silent about other barriers throughout the world. They, and Robert Frost too, have not accepted that Israel has demonstrated that "good fences make good neighbors."

8. Israeli Settlements Are Not an Obstacle to Peace

One does not have to be an apologist for Israeli settlements in disputed areas to recognize that the obsessive criticism that has developed around them is unproductive for reaching a peace settlement between Israel and its Arab neighbors. It is more important and useful to speak of a peaceful settlement rather than concentrate on settlements. The settlements may be seen as a problem, but they are not a serious problem. Altogether, they occupy less than 3 percent of the area of the West Bank and have a population of about 330,000 there, and another 20,000 in the Golan Heights, and 200,000 in east Jerusalem, with twelve neighborhoods including French Hill, Ramat Shlomo, and Gilo. Whether some or many of these settlements will be evacuated by Israel will depend on the nature of the peace settlement.

The settlements themselves cannot be seen as a real obstacle to that settlement.

Recent events support that conclusion. In spite of the settlement freeze suggested by former Israeli Prime Minister Ehud Olmert in 2008, and the ten-month moratorium on new construction announced by Prime Minister Benjamin Netanyahu in 2010, the Palestinians still refused, at least for over nine months, to enter into peace talks. The number of settlers in the West Bank began to grow substantially starting in the 1980s with the failure of those peace talks.

Settlements are of various kinds. Of these, 121 are government authorized: urban suburbs (Har Gilo); frontier villages (along the Jordan River); blocs (Gush Etzion and the Nablus area); and in east Jerusalem. About one hundred settlements in the West Bank, small outposts, are not officially recognized. Some settlements were built for security reasons, establishing "facts on the ground" and for military protection, such as the three Nahal army camps which later became civilian settlements. Ultra-Orthodox religious groups established some settlements around the Jerusalem area, primarily to obtain affordable housing. Some settlements were built by national-religious individuals who were fulfilling what they perceive as the claims to Judea and Samaria based on the Bible.

In the Golan Heights the first consideration was security. Some settlements were reestablished on sites that had been settled by Jews before they were displaced by Jordan, which forbad Jews to live in the West Bank or east Jerusalem after the 1948–49 War; they include the Silvan area in Jerusalem, Gush Etzion, Hebron, Kalia, and Beit-HaArava. The largest settlements are really suburbs of Jerusalem. Ma'ale Adumim is about three miles from the Green Line, and Modi'in Illit and Beitar Illit, each with about forty thousand people, are less than a mile from the Green Line.

Though the settlements have been subjected to criticism, they have not been built on land owned by Arabs. They have not destroyed any Arab homes or expelled any Arab residents. The Israeli courts have rule that the Israeli government cannot confiscate land owned by Arabs for construction of settlements.

The immediate problem is the question of who can legitimately claim sovereignty over the disputed areas of east Jerusalem and the West Bank, a term coined by Jordan when it controlled the area 1949–67. These areas were, for over four centuries, provinces of the Ottoman

Empire, and then from 1922 until 1948 were ruled by Britain under the mandate given it by the League of Nations. The areas were never under any kind of Arab sovereignty.

Jordan declared it had annexed the West Bank after the 1948–49 war. It was not until July 1988 that Jordan disavowed any claim to the land of the West Bank it had lost as a result of the 1967 war. Jordan had no valid legal claim to the area and to east Jerusalem, nor does the Palestine Authority. The Palestinians have never had a political state of their own and refused to create one when offered the opportunity by the United Nations General Assembly in November 1947. The Golan Heights, about four hundred square miles, was ceded to Syria by a Franco-British agreement.

The boundaries of Palestine and the decision about the exercise of sovereign power over it remain to be determined in an overall peace settlement. This was made clear in UN Security Council Resolution 242 of November 22, 1967. What is important in this regard is that the land captured by Israel in 1967 was not determined to be the accepted legal territory of any particular people or country, since the West Bank and the Gaza Strip, about 140 square miles, were unallocated parts of the British Mandate. Moreover, Jewish settlement in the West Bank was not seen as an intrusion into alien territory as a result of war, nor as a violation of international agreements, either of which would have made settlements illegal.

International law gives no clear answer on the issue of Israeli settlements. The Fourth Geneva Convention does forbid government deportation or "individual or mass forcible transfers" of population into territory it occupies. This convention was formulated because of the activities during World War II of the Nazi regime, and by inference the Soviet Union, in transferring population into occupied territory for political or racial reasons, or for colonization. As a result of those activities, millions were subjected to forced migration, expulsion, slave labor, and extermination.

On this issue two factors are pertinent. One is that Israeli governments have not aimed at displacement of population in the disputed areas. The other is that neither the Geneva Convention nor any other law prevents the establishment of voluntary settlements on an individual basis, nor on their location, if the underlying purpose is security, public order, or safety, and as long as the settlements do not involve taking private property. It is absurd to suggest that the State of Israel did deport or transfer its own citizens to the territories. Settlement in the West Bank had been voluntary by private citizens and not as a result of government force or pressure.

This conclusion has been buttressed by the report of the three-member committee headed by former Supreme Court Justice Edmund Levy in July 2012, which held that the classic laws of occupation cannot be considered applicable to "the unique and sui generis historic and legal circumstances of Israel's presence in Judea and Samaria spanning over decades." Consequently, it held that Israelis have the legal right to settle in Judea and Samaria, and that the establishment of settlements is not in itself illegal. According to international law, captured territory is seen as foreign if another state has sovereignty over it. No recognized state, neither Jordan nor any other state, held any claim or territorial sovereignty over the West Bank since the British Mandate ended in 1948.

Israel has made concessions in the hopes of peace, although scant recognition has been given to them. Israel withdrew all forces and settlers in Sinai after the peace treaty with Egypt in 1979. All twenty-one Israeli settlements with nine thousand residents in the Gaza Strip, as well as Israeli forces there, were withdrawn by Israeli unilateral decision in 2005. This action did not result in any positive response and has not yet stopped Hamas, the ruling group in Gaza, from continuing military activity against Israeli civilians.

The settlements in the West Bank, east Jerusalem, and in the Golan Heights remain as a source of contention, whether regarded as illegal or merely ill advised. Certainly there should be legitimate discussion about them and about the actions of the Israeli government in legitimizing unauthorized outposts in the West Bank. The government distinguishes between the settlements that have been officially sanctioned, and outposts, some on hilltops for security reasons, that settlers built without permission. About one hundred outposts, usually on hilltops, were built between 1991 and 2005 without government permits or planning approval. The activists in these outposts believed they were creating "facts on the ground."

It should be noted that Israeli authorities are concerned about abuses regarding settlements. The Israeli Supreme Court in June 2012 ordered the dismantling of an outpost named Migron that contained fifty families because it was built on private Arab land. Legal decision has made clear that settlements were never intended to displace

Arab residents of the territories. They have been established for a combination of economic, religious, and military reasons, not for purposes of colonialism, or even colonization. Only a peace settlement between Israel and the Palestinians will decide on the fate of those settlements.

9. The Unbearable Silence about the Jewish Refugees

In the Palestinian narrative of victimhood, a central focus is the emphasis on the existence and pitiful condition of Palestinian refugees. This emphasis has convinced many in the international community to accept a version of the unfortunate plight of those refugees and the injustices done to them. This narrative, essentially one of historical revisionism, portrays the Palestinians as the world's major refugee problem. It also denies the truth that the Jews who left, fled, or were expelled from Arab countries can really be regarded as refugees.

The story of these Jewish refugees has been much less well-known than that of the Palestinian refugees, about whose fate international resolutions have been passed, and on whose behalf thirteen UN agencies and organizations have provided aid of some kind. The issue of the legitimate rights of the Jewish refugees and the individual and collective loss of their assets have not yet been satisfactorily addressed. Nor have there been any real attempts at restitution of their rights and assets in international forums.

The contrast is startling. Between 1949 and 2009 there were 163 resolutions passed in the UN General Assembly dealing with Palestinian refugees; there were none on Jewish refugees. Similarly, the UN Human Rights Council (formerly Commission) since 1968 has adopted 132 resolutions dealing with the plight of the Palestinian refugees, but none directed to the Jewish refugees from Arab countries. Other specialized agencies of the UN have been specifically established, or have been charged, to pay attention to the Palestinian refugees. Those refugees have benefited by international financial assistance; the UN Relief and Works Agency (UNRWA) since 1950 has provided over $13 billion (in 2007 prices). Jewish refugees received nothing from the UN High Commissioner for Refugees, (UNHCR), the international organization dealing with refugees all over the world except Palestinians, who have the UNRWA solely devoted to them.

Though it has been challenged, the status of those Jews as refugees is in accordance with the United Nations Convention on the Status of

Refugees, adopted in July 1951 and entered into force in April 1954, which wrote the definition of refugee.

Jews had been living in what are today Arab countries over more than 2,500 years, going back to the Babylonian captivity. In 1948 they still accounted for 3.6 percent of the population in Libya, 2.8 percent in Morocco, and 2.6 percent in Iraq. Their place varied in the different countries. In Iraq and Egypt some Jews were successful in occupations and professions, and played some role in their societies; in Yemen and Morocco they were generally poor and not educated.

However, though there were differences of opinion on the issue, and conditions varied depending on time and place, Jews under Islamic rule were treated as dhimmis in Arab countries, second-class citizens, often obliged to pay a ransom in order to remain in the country. They were at times allowed limited religious, educational, and business, opportunities but at other times were denied civil and human rights, suffered legal discrimination, had property taken, and were deprived of citizenship.

In the twentieth century, before as well as after the creation of Israel, Jews were threatened physically, economically, and socially in a number of Arab countries. They experienced riots, mass arrests, confiscation of property, economic boycotts; limits on employment in many occupations, on admission to colleges, and on personal movement, as well as pogroms. The pogroms occurred in Libya, Syria, Morocco, and especially Iraq, where in the space of two days in June 1941 the pogrom, known as the Farhud, took place in Baghdad, during which 179 Jews were murdered and 600 injured by rioters in the pro-Nazi regime of Rashid Ali al-Gaylani. In Libya, rioters in Tripoli killed more than 140 Jews in 1945. In a number of other Arab countries Jews were murdered or kidnapped and in general encountered discrimination, expulsion, and exclusion from citizenship.

The Arab League decided to take away citizenship of Jews in their countries. Iraq deprived Jews of citizenship in 1950 and their property in 1951. Egypt and Libya issued laws that Zionists were not nationals. They disregarded the reality that Jews had lived in those countries for more than a thousand years before the birth of Muhammad in 570 and the emergence of Islam in the seventh century.

With the creation of Israel, Jews experienced spoliation, and organized discrimination, and violence and attacks and pogroms, in Arab and Islamic Middle East countries. Libya in 1961 deprived the less than 10 percent of Jews who had remained there of their citizenship, as did

Algeria in 1962. Iraq seized the property of Jews. As a result Jews began leaving them, were driven out, or were brought out of them. By the mid-1970s almost all Jews, more than 850,000, had left those countries. According to figures and analysis provided by the organization, Justice for Jews from Arab countries, and by Stanley Urman, its executive vice president; the largest numbers came from Morocco (265,000), Algeria (140,000), Iraq (135,000), and Tunisia (105,000). From Yemen almost all of the 55,000 living in Yemen were taken to Israel by the air operation named Magic Carpet. About 130,000 Jews were airlifted from Iraq to Israel. Today, fewer than 4,500 Jews remain in Arab countries. Israel has absorbed and integrated 600,000 of the more than 850,000 who left.

It is high time to end the virtual silence and unwillingness to consider the question of Jewish refugees, and to recognize that they should be part of any final resolution of the Middle East refugee problem. The crucial United Nations Security Council Resolution 242 of November 22, 1967, mentioned that a comprehensive peace settlement should include "a just settlement of the refugee problem." It was Arthur Goldberg, the US representative to the UN who was largely responsible or drafting the Resolution, who clarified that the language referred "both to Arab and Jewish refugees, for about an equal number of each abandoned their homes as a result of the several wars." The implication was that any arrangements made would apply to all, not only Arab, refugees in the Middle East.

This point of view appears to have been accepted by both bilateral and multilateral agreements. The Camp David Framework for Peace in the Middle East of 1978, the Israel-Egypt Peace Treaty of 1979, the Israel-Jordan Peace Treaty of 1994, the Madrid Conference of 1991–92, and the Israel-Palestinian Agreements beginning in 1993—including the Declaration of Principles of September 1993 and the Interim Agreement of September 1995—all articulated similar language.

Similarly, the UNHCR announced on two occasions, in February 1957 and in July 1967, that Jews who had fled from Arab countries "may be considered prima facie within the mandate of this office," thus regarding them as bona fide refugees according to international law.

In any settlement, the property abandoned by Jews would need to be taken into account. Calculation of this is not easy, but it has been assessed as some $300 billion, and Jewish-owned real estate, about four times the size of Israel, at about $6 billion.

The time is long overdue for the international community, if and when it deals with the Palestinian refugees, to see that equity prevails.

It must be conscious of the rights of Jewish refugees, who have suffered by being deprived of rights and property as a result of Arab and Islamic behavior. It should also call for redress on their belief or that of their descendants. Some form of compensation is due the Jewish refugees, and discussion of it should be part of final status talks and the normalization of relations of the parties in the Arab-Israeli conflict.

Notes

1. Ruth Gavison, "Jewish and Democratic? A Rejoinder to the 'Ethnic Democracy' Debate," *Israel Studies*, vol. 4, no. 1 (Spring 1999): 53.
2. Arthur Koestler, *The Thirteenth Tribe: the Khazar Empire and its Heritage* (London: Hutchinson, 1976).
3. Anita Shapira, "The Jewish-people deniers," *The Journal of Jewish History*, vol. 28, no 1 (March 2009):71.
4. Israel Bartal, "Inventing an Invention," *Haaretz*, July 6, 2008.
5. Albert Einstein, *Collected Papers*, vol. 7 (Princeton: Princeton University Press, 1987), p. 236.
6. Isaiah Berlin, Memorandum of January 23, 1959 to David Ben-Gurion, *Israel Studies*, vol. 13, no. 3, (Fall 2008):170–177.
7. Stephen Schwebel, "What Weight to Conquest?" *American Journal of International Law*, 64 (1970): 344–7.
8. Susan Lee-Hattis, "Jabotinsky's Parity Plan for Palestine," *Middle East Studies*, vol. 13, no. 1 (1977): 93–94.
9. Avraham Sela, "Transjordan, Israel and the 1948 War," *Middle East Studies*, vol. 28, No. 4 (October 1992: p. 631.
10. Anita Shapira, "The Past is not a Foreign Country," *The New Republic*, November 11, 1999: 26–37.
11. Yitzhak Gil-Har, "Political Developments and Intelligence in Palestine in Palestine, 1930–40," *Middle East Studies*, vol. 44, no. 3 (May 2008): 419–434.
12. Thomas Mayer, "Arab Unity of Action and the Palestine Question, 1945–48," *Middle East Studies*, vol. 22, Issue 3 (1986): 331–349.
13. Wolfgang G. Schwanitz, "Germany's Middle East Policy," *The Middle East Review of International Affairs*," Vol. 11, no. 3 (September 2007): 31.
14. Benny Morris, *1948: A History of the First Arab-Israeli War* (New Haven: Yale University Press, 2008), p. 393.

Epilogue:
Ironic Reflections

1. Middle East Glossary: Language and Politics
in the Middle East

"When I use a word," Humpty Dumpty said in *Alice in Wonderland*, "it means just what I choose it to mean, neither more nor less. Can you make words mean so many things?"

For some time now, a combination of international organizations and a considerable part of the media have accepted Lewis Carroll's challenge; they inhabit a linguistic Wonderland of their own in their abuse of language and their willingness to accept and repeat misleading information if it can be used to criticize and condemn the State of Israel. Their utterances, whether fashionable, thoughtless, ignorant, or part of a deliberate campaign, epitomize the famous remark of George Orwell: "Political language is designed to make lies sound truthful and murder respectable, and to give an appearance of solidity to pure wind."

To understand the Middle East societies and politics, it might be helpful to examine some of the language frequently used in the relentless nonmilitary campaign of trying to destroy Israel through diplomacy. Here are the authentic definitions of words and phrases with some apologies to the Great American Songbook.

Disproportionate . . . Any action taken by Israel in its self-defense.
Blasphemy . . . Any criticism of Islam or of the Prophet.
Extremist Arabs . . . Throw journalists who tell the truth in jail.
Moderate Arabs . . . Throw some journalists who tell the truth in jail.
Post-Zionism . . . Elimination of the State of Israel.
Catastrophe (Nakba) . . . We should not have attacked Israel in 1948.
Palestinian Refugees . . . Great-great grandchildren of people who left
    what is now Israel in 1948.

Jewish Refugees . . . Forgotten 850,000 Jews who were forced to leave Arab countries in 1948–49.

Arab States . . . Tribes and ethnic groups with flags.

Arab Spring . . . Spring will be a little late this year.

Arab "Peace Now" Group . . . Address unknown.

Turkish Foreign Policy . . . Let's take Cyprus.

Power Sharing in Arab Political Systems . . . Some other time.

Palestinian Textbooks . . . Do you like antisemitic propaganda?

Muslim Heroes . . . Suicide bombers.

Goliath and David . . . Mighty, treacherous seven million Israelis confronting courageous four hundred million Arab and Muslim victims.

Barrier in West Bank . . . A provocative, insulting attempt by Jews to make it more difficult to blow them up.

Jihad . . . Eliminate the negatives.

Arab Suicide Bomber . . . Someone who loves death more than you love life.

New York Times . . . Don't let sleeping dogmas die.

BBC Interview . . . Speaking nontruth to power.

United Nations Human Rights Council . . . Prejudice without pride.

United Nations General Assembly . . . A majority of tyrannies.

United Nations Committee . . . A body that keeps minutes and wastes hours.

Boycott . . . War by other means.

Deplore the Violence in Syria . . . How long has this been going on?

Deeply Disturbing . . . Any Israeli defensive action.

Goldstone Report . . . Sorry, retraction to follow tomorrow.

Occupation . . . When are the Chinese going to leave Tibet?

Israeli-Palestinian Peace Talks . . . Where or when?

West Bank . . . Invention of Jordan.

Jordan . . . Invention of Winston Churchill.

Moment for Moral Clarity . . . Wait till the fighting stops.

Israel as a State . . . Miracle in the Desert?.

Massacre in Syria . . . Just one of those things.

"Hour of Redemption" . . . Muslims must fight until we eliminate them.

Shabiha Fighters for Assad . . . Syrian militia killers.

Muslim Honor Killing . . . Poor butterfly.

Human Rights Watch . . . Bewitched, bothered, and bewildered.

Palestinian Authority (PA) . . . Hamas, can we talk?

J Street . . . Undermining Israel "for its own good."

All Options Are on the Table . . . Are any available under the table?

Let Diplomacy Work on the Issues . . . Do nothing.

A Matter of Grave Concern . . . Do nothing.

Multilateral Contact Group . . . Blame someone else.

Six-point Plan . . . Details to follow

Cease-fire Proposal . . . A pause to rearm.

Russian Proposal for Peace . . . Send arms to Syria!

Russian Conscience Will be Shocked . . . Does the name Pavlov ring a bell?

The United Nations Will Help . . . Send in the clowns.

Hamas Report on Palestinian Abuses 2012 . . . Somewhere over the rainbow.

UNESCO . . . Is there a Jewish cultural heritage in Israel or Palestine?

Lawfare . . . Abuse and misuse of universal jurisdiction.

The Big Lie . . . Israel is an apartheid state.

Protocols of the Elders of Zion . . . We'll take Manhattan, the Bronx, and Staten Island too.

Caliphate . . . Stormy weather expected .

Jewish "provocation" of May 1948 . . . Israel invites five Arab states to attack the new state.

The Power Group in the US . . . The Jewish Lobby.

The Nonexistent Interest Group in the US . . . "The Arab Lobby" of oil interests.

Prime Minister Netanyahu Insults President Obama in the White House . . . They disagree.

Kurds . . . Making the Turks unhappy.

Even-handed US Policy in the Middle East . . . The best is yet to come.

Justice in the US . . . Khalid Sheik Mohammed is read his Miranda rights.

Intifada . . . A spontaneous uprising after the television crews arrive.

Jewish Racism . . . The grandson of boxer Muhammad Ali bar mitzvahed in Philadelphia, June 2012.

Jewish Treachery . . . Defending themselves from attacks.

Gaza Tunnels to Help Starving Citizens . . . Arabs smuggle in weapons.

Syrian Democracy . . . Bashar Assad gets 70 percent of the vote of the terrified Syrian public, of whom seventy thousand are killed.

Combating Intolerance . . . Combatting criticism of Islam.

UN Human Rights Council . . . Never-never land in Geneva.

Peace Policy of President Gamal Abdel Nasser . . . "I announce on behalf of the United Arab Republic that we will exterminate Israel" (1959).

Jewish and Israeli Control of the Media . . . Welcome to the BBC, MSNBC, CNN, PBS, *New York Review of Books*, *London Review of Books*, *The Independent*, and *The Guardian*.

Arab Tolerance . . . Inferiority and persecution of Jews and Christians in the Middle East. "First the Saturday people, then the Sunday people."

Women . . . Koranically, worth less than half a man.

Israeli Discrimination . . . The Certificate Law, 1982, requires all Israeli nationals over the age of sixteen, whether Jews or Arabs, to carry an "identity certificate."

Israeli Arab Discontent . . . The index of Arab-Jewish Relations for 2011 states that 63.3 percent of Israeli Arabs polled said they preferred to live in Israel than in other countries.

No Room at the Israeli Inn . . . Israel has 250,000 foreign workers, half of whom are illegal. Israel has integrated 350,000 non-Jewish immigrants from the former Soviet Union and 120,000 from Ethiopia. Over 120,000 Arabs have citizenship, 20 percent of the population.

Zionist Aggression . . . Arab leaders rejected the 1947 UNGA Partition Resolution and began the 1948 war against Israel, as well as four subsequent wars.

Israel Is Economically Isolated . . . Warren Buffet is the largest investor in Israel, with an 80 percent share of Iscar.

Jimmy Carter . . . Poor wandering one.

Roadmap for Peace Talks . . . Detour ahead.

Treaties . . . Are they worth the paper they're written on?

International Tennis Tournament . . . We'll play Israel, but not in public.

Allahu Akbar . . . Run for your life.

President Ahmadinejad of Iran . . . President of the International Conference of Holocaust Deniers.

President of J Street . . . Some of my best friends are Jews.

Al Jazeera . . . Islamist Outreach.

European Left . . . Hamas is good for you.

Borders of 1967 . . . Who threw away the yardstick?

Mixed Marriages . . . Environmentalists and nongovernmental organizations join with Islamists.

The Peace Process . . . Here's that rainy day

Osama bin Laden . . . You gain martyrdom by suicide, but not me.

The Cause of Terrorism . . . Terrorists.

2. Europe Faces a Crisis

The English are watching on television the brutal massacres in Syria where seventy thousand have been killed. They have raised their security level from "miffed" to "peeved." They may raise it again to "really irritated," or even "a bit cross." This should be a warning to foreigners because the last time the British felt "a bit cross" was in 1588 when they had to defeat the Spanish Armada.

The Spanish at the same time have their new submarines to meet the threat. These are beautiful vessels with glass bottoms so the Spanish navy today can see the vessels of the old Spanish navy.

The Scots have raised their threat level from "damn it" to "let's go get them." The latter level was last used when Bonnie Prince Charlie pretended to claim the throne in 1745.

The French, who had promised to help Charlie but never did, decided after an existential moment to raise its alert level from "hide" to "run." They are considering the other levels, "surrender" and "collaborate." They continue to adore Joan of Arc as French because she was maid in France.

The Italians have changed from "shout loudly" to "does my uniform fit after all this pasta?" They plan to sing *che bella cosa* as they change sides.

The Germans have increased their alert from "lofty arrogance" to "how dare they?" The next level is "why does the neighbor want us to invade us?"

The Irish changed from "let's stop drinking Irish whiskey" to "we'll clobber them when we're sober."

The Swiss wanted to meet the threat by a painful thought: "Let's close the banks." Then they thought, "Let's face them with the Swiss navy."

The European Union met and decided "We are neither for or against apathy."

The Belgians replied to the threat: "We hear what you say." Then went on to say, "We disagree and don't want to discuss it further."

The Dutch replied to the threat with "Could we consider some other options?"

The Poles said, "We will fight fire with fire." Then they remembered that their fire department uses water.

The Czechs replied with excessive irony because they are used to rye bread.

The Welsh replied, "Be careful about dangerous cults. Practice safe sects."

The Icelandic response was, "Be aware of the assistants of Santa; they are subordinate Klauses."

The Norwegian rejected the threat: "You must have taken Leif off your census."

Index

Norway, 250
Nuremberg trials, 10, 28

Obsession with Israel, xi, xiii, xiv, 60
Occupation, xiii, xiv, 7, 8, 14, 16, 19, 22, 28, 30, 41, 52, 176, 180, 230, 243, 255
Oil, xv, xxiii, 13, 106, 110, 187
Oklahoma, 154, 155, 156
Olmert, Ehud, xxxv, 229, 253
Operation Cast Lead, xxxi, xxxiii, 9, 75
Organization of African Unity, 13
Organization of the Islamic Conference (OIC), 17, 162, 172
Orwell, George, 32, 70, 208, 261
Oslo Accords, xxx, xxxv, 216, 217, 228–230, 238, 243
Ottoman Empire, 27, 47, 48, 54, 56, 127, 169, 174, 179, 209, 210, 211
Ottoman Vilayets, 210

Palestine Liberation Organization (PLO), xxx, 26, 29, 32, 33, 37, 41, 55, 167, 210, 217, 224, 228, 229, 236, 237, 238
Palestinian Authority, xvi, xviii, xxx, xxxv, 6, 24, 29, 30, 37, 172, 180, 217, 219, 228, 230, 234, 238, 243
Palestinian Covenant, 217
Palestinian Narrative, xxix–xxx, 19, 23, 184, 185, 186, 205–209
Palestinian Refugees, xxxv, 1, 205, 211–216
Palestinian State, xxxi, 29, 55, 56, 58, 180, 185, 209, 210, 211, 216–222
Peace of Westphalia, 200, 201
Peace treaties, xxxiv, 29, 56, 190, 200, 227, 231, 233, 234, 255, 258
Peel Commission Report, 1937, 98, 232, 246
Pepy, Guillaume, 121
Pétain, Philippe, xxi, 95, 113, 121
Pinsker, Leo, 43–45
Pluralism in Israel, xvii
Pogroms, 43, 46, 49, 80, 128, 212
Potemkin Village, 64, 65, 66
Poland, 41, 79, 81, 82, 119, 128, 212
Political left, xii, 40, 83, 129
Polonium, 223
Post-Zionism, 40, 41
Power, use of, xxviii
Presbyterians, 185
Protocols of the Elders of Zion, 127

Qatar, xxvii, 4, 67, 192, 198, 225
Queen Elizabeth II, 190
Qutb, Sayyid, xxv, 203, 204

Rabin, Yitzhak, 52, 228
Race, 14, 15, 45, 78, 97, 126, 127, 132, 164, 193, 240, 241
Rachel's Tomb, 225
Racial discrimination, 6–8, 13, 23, 51, 167
Racism, xiii, 6–8, 13, 14, 23, 24, 27, 51, 68, 71, 73, 80, 116, 165, 167, 209, 230, 238
Rasmussen, Anders Fogh, 63
Red Cross, 10, 243, 252
Refugee camps, 10
Relativism, 34, 64, 117, 154, 171, 207
Revisionists (New Zionist Organization), 41, 42, 226
Right of Return, 213–217
Rocket attacks, xxv, xxx, xxxiv, 30, 103
Rohling, August, 131, 133, 136, 138, 141
Romania, 83, 84
Romans, 54, 55, 226
Rommel, Erwin, 101
Rose, Flemming, 72
Rothschild, Lord, 249
Round Table Conference, 1939, 232
Russell, Bertrand, 34
Russia, xxxiii, 4, 8, 21, 27, 43, 45, 48, 51, 62, 66, 70, 79, 127, 128, 189, 224, 240, 251

Sadat, Anwar, xxv, 166, 188, 204
Salafist, xxiv, xxvi, 189
San Remo Conference, 54
Sarah's Key, 117
Sarkozy, Nicholas, 69, 76, 182
Sartre, Jean-Paul, 88, 90
Saudi Arabia, xvi, xxiii, xxv, xxviii, 3, 4, 13, 27, 67, 79, 127, 154, 161, 175, 189, 193, 197–200, 220, 251
Schwebel, Stephen, 244, 259
Sephardim, 240
Settlements, xv, xxxi, xxxiv, 4, 5, 7, 16, 20, 30, 37, 42, 66, 184, 228, 229, 243, 248, 252–256
Sèvres, Treaty of, 56, 103
Sharia law, xxv, xxvi, xxvii, 69, 72, 151–161, 170, 174, 180, 192, 202
Sharon, Ariel, xxi, xxii, 10, 52, 244
Shaw, George Bernard, 64
Short, Clare, xii
Shuqairy, Ahmad, 210